"This fascinating product of Jayna Davis's near-decade of brave, thorough, and dogged investigative reporting effectively shifts the burden of proof to those who would still contend that McVeigh and Nichols executed the 1995 Oklahoma City bombing without the support of a group or groups from the Middle East."

—R. JAMES WOOLSEY
*Director of Central Intelligence, 1993-95*

"With the publication of this fascinating account, Jayna Davis will be recognized for what she is: an outstanding journalist willing to risk everything—her career, her financial security, even her life—to discover and illuminate the facts about foreign complicity in the murderous 1995 bombing in Oklahoma City. Thanks to her book, these facts can no longer be ignored, or concealed. And those who Ms. Davis reveals have systematically done both for nearly a decade must be called to account."

—FRANK J. GAFFNEY JR.
*President of the Center for Security Policy*

"With enormous skill, courage, and persistence, Jayna Davis pursued the foreign terrorist connections to the tragic attack on the federal building in Oklahoma. Now her fast-paced book reveals the facts that the Clinton administration did not want to confront. This is a must-read for all who want to see beyond the headlines."

—DR. CONSTANTINE C. MENGES
*Former Special Assistant to the President for National Security Affairs and former National Intelligence Officer, CIA*

"This is a must-read for anyone trying to figure out what our government has been doing (or not doing) for the past decade to protect this country from international terrorists. Jayna's book will chill your blood then make it boil."

—DAN VOGEL
*FBI Special Agent (retired)*
*Former Public Information Officer for Oklahoma City FBI field office*

# THE THIRD TERRORIST

## THE MIDDLE EAST CONNECTION TO THE OKLAHOMA CITY BOMBING

### JAYNA DAVIS

**WND BOOKS**
A Division of Thomas Nelson Publishers
*Since 1798*

www.thomasnelson.com

Published in Nashville, Tennessee, by WND Books.

**Library of Congress Cataloging-in-Publication Data**

Davis, Jayna.
    The third terrorist : the Middle East connection to the Oklahoma City bombing / Jayna Davis.
       p. cm.
    Includes bibliographical references (p.   ).
    ISBN 0-7852-6103-6
    1. Oklahoma City Federal Building Bombing, Oklahoma City, Okla., 1995. 2. Terrorists—Middle East. I. Title.
    HV6432.6.D38 2004
    976.6'38053—dc22                       2004001675

*Printed in the United States of America*

04 05 06 07 QW 5 4 3

To our brave servicemen and women and their families, who have nobly sacrificed to conquer global terror. I pray the Lord's divine protection over our nation's troops.

# CONTENTS

## FOREWORD

On the morning of April 19, 1995, my tranquility and feelings of security were demolished in one horrific explosion. I, together with millions of other Americans, watched in torment, as what had once been the Murrah Federal Building in Oklahoma City, collapsed into a mass of smoking ruins. I listened intently to the reports of an obvious terrorist bombing in the United States. My eyes filled with tears as the images of dead children and bloody victims appeared on the television screen.

Along with many other citizens, my suspicions initially focused on a possible Middle Eastern connection. The bombing and murder of innocents was a classic operation of Arab terrorists, and the method conformed to the 1993 bombing of the World Trade Center in New York and the attack on the Khobar Towers in Saudi Arabia. Those suspicions were later buttressed when it was learned that the FBI was looking for several Middle Eastern men—in particular, an individual known as "John Doe 2." A sketch of that individual was distributed throughout the media and an all-points bulletin went out calling for his apprehension. Then, within a week, the entire objective of the investigation changed dramatically and without explanation.

Shortly after the disaster, Timothy McVeigh was arrested by the FBI and charged with the crime. With that arrest and the subsequent apprehension of Terry Nichols, it seemed that all further leads dissipated. The investigation came to an abrupt end. They had their perpetrators, so there was no need to look further. The manhunt for John Doe 2 was abandoned, and the public was led to believe that the initial lead had failed to pan out. No longer was there any official suggestion that there may have been some Middle Eastern involvement. On the contrary, the Clinton administration adopted the party line that the bombing was planned and executed by two white male types. The president himself predictably attacked "two right-wing fanatics" and indicted conservative talk show hosts for their incendiary language calculated to incite the Timothy McVeighs of the nation to launch such attacks.

Once McVeigh and Nichols were in custody, the whole tenor of the bombing investigation did an about face. The government and the media dropped all references to possible state sponsorship and labeled anyone who thought otherwise as a "way-out conspiracy cuckoo." All efforts were redirected to insure, at any cost, the conviction of the two men in custody. The glaring questions that remained unanswered were shoved under the table and ignored. We who were forced to rely upon the reports emanating from the compliant media were convinced that the crime had been solved completely and all the loose ends had been dealt with successfully. I, for one, had been completely misled, but I didn't learn of it until almost six years later.

Everyone swallowed whole the false story put out by the government. That is, almost everyone. A young and beautiful investigative reporter at KFOR, an Oklahoma City television station, was not satisfied with the official account. Jayna Davis was on the scene within minutes of the bombing. She saw the devastation and lived the human suffering. She possessed those rare qualities in a television reporter: honor, integrity, and a willingness to work hard for the full story. Rather than waste her time attending insipid news conferences, Jayna elected to conduct her own independent investigation. And what an investigation it was! Despite adversity, roadblocks, and being told outright lies, Jayna persevered and did, in fact, get to the truth of the Oklahoma City bombing. The startling result of that investigation is reported fully in this book.

Over the next five years, Jayna made every attempt to share the results of her efforts with law enforcement. But to no avail. Nobody wanted to be bothered with the truth because it might cause doubt about the official story. Disillusionment and frustration descended like a pall upon Jayna Davis and her husband, Drew. They began to lose their respect and reliance on the Rule of Law. Then they had an idea.

In early October 2000, I received a letter from Jayna Davis. In it she recounted, in general, the results of her six-year investigation, together with an account of the attacks and stonewalling she had encountered. She told of the careless indifference of the FBI and the supine acceptance of the party line by others to whom she had brought her evidence.

I frankly admit that because I did not know Jayna Davis, I was slightly dubious. Actually, my first reaction was that she was just another conspiracy nut coming out the woodwork. I noted, however, that the letter was extremely well written, articulate, and concise. More important, the letter identified just enough details to suggest that the author possessed much more information than she had revealed.

My interest was stimulated, so I placed a phone call to Ms. Davis. She sounded not only rational but extremely intelligent as well. During the ensuing conversation, she revealed additional facts and assured me that every allegation made was fully confirmed by filmed interviews, affidavits, and unimpeachable documents. When I asked Ms. Davis to send some of the confirming material to me, she responded that she would prefer to bring it to me personally.

On the morning of March 15, 2001, that vivacious lady entered my office in Chicago, accompanied by her husband, Drew. They were carrying three large loose-leaf binders stuffed with documents, which they placed in front of me. As I paged through the reports and affidavits, Jayna and Drew quietly narrated the events surrounding the bombing. After no more than fifteen minutes, I realized that I was sitting in the presence of a true patriot and a courageous young woman, who had accomplished an astounding feat of investigation.

Since then, Jayna Davis has tried over and over to bring her evidence and conclusions to the attention of those responsible for the safety and security of the nation. Time and time again, she has been rebuffed, ridiculed, and ignored. Finally, she has decided to place her findings before the country in the form of a book. She will be ignored no more!

This is a book that needed to be written; the American people deserve it. Jayna Davis writes with the clarity and precision of a seasoned investigative journalist. The facts are riveting, and her narration of the nine-year quest for justice and truth flows as would a novel. If ever there was a page-turner, this is it.

I predict that *The Third Terrorist* will drop like a missile on the federal bureaucracy. No doubt the response will be both immediate and vicious, as is the case whenever a citizen demonstrates the temerity to question the actions or the powers of officialdom. Ms. Davis will certainly suffer personal vilification and false accusations as she has in the past. Her motives and her veracity will be attacked by those who do it so well. I know that Jayna fully expects all that and has the intrepidity to endure it. Let it be known, though, that every attempt to denigrate Ms. Davis and her conclusions is doomed to failure. Why? For the simple reason that there is contained in this book not one fact, not one allegation, not one accusation, not one conclusion that is not supported and corroborated by evidence sufficient to constitute proof in a court of law.

If you are a citizen who is seriously concerned over your own security and that of the United States, it is critical that you read this book cover to cover. I can say with certainty that you will be astounded by the investigative ability of Jayna Davis; dismayed by the ineptitude, if not outright incompetence, of those charged with investigating the Oklahoma City disaster; and, above all, enraged by the inexplicable policy adopted by our government to cover up a state sponsored Middle Eastern terrorist act in the American heartland six years before 9-11.

It is my honest opinion that if the Department of Justice and the federal investigative agencies had not ignored Jayna Davis and instead accepted the mass of creditable evidence compiled by her, indicating direct Middle Eastern involvement in the bombing, the course of future events may have been altered. Had those investigators taken their duty seriously and followed up on the investigation of that information, it is entirely likely that the Twin Towers would still be standing.

I count it as a singular honor to have been asked to contribute this foreword to what may well turn out to be perhaps the most vital exposé of the young twenty-first century. My respect and admiration for Jayna Davis and what she has accomplished is unbounded. She is, without question, the finest and most thorough investigator that I have ever known, and I have known literally thousands. Her professional abilities and technical competence, though, pale in the light of her heroic courage. She endured the wrath of the FBI, the disdain of the Department of Justice, and the snickers of her fellow journalists. Yet she did not waver but continued to pursue the truth. The culmination of that pursuit is this book.

It has been said prophetically that someday the American people will realize what Jayna Davis has been through for her country. Then will she be honored and then will her unselfish labors be finally recognized. Let that day come sooner rather than later. *Una donna non conoscei mai simile a questa.*

—DAVID P. SCHIPPERS
Fmr. Chief Investigative Counsel
for the impeachment trial of
President Bill Clinton

# THE SUSPECTS

Hussain Hashem Al-Hussaini publicly identified himself as the man whom multiple eyewitnesses implicated in the bombing of the Alfred P. Murrah Building in Oklahoma City. As a result, his true name appears in the text of the book. Although a compelling body of evidence inculpates several of Al-Hussaini's Middle Eastern cohorts in the commission of the crime, these individuals have not been arrested or charged. Therefore, the following pseudonyms (exceptions noted) have been selected for the subjects who have been depicted as suspects.

DR. ANWAR ABDUL: A Palestinian immigrant from Tel Aviv who pleaded guilty to insurance fraud in the early 1990s and served time at the federal penitentiary in El Reno, Oklahoma. Court records revealed that the FBI suspected the Palestinian expatriate, who operated under eight known aliases, of having possible connections with the Middle Eastern terror group, the Palestinian Liberation Organization. Six months prior to the bombing, the real estate mogul hired Hussain Al-Hussaini and a handful of ex-Iraqi soldiers to do maintenance work for his property management company, Salman Properties (pseudonym).

MAJID AJAJ: Employee of Dr. Anwar Abdul whom witnesses tied to the bombing plot.

HUSSAIN HASHEM AL-HUSSAINI (true name): The former Iraqi soldier identified in sworn witness statements as Timothy McVeigh's mysterious accomplice, John Doe 2—*The Third Terrorist* whom many Americans believe has eluded justice in the heartland massacre.

EDWIN ANGELES (true name): Cofounder of the Philippines-based terrorist organization, Abu Sayyaf, who asserted he witnessed Terry Nichols's meeting with notorious Middle Eastern terrorists such as Ramzi Yousef.

JOSE GONZALES: An employee of Salman Properties (pseudonym) who was assigned to the same job site as Hussain Al-Hussaini on the morning of April 19. However, Gonzales stated he did not know if Al-Hussaini had reported to work before the bomb went off.

ALI KAMEL: The owner of the Oklahoma City garage, International Auto Mechanics (pseudonym), where witnesses reported suspicious activities in the weeks leading up to the bombing.

ADNON KHAN: A New York City taxi cab driver who purportedly entered into a business partnership with Rizwan Sidiqqi in order to acquire ownership of International Auto Mechanics (pseudonym) from Ali Kamel.

ABU MAHMUD: An Iraqi army veteran with whom Hussain Al-Hussaini resided when he immigrated to the United States. According to witness testimony, in the fall of 1994, Mahmud and Al-Hussaini requested a tour of the downtown business district where the Murrah Building was located.

MARWAN MAHMUD: The brother of Abu Mahmud and former Iraqi army veteran with whom Hussain Al-Hussaini lived upon his entry into the U.S. through Boston's International Rescue Committee.

ABDUL HAKIM MURAD (true name): The partner of internationally renowned bomb maker Ramzi Yousef who was convicted of conspiracy in a foiled 1995 plot to blow up United States commercial airliners shortly after takeoff from the Philippines. Murad claimed credit for the Murrah Building explosion as a member of the Philippine Liberation Army.

RIZWAN SIDIQQI: A Pakistani college student who claims to have purchased International Auto Mechanics (pseudonym) from Ali Kamel and allegedly shut down business operations a few months before the Oklahoma City attack.

RAMZI YOUSEF (true name): The convicted mastermind of the first World Trade Center attack whom a jailed Filipino terrorist accused of collaborating with bombing convict Terry Nichols in the Philippines during the early 1990s.

# THE WITNESSES

Pseudonyms have been used to protect the witnesses from terrorist reprisals and intimidation. These courageous Americans have signed sworn affidavits attesting to the veracity of their stories. They remain steadfastly committed to delivering their testimonies in a court of law if the Middle Eastern suspects they believe perpetrated the April 19, 1995, slaughter of innocents are brought to justice.

HELEN ABDUL: The daughter of Dr. Anwar Abdul who admitted in a hidden camera interview that she fabricated Hussain Al-Hussaini's April 19 time sheet, which alleged the Iraqi national was working at Salman Properties when the bombing occurred.

KAREN ABDUL: The ex-wife of Dr. Anwar Abdul, and mother of Helen Abdul, who perished in the federal building on April 19, 1995.

MANUAL ACOSTA (true name): A Mexican migrant worker who recounted to the FBI his close encounter with a brown Chevrolet pickup which was occupied by two Middle Eastern males that peeled away from the north side of the federal complex the morning of April 19. Acosta narrowly escaped death when the truck bomb erupted minutes later.

KEN BANKS: An Oklahoma City gas station attendant who stated he sold one hundred gallons of diesel fuel to Hussain Al-Hussaini after the Iraqi driver pulled up to the pump in a large Ryder moving van on April 18, 1995.

MIKE BENTON: An Oklahoma City executive who chose Hussain Al-Hussaini from a photo lineup as the man he witnessed timing his run at a rapid rate of speed from the Murrah Building shortly before daybreak on April 19, 1995.

DAINA BRADLEY (true name): A bombing survivor who identified Hussain Al-Hussaini stepping out of the Ryder truck at ground zero moments before the massive fertilizer/fuel oil bomb destroyed the Alfred P. Murrah Building.

ELIZABETH BROWN: A bartender who witnessed Timothy McVeigh drinking beer with Hussain Al-Hussaini at an Oklahoma City tavern on the evening of April 15, 1995.

LANCE CARMICHAEL: A downtown employee who witnessed Timothy McVeigh conversing with a disheveled, shabbily dressed pedestrian while John Doe 2 sat stoically in the cab of the nearby Ryder truck at 8:45 A.M., moments before the terrorist bomb ignited.

RANDY CHRISTIAN: The owner of the Cactus Motel (pseudonym) where he claimed to have observed Timothy McVeigh in the presence of Hussain Al-Hussaini and his Iraqi coworkers in the months, weeks, days, and final moments leading up to the fatal nine o'clock hour on April 19.

LORI CONNER: The wife of Luke Conner and witness to the FBI's statement that their stolen pickup was suspected of involvement in the Oklahoma terror operation.

LUKE CONNER: The owner of the brown pickup, which had been stolen in December 1994, spray-painted yellow, and recovered from an Oklahoma City apartment complex in the wake of the bombing. Conner claimed the FBI initially confirmed that his vehicle was used in the Murrah Building attack.

JEFF DAVIS (true name): The witness who testified that the Dreamland Motel customer in Junction City, Kansas, to whom he delivered Chinese food on April 15, 1995, was not Timothy McVeigh, even though the Oklahoma City bomber was registered as the occupant of the room.

ELVIN DEVERS (true name): An Oklahoma City retiree who resided next door to the house where Hussain Al-Hussaini claimed to be painting the morning of April 19. Devers testified that the Iraqi soldier was not seen on the premises at the time in question.

RITA EDWARDS: An Oklahoma City nurse who socialized with Hussain Al-Hussaini and his Iraqi colleagues prior to the terrorist strike. Edwards recounted the unusual request posed by Al-Hussaini and Abu Mahmud to give them a driven tour of downtown upon their arrival to Oklahoma City in November 1994.

DAVID ELMORE: The Cactus maintenance man who stated he saw Timothy McVeigh crossing the motel parking lot with Hussain Al-Hussaini's Arab coworker as the pair approached a large Ryder truck that reeked of diesel. The sighting took place shortly before 8:00 A.M. on April 19.

ROSANNA ELMORE: The wife of David Elmore who corroborated that Hussain Al-Hussaini's Iraqi friends visited the Cactus Motel (pseudonym) in the weeks and days preceding the bombing.

GARY HAMMERSTEIN: The Cactus Motel (pseudonym) manager who witnessed several Middle Eastern men drive off the property an hour before the bombing in a caravan of vehicles which included a Ryder truck.

GEORGIA HAMMERSTEIN: The Cactus Motel (pseudonym) desk clerk who testified she was on duty when Timothy McVeigh and Hussain Al-Hussaini's former Iraqi army buddy registered for a room on the evening of April 18, 1995.

HENRY JOHNSON: The assistant manager of the Oklahoma City restaurant where Hussain Al-Hussaini performed janitorial duties. Johnson confirmed that Al-Hussaini did not work April 17-20 during the week of the bombing, and stated that the ex-employee resigned his position in May 1995, then re-applied in June. At the time, Al-Hussaini complained to local reporters that he was too busy working a second job to be involved in the bombing. Johnson said Al-Hussaini promptly quit his position again on June 19, just two days after he interviewed with several Oklahoma City reporters.

HERB JOHNSON (true name): Former chief of staff for Oklahoma Senator Jim Inhofe who asked the FBI to officially clear Hussain Al-Hussaini as a suspect in the Oklahoma City bombing, but the Bureau refused, stating it could not comment on a "pending investigation."

JOE KING: The husband of Virginia King and witness to the yellow pickup driving through his Oklahoma City apartment parking lot a few days after the bombing. King asserted that the FBI assured him the abandoned pickup was, in fact, the subject of the official all-points bulletin the Bureau had issued targeting foreign suspects.

VIRGINIA KING: An Oklahoma City resident who named Hussain Al-Hussaini's Middle Eastern coworker as the man she witnessed sitting in the driver's seat of a yellow pickup that was found abandoned at her apartment complex on April 27, 1995. Federal records and police reports prove the FBI theorized the deserted truck served as a getaway vehicle for Arab suspects, which several downtown witnesses saw fleeing the bombsite.

BRENT MARTIN: Coworker who verified Jesse Pearce's testimony that a Ryder truck with two occupants pulled into Johnny's Tire Store thirty minutes before the deadly cargo was delivered to the Murrah Building.

STACY MCBRIDE: The former girlfriend of Hussain Al-Hussaini's Iraqi coworker, Majid Ajaj. McBride testified in an affidavit that Ajaj confessed to involvement in the 1995 Oklahoma City bombing and inferred complicity in the holocaust of September 11, 2001.

LARRY MONROE: Former company foreman for Salman Properties (pseudonym) who disproved Hussain Al-Hussaini's claims to the Oklahoma City press that he was painting a garage at 2241 NW 31$^{st}$ Street when the bomb detonated. Monroe was assigned to perform carpentry work at the same location and vowed that Al-Hussaini was not there on that fateful day.

JERRY NANCE: *The Journal Record* printing press operator who, moments before the explosion, stood in the path of a speeding Mercury Marquis that he believed was driven by Timothy McVeigh with a swarthy companion by his side.

DAN NELSON (true name): An Oklahoma City attorney who identified one of Hussain Al-Hussaini's Iraqi associates in the driver's seat of a pale yellow sedan as it sped away from the vicinity of the Murrah Building minutes before 9:02 A.M.

COLE O'BRIEN: A Cactus customer who testified that he saw one of Hussain Al-Hussaini's Middle Eastern cohorts performing repairs to a 1980s Mercury Marquis with Timothy McVeigh on the motel grounds the evening of April 18, 1995.

RICHARD PARNELL: The Cactus maintenance worker who identified several Middle Eastern employees of Salman Properties (pseudonym) and a malodorous Ryder truck at the motel during the time of the bombing.

JESSE PEARCE: The downtown tire salesman who testified he gave Timothy McVeigh directions to Fifth and Harvey Streets where the federal offices were located approximately thirty minutes before detonation. The witness pegged Hussain Al-Hussaini as the dark-haired stranger whom he saw sitting in the passenger seat of the Ryder truck when McVeigh drove into the parking lot of Johnny's Tire Store at 8:30 A.M. on April 19.

CINDY PRESTON: An Oklahoma City businesswoman who identified Hussain Al-Hussaini as the mysterious jogger she observed running at a breathless pace near the federal complex before sunrise on the morning of the bombing.

TIM RAINS: A former investment partner of Ali Kamel, owner of International Auto Mechanics (pseudonym), who detailed Kamel's shady business practices and the strange circumstances surrounding the hasty sale of his auto garage in the months preceding the bombing.

LEON RHODES: An Oklahoma City resident who witnessed unusual activities at the neighborhood garage, International Auto Mechanics (pseudonym), in the spring of 1995 during a time frame in which the business was reportedly nonoperational.

RACHEL SEALY: An Oklahoma City computer programmer who, moments after the blast, was nearly run down by a speeding brown

Chevy truck with two Middle Eastern occupants in its mad getaway from the kill zone. Sealy named Hussain Al-Hussaini as the driver with whom she locked eyes as the pickup barreled breathlessly close.

BERNIE STANTON: Dr. Anwar Abdul's former employee whose sworn testimony refuted Hussain Al-Hussaini's alibi for April 19, 1995.

JOAN WHITLEY: An Oklahoma County elected official who witnessed a Middle Eastern looking man racing on foot from the vicinity of the Murrah Building in the early morning hours of April 19, 1995.

JOHNNY WILBORN: A patron who identified Timothy McVeigh in the company of Hussain Al-Hussaini at an Oklahoma City night club on the evening of April 15, 1995.

DARBY WILLIAMS: The former secretary of Dr. Anwar Abdul who discredited the authenticity of Hussain Al-Hussaini's time sheet which alleged he was on the job prior to 9:02 A.M. when the Murrah Building bomb exploded.

# CHAPTER 1

# A VIEW OF HELL

APRIL 18, 1995

"Mama, I want to come home," the trembling twenty-year-old softly spoke into the telephone.

A tender answer reached her ears, "Okay. You're ready to come back. Your sister and I miss you."

Daina Bradley had not spoken to her mother in a year. Her life had changed dramatically in just twelve short months. As a teenage runaway sleeping on the streets, she had confronted the danger and vulnerability of living on her own. She resolved to emerge from the sinkhole of self-destruction and voluntarily commit herself to a drug rehab program to overcome an addiction to methamphetamines.

Now the teen mother wrestled with the responsibility of being the sole provider for her three-month-old son. The emotional and financial burden of parenthood threatened to destroy Daina's devotion to the child's father, her first love and high school sweetheart. Living together outside the bonds of marriage and the insecurity that represented was more than she could endure.

"Gabreon, we're going to live with my family," Daina whispered to the slumbering baby as she climbed into her mother's car.

Cheryl Hammons reached over and embraced her daughter, "No matter what has happened between us, I'm here for you. I love you. Nothing will ever change that."

Tears and regrets stained the past. Cheryl was a dedicated mother who raised two girls while juggling around-the-clock jobs as a licensed nurse and housekeeper. But the burgeoning pressure of single parenthood became overwhelming. Alcohol and romantic relationships substituted as a distraction to ease her anxieties. Daina never doubted her mother's love, but she deeply resented the physical abuse she suffered at the hand of Cheryl's live-in boyfriends. She complained, but her mother refused to believe her stories.

At the tender age of eight, Daina began to lash out. She became physically aggressive toward classmates, then turned her rage inward, attempting suicide. Mother and daughter reached an impasse. The state interceded. Daina was institutionalized until her sixteenth birthday. Upon returning back home, the troubled teen returned to a life of revelry—imbibing alcohol to anesthetize suppressed hurts. Resentment and a sense of abandonment had obliterated her hope for the future.

Searching for love and security, she soon found herself pregnant, unwed, and emotionally incapable of caring for her infant daughter, Peachlyn. She buried her fears in pills. What began as momentary escapism quickly turned destructive. She had a drug habit which enflamed a rebellion within. Her mother and older sister, Falesha, raised her child while she grappled with premature adulthood.

"I've made a lot of mistakes, Mama," Daina said with a tear-streaked face that conveyed a daughter's profound regret. "I put you through a lot. I see now how rebellious and disobedient I was. I'm sorry. But I made sure I never got in trouble with the law. You raised me right. I guess I'm trying to say thanks for disciplining me."

"You know I let the state care for you all these years because I was trying to protect you. It tore me apart to be separated from my baby girl. But you were more than I could handle at the time," Cheryl confessed. "I know that you also had a tremendous burden dealing with my drinking. I hope you can forgive me."

The family reunion of April 18 seemed dreamlike. An inner peace and contentment replaced what was once a perceptibly tense environment where tempers were quick to flare. For the first time in years, Daina was together with her mother, sister, her daughter Peachlyn, and her newborn baby Gabreon.

Daina smiled with quiet reassurance. "Living with my family is going to work out this time," she thought.

APRIL 19, 1995, 6:45 A.M.

Clark Peterson stirred from sleep. For some unexplained reason, a palpable uneasiness invaded his morning prayers. Something was amiss, foreboding. His thoughts quickly became preoccupied with the hectic workload awaiting him at the U.S. Army recruiting office. Clark had planned to take vacation time on April 19, but he confronted too many pressing deadlines. He glanced at the clock and grimaced. He was behind schedule. The brisk one block walk from his apartment complex to the Murrah Building landed him in his fourth floor office at the stroke of 7:30 A.M.

7:00 A.M.

"You're happy and you shine," Cheryl Hammons hummed with a light-heartedness that was reminiscent of school mornings when she would rustle Daina from bed singing a familiar tune.

"You sleepy heads need to get up and get going," she repeated as she opened the blinds. "We have to be there by 9:00 A.M. to beat the crowd."

Daina slipped back under the covers. She and her mother had stayed up late playing video games and catching up on the events of the past year. The family planned to visit the federal building in downtown Oklahoma City to obtain a Social Security card for Daina's son, Gabreon. But as the daylight began to bathe the windows and bedroom, Daina felt an inexplicable reticence to initiate the day's plans.

Her sister Falesha voiced a similar discomfort moments later, "Mama, I don't feel right. I want to stay home."

"I need you to go so you can help watch the children, or I can just leave you here to baby-sit Gabreon," Cheryl instructed.

Falesha relented. "I'll go."

7:36 A.M.

"I'm exhausted. I'm going to turn off the phones and crash for a few hours," Steve Bowers told his wife Teresa. He hung up the phone, flipped off the ringer, and melted under the bed covers. He had just returned from the graveyard shift at the Bethany Fire Department, running breathlessly from one ambulance call to the next throughout the pre-dawn hours. For the past two years, Steve had been juggling college and full-time duty as a firefighter and emergency medical technician. His energetic passion for his profession normally enabled him to endure the sleepless nights. But today was one of those rare occasions when his body craved rest. Within seconds, he slipped into deep slumber.

9:00 A.M.

"The girls are elated about starting college next semester," said Dorothy Hill, a forty-three-year-old purchasing agent for the General Services Administration. "Dot," as she was affectionately known by family and friends, enjoyed bantering about her daughter's career ambitions with coworker Steven Curry. The two shared a common bond. Both their daughters were high school seniors who aspired to attend the same state college to earn a degree in physical therapy.

As the work colleagues stood chatting at the office copier, Dot glanced at the clock. It was 9:00 A.M.—time for her morning break. She crossed the room to her desk, which stood flush against the wall of plate glass that framed the front plaza of the Murrah Building. A large Ryder truck, parked just fifty feet away, eclipsed the rays of light that streamed through the window where Dot stood. Oblivious to the bustle of rush hour traffic just outside her office, Dot headed toward the back entrance, crossed the hall, and entered the company break room. After turning on the television, she sat down to savor a moment of escapism in her harried work week.

9:02:13 A.M., ZERO HOUR

Daina turned from the line of waiting patrons on the ground floor of the Social Security Administration office and headed back to the chairs where her children quietly waited. Seconds later, a brilliant white light blinded her. A thunderous concussion thrust her downward. Unconsciousness seized Daina as her world faded to black.

A Ryder moving van parked twelve feet from where Daina and her family stood exploded, instantly transforming the nine-story structure into a smoldering cauldron of flames and acrid smoke. The terrorist bomb unleashed a searing shock wave that shredded concrete, cable, steel, and glass at the blinding rate of seven thousand feet per second, more than two times the muzzle velocity of an M-16 assault rifle. A crushing force field indiscriminately sought its victims with an immeasurable fury—lacerating human flesh, shattering bones, dismembering limbs, and compressing internal organs. The cold hand of death clutched many without delay. For others, the end was less merciful, suspended in mind-boggling horror, as they felt their bodies free-falling after the floor beneath their feet instantly vaporized.

The propulsion of the bomb simulated a giant dagger plunging into the belly of the building, severing it in two. The majority of federal workers located in the northern sector died as one floor after another collapsed, sending countless employees plummeting into the debris pit at ground zero. The monstrous, explosive pressure wrenched the cement-encased edifice from its foundation, peeled back the roof like cardboard, and hurled office workers out of windows. Several victims landed in the thirty foot wide crater the truck bomb had carved out of the earth below. Inside the Federal Employees Credit Union, director Florence Rogers was instructing a group of six female employees who were sitting just a few feet away when suddenly, the women vanished. The bomb's fatal course viciously devoured the floor of Rogers's office, stopping three inches shy of her desk.

A spark of electricity surged through Clark Peterson's computer as an impenetrable darkness flooded the room. The agonizing sound of moaning metal screeched inside Clark's ears. Glowing objects, illuminated by intense white heat, flew past at incalculable speeds. Fractions of seconds moved in slow motion as Clark's eyes recorded the last breath of a female coworker standing just ten feet away. The woman screamed into the black abyss as the stranglehold of gravity violently pushed her arms heavenward. In that harrowing moment, both she and Clark spiraled downward into death's dungeon.

The scorching fireball that erupted from the enclosed cargo hold of the moving van incinerated the daycare center located on the second floor. Several toddlers were burned beyond recognition. One child was decapitated. Fifteen youngsters and three workers perished. The glass façade that lined the north side of the federal building disintegrated into a shower of razor-sharp rain. Cement slabs were minced into white powder that coated bleeding corpses with a ghostly white pallor.

The fractured carcass, which housed federal agencies, spewed columns of rapidly rising smoke as wounded survivors staggered from the choking black mist. Many were partially clad, stripped down to their underwear, seemingly unaware of streaming blood that saturated their torn clothing. They scampered barefooted across a blanket of shimmering slivers of glass before collapsing on sidewalks. A trembling woman quietly awaited medical treatment as she bled profusely—her trachea and jugular vein slashed. A female coworker clutched the victim's hand, unconcerned that she too had been gravely wounded. Shock obviously had masked the excruciating pain.

On the north side of the building, gas tanks and tires of parked cars ignited and exploded. Blistering heat from rows of burning vehicles crackled in the chilly morning air. The tremendous vacuum at the core of the explosion caused surrounding buildings to shudder and buckle, violently shattering windows and tossing people about like rag dolls. At the nearby YMCA, the vibration from the detonation lifted a two-hundred and forty pound man from his bed, thrusting him through a window like a battering ram. Before Trent Smith could comprehend what was happening, he was dangling halfway out of a gaping hole encased by jagged glass, thankful his sizeable frame prevented him from being completely expelled from the building.

### 9:02:19 A.M.

For several interminable seconds, time remained suspended. Falling ceiling tiles pelted Dot as opaque darkness coated the break room where she was trapped. Thankfully, an adjacent elevator shaft had served as a firewall, insulating her from the deluge of bone-crushing debris. Yet no one was shielded from the torrential current that surged from the bowels of the terrorists' lethal instrument. The noxious airflow consumed Dot's body and instantly siphoned the life's breath from her lungs. A paralyzing fear of suffocation accompanied the peculiar sensation.

"What is happening?" she thought. "The TV blew up. The air conditioner on the second floor must have fallen. Surely we haven't been bombed?" Dot winced in pain as she opened her eyes to seek out an escape route. Abrasive dust scratched her corneas with knifelike jabs. "I can't see. I can't breathe. Am I going to die?"

"Help me, help me!" a frightened survivor cried out, shaking loose the anxiety that had seized Dot.

"Hold on, I'm coming," she answered. Navigating by hand, Dot felt her way through the black hole of destruction. Seconds later, she clutched the trembling hand of a young female janitor pinned in the debris outside the break room doorway.

"Follow me, I'll get you out of here," Dot promised. The two women began edging their way along the granite walls that lined the hallway when they met Dot's boss, Don Rogers. A stream of faint light guided them to an exit on the west end of the building.

### 9:03 A.M.

Dazed and traumatized children from the nearby YMCA daycare center wandered into the chaos searching for their parents. Within seconds, passing strangers embraced the trembling youngsters who had just been brutally slashed by shards of glass that had been converted into flying shrapnel. Frantic mothers and fathers darted through the pandemonium, hysterically crying out their children's names, but few reunions would take place. In desperation, one woman repeatedly begged passersby, "Have you seen my daughter?" No one answered.

9:05 A.M.

Daina lay entombed in a cement coffin. Her body immobilized. Her ears deafened by the haunting wails of her mother, "No, No, No," Cheryl cried.

"Mama, Mama, where are you?" she screamed. Suddenly, she heard the faint whimpers of her children, Gabreon and Peachlyn, who had been seated just inches from her when the bomb detonated. But now their tiny bodies were unreachable. Suffocating black smoke stung Daina's lungs with every labored gasp for air. As she lay buried in a shroud of petrifying darkness, Daina's only comfort was her loved ones' tortured voices. Though agonizing to hear, at least her family had survived.

Seconds later, a dangling section of the building collapsed, muffling the cries of her mother and children. The only sound Daina could distinguish now was the distant moaning of her sister Falesha. The omnipresence of death enveloped her as she drifted back into unconsciousness.

9:06 A.M.

"What the hell happened here?" Dot shrieked.

"I don't know," coworker Don Rogers answered in amazement.

"It looks like the war zone in Bosnia!" Dot exclaimed. Immediately, she was reminded of the daycare center on the second floor. She was grateful that her eighteen-month-old grandson had stopped attending the facility six months ago, but Dot continued to visit several youngsters at the daycare to whom she had grown emotionally attached. She ached at the thought of their cruel fate.

"My God, Don, the babies," Dot sobbed.

"They're gone," Don replied in grief-stricken resignation.

"No . . . No, that can't be."

At that moment, Dot spotted an Oklahoma City policeman racing toward the gaping hole where her office once stood. "Officer, there are children in that daycare," she shouted.

"What daycare?" Officer Terrance Yeakey apprehensively inquired.

"On that second floor, there's a daycare center."

"How many kids?"

"Not more than twenty-five," she answered as pressing heaviness clawed at her heart. The officer grabbed his dispatch radio, reported the position of the daycare center, then disappeared into the crumbled remains of the General Services Administration office, which had shouldered the brunt of the blast. Dot followed him in.

9:08 A.M.

Two policemen, who were among the first to arrive at the scene, ventured into the bowels of the smoldering structure. Their flashlights illuminated the massive destruction inside the Social Security office. Wading through rising water from burst pipes, the officers navigated through a minefield of live electrical wires. A short time later, they emerged from the suffocating darkness and dust, carrying an unconscious woman by the upper torso and legs. As Officer Keith Simonds's eyes adjusted to the bright morning sun, he immediately noticed he had been holding an exposed bone of the victim's upper arm. He feared her wounds might be mortal. Days later, Simonds and his partner, Sergeant Richard Williams, learned the Jane Doe who they extricated from the rubble had survived. Her name was Falesha Bradley.

9:10 A.M.

Panicked shrieks of petrified children resonated inside the skeletal remains of the Murrah Building. Don Hull, a homicide detective with the Oklahoma City Police, spotted a small foot and started digging. Minutes later, he embraced twenty-month-old Joseph Webber. A large laceration lined the toddler's face, yet amazingly, the wound was not bleeding. The officer tenderly lifted the child's broken arm. A promising sign followed. The seemingly lifeless boy gasped for air, causing blood to pour from the gash on his head. Little Joseph stopped breathing twice during the short dash to the medics waiting to transport the most critical victims. On both occasions, the quick-thinking officer administered CPR and revived him.

"That's my baby. That's my baby," a woman yelled from behind. Realizing the child might be dying, Detective Hull hid the fragile patient from the young mother's view as she clamored to see her injured son.

"He will be all right, but he needs to go to the hospital now," Hull reassured the hysterical parent as he scrambled to the back of the ambulance. Suddenly, the child's head fell limp and his eyes rolled back. There was no respiration. Once again, Hull anxiously blew air into the child's tiny lungs, begging him to breathe. His prayerful pleas were answered. Joseph Webber would be counted among the handful of survivors of the federal complex daycare center.

9:12 A.M.

Disbelief and shock seized rescuers as they scoured the ruins of the Murrah Building daycare. They uncovered tiny, lifeless forms imprisoned under layers of jumbled toys, mangled cribs, and crushed chairs. After disposing of several bricks and concrete rocks, Oklahoma City Police Sergeant John Avera unearthed a baby girl. He gently scooped her up and scurried through the parking garage. The child lay motionless in the officer's hands. He carefully placed his precious cargo in the outstretched arms of a firefighter. At that moment, a photographer peering through his viewfinder flashed his camera. The dying little girl with the blood-spattered head and broken body would be forever memorialized. The most defenseless victim, one-year-old Baylee Almon, would become the universal symbol of April 19, 1995, and America's innocence lost.

A grievously wounded survivor valiantly attempted to assist the victims within his reach. The man's arm had been blown off, but shock prevented him from noticing. The macabre surrealism witnessed by scores of survivors and rescue personnel generated impulses of adrenaline, while numbness and denial set in. During the initial hours of the rescue operation, that numbness insured the sanity of the hundreds of firefighters, police officers, paramedics, physicians, nurses, structural engineers, clergymen, and citizen volunteers who confronted unfathomable carnage to save lives. Local emergency rooms overflowed with the walking wounded as more than five hundred people sought medical treatment for injuries. Some drove themselves to the hospital while the very critical arrived on bloodstained gurneys; unconscious and unaware they were slipping dangerously closer to death.

## 9:17 A.M.

"Ma'am you will have to move. You're standing on someone," Officer Yeakey yelled.

Dot looked down but saw nothing—not a hand or foot, no sign of life. However, just inches beneath Dot's feet, a coworker had been buried alive. Another colleague staggered from the depths of the annihilation bleeding from a severed jugular vein. Miraculously, eleven of Dot's fellow employees survived, but the death count would have been much greater had the building manager, Don Rogers, not postponed a 9 A.M. employee meeting. If the morning activities had proceeded as planned, the entire staff would have been in the GSA conference room that was virtually obliterated in the explosion.

During Dot's frenzied search for friends and coworkers, she could not help but contemplate the enigmatic circumstances that snatched her from death's grasp—a rescheduled staff meeting, leaving her desk two minutes before the bomb detonated, and entering the break room, which in turn became an enclave of protection.

"Thank you, God, for saving my life," she prayed in silent reverence. But the serenity of that poignant moment was short-lived. As an employee of the federal agency that managed the Murrah Building, Dot bore an immense burden for the safety of each and every tenant. An unrelenting drive pushed her forward. She had to reach the babies on the second floor, but how? A large unidentified man scaling a wooden fence that had been propped up against the southeast side of the crippled structure provided the lead. Despite her inherent fear of heights, Dot mounted the makeshift ladder.

"You don't need to be up there," hollered John Creswell, a maintenance man whom Dot knew well.

"But I have got to help," Dot insisted. "My husband Chris says I have a weak mind and a strong back. Let me do what I can." As she climbed skyward, she spotted a man trapped several floors above her. His piercing, unflinching stare silently communicated a yearning to get out of there.

"You don't need to be up there," John bellowed emphatically. But Dot was impervious to the warning. Mesmerized by the stranger's engaging eyes, she continued to ascend. The lively, strong-willed, forty-three-year-old refused to abandon the rescue.

"He's gone, Dot. There's nothing you can do for him," John shouted from below. Dot froze. Her efforts were hopeless. Later, she learned the morbid details. The torrential downpour of splintered concrete had sheared off the victim's legs. She was spared the ghastly sight; however, the man's penetrating gaze burned an indelible mental picture that would never fade.

Weakened by despair, she slowly descended the wooden fence. Glancing downward, she noticed a woman trying to pry open the door to the second floor. "Ma'am you can't go in there. It's blocked," Dot yelled. "Do you have a child in there?"

A tear-streaked face looked upward, "Yes."

"What's his name?"

"It's Blake."

"Blake Kennedy?"

"Yes."

"I know Blake. Do you pray?"

"Yes, I do."

"Let's pray for your little boy to be safely returned to you," Dot said. Fear of the unknown seemed almost bearable as the two strangers sought strength in their faith. But their prayers came too late. At 9:02 A.M., the truck bomb had savagely ended the life of the fair-haired eighteen-month-old toddler.

9:20 A.M.

"Someone just blew up the Murrah Building! They need you down there right now," a woman shouted just outside Steve Bowers's bedroom window. He was jarred from his sleep moments earlier when the foundation of his home shook violently, but he figured it was probably a plane crash. He was so exhausted, he drifted back to sleep, comfortable in the assumption that emergency personnel working the day shift could handle the crisis.

"Wake up. They need you," the woman persisted, as she tapped forcefully on the glass. His wife Teresa had contacted a next door neighbor to wake Steve because he had turned off the ringers on the phones.

Steve sat up to shake off his grogginess. "This can't be possible," he thought. "A bomb has leveled the federal building!" His drowsiness gave way to overwhelming dread. As a former U.S. Navy combat medic who served in the Middle East, he had witnessed the butchery of terrorist bombings. Grisly flashbacks invaded his consciousness. He envisioned 1983, Beirut, and an unspeakable bloodbath. A crazed suicide bomber crashed an explosives-laden truck into the Marine barracks, killing two-hundred forty-one sleeping servicemen. For seventy-two grueling hours, Steve directed morgue operations where he tagged more than one hundred corpses that had been crushed beyond recognition.

Steve jumped into his pickup and sped downtown. Within minutes, he caught the first glimpse of the smoke-filled horizon. The Murrah Building, where he once worked as a Navy recruiter, had been nearly erased from the landscape.

"I was trained to deal with this overseas, but not here in the heart of America. This is Oklahoma City, not a war zone. Not here. No way!"

9:21 A.M.

Convulsive shivers awakened Daina. She realized she was submerged in freezing water and the level kept rising. The blast had severed a pressurized pipe that provided chilled water to the air conditioning system. The temperature gauge was set at forty-two degrees Fahrenheit. Panic gripped her as the cold liquid seeped into Daina's ears. She feared she would drown.

Escape eluded her. An immovable concrete beam pinned her lower right leg, shattering the bone. Steel reinforcement rods crisscrossed her body like prison bars. Concrete shards buried her petite frame, rendering her nearly invisible to rescue workers who were combing the building for survivors. Miraculously, a firefighter heard her muffled cry from beneath the rubble. Within minutes, she was in a blanket and fitted with an oxygen mask.

Rescuers were forced to saw through steel rebar in order to assess the grim condition of the barricaded, shivering woman. The blast caused several floors to pancake like an accordion, compacting nine floors to the height of only two. Tons of debris teetered above the immense cement column that held Daina's leg captive at ground level. To move it would surely trigger an avalanche and certain death for nearby emergency crews. The only way to free her limb would be to carefully saw through the beam, but attempting such a precarious feat presented tremendous risk. Nevertheless, the sawing began and the rescue effort continued.

### 9:37 A.M.

The ceaseless howl of sirens roused Clark Peterson from unconsciousness. He was sitting on a ceiling tile that rested upon a three-story pile of rubble. The tile prevented him from being impaled by protruding table legs and wooden spikes. The swirling debris cloud that enveloped Clark slowly dissipated, revealing a sheer drop-off extending from the ninth floor to the cavernous crater at the base of the building. Drained and disoriented, he realized he was situated inches from a precipitous ledge. His arms and legs moved without noticeable pain; however, blood seeped from a slash in the back of his head.

An interminable thirty minutes passed before helping hands grasped Clark's wrists and lifted him from the third to the fourth floor. Gazing at the mind-numbing destruction that encompassed him, Clark pondered the awe-inspiring evidence of divine protection.

"How could I be alive when the five floors above me collapsed, leaving nothing but air and sky above? God's angels must have been watching over me."

Clark was seated just seventy feet above the bomb, yet his eardrums did not rupture. The ceiling tile that broke his fifteen foot fall remained level. Had it tipped over, he would have plunged several more stories—the tragic fate of many. Most significantly, Clark was working directly in the bull's eye of the kill zone. However, he was among the few who eluded death within the deepest penetration of the blast. Three of his colleagues were not so fortunate.

### 9:40 A.M.

Steve adeptly evaded roadblocks, zigzagging through familiar shortcuts and alleyways before parking his truck a block from the bombed out building. As he sprinted to the garage entryway, he prayed, "Lord, don't let me find the dead bodies of anyone I know."

"Sir, we could use you in the basement area. We've located a woman screaming from beneath the wreckage, but it's going to take some work to get her out," said an Oklahoma City fireman who was standing post at the southwest entrance. Steve nodded his acceptance of the assignment and headed through the parking garage. As he surveyed the rows of parked cars, an eerie feeling overcame him. Just a few steps to the north, Steve looked upon untold death and devastation, yet hundreds of vehicles remained untouched, quietly draped in a fine white mist of ash and pulverized cement.

"Each one of these cars has a family attached to it, and some of them are never going to return home," he thought.

### 9:55 A.M.

"Where are my babies? Where are my mama and my sister?" Daina begged. Steve Bowers looked on with a sinking feeling. He cringed at the sound of the victim's tormented cries. The former battlefield medic had barely tolerated the shrieks of wounded Marines years earlier, but now he confronted the unbearable—the wails of a helpless woman in anguish.

"Hang in there. We don't know about your family just yet, but we're going to get you out soon," Steve gently reassured Daina. His attention was then immediately drawn overhead to the cement slab hanging precariously by a couple of two-inch pieces of rebar. The lives of rescuers hinged upon the jagged, weakened steel holding its grip as a fireman sawed through the beam to release Daina's trapped leg. Suddenly, the concrete snapped and spider webbed.

"It's giving way!" a rescuer yelled. Hearts stopped. Everyone stood motionless. Wary eyes looked upward. Yellow hardhats below slowly turned crimson, as thick red droplets of blood steadily dripped through the fractured concrete.

"Will someone check above us and see whether there's a live victim trapped up there?" a doctor on the scene asked.

"I'll go, sir," Steve volunteered. He attached his flashlight to his fireman's helmet, climbed an embankment of debris, and entered the confined crawl space. Inside the narrow tunnel, he noticed what appeared to be a rolled up section of carpet. But as he inched closer, the indistinguishable object came into focus, revealing the severed torso of a young woman. Steve closed his eyes for a moment in an attempt to block the grisly image from his mind.

He delivered the tragic news to the doctor. "It's a fatality," Steve said solemnly.

10:30 A.M.

All options had been examined and ruled out. Amputation was unavoidable in order to save Daina. An orthopedic surgeon from Oklahoma City's Children's Hospital answered the call for help. Now, Dr. Andrew Sullivan must tell the trembling young woman the only way she was coming out of the building alive was without her leg.

"No, I can't do it. I won't do it," Daina cried in horror and shock. Her pleas did not diminish the doctor's resolve. This was a life or death dilemma. He calmly explained that if she refused, they had no choice but to leave the building. The structure was unstable and could cave in without warning. Tears filled her large brown eyes as she grappled with the inevitability of the doctor's dire prognosis. There was no alternative. Daina conceded to the operation.

"Do what you have to do. I want out of here," she whispered reluctantly.

Maneuvering inside the slim crevice that encased Daina posed tremendous obstacles. Dr. Sullivan struggled to reach his patient, crawling combat style on his stomach.

"There's another bomb in the building. All companies, come out of the building. Right now! Everybody evacuate," a fireman bellowed over a loudspeaker. Medical teams and rescue crews confronted the unthinkable. They must leave behind trapped survivors.

"Don't leave me. Don't leave me. I'm going to die," Daina beseeched Dr. Sullivan as he reluctantly pulled away. Abandoning her tore at the very fiber of his heart. He had dedicated twenty-three years to healing people. How could he desert a terrified woman as she lay dying?

The bomb scare proved innocuous. However, an agonizing forty-five minutes passed before rescue teams were permitted to return. Then came the arduous task of carving out enough room for Daina's surgery. During the next few hours, fireman Jeff Hail worked tirelessly to saw through rebar and remove the wreckage that impeded access to her crushed leg. Meanwhile, several physicians collaborated. The situation was bleak. The operation would be perilously delicate, with the odds stacked against the patient. Daina was in shock and hypothermia had set in due to the frigid water. Dr. Sullivan later learned her condition was graver than he was able to diagnose at the scene. Several of her ribs had been broken. One lung had collapsed and blood was quickly filling both lung cavities.

The emergency room physician who assisted Dr. Sullivan feared that the use of any anesthetics, such as morphine or Demerol, would shut down her respiration. She would likely lapse into a coma and die. Instead, she would be administered a barbiturate sedative that had a hypnotic, amnesic effect. It would erase her memory of the pain but do little to deaden the sensation. While Dr. Sullivan anxiously waited for the drug to take effect, he silently prayed. Would she bleed to death in his hands? Would he die in a building that threatened to crumble at any moment? Working under such austere, precarious conditions made such fears insuppressible.

Limited access to Daina's leg further compounded the crisis. Dr. Sullivan was forced to lay on top of her, performing the gruesome procedure with just one hand. Once the tourniquet was securely in place, the surgeon skillfully sliced through her knee to avoid cutting through dense bone. With the first incision, Daina began to thrash about and scream in inexorable torment. Dr. Sullivan had to brace her left leg as he continued the amputation, severing the ligaments, tendons, and muscles.

"Please just let her pass out," Steve prayed as he held tightly to the backboard to which Daina was harnessed throughout the procedure. He was poised to extricate her the moment the surgery was complete, but the wait seemed interminable. Twice, Daina was pulled out as she let out an agonizing screech. Steve, the doctors, and the firemen were aghast to discover her leg was still attached. Four scalpels had been broken, and the amputation knife dulled to the point of ineffectiveness. Dr. Sullivan remembered he had brought his personal pocketknife. He made the last cut.

Daina survived the crude operation that normally would be performed only under battlefield conditions. Days later, the twenty-year-old awakened from her traumatic ordeal to learn her mother, daughter, and newborn son did not survive. Their final screams of terror echoed in her mind.

1:00 P.M.
"This is unbelievable. No one could survive this," a fireman muttered as he shook his head in despair.

"No, I've seen this before. I've been there before. There are going to be voids where people are trapped alive. We've just got to find those pockets," Steve explained. He had experienced the miracle of locating someone tucked inside a void days after the Beirut bombing. He stubbornly clung to the promise the same would happen here. But as the hours ticked by, early glimmers of hope waned. Excavating the mound of rubble at ground zero seemed insurmountable. Every scrap and fragment had to be removed by hand in five-gallon buckets, a painstaking and frequently frustrating process.

As he scoured the devastation, Steve feared he would unknowingly step on someone's grave, desecrating sacred ground. Whenever he felt a spongy sensation beneath his feet, he jumped backwards and dropped to his knees. Leaning over, he listened intently for faint whimpers. He refused to allow the ensuing silence to dampen his eagerness to dig feverishly. Yet time after time, he labored in vain. He often uncovered padded office partitions where he expected to find an unconscious survivor. On other occasions, he unearthed the dead.

5:30 P.M.
Looming thunderclouds greedily devoured the fading glow of daylight as a hard driving spring rain ushered in nightfall. The tortured remains of the federal complex groaned and swayed, powerless to withstand cruel wind gusts. Structural instability plagued the thoughts of fatigued rescuers. Lightning crackled. Thunder raged and roared. Heaven sounded a mournful cry, but threatening weather did not dampen Oklahoma's collective prayer to hear yet another voice from the mass grave.

10:00 P.M.
"We were able to free a young female from the basement area. In fact, she is being brought out as we speak. It took us an hour or so to rescue her. We had to remove some bodies and debris," explained an elated fire official during an internationally televised interview. Fifteen–year-old Brandi Liggons endured twelve terrifying hours entombed with several friends who died before help arrived.

But there would be no more rescues. No more survivors. Instead, the dead were delicately retrieved, identified, and tallied. The staggering number of casualties carved a grievous wound in America's heartland. The April 19, 1995, bombing of the Alfred P. Murrah Building became the 20th century's deadliest act of terrorism on U.S. soil. In the coming days, Oklahomans buried their children, mothers, fathers, siblings, husbands, wives, aunts, uncles, cousins, and precious friends.

The dark annals of history recorded one-hundred seventy-one dead, including three unborn babies. One terrorist bomb orphaned thirty children while two hundred nineteen others would grow up in a single parent household. More than five hundred survivors injured in the explosion would bear the scars of that fateful day. Some were permanently maimed or disabled by the loss of limbs. Others healed externally, but never internally, carrying with them the debilitating fear and horror of 9:02 A.M.

# CHAPTER 2

# MANHUNT

APRIL 19, 1995, 8:45 A.M.

Broke and jobless, thirty-four-year-old Manuel Acosta set out from an Oklahoma City homeless shelter to earn a day's wages. The once successful businessman made a daring sacrifice to escape the political corruption and poverty of Mexico. Self-educated and driven by tireless ambition, Manuel was determined to live the American dream and make a new life for his son. However, he could not ignore the hampering influence of his language barrier. While studying English, soliciting construction work presented the only viable means of earning survival pay. Manuel climbed inside the cab of his old pickup, which displayed Mexican license tags, and launched his morning ritual of locating a building contractor who was in need of hiring cheap labor to avoid project delays.

Shortly before 9:00 A.M., he rolled into the downtown area, parked his truck and continued his quest on foot. As he approached NW 5th Street, he spotted what appeared to be a potential construction site manager parked in front of the Murrah Building. He had developed an eye for their expensive new pickups and this one was a later model Chevrolet with a shiny, brown finish, tinted windows, and a bug deflector on the front hood. Encouraged by the prospect of scoring a job assignment, he moved closer.

Suddenly, a flurry of activity ensued. Manuel observed a Middle Eastern man waving a hand signal to a foreign looking male who was standing on the north side of 5$^{th}$ Street. Both individuals were dark-complexioned with black hair. One of the men wore blue jogging pants, a black shirt, and black jacket. Manuel stood close enough to discern strands of gray hair in the beard of the second Middle Easterner.

Fractions of a second later, both men sprinted and jumped inside the brown Chevy pickup that had grabbed Manuel's attention moments earlier. Darkly tinted windows obstructed his view of the driver as the pickup peeled away from the curb. Five minutes later, a concussive wave of fire erupted beneath the shadow of the towering federal building.

9:15 A.M.

Shockwaves rocked homes and businesses within miles of the explosion's epicenter. Minutes later, news helicopters hovered above the harrowing scene. The choppers' blades sliced through dense black pillars of smoke that spewed skyward in the ominous shape of an Oklahoma twister. Photographer Mike Duncan and I arrived downtown as the local television news crews transmitted the first recorded images to Oklahoma, CNN, and the world.

We parked our KFOR-TV news vehicle and trekked on foot several blocks southward to the Murrah Building, hoping to slip through law enforcement blockades. Glass shards crackled and snapped beneath our shoes as we sprinted across shimmering sidewalks and roadways that eerily reflected the radiance of the morning sunlight. The explosion had blown out windows in every office building and high-rise within our immediate range of sight and beyond. My eyes drank in the staggering devastation, but my mind could not comprehend the possible cause.

"This quite likely was a natural gas explosion," I reasoned. "Terrorism is out of the question, not in Oklahoma."

A block north of the federal building, Mike paused to shoot more video. We had encountered property damage, but no victims. Now, just feet away from our camera was a blood-drenched woman trembling in unimaginable pain. I watched in horror as her friends and coworkers huddled around, offering gentle reassurances help would arrive soon. Minutes passed and still no ambulance, no paramedics. Blood continued to pump forth from deep gashes that crisscrossed her delicate face, arms, and torso.

"This is unreal," I cried out to Mike, emotionally charged by the intensity of the moment. "We are surrounded by emergency crews, but there are too many victims and not enough paramedics to help this badly wounded woman."

Mike nodded in agreement.

For the first time in my reporting career, I felt like a voyeur looking upon human suffering, recording the agony, then moving on, helpless to assist. Within seconds, we were standing at the intersection of Robinson and 6th Streets, one block north of ground zero. Mesmerized by the steady flow of trembling passersby with blood-streaked faces, I stood motionless, overcome by the enormity of what had just transpired.

"One man—just one man—is coming out of that building. Are there no more survivors?" I observed aloud. A silver-haired, wiry framed gentlemen zealously clutched the fireman's ladder as he cautiously descended several stories, guided by the coaxes of a rescuer inches from his reach.

"Thank God I'm alive," Brian Espe exclaimed before a throng of cameras and microphones. His hollow stare and ashen complexion communicated bewilderment and fear. Less than thirty minutes before, the fifth floor offices of the U.S. Department of Agriculture instantaneously eroded before Espe's eyes.

"I went under a table when the ceiling started falling in. That's what saved me I guess, except there was a floor still where I was," Espe breathlessly explained. KFOR-TV's videotape capturing that poignant moment would replay again and again on international airwaves. From that point onward, our coverage of the 1995 terrorist massacre became a haze of blood, tears, and human sorrow. One interview ran into the next. Each time, the shaken witnesses recounted horrors the mind cannot fathom.

## 9:30 A.M.

Spine tingling flashbacks of El Salvador, brutal revolution, and street massacres burst forth from the dark corridors of Claudia Rossavik's mind. The forty-year-old doctor immigrated to America nearly a generation ago. She assumed time and distance had neutralized her haunting childhood memories of torture and mass executions by government soldiers. But those once suppressed snapshots of death flickered to life as she observed the April 19 butchery, administering first aid to the bloodied, disoriented survivors in her midst.

"Do you speak Spanish?" a voice spoke softly in Spanish, Claudia's native language.

Engrossed in her task of bandaging a patient, the physician glanced upward to see a distinctly foreign looking man with prominent, dark features. His unkempt hair and tattered coat, which bore witness to the blast's fury, made him appear to be a homeless vagrant. The courteous stranger then introduced himself as Manuel Acosta.

"Yes, I speak Spanish," Claudia answered.

He smiled exuberantly. "Then I can help you. You are small, and if you don't mind, I would like to carry the seriously wounded to the ambulances for you."

Claudia welcomed the gentlemanly offer. For the next hour the two treated the injured, many of whom were retirees who resided at a nearby apartment complex. Their frail bodies trembled in the chilly morning air. "Everyone move it back now! There's another bomb," an anonymous cry roared through the chaos at the makeshift clinics near the bombsite.

Stricken with panic, Claudia and Manuel joined the throng of medical workers who instinctively sprinted to safety. But after running just a few yards, Manuel abruptly stopped. "We can't run. Look at all these helpless elderly people. We can't leave them!" he exclaimed. He then turned back and attempted to carry a fragile eighty-year-old woman.

11:15 A.M.
"Dr. Rossavik, there is something I must say," Manuel confessed in a contrite tone. "I cannot bear to see all this bloodshed and not tell what I know."

"What is it?" Claudia asked, noticing his serious demeanor. "Before the explosion, I was downtown and I think I saw the people who did this terrible thing. I must tell the authorities," he declared.

Claudia motioned a nearby police squad car. An FBI agent was quickly dispatched to the scene, and within thirty minutes, Claudia found herself translating Manuel's brush with the Middle Eastern men whom he witnessed fleeing the scene in a brown Chevy pickup. The next day, the FBI presented Manuel a photographic line up of potential suspects. He did not recognize any of the subjects featured. However, agents requested he remain in the United States to appear before the federal grand jury. But the subpoena for his testimony would not be issued. After a year of washing dishes and barely scraping together a living, the Mexican alien could wait no longer and returned to his homeland. The immigrant who risked deportation to report his close encounter with foreign terrorists would never know the far-reaching impact of his noble deed.

Manuel Acosta's account marked the first solid lead in a manhunt that stretched worldwide. Enterprising reporters wasted no time tuning in to police scanner traffic to monitor the all-points-bulletin that flooded law enforcement channels. The bulletin would be repeatedly broadcast the morning of April 19.

"Be on the lookout for a late model, almost new, Chevrolet full-size pickup, will be brown in color with tinted windows and smoke-colored bug deflector on the front of pickup." Acosta and several downtown witnesses who had seen the suspects speculated that the men riding in the cab of the speeding brown pickup were of Arab descent. One male was reported to be in his mid-twenties; the second was described as thirty-five to thirty-eight-years-old. The truck's darkly tinted windows obscured the identity of a possible third terrorist—the driver.

"Middle Eastern male, twenty-five to twenty-eight years of age, six feet tall, athletic build, dark hair and a beard, dark hair and a beard, break," the dispatcher for the Oklahoma County Sheriff's repeated throughout the morning.

When an officer in the field questioned the authenticity of the information, the dispatcher responded firmly, "Authorization FBI."

**4:30 P.M.**

The FBI mysteriously withdrew the APB and issued a directive to local law enforcement agencies to immediately terminate its broadcast. A veteran officer with the Oklahoma County Sheriff's department demanded to know why the Teletype had been abruptly cancelled.

"Just pull it!" the federal agent barked through the phone line. The conversation ended.

**5:30 P.M.**

By nightfall, the APB for foreign terrorists dominated the evening news.

"Police were told by one witness that he saw at least two men in blue jumpsuits running away from a minivan outside the courthouse just before the blast. The witness told investigators the two men fled in a brown pickup," asserted NBC news correspondent Jim Cummins.

"This information is not a rumor," explained Oklahoma City's KWTV news anchor Jennifer Reynolds. "This was a radiogram, authority of the FBI, which was issued over radio channels to law enforcement authorities in central Oklahoma, and it was read aloud to law enforcement authorities."

**11:30 P.M.**

Shortly before midnight, FBI agents, armed with a sealed search warrant, raided a North Dallas apartment home where two Middle Eastern men were taken into custody for questioning. Meanwhile, authorities apprehended a third Arab male at an Oklahoma City motel. According to CNN, federal agents serving on the newly dubbed "Bombing Task Force" subjected all three men to intense interrogation. The Immigration and Naturalization Service (INS) then arrested the men for immigration violations.

Earlier that day, the Oklahoma Highway Patrol (OHP) issued an all-points-bulletin characterizing the trio as possible bombing suspects. The Middle Eastern subjects had been driving around Oklahoma City in a Chevy Blazer or Suburban shortly before the blast. According to news accounts, the men flagged down an OHP trooper to ask for directions. Before the vehicle pulled away, the suspicious officer jotted down the license number and later traced the tag to a blue Chevrolet Cavalier that had been rented from National Car Rental at the Dallas/Forth Worth International Airport. The tag did not belong to the vehicle the men were driving. Naturally, this discovery raised red flags among law enforcement. Why were three Arab men from Dallas traveling through Oklahoma City in the wake of the country's largest terrorist attack with a switched license plate from a rental car?

The OHP Teletype hit the wires at 2:28 P.M. warning lawmen to "locate possible suspects and vehicle involved in bombing Oklahoma City 04/19/95 0900 hours." The bulletin targeted a Chevy Cavalier or Blazer that "may be a rental car from National Car Rental Systems, D/FW Texas, possible tag of PTF-54F."

In the predawn hours of April 20, authorities eventually tracked down the blue Cavalier parked outside an Oklahoma City motel where one of the Arab men had rented a room. Meanwhile, the Blazer was found at a Dallas residence that was thoroughly searched for evidence of bomb making materials. Unnamed federal officials told the *Dallas Morning News* that investigators seized several duffle bags from the North Dallas apartment and "sent them to a federal laboratory near Washington after a bomb-sniffing dog indicated the bags may have been exposed to chemicals used in explosives."

Staff reporter Alexei Barrionuevo flushed out the lead even further and knocked on the alleged suspects' door at the Foxmoor apartments. An unnamed Middle Easterner, who claimed he was terribly shaken by sixteen hours of questioning by the FBI, spoke from behind a closed door and refused to show his face to the interviewer. The unseen man vehemently denied involvement in the bombing, explaining that his brother and roommate were in Oklahoma City on April 19 to obtain a document that "the Dallas (immigration) office had rejected him for." He claimed that his brother recently came to Dallas from New York to get immigration documents that were difficult to obtain from the New York branch of the INS.

The reporter inquired, "What documents?"

But curiously, the evasive stranger hidden from view offered no explanation. "I do not know. I come here for education," he answered.

The Middle Eastern man also refused to address questions about the contents of several boxes that federal agents had confiscated. However, the unidentified man did admit that the apartment had been extensively dusted for fingerprints. He also volunteered that he had been administered a polygraph examination during questioning. Within twenty-four hours, the remaining two detainees were released.

APRIL 20, 7:00 A.M.

Stunned Americans awoke to the continued replay of nightmarish television images in which each video frame communicated the dank, stifling spirit of widespread death. The bloodstained panorama unfolding live and unedited before a nationwide audience undoubtedly evoked feelings of defenselessness against unknown mass murderers. Once the sting of disbelief and shock subsided, the country would demand to see the faces behind this act of savagery. Meanwhile, the press corps remained eagerly poised to feed the masses' burgeoning appetite for an inside scoop.

In a succession of nationally televised press conferences, a handful of reporters pelted the top brass at the U.S. Department of Justice and FBI with questions about the all-points-bulletins for the brown Chevrolet pickup, blue Chevy Cavalier or Blazer, and Middle Eastern suspects. But that line of questioning would be instantly shut down with the clichéd "no comment." The freshly appointed on-site commander, FBI Special Agent Weldon Kennedy, stood staunchly behind the microphone, deflecting the probing queries. "Some people were detained last night who were riding in a Chevy Cavalier. Are they considered suspects?" a reporter shouted from behind the cameras' purview.

"I cannot confirm that we have questioned any suspects, no," Kennedy answered.

"There were confirmed reports that there was an APB out on three Middle Eastern suspects. And we have heard rumors in all of this, but we were able to confirm that in the state of Kansas they were looking for those three suspects, what is your response to that?" inquired a female journalist.

"The question is that there was an APB out on three individuals and you are asking if I can confirm that. No, I cannot confirm that at this time," Kennedy stated firmly.

Twenty-four hours after that news conference, on April 20, Agent Kennedy was barraged once more with queries about the apprehension and interrogation of the Arab men driving a Chevy Blazer that displayed a switched license tag from a rental vehicle.

"I have been informed that the news media has been reporting that two individuals were arrested in Dallas. The FBI is unaware, at least at my level, of those arrests. I have no idea what they may be about," Kennedy claimed.

Meanwhile, at a news conference in Washington, D.C., Kennedy's boss, Attorney General Janet Reno, faced the same avenue of questioning, only this time, the unfaltering persistence of a male journalist cast a dubious light on her purported ignorance of the string of arrests.

"General Reno, there are broadcast reports of two men arrested in Dallas and one in Oklahoma. Are those reports incorrect?" the reporter asked.

"I could not confirm that. I have no knowledge of that," Ms. Reno responded with a tinge of observable annoyance.

Undaunted, the journalist pressed further. "Reports concerning a New York City cab driver and his brother and another man named Mohammed . . ."

"Neither [FBI] Director Freeh or I have information to that effect," Ms. Reno affirmed as she signaled another journalist to ask a question.

Minutes later, the same reporter interjected, "Will you go back for a second to the report of the two arrested in Dallas? You said you had no information on that. I assume you would know if anyone had been arrested. Are you saying that report is therefore false?"

Reno paused and then parsed her words with measured caution, "Unless there is immediate information, but we have checked the reports and do not find any information at this time."

Feigning ignorance of law enforcements' sedulous pursuit of radical Islamic tentacles in this unprecedented crime would not hold the press at bay for long. By 2:41 P.M. on the afternoon of April 20, Attorney General Reno's moratorium on acknowledging unauthorized reports of suspects currently in custody collapsed when British immigration officials confirmed they had prohibited a Jordanian national arriving from the United States from entering the country.

The spin machine was now spiraling out of control. In Washington, Justice Department spokesman Carl Stern portrayed the man being returned from London as a "possible witness who was refused admittance to Britain." When the London Associated Press inquired if the detainee was considered a suspect, Stern replied, "You never know what's down the road."

CHAPTER 3

# 48 HOURS

A radiant afternoon sun illuminated the face of terror as law enforcement officers paraded their stoic, shackled prisoner past a throng of cameras stationed on the lawn of the Noble County courthouse in the sleepy Oklahoma town of Perry. It was April 21 and the FBI dragnet had already caught its prey—a Gulf War veteran assisted by antigovernment zealots. On August 10, 1995, a federal grand jury sealed the case. Timothy McVeigh and Terry Nichols, aided by Michael Fortier, conspired to murder innocents, apparently motivated by a maniacal desire to avenge the deaths of the Branch Davidians during the April 19, 1993, fiery standoff with the ATF and FBI at Waco, Texas.

Had this trio of "homegrown" terrorists single-handedly pulled off the crime of the century? Some in the highest levels of the Department of Justice keenly desired the ink to dry on one of the darkest chapters in U.S. criminal history, putting to rest lingering questions and speculations. However, the apprehension of American suspects did not dissuade the federal government from furtively pursuing the theory of foreign collaboration. On April 19, CBS News reported that eight organizations contacted the FBI, professing responsibility for the heartland strike. Seven of the claimants had ties to the Middle East.

As blood-soaked victims streamed from the devastated Murrah

Building, a crisis team had already begun assembling in the White House Situation Room, bringing to the table the prodigious intelligence files of the Federal Bureau of Investigation, Bureau of Alcohol Tobacco and Firearms, National Security Agency, Central Intelligence Agency, and Defense Intelligence Agency. McVeigh's defense team later discovered the kinetic mobilization of federal law enforcement and intelligence agencies focused principally on Middle Eastern terrorists "with no limit on available man-power, assets, technology, and without regard to geographical borders."

A series of sobering facts that were leaked to the media within the first forty-eight hours underscored the government's early inclination to seek out suspects of Arab origin embedded in the homeland. The stack of telling clues included sensitive military communications in which the FBI urgently requested on April 19 that the Pentagon provide ten Army linguists profi-cient in Arabic to assist in monitoring radical Islamic sects in several major metropolitan areas. Within days, the mission quickly evolved from analyz-ing recordings of FBI wiretaps of suspected Middle Eastern extremist groups to listening and translating live conversations.

The Department of the Army Headquarters Forces Command at Fort McPherson, Georgia, issued a memorandum on April 22, 1995, asserting that federal law strictly prohibited military involvement of this enormity and scope in a domestic criminal investigation, except under the rare circum-stance where the president's life was imperiled. Such a danger was not only deemed to be real, but imminent. In a unique correspondence, the FBI director contacted the secretary of defense to request the Army Arabic lin-guists continue to monitor live wiretaps in an effort to "protect the president from possible attack during his attendance of the memorial service in Oklahoma City on Sunday, April 23."

By this time, the chief culprits had been profiled as right-wing fanatics, ostracized by their own kind. Not even the citizen militia movement, which spawned from paranoia over government encroachment upon civil liberties, embraced McVeigh and Nichols's brand of extremism. Therefore, if a duo of rogue domestic terrorists was solely to blame, why was the Department of Justice so intent on obtaining such an unusual waiver of federal law? Without it, the Army linguists would be ordered to cease translating inter-cepted "chatter" between Middle East terrorists on domestic soil, leaving Bill Clinton vulnerable to a potential foreign assassination attempt during his forthcoming trip to Oklahoma City. What did two disgruntled malcontents and radical Islamists have in common? *Plenty.* And the FBI, CIA, DIA, and all other organs of the U.S. law enforcement community were collectively acting on far more than an educated hunch.

APRIL 19, 9:30 A.M.

A conspicuously nervous passenger with distinct Middle Eastern features piqued the interest of vigilant employees posted at the American Airlines ticket counter. By the time the FBI was notified, the man's flight had already lifted off from Oklahoma City's Will Rogers World Airport; his final destination—Amman, Jordan. During a scheduled stopover at Chicago O'Hare International Airport, federal agents placed the shifty traveler, Jordanian national Abraham Ahmad, under temporary arrest. After a cursory interview, the thirty-one-year-old naturalized American citizen was released, allowing him to resume his international flight.

Upon arrival at London's Heathrow Airport, British authorities seized him for further interrogation. Meanwhile, Ahmad's luggage was rerouted to Rome, where Italian officials rifled through the commuter's overstuffed bags, yielding a provocative inventory of materials. Ahmad had stockpiled multiple car radios, shielded and unshielded wire, a small tool kit, solder, and caulking—items which authorities theorized could be used to assemble a crude, "homemade" bomb. The vise of suspicion tightened with the discovery of blue jogging suits matching the description of the clothing worn by the Middle Eastern men profiled in the FBI's bulletin.

12:07 P.M.

"If you look at the nature of the destruction, this looks very similar to the destruction of the Israeli Embassy in Argentina and even the U.S. Embassy in Beirut," a former Oklahoma congressman asserted in an interview with CNN.

During his fourteen-year career as U.S. representative, Dave McCurdy previously chaired the House Intelligence Committee, enjoying unfettered access to national security threats. Today, amidst the widespread slaughter of fellow Oklahomans, the gloves came off. Diplomatic measurement of words did not figure into the retired lawmaker's clarion call for America's heartland to wake up to the terrorist infrastructure flourishing from within.

"My first reaction when I heard of the explosion was that there could be a very real connection to some of the Islamic fundamentalist groups that have, actually, been operating out of Oklahoma City. They've had recent meetings, even a convention, where terrorists from the Middle East who were connected directly to Hamas and Hizbollah participate," he passionately preached, touching off a media backlash.

The local press scourged McCurdy for demagoguery, prompting him to defend his remarks in an opinion column published by the *Oklahoma Gazette*. While acknowledging that prime suspects Timothy McVeigh and Terry Nichols fit the profile of "right-wing extremists," the man who once held security clearances to classified intelligence waxed unapologetic for his earlier statements pointing to Middle Eastern complicity.

"Based on recent bombings that occurred in the U.S.—such as the one at the World Trade Center in New York—and known capabilities of existing Islamic terrorist groups, the authorities began to assess recent threats against the U.S. government," McCurdy argued before unleashing widely over-looked, but unnerving evidence of an enemy living among us.

"With recently acquired information about Hamas demolitions experts living in the Oklahoma area, the FBI almost immediately focused on militant fundamentalists as the primary suspected culprits," he continued, dropping a bombshell that the media collectively ignored. The former legislator went on to commend the investigative findings of journalist Steven Emerson, who produced the award-winning PBS documentary *Jihad in America*.

Posing as an inquisitive journalist exploring the tenets of Islam, Emerson recorded rare footage of Middle Eastern terrorists congregating on U.S. soil. In one scene after another, radical Muslim leaders incited enthusiastic disciples to carry out holy "jihad" against Jews, Christians, and infidels. December 1992 marked Emerson's introduction to militant Islam's entrenched networks in the American Midwest. At the time, he was working as an investigative reporter for CNN.

Emerson had been assigned to cover the Oklahoma City press conference of the former special prosecutor for the Iran-Contra affair. Venturing out of his downtown hotel, the observant reporter noticed a sizeable gathering of men adorned in traditional Muslim attire. Curious about the unusual scene, he casually followed the group into the city's convention center. Inside he encountered the Moslem Arab Youth Association, whose membership reputedly includes the terrorist network Hamas. A crowd of six thousand participants enthusiastically cheered militant leaders who called for the killing of Jews and infidels. According to former *New York Times* executive editor and columnist A. M. Rosenthal, Khalid Meshal, the military and terrorist commander of the Hamas political department which is headquartered in Jordan, was among the featured speakers who advocated jihad during the 1992 Oklahoma City convention.

Three years later, a terrorist bomb would obliterate the federal complex situated just a few blocks from the religious rally which was energized by mantras to "destroy the West." Just twenty-four hours after the bombing, Steve Emerson reflected upon this disturbing event.

"Oklahoma City is probably considered one of the largest centers of Islamic radical activity outside the Middle East," the fiercely independent journalist told the *Boston Herald*.

"Well, Oklahoma City is a target of opportunity and is a place where militants have been able to establish an infrastructure over the past dozen years. I know it's surprising to a lot of people. They expect it to be on the east coast or the west coast, but Oklahoma City, Tucson, Phoenix, Kansas City have all been places where radical Islamic leaders from around the world have hosted and organized conventions featuring Hamas, Islamic Jihad and almost every other Middle East radical group," Emerson bluntly outlined in a candid discussion with the morning anchors of NBC's *Today Show*.

"I attended the meeting in 1992 in December of that year, where I actually could have envisioned that I was in Beirut considering who attended. I remember listening to a speech in which this speaker got up—he was a radical from Egypt—and basically said, 'We will destroy the West.' This was in the Oklahoma City Convention Center."

Steve Emerson's courageous pursuit of a story no mainstream journalist dared broach laid bare the FBI's apparent ignorance of the ubiquitous presence of Islamic terrorism. But the rewards were bittersweet. The events of April 19 confirmed every nightmarish eventuality forecasted in Emerson's 1994 documentary. But ultimately, his vanguard research prompted no change toward greater national security. Constitutional constraints forbade law enforcement from infiltrating the inner sanctum of the local networks which designated themselves as religious groups, thereby gaining immunity from surveillance. Moreover, budgetary cutbacks had gutted police intelligence units, and the foreign agents of terror knew it. In the case of Oklahoma City, they planned to slither back into obscurity, leaving their American counterparts, McVeigh and Nichols, to take the fall.

## MORNING HEADLINES, EVENING NEWS, AND INTELLIGENCE LEAKS

The compelling indicators of a Middle Eastern signature would not escape detection altogether. "This is the work of Hamas," Israeli Prime Minister Yitzhak Rabin emphatically decreed across international airwaves, a charge echoed by a chorus of authoritative voices.

William Webster, the former director of both the CIA and FBI, noted that the bombing had all the hallmarks of Mideast terror in an interview with *USA Today*. The Oklahoma attack harkened back to the July 1994 bombing of the Argentine Israelite Mutual Aid Association (AMIA) Jewish community center in Buenos Aires, Argentina, and the 1993 truck bombing of the World Trade Center. In both cases, the perpetrators parked a vehicle packed with explosives composed primarily of fertilizer and fuel oil near the intended target, then detonated the bomb amidst a mad getaway.

"I think what we've got here is a bona fide terrorist attack," Oliver "Buck" Revell told the *Baltimore Sun*. The former FBI assistant director and counterterrorism expert did not mince words. "I think it's most likely a Middle East terrorist. I think the modus operandi is similar. They have used this approach."

The *Dallas Morning News* published the contents of an FBI internal communiqué circulating within hours of the blast which suggested "the attack was made in retaliation for the prosecution of Muslim fundamentalists in the bombing of the World Trade Center in February 1993 . . . [and] we are currently inclined to suspect the Islamic Jihad as the likely group."

But while the tentacles of investigative leads stretched worldwide, the Middle Eastern mercenaries of death were believed to be hiding in plain view. On April 20, the *Associated Press* dispatched to newsrooms nationwide the startling comments of Yigal Carmon, a counterterrorism advisor to former Israeli Prime Minister Yitzhak Shamir. The news report claimed Mr. Carmon asserted that "Islamic militants have set up a well-funded infrastructure throughout the United States, and stated further that he knew of fundraising efforts in Oklahoma City."

## IRAQI HIT SQUAD

ABC's *World News Tonight* opened the April 19 evening newscast exploring the probable involvement of inveterate terrorist factions. "Sources say the FBI has been watching dozens of suspicious Islamic groups throughout the American Southwest and several right in Oklahoma City," national security correspondent John McWethy reported.

Vincent Cannistraro, the former chief of operations for the CIA's counterterrorism division, corroborated the legitimacy of McWethy's intelligence sources. "This is something professional. It really implies that the person who constructed the explosive device had experience, was trained in the use

of explosives, [and] knew what they were doing," Cannistraro postulated in
the ABC broadcast.

But the former spymaster's public conjecture belied his familiarity with
far more specific, albeit classified, information. Within a few hours of the
bomb going off in downtown Oklahoma City, the phone rang at
Cannistraro's private residence. The man on the other end of the line was
calling from Jeddah, Saudi Arabia. The overseas conversation lasted only
minutes but yielded a golden nugget of intelligence that would wrinkle the
government's neatly packaged case of "domestic" terrorism. Without delay,
Cannistraro, who was then employed as an *ABC News* consultant, notified
the FBI's Washington Metropolitan Field Office of what he had learned.
Happenstance played no role in the call being patched directly to FBI
Special Agent Kevin Foust, the Bureau's top investigator in charge of appre-
hending and prosecuting international terrorists.

The longtime CIA operative instinctively safeguarded the name of his
informant, only disclosing that the Saudi citizen served as a "counterterrorism official" responsible for protecting the Saudi royal family from terrorist
attacks. The source professed to have intimate knowledge of a foreign plot
specifically aimed at the Alfred P. Murrah Building. Agent Foust noted the
following information in an FBI interview report which is officially cata-
logued as a "302":

> The Saudi official told CANNISTRARO that he [the source] had infor-
> mation that there was a "squad" of people currently in the United States,
> very possibly Iraqis, who have been tasked with carrying out terrorist
> attacks against the United States. The Saudi claimed that he had seen a list
> of "targets," and that the first on the list was the federal building in
> Oklahoma City, Oklahoma. The second target was identified as the INS
> office in Houston, Texas, and the third target was the FBI office in Los
> Angeles, California.

The Saudi citizen's trustworthiness was never in question given the fact
that Cannistraro had known this individual for "fifteen to twenty years." Be
that as it may, FBI Agent Foust noted that Cannistraro "could not comment
on the reliability of the information, nor could he corroborate it." But the
Bureau did have confirmation, despite a tacit policy to ignore it.

In the earliest days of 1996, the "Cannistraro 302" found its way to the
law offices of Stephen Jones, Timothy McVeigh's lead defense counsel.
Buried in a batch of several hundred documents federal prosecutors had

marked "non-pertinent." The odds of the formal report ever being discovered bordered on miraculous. But once in the hands of the unflappable Mr. Jones, the retired CIA chief was no match for the shrewd litigator. In his book *Others Unknown*, Jones recounted how Vincent Cannistraro feigned memory loss when he inquired about the April 19 call from the Saudi Arabian counter terror official.

"Vince," Jones interrupted, "I've got a copy of the FBI insert sitting right in front of me."

Boxed in, with little room to maneuver, Cannistraro conceded he had spoken to the Saudi source, but didn't know if the tip "was credible or not."

The tepid response was obviously intended to douse Jones's curiosity, but instead, stoked the flames of fascination all the more. The introspective attorney contemplated why a man with such an illustrious career, which included the directorship of intelligence programs for the National Security Council, would inform the FBI and CIA of "dubious" intelligence of this magnitude. If true, Iraq might have controlled and orchestrated the Oklahoma attack, a provocation tantamount to an act of war.

The next conversation with Vincent Cannistraro took place on January 15, 1996, inside the Washington beltway, face-to-face.

"The government is not interested in a foreign plot. It has its perpetrators and they don't want anyone or anything complicating it," Cannistraro postulated in a bold departure from his previous fence-sitting comportment.

Stephen Jones and his research assistant Ann Bradley took copious notes as the counterterror authority bluntly outlined the telltale Middle Eastern footprints taking shape in the ashes of Oklahoma City. Months later, in October 1996, his "off-the-record" commentary was memorialized in McVeigh's sealed defense filings, legal briefs that were never intended to be leaked.

The closed-door session opened with Cannistraro's skilled analysis of the Murrah Building destruction which he likened to the 1983 bombing of the Marine barracks in Beirut, Lebanon. He also drew a striking comparison to the 1993 World Trade Center bombing which was "originally seen as the work of a few 'woe-be-gone-zealots' when in fact it turned out to be carefully and methodically organized with a group of 'cut aways' who appear to be 'keystone cops' and were quickly arrested while the real leaders got away." He publicly agreed with the late James Fox, the former director of the New York City FBI, that "Iraqi intelligence may very well have been behind the [first] World Trade Center bombing."

Cannistraro depicted the bomb encased in the Ryder truck as "medium tech," hypothesizing that Iraqis were motivated to retaliate with terrorist acts because Saddam "Hussein has unbounded vitriol and has done desperate things in the past. There are huge stockpiles of unconventional and biological weapons which are still unaccounted for by the United Nations . . . from a terrorist's point of view, all non-Washington, D.C., federal buildings are vulnerable."

## CONTRACT KILLERS

It wasn't long before the scramble to shut down this avenue of inquiry into possible Iraqi sponsorship and the Saudi intelligence report digressed into shamelessness. Federal prosecutors audaciously posited that Cannistraro might have embellished the Saudi message or simply "made it up out of thin air." The very suggestion dripped with pomposity, fueling the Oklahoma lawyer's immense frustration with government obfuscation. But Stephen Jones's gut told him there was more to the story, and eventually his perseverance paid dividends.

The McVeigh defense team worked tirelessly to perform the impossible, plucking from a cascade of discovery documents two FBI reports which independently corroborated the terrorist plot described by the Saudi contact. The first insert referred to an April 19 call to the FBI's Los Angeles Crisis Center from a purported member of an "Islamic group (NFI)" that claimed credit for the terrorist assault. The unknown caller "stated that the FBI and INS offices in the Houston and Los Angeles were also targeted."

A second FBI Teletype conveyed urgent information about a terrorist hit list that encompassed not only the federal building in Oklahoma City, but government offices in Houston and Los Angeles as well, mirroring the plan the Saudi source independently disclosed to Vincent Cannistraro. The author of the emergency bulletin, a "Supervisory Special Agent" whose name had been redacted from the photocopy given to the defense team, wired the warning to the FBI's Washington headquarters and other "concerned government agencies." The source was not named.

Once again, the finger of blame pointed directly at Iraq. The source reported "the Oklahoma City bombing was sponsored by the Iraqi Special Services, who contracted seven (7) Afghani Freedom Fighters currently living in Pakistan." As expected, the identity of the confidential informant was purposely concealed, revealing only that the source maintained close ties with the Saudi Arabian Intelligence Service and had a track record of providing "accurate and reliable information," strikingly similar to the credentials of Cannistraro's Saudi informer.

The two unnamed Middle Eastern informants provided overlapping evidence regarding Iraqi sponsorship; however, the man who reached out to the CIA's ex-director of counterterrorism accused a squad of Iraqis currently living in the United States. The parity was enough to satisfy Stephen Jones that the warnings were genuine, but convincing the court to order the blanket unsealing of national security files in a wide scale hunt for corroborative intelligence eluded his grasp.

## PRIOR KNOWLEDGE REVEALED

"No press allowed! No one but authorized personnel gets a pass and absolutely no cameras," barked a U.S. Marshal. Oklahoma County deputy reservists Don Hammons and David Kochendorfer had explicit orders to secure the northwest perimeter of the crime scene the night of April 19, rendering it impenetrable to voyeurs and opportunists seeking surreptitious snapshots of exhumed bodies. Fortunately, few had attempted such a callous exploit.

The evening deluge of cold rain had momentarily subsided when an entourage of dignitaries filed in. The first arrival included the Oklahoma City mayor and staff, followed by the local district attorney, and governor—each soaking in the enormity of human suffering through the misty night air.

After handing out hard hats to the visiting officials, deputy Don Hammons scanned the fenced in area for unwelcome intruders. The forty-two-year-old business entrepreneur routinely dedicated twenty to thirty hours monthly to the sheriff's department. However, as a reserve deputy, he was unaccustomed to standing post at a homicide scene, and undoubtedly never fathomed witnessing one of this magnitude.

Suddenly, a camera flickered. A rapid succession of flashes followed. A nearby stationary backhoe partially obscured a photographer who was snapping pictures. Don jogged closer to investigate.

"M'am, no pictures allowed. I must order you to stop," he shouted as he approached a middle-aged woman with sandy blonde hair.

She paused to introduce herself. "I'm Lana Tyree, and I'm accompanying Oklahoma Congressman Ernest Istook. I'm a local attorney and amateur photographer. The Congressman asked that I meet him here and take some pictures of the bombsite for him."

Ms. Tyree then offered a business card confirming her identity. Don glanced eastward and noticed Congressman Istook standing just a few feet away, conversing with his colleague, reserve deputy David Kochendorfer.

"There are photosensitive law enforcement officials here who work undercover," the deputy advised. "They cannot be photographed under any circumstances. Please limit your shots to the building. Avoid movement of bodies and retrieval of victims."

Ms. Tyree agreed to respect the guidelines as Don escorted her on the brief photo taking session. He immediately sensed she was visibly shaken by the cataclysm before them. After twenty minutes of somber dialogue, emotion seized Ms. Tyree.

"Congressman Istook told me there had been a bomb threat called in on April 9!" she exclaimed as she gazed through the camera's viewfinder at the ravaged structure. Her eyes remained fixated on the building.

"A prior warning?" Don gasped under his breath. "The government was warned ten days ago and no action was taken." He reasoned if Ms. Tyree had confided potentially classified information to a uniformed officer she had just met—a virtual stranger—surely this revelation would surface in the national headlines.

As Ms. Tyree and Congressman Istook departed the bombsite, Don unburdened himself to friend and partner David Kochendorfer. The pair often shared patrol duty since joining the volunteer reserves in the early 1990s.

"What's going on here? Congressman Istook's attorney friend just admitted that the government was warned about this attack and ignored it," Don commented.

"I already know," David uttered with an expression of bewilderment.

"How's that?"

David recounted how Congressman Istook introduced himself and made small talk about the tragedy. Then came a startling admission.

"Istook said, 'Yeah, we knew this was going to happen.' I was shocked. I looked at him and said, 'Sir, excuse me? How did you know that?'"

The fifty-one-year-old Air Force veteran grimaced as he pondered Congressman Istook's next remark. "Istook told me 'we knew it and we blew it.' He said 'we heard that there was a threat from some Islamic extremist group operating in Oklahoma City and they were going to try to bomb a federal building in Oklahoma City.'"

"That may explain why the FBI issued an all-points-bulletin for Middle Eastern suspects," Don observed. Both expected to discover more about the prior warning of a possible foreign terrorist attack as the case against whoever did this monstrous, unforgivable deed unfolded. But years passed, and still, a mysterious silence. The U.S. Department of Justice vociferously debunked allegations of a prior warning as baseless, branding anyone who seriously entertained the notion a "conspiracy nut."

During the summer of 1997, Oklahoma State Representative Charles Key's citizens' petition drive culminated in the seating of a grand jury to delve beyond the government's case. The panel probed rumors of forewarning, setting local talk radio abuzz. The broadcasts of the DOJ's repeated blanket denials inflamed the ire of both Don Hammons and David Kochendorfer.

"This is starting to smack of a cover-up," Don thought. He and David agreed they owed it to the people of Oklahoma and their own consciences to tell what they knew. The political stakes were high. They were alerted to the potential fallout. But the decision to speak out was final.

On January 15, 1998, the two reserve deputy sheriffs stunned the Oklahoma City media with their story. Before the news hit the wires, Washington, D.C., had already delivered a furious backlash. Congressman Istook's temper flared.

"It is garbage and a total fabrication to suggest I have information that the government supposedly had prior knowledge of the Murrah Building bombing," he fired back in an interview with the *Denver Post*. "Any such suggestion is the product of somebody's sick and warped imagination."

Local reporters discounted the claims of the two unknown law officers as wild and outrageous. The national media failed to take notice. The prospective government forewarning of a radical Islamic terrorist cell threatening to strike the heart of Oklahoma City had been summarily dismissed without a fair hearing.

The Oklahoma County Sheriff's department and FBI interrogated both deputies, debunking their testimony as "rumor" and "hearsay." Publicly disgraced and humiliated, both men grappled with disillusionment. But unbeknownst to them, the precisely worded prior warning implicating Islamic sponsorship, the existence of which Congressman Istook vehemently denied, had already been leaked and had fallen into my hands. Harboring this secret knowledge would torment me for years to come, muzzled by a journalistic pledge to keep the document confidential.

## POTENTIAL MATERIAL WITNESS IN CUSTODY

British authorities informed the FBI Command Center of Abraham Ahmad's London arrest, prohibiting the immigrant from entering or transiting through England. The detainee flew back to Washington, D.C., directly into federal custody. The next two days brought nail-biting questioning. The

Jordanian national zealously professed his innocence, categorically rejecting any affiliation with groups that advocate violence against the United States, emphasizing that he was unaware of where the Murrah Building was located. He produced a birth certificate from the Hashemite Kingdom of Jordan, Oklahoma driver's license, business cards, and personal telephone book, voluntarily discussing his immigration to the U.S. in 1982 on a student visa.

His tumultuous two-year marriage to Oklahoma City resident Pamela Plumber was racked by domestic violence. On the heels of divorce, Ahmad married Martina Quiniones, a Mexican woman from El Paso, Texas. In 1990, he graduated from Central State University with a Bachelor of Arts degree in Computer Science. However, he emphasized that he did not study engineering and scored poorly in basic chemistry. In 1992, he landed a job as a computer technician for Seagate Technologies in Oklahoma City. But after three years of steady employment, he resigned for unspecified reasons.

A few weeks later on January 2, 1995, Ahmad traveled to Jordan, ostensibly to visit relatives. He flew back to Oklahoma City on March 26, but a "family crisis" necessitated his immediate return. His father reportedly became engaged to marry a second time, but intended to continue residing with his first wife. He claimed chance dictated the uncanny timing of his next excursion. On the morning of the bombing, the thirty-one-year-old father once again boarded a plane bound for his homeland, leaving behind his wife and two young daughters.

FBI agents wondered how the unemployed computer technician afforded two pricey roundtrip tickets to Amman, Jordan. Ahmad claimed his brother who worked as an accountant for a relief agency in Vienna, Austria, wired him $3,000 for airfare. Still puzzled by his lack of financial resources, agents queried the unemployed computer technician about how he afforded to make house payments. He explained that he had paid $7,000 for his home and covered mortgage installments and living expenses from savings.

A title search on Ahmad's Oklahoma City home revealed that just ten days after Ahmad resigned his position at Seagate Technologies, he purchased a house from Palestinian immigrant Dr. Anwar Abdul. Why would Dr. Abdul sell a home to a renter who was unemployed? The financial transaction obviously piqued the FBI's curiosity, prompting a phone call to Dr. Abdul's property management company.

Curiously, Ahmad never mentioned Dr. Abdul when providing a long list of associates living in the United States.

# CHAPTER 4

# "HOMEGROWN" TERRORISM

The blare of the alarm clock pulsated inside Darby Williams's aching head. She missed work on April 19, nursing flu-like symptoms, but the thirty-five-year-old office assistant was determined not to press her luck. Her boss exercised no magnanimity toward racking up sick days. Since 1992, Darby had been earning a steady paycheck administrating Dr. Anwar Abdul's multi-million dollar property management company. Fielding never-ending complaints from renters residing in hundreds of dilapidated housing units made for a taxing job, but a twenty-four hour bug was not going to send the unmarried secretary back to the unemployment lines.

Upon entering the office the morning of April 20, she noticed the message light blinking on the company answering machine. An FBI agent investigating the Oklahoma City bombing requested to interview Dr. Abdul about Abraham Ahmad.

"Why is the FBI interested in Abraham?" Darby wondered, contemplating the sudden and frequent visits Dr. Abdul's Jordanian friend had paid to the company headquarters since late March. She knew that Ahmad had performed contract repair work for Dr. Abdul's real estate business years ago, but only on a few occasions.

Hoping to unravel the mystery, she flipped on the television near her desk to monitor breaking news on the bombing.

"Oh, my God," Darby gasped aloud. "Abraham Ahmad has been arrested as a possible suspect!"

While the published details surrounding the Oklahoma City man's apprehension were sparse, the FBI wasted no time filing a confidential material witness warrant with the United States District Court for the Western District of Texas. FBI Agent Henry C. Gibbons submitted a sworn affidavit under seal requesting Ahmad "be held without bail to assure his presence before the Federal Grand Jury." Agent Gibbons noted that the "material witness" had been detained and questioned because he had a blue jogging suit packed in his luggage which was similar to the description of the clothing worn by several Middle Eastern suspects seen "running from the area of the Federal Building toward a brown Chevrolet truck" shortly before the explosion.

## TWO FACES OF TERROR

But within twenty-four hours, the full throttle global search for foreign terrorists shifted into reverse, settling squarely on domestic culprits. The roadmap leading to homegrown villains began with an investigative coup that veteran lawmen commonly characterize as serendipity; only this time, many perceived divine providence. A sharp-eyed police officer spotted the charred rear axle housing of a large truck which the force of the blast had ejected one block west of the bomb site. The vehicle identification number paved a path northward to Eldon Elliott's body shop in Junction City, Kansas, where the explosives-laden Ryder truck was rented. The shop owner and employees claimed two men leased a large moving van on April 17 using a driver's license bearing the alias "Robert Kling." The witnesses assisted in drafting artist renderings of the Oklahoma City bombers which were subsequently dubbed John Does 1 and 2.

Sketches in hand, FBI agents canvassed Junction City, scoring yet another extraordinary breakthrough. Almost instantly, the owner of the Dreamland Motel, Lea McGown, recognized the fair-complexioned, clean-shaven suspect with the military crew cut. "This is Mr. McVeigh. He stayed in room 25," the German native asserted with calm composure.

"You mean his name is Bob Kling," the FBI agent smirked with an air of disbelief.

McGown placed the document on the desk. "I have the gentleman's registration card right here. He checked in on April 14 and signed the name Tim McVeigh," she insisted while reflecting upon McVeigh's peculiar reaction when she asked to see a photo ID. He pulled out his wallet, but decided not to present his driver's license after glancing at the name on the registration log. McGown believed she may have distracted McVeigh with conversation during check-in, causing him to instinctively sign his real name.

The FBI investigator evidently had no idea he had stumbled upon the blockbuster lead, uncovering the true identity of Bob Kling. Another twenty hours slipped by before the information on the Dreamland Motel guest was entered into the National Crime Information Computer at 10 A.M. on April 21. Within seconds, the screen flashed the arrest record of "Timothy McVeigh" who was currently confined at the Noble County jail in Perry, Oklahoma. The home address of Decker, Michigan, which was entered on the police report, matched the motel log. The FBI found their man with only minutes to spare. An ATF agent placed an urgent call to Sheriff Jerry Cook, ordering prisoner McVeigh to be put "on federal hold." The bomber was a hairsbreadth away from posting bail and walking out of the jailhouse.

Was McVeigh jinxed by the hand of fate, or was he a dupe in a larger conspiracy, set up to get caught? With the smoldering building in his rearview mirror, McVeigh drove north up Interstate 35. His getaway seemed assured, that is, until Oklahoma Highway Patrol trooper Charlie Hanger noticed his 1977 Mercury Marquis had no license plate and signaled him to pull over. It was 10:17 A.M. on April 19 as McVeigh stepped out of the driver's seat to meet the approaching officer. Upon learning he had no license tag, the fugitive terrorist glanced back at his car, unable to mask his utter surprise.

"I just bought the car and don't have a tag yet," he nervously explained as he reached into his pocket to retrieve his driver's license. The motion exposed a bulge under his blue jean coat.

"Take both hands and slowly pull back your jacket," Officer Hanger ordered.

"I have a gun," McVeigh volunteered, impelling the trooper to seize the .45-caliber Glock pistol McVeigh had concealed in a shoulder holster.

"Get your hands up and turn around," the patrolman directed as he thrust his weapon to the back of the suspect's head. McVeigh felt handcuffs clamp around his wrists. His escape lasted sixty miles and little more than an hour. If he had not been carrying a concealed weapon, the bomber would have been released with a few traffic citations for driving without a tag or insurance.

Trooper Hanger's divine providence. Timothy McVeigh's bad luck.

In the days that followed, lawmen on horseback scoured the sixty mile stretch of highway, retracing McVeigh's trek northward to Perry in search of the missing license tag. I would later hold that very plate in my hands.

Tracing its origins legitimized eyewitness accounts of a dark-haired passenger seen in the Mercury Marquis as it screeched away from the blast zone, poised to erupt in less than five minutes.

"I knew there were reports that people had seen a car with two people in it, not one. That has always bothered me . . . and all of a sudden that kind of drops out," Danny Coulson revealed in a June 2003 interview with PBS. In a singular moment of candor, the redoubtable founding commander of the FBI's Hostage Rescue Team unveiled grave personal concerns about vexing questions that beleaguer the FBI's handling of critical leads.

"Was everything done right in that investigation? I had my questions about it," the thirty-one year career agent grimaced as he excoriated Attorney General Janet Reno's decision to suddenly remove the Bureau's "most experienced crisis managers" during the early stages of the case. He was among a handful of agents appointed to the initial task force. After "flipping" Michael Fortier and securing his testimony as the government's star witness, he was inexplicably yanked. "The FBI is no longer an independent organization. It has not been since Janet Reno."


## PARTNER IN CRIME

Driving home from the local lumber yard, the forty-year-old military surplus salesman flipped on the car radio. "James and Terry Nichols," two brothers from Michigan known to be associated with prime suspect Timothy McVeigh, were wanted for questioning in connection with the April 19 attack, the radio announcer reported.

"That's me!" Terry Nichols choked as he parked outside his Herington, Kansas, home. Bursting through the front door, panic set in.

"Have you heard anything on the news about the FBI looking for me?" he asked his young Filipino bride, Marife.

"You're not serious," she stammered.

Her husband stood transfixed, watching Attorney General Janet Reno announce at a national press conference the apprehension of a suspect named Timothy McVeigh for traffic violations. The pair met in 1988 during basic training at Fort Benning, Georgia. Both were assigned to the 1st Infantry Division stationed at Fort Riley, Kansas. A year later, Nichols acquired a hardship discharge to raise his six-year-old son, Joshua, following his divorce from his first wife, Lana Padilla.

Although his Army buddy was thirteen years his junior, a friendship took root based on a mutual distrust of the federal government. In 1993, McVeigh briefly resided with Nichols at the family farmhouse in Decker, Michigan, which was owned by his brother James.

Outwardly unmoved by the April 21 news bulletins broadcasting his name, the Kansas farmer turned small-time gun trader robotically carried out his daily errands, visiting a surplus store to barter some tools for shingles. But after loading his wife and toddler Nicole into his truck, his collected, calm façade cracked. Paranoia seized his thoughts.

"I'm being followed," he imagined. "I must turn myself in to authorities, or risk another showdown like Waco."

Nichols drove directly to the Herington Police Department, walked through the doors at 3:15 P.M., surrendered to the FBI, and agreed to unrestricted questioning. The man classified at the outset as a potential "material witness," unwittingly delivered a rambling confession of sorts. Nichols assumed his intellectual prowess would persuade federal agents he was not McVeigh's criminal collaborator, but a dupe, victimized by a string of bizarre coincidences. They were unconvinced.

"Describe your most recent contact with Timothy McVeigh," the lead investigating agent ordered, opening the dialogue.

"He called me on April 16, Easter Sunday, upset that he was experiencing car problems," Nichols recounted. "He said he was pressed for time to get back East to see relatives."

Nichols claimed McVeigh offered to return a television set belonging to Nichols's son in exchange for a ride home from Oklahoma City. Nichols agreed, but lied to his wife Marife, claiming he was headed to Omaha, Nebraska, at McVeigh's insistence. Five hours later, the men crossed paths in an Oklahoma City alleyway near NW 8th Street.

"I went past that building a couple of times," he admitted, referencing the targeted federal complex. A videotape from a nearby apartment security camera subsequently confirmed his story. Despite the degraded quality of the footage, the recording captured blurry images of Nichols's 1984 blue GMC pickup whizzing eastward along NW 5th Street presumably while looking for his marooned friend.

"When McVeigh climbed into the cab of my truck, he seemed hyper or nervous," Nichols said. "He told me, 'You will see something big in the future,' so I asked if he was going to rob a bank. He responded, 'Oh no, I got something in the works.' But I did not know anything."

When asked if he thought his former Army colleague was capable of terrorist acts, Nichols stated unequivocally, "I cannot believe it was him. I cannot see why he would do it." But later, he waffled, openly contemplating underlying motives such as McVeigh's seething rage over the deadly government raids at Waco and Ruby Ridge.

"He could be capable of doing it. I must not have known him that well for him to do that."

During nine hours of interrogation, Nichols portrayed his five-year friendship with McVeigh as benign, cultivated by common business ventures as military surplus traders. The duo would often "pool their money, deduct their expenses, and then split the proceeds."

With contemplative, deliberate forethought, the interviewee frequently hesitated for lengthy pauses before answering damning questions. He methodically outlined how he acquired limited knowledge about assembling explosives from agricultural compounds while traveling the gun show circuit attended by right-wing militia enthusiasts clad in "full battle dress." But he claimed he lacked the expertise to design a terrorist bomb.

Eventually, his clumsy explanations of innocence backfired, exposing a premeditated plan to fashion an ironclad alibi, absent the common sense to eliminate an indelible trail of evidence. In an effort to appear cooperative, Nichols signed consent forms granting the search of his home and vehicle, without the benefit of legal counsel. However, he stopped short of submitting to a polygraph examination, claiming lie detector findings are unreliable.

"In my eyes, I did not do anything wrong, but I can see how lawyers can turn stuff around," he complained while suggesting innocent uses for some cleaning solvents stored at his house that could be misconstrued as bomb ingredients. He pointed out that he had just purchased two bags of ammonium nitrate fertilizer to spread on his lawn and to repackage it as plant food to sell at gun shows.

## FORENSIC FINGERPRINTS

Teams of federal technicians swarmed the Herington residence, effortlessly harvesting a treasure trove of clues in plain sight. The most significant discoveries included plastic barrels consistent with the 55-gallon drums demolition experts theorized contained the truck bomb's deadly mixture, fertilizer prills strewn across the property, a fuel meter, a hand-drawn getaway map of downtown Oklahoma City, and a sales receipt bearing McVeigh's fingerprint. The pink slip documented the purchase of one ton of ammonium nitrate fertilizer from the Mid-Kansas Co-op in McPherson. The manager of the farm supply store, Fred Schlender, and salesman Jerry Showalter vaguely remembered the nondescript customer who went by the name "Mike Havens," a known alias of Terry Nichols. Using phony identification, the bombers rented storage lockers throughout Kansas, Arizona, and Nevada to hide their loot until the time came to blend the lethal concoction of fertilizer and diesel fuel.

Rifling through Nichols' basement, FBI Agent Larry Tongate found five Primadet non-electric blasting caps with sixty-foot cords stashed under a stack of boxes. From there, investigators linked the suspect's cordless drill to a padlock drilled open during a burglary of explosives from a Marion, Kansas, rock quarry.

The October 1994 break-in occurred near a ranch where Nichols was once temporarily employed. Experts speculated the blasting caps and gel explosives stolen in the theft were similar to those employed in the Oklahoma operation. The pockets of the blue jeans McVeigh wore when arrested tested positive for residue from Primadet cord classified as PETN. Lab analysis also detected particles of ammonium nitrate on his shirt.

Moreover, the raid yielded a telephone calling card issued under the alias "Daryl Bridges." From that point on, connecting the circumstantial dots of the criminal case fell into place with the ease of assembling a toddler's jigsaw puzzle. McVeigh purchased the Daryl Bridges phone debit card in 1993 from *Spotlight* magazine, a populist publication espousing virulent anti-government rhetoric. By using money orders to purchase more long distance minutes on the same card, the neophyte terrorists figured they had covered their tracks. But once the card fell into the hands of authorities, FBI computer technicians labored to reconstruct the quest to purchase bomb components, successfully resurrecting a surfeit of calls to manufacturers of barrels, demolitions, chemicals, racing fuel, motels, and the Junction City Ryder rental shop.

## CUTTING THE PLEA

He portrayed himself as a shocked observer, stunned along with the rest of the nation, by the horror of April 19. A raised yellow flag emblazoned with the warning, "Don't Tread on Me," greeted FBI agents as they approached Michael Fortier's trailer in the arid Arizona desert. From the outset, the former McVeigh Army pal emanated a loyal front. The twenty-six-year-old hardware store clerk ranted about the arrest of the soldier who recently served as the best man at his wedding. Fortier's outrage over the inference of McVeigh's guilt dominated network news for days. His long, black scraggly hair danced in the breeze as he campaigned for his imprisoned, anti-government soul mate.

But the bellicose indignation soon subsided. By May 1995, officials threatened to charge Fortier with conspiracy. If convicted at trial, he could have faced a possible death penalty. After months of playing hardball with unflinching prosecutors, the pressure-cooker became more than Fortier could bear. The dam broke, spilling out his intimate prior knowledge of the murderous plot. The young newlywed cut a plea that eventually led to a reduced twelve-year prison term in exchange for testifying against the bombing defendants. The deal also secured immunity for his bride Lori who later told the court McVeigh stacked soup cans in her kitchen, demonstrating the arrangement of the barrels of explosives inside the Ryder truck. She admitted to laminating the phony driver's license bearing the alias Robert Kling.

"McVeigh told me about plans he and Terry Nichols had to blow up the federal building in Oklahoma City," Fortier penned in a handwritten confession. April 19 marked the forthcoming day of destruction to avenge the two year anniversary of the FBI's fiery stand-off with members of a religious compound near Waco. Seventy Branch Davidians perished as the buildings burned to the ground. In December 1994, while driving through Oklahoma City with McVeigh, the pair scouted out the Alfred P. Murrah Building.

"We've chosen that building because that was the building that the orders from Waco came out of," McVeigh ardently boasted. "I'm going to bring that building down."

Fortier asked, "What about all the innocent people? What about the secretaries and the people like that in the building?"

McVeigh's stolid response followed. "Well, even if they as individuals are innocent, they work for an evil system and have to be killed." In the next breath, the Gulf War veteran mapped out his battle plan to topple the "easy target" with pietistic vigor, drawing a diagram of the truck bomb and designating the placement of his getaway vehicle.

While acknowledging he initially "lied" to authorities, Fortier maintained he rebuffed McVeigh's borderline strong-arm tactics to recruit him. Nonetheless, the prosecution's star witness played an insider's role, dutifully obeying his cohort's instructions to transport "twenty-five (stolen) weapons" in a rental vehicle from Kansas to Arizona.

McVeigh supposedly confided that Nichols looted the guns in a daring armed robbery on November 5, 1994. The victim, affluent gun collector

Roger Moore, later testified the masked assailant, clad in military camouflage and combat boots, shoved a pistol-gripped shotgun in his face. However, the defense castigated Moore for telling contradictory stories of the hold-up to friends. At one point, he reportedly described the gravelly-voiced gunman as bearded, with "an extremely dark complexion," fueling the specter of a third conspirator.

More than eighty guns, jade, precious stones, coins, silver bars, and $8700 in cash were looted in the Arkansas heist. The cash-strapped cohorts ostensibly sold the purloined weapons at gun shows to finance their hellish scheme.

Fortier's testimony stitched together the patchwork quilt of circumstantial evidence, but under cross-examination, the witness's credibility hung by a tenuous thread. While traversing the Midwest, soaking in the rantings of an infantryman turned terrorist, Fortier was snorting and smoking crystal meth several days a week. He broke down under questioning, admitting that sometimes he even sold narcotics. Secretly recorded FBI tapes of the reformed drug addict's tapped phone conversations proved even more damning.

"I can tell stories all day," he bragged to friends and family. At the time, the unemployed salesman purposed to tell "fables" to strike it rich on his notoriety, unaware the feds were listening in.


## MILITIAMEN OR MERCENARIES?

The tall, lanky kid from a bedroom community in upstate New York grew up feeling the heartbeat of rural America, shaped by strong family values and faithfully attending Sunday church services. Born in Pendleton, the son of an auto plant worker, he grew up as one of three children. Neighbors in the suburbs of Buffalo came to know the McVeigh boy as easygoing, polite, and responsible. At age ten, the fair-haired youngster nicknamed "Timmer" chose to stay with his father when his parents split up. That year marked the first humiliating run-in with a bully, in a tussle over a baseball cap in which Tim came out the loser. The shy child sought comfort from the only adult with whom he could freely confide, his beloved paternal grandfather, Ed McVeigh.

In high school, he tried his athletic skills at basketball and track but never stood out.

"He blended into the woodwork," said a former track mate. He was a prisoner to anonymity; the stigma of ordinariness among his peers seemed unshakable. But while sports, academics, and social popularity proved disappointing, backyard target practice empowered the awkward teenager with the sense of achievement he so desperately craved. Under his grandfather's tutelage, he became an accomplished marksman with a rifle. By 1988, that love of firearms would drive the twenty-year-old McVeigh to enlist in the U.S. Army, marking the critical turning point in his meandering journey to Oklahoma City.

During the 1991 Persian Gulf War, the mediocre boy from Buffalo won the recognition he needed to nourish his ailing self-esteem. As a top-notch gunner on a Bradley fighting vehicle, McVeigh earned the Bronze Star Medal for battlefield valor. But his military colleagues would never have imagined the decorated soldier resented the commendation. He had killed two enemy combatants for whom he harbored a warped sense of empathy. Years later, courtroom evidence would profile the American terrorist as a man seeking revolution against a government he perceived to exercise totalitarian actions against its own citizens, not foreigners.

By 1998, that psychological mold would shatter when a window into the former Army sergeant's darkest thoughts opened wide. He publicly expressed unabashed disapproval of the U.S. bombing of Baghdad during the Gulf War. McVeigh's ire ignited as U.S. troops prepared to launch air strikes if Saddam Hussein continued to block the United Nations' weapons inspections. Brimming with righteous indignation, he passionately argued the Iraqi dictator's justification for "stockpiling weapons of mass destruction" in order to protect his people against neighboring hostile nations.

Not long after being sentenced to execution, the veteran of Operation Desert Storm fired off a jarring salvo from his death row cell, expressing outrage at opinion polls that showed widespread favor for bombing Iraq into compliance. In a published essay, which received little fanfare, the convicted terrorist accused the federal government and public of "blatant hypocrisy."

"Do people think that government workers in Iraq are any less human than those in Oklahoma City? Do they think Iraqis don't have families who will grieve and mourn the loss of their loved ones?" McVeigh asked with unambiguous sympathy for Iraq. By March 1991, the embittered noncommissioned officer, who was among the elite few assigned to stand post during General Norman Schwarzkopf's signing of the historic cease-fire armistice, had ventured across a psychological threshold. There would be no return.

Disillusionment over the impoverished plight of the war-ravaged Iraqi citizenry left him wrestling with profound misgivings. McVeigh confided to friends in letters from the war front how "trying it was emotionally" to helplessly watch Iraqi children starve. During a private conversation with a battlefield comrade, he hinted at a calculated means of venting his mordant hostility. He resolved to become the ultimate avenger—a soldier of fortune.

"He had mentioned before that he wanted to become a mercenary for the Middle East because they paid the most," McVeigh's former Gulf War bunk mate Greg Henry told ABC's *Prime Time Live* in April 1995. "Well, we just kind of took it as a joke," the soldier somberly reflected, "But he's the kind of person that would have become that."

In the wake of the Allied victory, the twenty-two-year-old received orders to promptly report to the rigorous Special Forces Assessment and Selection Course at Fort Bragg, North Carolina. The summons to join the military's most venerated soldiers comes once in a lifetime. But the selection process implemented by the U.S. Army Special Forces, more commonly known as the Green Berets, demanded the highest level of physical fitness. Candidates must demonstrate robust survival skills in order to endure the most daring missions. Months of wartime service during Desert Storm had hindered McVeigh's performance during the grueling testing regimen. The semi-sedentary lifestyle, though short-lived, had taken its physical toll. He failed the cut.

Despondent over his rejection from the course, McVeigh passed up a promotional offer to serve as his battalion commander's gunner. It was now late 1991 and the combat hero issued his final salute to the U.S. Army. He chose not to reenlist and went home to New York. In the years that followed, he lived as a nomad, drifting aimlessly from one dead-end job to the next, occasionally pitching a tent at Nichols' Michigan farmhouse and Fortier's Arizona trailer. All the while, the inner turmoil raged.

"America is on the decline . . . is a civil war imminent? Do we have to shed blood to reform the current system? I hope it doesn't come to that, but it might," McVeigh sounded off in a letter published by the Lockport *Union Sun & Journal* on February 11, 1992.

Lurking on the fringes of the citizen militia movement, McVeigh and Nichols spouted obsessive distrust of federal gun control legislation as well as the United Nations and its perceived Orwellian role in establishing a "new world order" with one currency and a universal police force. However, when Nichols and his brother James crossed an unspoken threshold by advocating violent retribution against the establishment, the Michigan militiamen ousted the twosome from their paramilitary membership. But the rejection did not impede the budding malevolence. Nichols's paranoia and ire culminated in March 1994 when he renounced his U.S. citizenship in a letter addressed to the Marion County, Kansas, clerk. The rambling diatribe depicted the federal government as a "fraudulent, usurping octopus." But above all, the FBI fiascoes at Ruby Ridge and Waco fomented the pair's warped philosophies. They believed law enforcement had violated the rules of engagement, murdering noncombatants and innocent children.

"McVeigh wrote letters declaring that the government had drawn 'first blood' at Waco," Assistant U.S. Attorney Joseph Hartzler thundered in his opening statements to the Denver jury that subsequently sentenced McVeigh to death. "He expected and hoped that his bombing of the Murrah Building would be the first shot in a violent, bloody revolution in this country."

Federal prosecutors alleged that during McVeigh's season of violent sentiment he became a disciple and promoter of the subversive novel *The Turner Diaries*, a fictionalized account of disenfranchised "patriots" who overthrow the federal government by force. A fertilizer truck bomb explodes in front of a federal building in Washington, D.C., murdering hundreds of government employees. Prosecutors earmarked several passages from the book depicted as the "blueprint" for McVeigh's master plan. He then augmented his do-it-yourself training with a mail-order manual entitled *Homemade C-4*. The term "C-4" refers to a form of plastic explosives.

"This book provides essentially a step-by-step recipe as to how to put together your own fertilizer fuel-based bomb. . . . In fact, it shows how unbelievably simple it is to make a hugely, hugely powerful bomb," U.S. Attorney Hartzler told the jury in 1997.

During this time frame, the apprentice bomb makers embarked on experimentation, mixing small bottle explosives at Nichols' Michigan farm. McVeigh eventually graduated to detonating a pipe bomb in the Arizona desert. However, the device did not pack a very powerful blast; the detonation only managed to crack a boulder.

"Tim couldn't blow up a rock. Then Terry goes to the Philippines and Tim says he builds the bomb," McVeigh's lead attorney Stephen Jones preached in and out of the courtroom. The defense team grew enormously frustrated with their client's failure to elucidate how he acquired the technical skills to create a terrorist bomb that detonated flawlessly.

"He told us that he read it in a book. . . . Some of the things he said simply did not add up with what our experts told us. We thought he was basically memorizing what somebody else told him," the Oklahoma lawyer wryly pointed out, confident the duplicitous McVeigh was covering for Nichols' liaisons with Middle Eastern bomb experts in the Philippines, a mecca of international terrorism.

## NICHOLS'S PHILIPPINES "COVER STORY"

Enterprising defense investigators latched on to the Kansas farmer's frequent forays to the South Pacific, ostensibly to marry a mail-order bride. He eventually wed Marife Torres, a seventeen-year-old Filipina, but before he escorted his new wife back to the United States, she became pregnant with another man's child. Nichols overlooked her infidelity.

The mail-order bride was likely a "cover story," ex-wife Lana Padilla speculated in an interview with me in July 1995. The Las Vegas realtor remembered that "Tim (McVeigh) bought Terry's first ticket" to Cebu City. That trip took place in 1989, just one year after the two men met during Army basic training. Nichols' passport records, which were presented at the 1997 federal trial, documented five trips to the Philippines, but Jones's detectives located island witnesses who attested to dozens of visits.

In November 1994, Padilla drove her ex-husband to the airport prior to his final excursion to Cebu City. His parting words to their son Josh before boarding the plane traumatized the youngster.

"Josh got in the car and started crying. He said, 'Mom, I'm never going to see my daddy again.' He was crying hysterically," she recounted.

Before departure, Nichols placed a mysterious parcel in Padilla's trunk. The attached note admonished her to open it only in the event of his death. Overwhelmed by curiosity, she ripped into the package. Inside, she found a will instructing her to distribute his personal property to their son, Josh, his second wife Marife, and infant daughter. The bag also contained directions to a secret compartment Nichols had built into her kitchen cabinet. The hidden drawer contained a stash of $20,000 cash.

Hoping to find some clue as to why Nichols feared he would not return, she read a sealed letter addressed to McVeigh. The note instructed him to clean out two storage units in Council Grove, Kansas. The closing line carried sinister implications. "You're on your own. Just go for it," he encouraged his coconspirator before signing off. "As far as heat, none that I know."

"Why would he write this letter? Why this trip? That is what is so suspicious to me. He has been there (the Philippines) so many times," Padilla thought. The conundrum deepened the more she sought an explanation. While exploring Nichols' Las Vegas storage shed, she found a ski mask, wig, coins, precious stones, gold, and silver. She had unwittingly stumbled upon the stolen goods taken during the Arkansas robbery.

Weeks later, in January 1995, the man with whom she once shared the intimacy of marriage returned from the overseas voyage a complete stranger. Paranoid and packing a concealed weapon, Nichols confided he flew back early because "somebody could get killed down there." He trembled at the thought of going back. Nichols had reached an impasse. He resolved to pull out of the bombing plot. But McVeigh wouldn't have it, or so he (McVeigh) said. The former gunner bragged to Michael Fortier that he could coerce Nichols's cooperation.

What precipitated Nichols's sudden cold feet? Was it a stroke of conscience or abject fear? The passage of time would prove the latter. My investigation uncovered Nichols' collaboration with Iraqi intelligence operatives based in the Philippines. The introverted farmer from the Midwest had gazed into the soulless eyes of a cold-blooded killer, Ramzi Yousef. Yousef, the macabre genius behind the 1993 World Trade Center attack, based his operations out of Manila. This Middle Eastern terrorist commandeered the role of general, not Timothy McVeigh. Nichols was in over his head with no way out.

After the bombing, Padilla contemplated the threat of retaliation if her jailed ex-husband shared all he knew to negotiate a plea bargain.

"Everything just seems like its going in the direction . . . that he knows something and why isn't he talking? Now I think the only reason why he's not talking is to protect us," she surmised in a direct reference to her family's vulnerability.

While the incarcerated terrorist never admitted to meeting with Muslim extremists, his accomplice Tim McVeigh cleverly hinted at his closet sympathies for Middle Eastern terror groups hostile to the United States. In an April 2001 letter to Fox News, McVeigh made known his tacit approval for the crimes committed by Ramzi Yousef. He shamelessly quoted the Muslim terrorist's statement to a New York court before sentencing. "Yes, I am a terrorist and proud of it as long as it is against the U.S. government," Yousef proclaimed during the January 1998 hearing. This telling reference was not the first time McVeigh zealously defended the murderous actions of our Middle Eastern adversaries.

During a March 2000 interview with *60 Minutes*, McVeigh vented his disgust over American foreign policy in the wake of the 1998 cruise missile strikes against Afghanistan and Sudan in retaliation for Osama bin Laden's bombing of the U.S. embassies in Africa. But for years prior to that, McVeigh's deranged identification with terror masters such as Ramzi Yousef, Osama bin Laden, and Saddam Hussein would remain locked in his innermost thoughts.

## THE UBIQUITOUS JOHN DOE 2

During the age of innocence, Josh Nichols transcended from obscurity to international fame. The twelve-year-old son of a notorious killer became an overnight celebrity, fiercely defending his father before the world press and dogged FBI interrogators. But deep within, he wrestled with secret knowledge, only allowing cryptic hints to slip out, and only to his mother.

"One thing Josh said to me, he said, 'Mom, there was supposed to be more than one bombing.' And I said, 'What do you mean?' He said there was going to be more than one bombing," Padilla shared. It was April 21, 1995, when the baby-faced schoolboy made the shocking disclosure, a fact which the former CIA chief Vincent Cannistraro learned from the Saudi intelligence source within hours of the explosion. But that information was unpublished, classified as top secret, and would remain sealed to this day had it not been leaked. Was Josh simply repeating grandiose chatter he overheard during weekend visits with his father and McVeigh? Or, had the child whom Nichols raised from the cradle to fifth grade already become indoctrinated and entrusted not to talk? The definitive truth may never be known, but strong indicators emerged during a hidden camera conversation with the boy's mother.

It was July 1995. Lana Padilla pledged to interview with KFOR-TV, given her heartfelt sorrow for the suffering of Oklahomans. But within minutes of our plane touching down in her hometown of Las Vegas, the shoot was spiked. Padilla callously informed me she had granted exclusivity to a television tabloid show in exchange for a speaking fee. Paying for information violated every tenet of credible journalism, and I was not about to cross the line. Instead, I persuaded the reluctant interviewee to meet me for an introduction and brief chat. She agreed. KFOR management and I decided to surreptitiously record the rendezvous at a local casino. Although the use of concealed cameras has been widely viewed as an invasion of privacy, the comfort level often invites the unfiltered truth. Such was this case.

The woman living under the microscope of national headlines relaxed, unburdened herself, and let the untold facts flow, information not yet disclosed during lengthy questioning by the FBI. Within hours of Channel 4's broadcasts airing Padilla's bone-jarring revelations, the Bureau rang the assignment desk requesting an unedited copy of the tape. The station complied.

"Josh stays locked up. Josh doesn't share a lot of what he knows with you. Is he trying to protect you?" I casually commented, not expecting what came next.

"I'm sure he's trying to protect me . . . because if he talks to me, I have to tell," Padilla acknowledged as she vowed to pull the plug on FBI access to her son, including permission to take fingerprints. Under the pretense of being a protective parent, she lauded Josh's decision to hold back what he might know about a third conspirator.

"Terry told Josh the other night on the phone, he said they (FBI agents) do not have John Doe 2," she said with a troubled look. I theorized that Nichols feared for his son's life if he implicated others.

"Your son hasn't picked out John Doe 2 yet, has he?" I asked.

"I was there when they (investigators) set the sketches out and Josh said, 'That's Tim McVeigh and I don't know who that is.' He didn't even look at it (John Doe 2 sketch)," Padilla recounted. "When Josh left the room, the investigator said to me . . . he knows who he is. He's just denying it."

Until the date of his execution on June 11, 2001, McVeigh steadfastly maintained he acted alone, with minimal participation from Terry Nichols. Yet even in death, the lingering suspicion of McVeigh's treasonous collusion with enemy soldiers, upon whom he had once fired as a Bradley gunner in the Gulf War, persists.

In October 2001, high-ranking defense department officials leaked to the national press that the Oklahoma City bomber was an "Iraqi agent, who collected Iraqi telephone numbers." According to the published account in *U.S. News and World Report*, several top men in the Pentagon believed the foreign connection to the Oklahoma bombing was part of a "cover-up."

By July 2003, the volume from the ranks of military hawks turned up a notch. A "longtime friend" and confidant of Assistant Secretary of Defense Paul Wolfowitz confirmed to a *Vanity Fair* reporter that the secretary seriously entertained the notion, "based on phone records and other evidence," that Saddam Hussein was behind the Oklahoma City bombing. It seems some in the hierarchy of Washington's intelligentsia refuse to dismiss as conspiracy theory the multiple sightings of McVeigh's foreign, dark-complexioned accomplice sitting in the passenger seat of the Ryder truck.

In 1995, the federal grand jury proclaimed in the official indictment that McVeigh and Nichols acted with "others unknown." Several members of the Denver jury who convicted Terry Nichols in the Oklahoma City bombing publicly expressed their strongly held beliefs that after months of examining every facet of the government's evidence, they could only conclude that the April 19 bombing was perpetrated by more than those who had been arrested and charged.

"I think we agree that there were more people involved, and I think most of the jury members feel that John Doe 2 is a definite possibility," juror Chris Seib told a swarm of reporters after delivering the guilty verdict. The panel failed to reach a consensus regarding the defendant's degree of culpability, so members convicted Nichols of conspiracy and involuntary manslaughter, not murder.

Lead defense counsel for McVeigh's federal trial, Stephen Jones, disclosed the American terrorist failed a polygraph examination when he denied that additional conspirators aided and abetted in the bombing plot.

"I believe Timothy McVeigh's role in the Oklahoma City bombing was a very minor one," Jones postulated in a nationally televised interview in 2003. "A member of the conspiracy? Yes. The leader? No. The financier? No. The organizer? No. Timothy McVeigh saw his role as the cover for everybody else, to be the person to fall on the sword. It served deep-seated emotional needs that he had, and it furthered the role of the conspiracy."

Dissatisfied with the "final" version of the story, when sentencing Terry Nichols to life behind bars, U.S. District Judge Richard Matsch remarked, "It would be disappointing for me if the law enforcement agencies of the United States government have quit looking for answers."

Driven by a belief that federal prosecutors presented only a partial picture of the awful truth, an Oklahoma state legislator spearheaded a citizens' petition drive to seat a grand jury to probe the looming presence of unindicted conspirators. In December 1998, after eighteen months of research and examination of one-hundred-seventeen witnesses, the Oklahoma County grand jury making inquiry into "conspiracy theories" swirling around the bombing returned no indictments. Yet the panel carefully worded this telling statement in its final report: "In spite of all the evidence before us, we cannot put full closure to the question of the existence of a John Doe 2."

Why do questions swirl about the official account of the massacre in the American Midwest? A *CNN/USA Today* poll taken in April 1996 tapped into a collective consciousness. Sixty-eight percent of Americans believed conspirators were still out there, somewhere. I found them hiding in plain sight.

CHAPTER 5

# REFUGEES OR AGENTS
# OF SADDAM?

"I want you, Jayna, to investigate who did this," ordered KFOR-TV News Director Melissa Klinzing while handing out reporter assignments on April 20. Had she abandoned her senses? How was I, a television journalist from a local Midwestern affiliate, going to find the parties responsible for murdering hundreds of Oklahomans? This was no rookie operation, but one that pundits depicted as sophisticated and flawlessly executed. Foreign and veteran news correspondents had been reporting from the outset that highly placed government sources suspected Middle Eastern terrorists.

I contemplated in silent amusement my limited options in tackling the impractical news assignment—pray for a miracle that a CIA case officer or the local Israeli Mossad agent would share with me classified intelligence about a possible foreign plot; or I could quit daydreaming and begin monitoring the satellite feeds of FBI press conferences. The latter was the only realistic alternative. That is, until one telephone call to the newsroom turned my journalistic lottery fantasy into a groundbreaking lead. One inside tip led me directly to the doorstep of what several esteemed intelligence experts later characterized as a Middle Eastern terrorist cell operating in the heart of Oklahoma City.

My odyssey began on April 22 when the Jordanian national, Abraham Ahmad, returned to his home in Oklahoma City. His high profile detention and questioning by authorities in two countries stirred up a media feeding frenzy. I joined a bevy of press people clamoring for a one-on-one interview. For an uninterrupted twenty-five minutes of taping, the unshaven, weary traveler delivered an exhaustive recitation of his FBI detention.

"I don't understand why they stopped me. It was so insulting, so humiliating. They put handcuffs on my hands and there were twenty to thirty policemen around me. I said, 'Please respect that I had nothing to do with it. I am innocent,'" Ahmad grumbled, eliciting compassion for his terrible ordeal.

"And personally I know somebody, his wife is still missing and I didn't go over there to tell him how sorry I feel about this. But I cannot leave the house. I have to stay and wait for the FBI."

Ahmad touted his cooperation, agreeing to take a polygraph examination and to testify before the federal grand jury investigating the bombing. His affable, forthcoming stance disarmed me. I understood why the media characterized him as the quintessential victim of circumstance, in the wrong place at the wrong time. But his testimony aroused my curiosity because selected portions seemed to defy common sense.

The erudite, college educated foreigner with superb command of English volunteered no explanation for quitting a decent paying job at a premier computer firm. For six months, he had been unemployed with a wife and two children to support. When I asked how he afforded two lengthy roundtrips to the Middle East with no source of income, he explained that siblings living overseas wired him thousands of dollars to travel home. Suspicious or coincidental, I figured the feds would not have released him were he complicit. Yet there was one thing I could not reconcile—his implausible insistence he was unaware of a terrorist strike until his plane landed in Chicago, Illinois, the afternoon of April 19.

Ahmad narrated his morning activities which included running errands in the northwest sector of the city to prepare for his trip to Amman, Jordan. But how did he miss the tremors? Witnesses within a fifty-five mile radius of downtown felt the powerful impact of the blast. Moreover, his flight did not depart Oklahoma City until 10:45 A.M. By that time, the airport was teeming with lawmen clad in the traditional blue windbreakers armed with walkie-talkies.

I decided to check out his story. After packing up our camera gear, I started knocking on doors. A woman living directly across the street said she watched as Ahmad loaded his luggage into the back of his pickup thirty minutes after the explosion. The neighborhood was located a few dozen blocks north of the blast zone where the thunderous roar and vibration were inescapable.

Racing a tight deadline, I voiced a short audio track while my photographer edited together portions of the interview, interspersed with comments from the neighbor. I delivered the story during the evening newscast from Ahmad's front lawn, unaware of its impact. That particular live shot would prompt a call to the newsroom that thrust me directly into the eye of a hurricane.

## MYSTERY CALLER

"I work for a man named Dr. Anwar Abdul who is close friends with Abraham Ahmad. He's Palestinian and owns hundreds of low-rent houses in Oklahoma City," the unidentified caller to the newsroom said with a dense southern drawl.

The lead seemed like a dead end. "What does that have to do with the bombing?" I retorted. "Mr. Ahmad was thoroughly vetted by the feds and released."

"I told the FBI about the bizarre activities of Dr. Abdul and Ahmad which took place in the days before the bombing," he answered.

"Who are you?" I asked.

"I would prefer to meet in person," he replied.

I expressed impatience with the cat-and-mouse tactic.

"Please don't cut me off. My name is Bernard Stanton. I promise you it will be worth your time to hear me out," the stranger pleaded. We set an appointment to meet at a local diner. Breaking protocol, I asked my husband, Drew, to come along. I was feeling a bit out of my element and wanted a second opinion about the witness's veracity. There was no rule book to which I could refer when it came to covering international terrorism. A fatiguing deluge of calls to our newsroom had already demonstrated that human tragedy encouraged emotionally disturbed individuals to spin outright lies, starving to steal a moment on the evening news.

While scanning the restaurant for the mystery caller, I noticed a ruddy complexioned man sitting in a booth tucked away from chatting customers. It was Bernard Stanton, only he didn't come alone.

"Thanks for meeting with us, Ms. Davis. You can call me Bernie," he nervously announced with a firm handshake. I felt the hard calluses of a laborer. His fellow employee, Larry Monroe, nodded a quiet hello, his eyes shadowed by the bill of a ball cap. At first, the pair seemed ill at ease and fear-ful. But as the lilac twilight sky blackened into night, the men's stilted pos-ture surrendered to indignation. Strong emotion steered the conversation.

A red flush bathed Bernie's tanned, weathered face. "Things started get-ting weird last fall when our boss, Dr. Anwar Abdul, hired a handful of Middle Eastern guys. He said they fought in the Iraqi military during the Gulf War. One time, he even warned if anyone ever got them riled up, then they could probably do some major damage."

Larry crossly interjected, "These Iraqis claimed they were refugees, but they openly bragged about the superiority of Saddam's army. Some of the Middle Eastern men I worked with that day cheered enthusiastically when we heard radio reports that Islamic terrorists claimed credit for the attack."

Bernie remembered one of the soldiers deliriously boasting about his shameless devotion to the Iraqi president.

"This guy said, 'I love Saddam. I would die for Saddam,'" he said. His piercing blue eyes squinted with disgust.

"Just because these Iraqis supported a maniac like the Iraqi dictator proves they are devoted to their homeland, but that doesn't make them ter-rorists," I noted.

Glancing at his troubled companion, Bernie opined, "We understand your point, but there are a lot of things that just don't add up."

"Can you be more specific?" I said impatiently.

"Why was there a brown Chevy pickup parked at Abdul's office that matched the truck the FBI was tracking right after the building blew up? I haven't seen it since," he reported.

"When was that?" I queried.

"Just about three to four weeks before the terrorists hit downtown. I remember the truck looked too expensive to belong to one of Dr. Abdul's low-income renters. It was a late model, with tinted windows and a bug shield, just like the police broadcasts for the getaway car reported on the news."

"Who was driving the vehicle?" I pressed.

"Well, I didn't see the man get out of the cab of the truck. But when I walked in the office, I saw Dr. Abdul and a clean-cut Middle Eastern look-ing guy talking. He handed the stranger what I figured was a check," Bernie responded.

"What did they say to each other?" I asked.

"I wouldn't venture to guess. They were speaking in a foreign language."
"Was it Arabic?"
"I suppose that's what you would call it," Bernie answered.

I turned to Larry. "Did you see a brown Chevy truck at Dr. Abdul's?"

"No, I don't recall seeing a pickup like that," he answered somberly. "I don't want to get in this thing too deep. My wife says talking to a reporter could put our family at risk."

Reluctance churned and I read the signs. "I understand. You both will remain confidential sources," I promised.

Though rudimentarily schooled, these construction workers possessed innate perspicacity. They presented a bold front, but their eyes communicated trepidation. As our conversation progressed, I became more persuaded that the strange occurrences surrounding Dr. Anwar Abdul added up to more than mere coincidence.


## PLO CONNECTION?

For the past few years, Bernie and Larry had performed maintenance, repair, and clean-up work for Dr. Anwar Abdul's multi-million dollar real estate company known as Salman Properties. I quickly accessed federal court records which made the affluent émigré appear all the more inscrutable. In 1968, the Palestinian expatriate left his homeland in Tel Aviv in search of the proverbial American dream. Within a decade, he had earned a PhD in psychology from the University of Oklahoma. Soon thereafter, the Oklahoma Department of Human Services hired the foreign born graduate as a staff psychologist, granting him a modest annual salary of approximately $40,000. During the early 1980s, Dr. Abdul's investment portfolio multiplied exponentially with the purchase of nearly $4 million in low-income rental houses throughout Oklahoma City's crime-ridden neighborhoods.

During his swift journey from rags to riches, Dr. Abdul's business practices illuminated the radar screen of federal investigators. FBI agents identified eight known aliases under which the real estate mogul operated. He attributed his newfound wealth to generous contributions from "siblings living in Baghdad; Dhahran, Saudi Arabia; Amman, Jordan; and Jerusalem." But the Department of Justice suspected a more illicit source of revenue. On February 11, 1991, Dr. Abdul pleaded guilty to two counts of a four count indictment for federal insurance fraud, sentencing him to eight months in the penitentiary. The company plumber delivered the most damning evidence, accusing Dr. Abdul of enlisting him in an arson-for-hire scam that led to the filing of illegal property claims.

White collar crime fueled the FBI's obsession with the Palestinian doctor, but only in part. While sifting through the lengthy court dossier, I found a telling reference to the government's belief that avarice was not the confessed felon's driving motive. The FBI alleged Dr. Anwar Abdul had ties to the Palestinian Liberation Organization, a charge the indignant defendant denied. The legal reasons why federal investigators suspected this man of links to a Middle Eastern terrorist organization would remain permanently sealed from public disclosure.

Dr. Abdul was paroled from prison not long after the Gulf War ended. He immediately resumed operating his rental empire, but continued to run his business *sub rosa*. Scouring the company registrations with the Oklahoma Secretary of State, the Southwestern Bell phone book, and directory assistance, I found no official record of Salman Properties.

## ARMY DESERTERS OR UNDERCOVER INFILTRATORS?

In the fall of 1994, Dr. Abdul hired a half dozen ex-Iraqi soldiers who were purportedly seeking political asylum from a tyrannical regime. Bernie and Larry remarked that all of their Iraqi coworkers were conspicuously absent from work on April 17, the day McVeigh rented the Ryder truck that transported the bomb. One of the Iraqis missed several weeks, claiming he was recovering from injuries sustained in an automobile accident. Furthermore, two Jordanian employees simultaneously separated from their American wives and ceased reporting to work in late March. One of these men claimed he was returning to Jordan to find a new bride, the other said he was tending to a sick child.

"These Iraqi workers had no construction skills whatsoever. It was unbelievable. All they were qualified to do was to throw paint on the walls. But the boss gave these foreigners special treatment like buying them new and used cars for personal use," Bernie flared.

"I noticed the same thing," Larry agreed.

I tested their motives at every juncture. "I don't want to sound offensive, but this could be interpreted as sour grapes."

"I was the company foreman for eight years with a pretty good track record," Bernie said with mounting agitation. "But for no reason, Dr. Abdul started making insulting comments that told me loud and clear he wanted me to quit my job. After the bombing, I knew I had no choice but to resign."

"I still have to go back there and act like it's business as usual. I can't afford to lose my paycheck," Larry apprehensively explained.

The witnesses came across as sincere, but misjudging their character could invite disaster. I sized them up as transparent. Bernie wrestled with anger; Larry grappled with fear. Yet they were not crackpots. Their suspicions seemed justified in light of Dr. Abdul's apparent link to a vehicle that bore an uncanny resemblance to the brown Chevrolet pickup seen speeding away from the bomb site.

Bernie contacted the FBI while Larry gave a statement to the Oklahoma State Bureau of Investigation within forty-eight hours of the bombing. Each shared their grave concerns with authorities, independently and unknown to each other. The pair itemized a litany of disturbing events which cast their employer—who expressed vehement distrust and hatred for the United States government—in a dubious light. The story grew even more engrossing as I explored Dr. Abdul's close relationship with the man collared as a potential material witness, Abraham Ahmad.

"A long time ago, Ahmad did some contract remodeling work for Dr. Abdul. But in the weeks before the bombing, he began showing up at the office everyday, pretty frequently too, sometimes three and four times a day," Larry observed.

"Maybe they're just friends." I commented.

"That's true, but I've worked for Dr. Abdul for eight years and have only seen Ahmad two or three times at the Salman Properties' office during that period." Bernie observed. "But there's something else that bothers me. Just a few days before the explosion downtown, Ahmad pulled up to Dr. Abdul's office, opened the trunk of his car, and all the Iraqi guys crowded around. I noticed a white box but couldn't see what was inside. They seemed really excited about it, laughing and talking in their foreign language."

"Did you walk over to see what was in the box?" I cut in.

"No, I got the distinct impression they weren't ready to share the moment with me," Bernie smiled sarcastically.

I observed, "Ahmad's peculiar behavior pattern hardly makes a case for terrorist involvement. But I am curious if you have any insight into the reasons why he was traveling to Jordan on the very day of the attack."

"He told me he was flying home to Jordan and had no intention of returning to the U.S.," Larry volunteered. "But the reason for his trip struck me as bizarre. He said he must fulfill a Jordanian tradition which required the oldest son to care for his parents once the youngest son moved out of the home."

Bernie chimed in, "He told me he had to deal with a family emergency. But Abraham supposedly told the company secretary, Darby Williams, that he had all that weird stuff in his luggage to build a house in Jordan."

"When can I interview Darby?" I asked. Both men grimaced. It didn't look encouraging.

"Darby is scared to death. And she's seen a heck of a lot more than we have. To be frank, she doesn't trust reporters," Bernie said.

"Well gentleman, I can't say I blame her. Here's my unlisted home phone number. Impress upon her the importance of trusting someone, even if she just makes a call to the FBI." The interview concluded with a handshake, but I wasn't sure where it was leading.

## Brown Pickup "Not Ruled Out"

The next morning, I contemplated strategy. Bernie and Larry had painted a mosaic of facts laced with intrigue, but absent a smoking gun. The evidence trail began and ended with the mysterious brown pickup that reportedly contained Middle Eastern suspects. While the pursuit started out white-hot, it quickly turned ice-cold. The FBI had cagily dodged the media's questions when asked why the lead was suddenly dropped.

I started dialing. First stop, the Federal Bureau of Investigation. The official spokesman for the Oklahoma City field office took the call.

"Is the FBI still investigating the all-points bulletin it issued on April 19 for the brown Chevy truck?" I asked, then braced for the bureaucratic lock down.

"It has not been ruled out," FBI Special Agent and Public Information Officer Dan Vogel confirmed in his trademark impassive, businesslike style.

I scribbled his quote without much thought, then stared at the notepad. Then it hit me. "Did he really say the truck had not been ruled out?"

The Bureau had publicly trampled any inference of foreign participation with the vigor of fire crews dousing a raging brush fire. Now a veteran agent, known to the local press as a straight shooter with a flair for understatement, struck the match and tossed it into the parched grass. With no time to waste, I paid an unannounced visit to a well-connected source.

"Little darling, you're treading in the no trespass zone that could stir up trouble," the career lawman presaged. I responded with a quizzical look.

"The FBI issued that Teletype at 11:56 A.M., and four hours later, ordered the Oklahoma County Sheriff's Department to cancel it," he claimed with careful precision.

"You mean all police radio broadcasts for the brown truck with foreign suspects would never be rebroadcast?"

"You got it. That's why I suggest you, young lady, be careful," he warned with a protective tone of fatherly advice. "I have been tracking suspects for thirty-five years and I have never seen the FBI so hot to drop an all-points bulletin."

"Did they give a reason?" I implored.

"I asked. The answer—just pull it!"

## THE FBI IS CALLING

Darby Williams tossed files trying to prioritize the urgent tasks from the not so pressing. A pink phone message slipped from the piles of paperwork. It was the note she jotted down to remind her boss the FBI had phoned the office.

"Did he return the call? What does this mean?" she shuddered.

The office door swung open with a thud, interrupting her racing thoughts. She glanced up. Abraham Ahmad stood trembling in the entryway, disheveled and unshaven. Dr. Abdul walked out to greet his unannounced visitor.

"I'm scared to f—-ing death!" Ahmad shrieked as Dr. Abdul whisked him behind closed doors. The rancorous harangue that ensued bled through the peeling Sheetrock which draped the walls of the small-framed house that had been converted to a company headquarters. Darby sat motionless, listening to the tempestuous argument, unable to decipher what was being said. The two had always communicated in Arabic.

Bernie entered and tiptoed softly to Darby's desk to avoid detection. "What's going on in there?"

Darby frowned. "I figure the FBI put Abraham through the rigors during these past few days. He looks pretty shaken up," she whispered, her tear-filled eyes downcast.

"I'm frightened. There are strange circumstances I just cannot explain," she sniffled.

Bernie knelt down and gently asked, "Would you be willing to trust a reporter from Channel 4? Her name is Jayna Davis and she guaranteed me whatever you say will remain confidential." Darby silently acquiesced.

## FULL DISCLOSURE

Before long, I was sitting face-to-face with the reluctant witness. Bernie provided a reassuring presence, sitting quietly by her side. Both were unaware I was surreptitiously recording every word. Darby Williams was far too skittish for the glare of cameras, but pinpoint accuracy was imperative if I was going to convince an exacting news director to navigate the minefields embedded in this story.

The interview evoked surges of deep emotion. Throughout, the naturally shy witness clutched a crumbled tissue as she dabbed intermittent streams of tears. Her fair skin accentuated the dark hue beneath her swollen eyes. She had endured a few sleepless nights reliving incriminating events and sightings that gnawed at her conscience.

"Dr. Abdul became secretive after he hired the Iraqi soldiers in November of 1994. It was as if he did not want me to monitor his daily activities," Darby reflected. By March, the secretary detected a marked increase in her employer's paranoia. He forbade her from leaving during her lunch hour and from running office errands. Dr. Abdul's controlling behavior struck Darby as irrational with no clear motivation. During this time frame, former employee and close friend Abraham Ahmad began paying unexplained daily visits to Salman Properties.

"Just today, Abraham came crashing into the office, yelling that he was 'scared to f——ing death.' I assumed he was strung out from FBI interrogations. But it's that mysterious pickup that haunts me the most," she softly proclaimed.

"When did you see it?" I asked.

"It was a few days before April 19," she answered.

Darby claimed to be peering out the office window when she observed Abraham Ahmad seated behind the wheel of a parked brown pickup. But this was no ordinary work truck. Darby now thought it was likely a Chevrolet which bore the distinct body markings detailed in the FBI's bulletin.

"I remember it had darkly tinted windows and a smoke-colored bug deflector."

Darby also recalled seeing Ahmad in the passenger seat of a vehicle similar to suspect Timothy McVeigh's dilapidated Mercury Marquis. She remembered the now famous getaway car was parked in Salman Properties' driveway a few days prior to the blast. She could not identify the driver. When she glanced at the faded yellow vehicle a second time, Ahmad and Dr. Abdul were leaning against the automobile conversing.

"I never saw the brown truck or the yellow car again after the bombing," she noted as her voice trailed off. A breathless hush followed. Silence filled the space between us. Darby pensively twirled her finger around a long lock of sandy blonde waves, then clenched her teeth. "I want to know why Dr.

Abdul didn't notify the authorities his ex-wife Karen was missing in the bombing?" she quivered, lifting her eyes to meet mine.

"When I saw what he did to his little girl, I resigned my job after eight years," Bernie fumed. "I just couldn't swallow working for a man like that anymore."

I stopped writing. "Slow down, folks. What on earth are you talking about?"

Darby's timid comportment evaporated. Suffused with indignation, the two bristled at their employer's insensitivity toward the fate of his ex-wife, Karen Abdul, who perished on the fifth floor of the federal complex. The Palestinian immigrant divorced his American wife in 1994, reaching a settlement in which she was awarded ownership of a large number of his rental properties. He remarried a Jordanian woman, Nadia.

"When I came into the office after the bomb went off, everyone was watching the television coverage of the collapsed building. Nadia was laughing at Karen's bad luck right in front of this missing woman's daughter, Helen. The poor kid was crying hysterically," Bernie seethed.

"I recall during my interview with Ahmad he expressed genuine regret for a friend whose wife was missing in the building. Keep in mind these people have foreign customs we don't understand," I admonished.

"No, it seems more sinister to me," Darby countered. Karen Abdul had made the regrettable decision to oblige her ex-husband's request to assist in preparing his business tax returns on April 17. As a result, she missed work on Monday and was obligated to report to the office on Wednesday, April 19, her regularly scheduled day off. Darby explained that auditors for the Internal Revenue Service had inspected Dr. Abdul's company books several times since the beginning of 1995. Bernie and Darby claimed their boss failed to withhold state and federal income taxes from their paychecks. The Oklahoma Employment Security Commission summoned both witnesses to testify at a hearing in which Dr. Abdul was accused of failure to pay state unemployment insurance taxes. Authorities eventually slapped the company owner with a $26,000 tax warrant. He settled before trial.

"If Karen had not helped Dr. Abdul with his taxes on Monday, she would be alive today. I can't conceive how Nadia thought that was amusing," Darby lamented. She related how she frantically scanned news footage for survivors, praying that her dear friend Karen would call. But the phone never rang.

"You mentioned earlier that your boss neglected to report his ex-wife's death. How do you know?" I asked.

"Check the newspaper. Her name has not been reported on the official list of dead and missing," she asserted. "And her body still has not been recovered. But that didn't stop Dr. Abdul from handing me a check to deliver to the insurance company."

"What was the check for?" I inquired.

"Dr. Abdul jokingly remarked it would be prudent to keep Karen's insurance current. I assumed he was paying an installment to avoid cancellation of Karen's auto or life insurance policy, but didn't dare ask."

## LAS VEGAS CROSSROADS

On the morning of April 20, Dr. Abdul arrived at the office unusually early, irate that his teenage daughter Helen had failed to report to work. Darby watched as he scurried around the office, then left without a word.

"A few hours later, he phoned me from Las Vegas to let me know where he could be reached. I was stunned by his cold heart. How could he leave his eighteen-year-old daughter alone to grieve the loss of her mother?" she wept.

Dr. Abdul's hasty departure delivered quite a jolt, but it was not uncommon for the Palestinian businessman to visit "sin city." Darby made travel arrangements for his monthly excursions. He routinely flew out of Oklahoma City on Thursday and returned Sunday evening, booking rooms at MGM Grand and Binion's Horseshoe casinos. He often left cash receipts for $10,000 to $15,000 in open view after his weekend sprees.

During the course of my investigation, I discovered the Oklahoma City bombing suspects also took weekend jaunts to Las Vegas, presumably to visit Terry Nichols's son Joshua, who resided there with his mother, Lana Padilla. At the time, the nomadic McVeigh lived in rural Kingman, Arizona, a short drive from the gambling mecca of the United States. I mulled over the likelihood that the trio had crossed paths. While I tracked down several promising leads that hinted at a liaison, the evidence was not concrete, with the exception of two cryptic phone calls.

On April 20, less than twenty-four hours after the bombing, the Palestinian property magnate boarded a plane in Oklahoma City bound for Las Vegas. The next day, Terry Nichols surrendered to federal authorities at the Herington, Kansas, police department. News of the material witness's interrogation flooded the international airwaves. Phone records revealed that just hours later, an unknown party placed two brief calls to Nichols's Kansas home at 11:01 P.M. and again at 12:30 A.M. from a payphone at the Las Vegas casino Circus Circus. That same night, Dr. Anwar Abdul was registered at

Binion's Horseshoe, located within walking distance of the Circus Circus casino where the calls to Nichols's residence had originated.

## THE QUICK AND THE (UNREPORTED) DEAD

In the days that followed, I considered every imaginable explanation that would cast an innocuous light on otherwise incriminating scenarios. The fallibility of the human memory had to be factored into the equation. But after poring over my notes, the amalgamation of the witnesses' stories resonated with malignant overtones. The final verdict on the complicity of these men would hinge in part on the veracity of Darby, Bernie, and Larry. I resolved to try their reliability by fire.

My fact-finding mission began with the death of Dr. Abdul's former wife. Day after day, I scanned the wire feeds from the Associated Press. The calendar turned from April to May and still Karen Abdul's name remained noticeably absent from the directory of recovered victims and missing federal employees. I dialed the number Bernie gave me for Salman Properties. A female with a girlish voice answered. It was Helen, Dr. Abdul's daughter.

"Good afternoon, my name is Jayna Davis. I'm a reporter from KFOR-TV. To begin, I would like to extend my condolences for your mother's death. I am truly sorry," I said.

"Thank you," Helen softly answered.

"We have received several inquiries from your mother's friends who are deeply concerned that Karen's name has not yet been added to the list of missing people. Can you tell me why?" I asked.

The distraught teen innocently explained that her father was trying to notify the proper authorities, but had been unable to get through. The story changed when I spoke to Helen's elderly grandmother who contended her ex-son-in-law, Dr. Abdul, volunteered to report Karen's fate to the medical examiner. My next call was to the coroner's office.

"There is no logjam when it comes to taking information from victims' families," an Oklahoma County medical examiner asserted. "At the risk of sounding gruesome, the majority of these corpses are so severely mutilated, we are dependent upon relatives to submit dental records in order to accurately identify victims' remains."

I hung up the phone and stared at Karen's name scrawled across my notes.

"Why would Dr. Abdul delay reporting his ex-wife to officials? After all, her death would elicit sympathy, not suspicion." I hypothesized.

The answer jumped off the page. "She kept her husband's last name after their divorce. The surname Abdul would have flagged FBI agents who previously investigated the Palestinian ex-con for possible ties to the PLO. And now his former spouse happened to meet a deadly fate on her regularly scheduled day off," I reasoned.

I gathered up my files and headed to my news director's office. I had reached the threshold to make the story pitch. After hours of deflecting Melissa's rapid-fire objections, the ever-skeptical newswoman gave me the green light.

"Grab a photographer and record hidden surveillance videotape of Dr. Abdul's Iraqi employees. But be discreet," she cautioned.

# CHAPTER 6

# DEAD RINGER

The news assignment seemed almost voyeuristic. A camouflaged camera captured their every move. The powerful zoom lens generated close range surveillance from our nondescript, white van parked several blocks away. The foreign handymen of Salman Properties carried out their daily tasks, oblivious to our watchful presence. At first blush, the men appeared industrious. But as the afternoon stakeout progressed, their perpetual motion became transparently inefficient. I noticed the Iraqi workers expended much of their energy chain smoking and bantering while pausing sporadically to toss a few branches or debris from the back of a broken down pickup into the company trash dumpster.

After returning to the KFOR-TV studio, I meticulously combed through every frame of the surreptitiously recorded video. I carefully compared the scowling faced sketch of John Doe 2 to each Iraqi subject and ejected the tape. None bore a striking likeness.

A week later, federal authorities unveiled a new artist's rendering of the elusive bombing suspect. FBI spokesman Weldon Kennedy noted that the most recent composite, which featured the suspect in profile donning a ball cap, was based on "additional witness interviews." Trusted friends I contacted in law enforcement pointed out the glaring disparity between the first two sketches (full-faced) and the latest depiction of the rugged-featured terrorist.

One of Dr. Abdul's Iraqi crewmen known as Hussain Hashem Al-Hussaini fit the physical description issued in the government's arrest warrant for John Doe 2. However, the émigré's buffoonish, protruding curly hair disqualified him as a match for the composite. I realized everything had radically changed upon the government's release of the third sketch. Back at the KFOR-TV newsroom, I carried the videotape to the director's booth, then anxiously sat back as he electronically overlaid the FBI sketch with a profile photograph of Al-Hussaini. A bank of television monitors mounted overhead displayed the government's illustration as it blended into the face of the ex-Iraqi serviceman with pinpoint precision, from the hairline to the jawline.

"If that man isn't John Doe 2, there is no John Doe 2," the director gasped. Several confidential police and sheriff sources echoed the same sentiment, describing the resemblance as "uncanny."

Al-Hussaini matched the height, weight, and physique of the man sought by the FBI with one possible snare. Witnesses described McVeigh's shadowy cohort as bearing a distinctive tattoo on the upper left arm.

I met with Bernie Stanton. "Do you recall seeing a tattoo on any of Dr. Abdul's foreign employees?"

He paused. The wait seemed interminable. "Yeah, I believe Al-Hussaini has a tattoo."

"What was it, and where was it located?" I eagerly asked.

"I don't recall exactly what it looked like. I just know it was located above his shirt-sleeve on his left arm."


## THE ALIBI

Reconstructing Al-Hussaini's movements for the critical hours leading up to the heartland massacre was paramount. Dead ringer or not, an ironclad alibi would instantly transform the spellbinding discovery into a dead end. Charting the Iraqi soldier's whereabouts for the morning of April 19 became one of the most challenging feats of the investigation.

My quest began with Bernie. At approximately 8:30 A.M., he arrived at 2220 NW 37th Street to perform remodeling work. Thirty minutes later, he realized his task required tools he did not have on hand. He decided to head home to retrieve the necessary equipment. No other workers had reported to the job site when he climbed into his pickup. He drove a few short miles to his house. As he clutched his front door knob, the earth shook. It was 9:02 A.M. Bernie flipped on his television to discover terror had ripped through his hometown. He watched the news briefly then decided to drop by Salman Properties' main office where he spoke to Dr. Abdul and his Jordanian wife, Nadia. It was some time after 10:00 A.M. when he returned to NW 37th Street. For the first time that morning, he witnessed Hussain Al-Hussaini's presence at the job site. He was painting the garage door side-by-side with coworkers Mohammed Amir and Jose Gonzales.

I could safely conclude Al-Hussaini had not shown up before 8:55 A.M., but what was his precise time of arrival? I immediately eliminated his Iraqi comrade Mohammed Amir as a trustworthy source. Mexican immigrant Jose Gonzales was my only alternative. I knocked on his door unannounced. He had just returned from a purported visit with family in Mexico. His "vacation" began immediately after the bombing.

"I was working with Hussain all day long, from 8:00 A.M. to 1:00 P.M. He did not leave my side the whole time," the petite-framed man stammered in broken English. My husband Drew, who had a working knowledge of Spanish, accompanied me to serve as an interpreter given the potential language barrier. Jose Gonzales exhibited overt anxiousness. I sensed deception.

"Where did you park your car when you arrived at the house on NW 37th Street?" I asked.

"Actually, now I remember the company plumber gave me a ride to work that day. He dropped me off sometime after 10:30 A.M.," he stated while nervously shifting his feet. In a matter of minutes, Jose had radically altered his time of arrival. If he was telling the truth, he had eliminated himself as Al-Hussaini's alibi witness.

I consulted with my news director. We both agreed any miscalculations of Al-Hussaini's location for fleeting lapses in time would swing the pendulum toward guilt or innocence. There was no room for error. Jose's inconsistent statements warranted further scrutiny. The presence of a reporter might have intimidated the witness. So I enlisted Bernie to question him in a friendly, relaxed fashion while wearing a concealed tape recorder.

The conversation grew heated in short order.

"You said you were on the job site at 2220 N.W. 37th Street that morning," Bernie casually remarked.

"Yeah," Jose acknowledged as the two men sat down on the curb during an afternoon work break.

"I arrived at 8:30 A.M. I had to go home to get a caulking gun. I left around 8:55 A.M., but ya'll were not there yet," Bernie firmly asserted.

Jose hesitated. "Who me?"

"Yeah you, Hussain Al-Hussaini, and Mohammed Amir. All ya'll were assigned to my job site that morning. But I left just a few minutes before the bomb went off."

"You go?" Jose queried.

"Yeah. I went to my house to get some tools. When I came back it was after 10:00 A.M. and that's when you three were painting the garage. Where were ya'll before that?"

"How many times you go?" Jose stalled again.

Bernie became agitated. "I only left once."

"What time was that?" Jose asked.

"It was about 8:55 A.M. when I left the job site and ya'll weren't there."

"Yeah," Jose conceded.

Bernie's patience snapped. He would no longer tolerate his colleague's evasiveness. "Ya'll weren't there all morning. Where the hell were you?"

Jose hung his head and stared at the pavement. No answer.

"Where were ya'll that morning. You tell me!"

Jose's eyes widened. "Maybe I was in the office, but I don't remember, I don't remember. I don't remember very good."

"What do you mean you don't remember very good? You don't drink," Bernie stoutly interjected.

"I don't drink."

"Then you should remember. A bomb went off that day. Where were you when the explosion happened?"

"Chad, the plumber, he dropped me off at the house on NW 37$^{th}$ Street. But I don't know what time," the prevaricative migrant hedged. He eventually estimated he showed up at the job site around 9:30 A.M. In the course of two conversations, Jose Gonzales's testimony had evolved from an immovable alibi witness to a reluctant admission that he did not recall his own location, let alone Al-Hussaini's, when the bomb detonated.

## FACE-TO-FACE WITH THE FBI

"Time to strategize where we go next." Melissa instructed as she spun her leather bound chair toward me. "Give me the rundown."

"You've seen the surveillance videotapes and witness interviews. Hussain Al-Hussaini bears a remarkable resemblance to John Doe 2's profile and several coworkers cast his alibi in a dubious light," I explained. "But at this point, we are still missing a tangible connection to the bombing suspects or the crime scene."

The forty-one-year-old supervisor wielded the authority to spike the story on the spot or stay the course. Her intuitiveness often served as the rudder which propelled KFOR-TV's news team into uncharted waters. This was yet another textbook case, albeit extraordinary. I marveled at Melissa's God-given brilliance as a journalist which was often subjugated by a paradoxical personality. Her German and Native American ethnicity produced a fearless adventurer with an iron will that clashed with a compassionate predilection for the underdog. Little did we know that her next decision would merge our collective destiny in becoming the pariah of the media, the underdog against all odds.

"Take the surveillance photographs of Dr. Abdul's Iraqi staff and canvass downtown businesses and restaurants. There's got to be a witness near the target who has seen McVeigh or Nichols with these Middle Easterners if they are truly involved," she said.

A sinking heaviness overcame me. "I realize we are far from putting the story on the air, but don't we have an obligation to tell the feds what we know?" I postulated.

"I agree. It's unconventional for journalists to open their notebooks to law enforcement, but there are one hundred sixty-eight people who have lost their lives. Maybe we have a piece of the puzzle, or maybe it's all just a mind-boggling series of coincidences."

I rifled through my files and located the name of James Strickland, the FBI agent who had spearheaded the insurance fraud case that landed Dr. Abdul behind bars. Within an hour of my call, Agent Strickland arrived at KFOR-TV accompanied by Agent James Judd, a polygraph expert. It was the afternoon of May 4, 1995. The pair thoroughly debriefed me while the station's private investigator silently observed the discussion. The agents peppered me with questions about my recorded interview with Jordanian detainee Abraham Ahmad. I emphasized my astonishment over Ahmad's self-professed ignorance that a bombing had occurred the morning he left town, and more importantly, his unexplained resignation from his computer job shortly before taking two costly excursions to the Middle East.

"How did he intend to support his Mexican wife and two children?" I contemplated aloud.

FBI Agent Judd's stoic veneer melted into frustration. "Do you really believe those kids are Mexican? Don't you think they look Jordanian?" I was stunned by the unexpected expression of sarcasm.

"Well, I suppose his polygraph exam would answer that question," I quipped.

Agent Judd stiffened with restrained annoyance. "Some people cannot distinguish the truth from a lie. It's a cultural thing." I surmised he was the federal agent who administered Ahmad's polygraph examination.

Capitalizing on the agent's unconventional candor, I broached the death of Dr. Abdul's ex-wife and her mystifying absence from the medical examiner's list of victims. I recounted my conversation with his daughter Helen who sincerely believed her father's excuse that a logjam of calls prevented him from contacting authorities.

"I phoned Karen Abdul's mother who said her ex-son-in-law volunteered to officially notify the coroner's office," I informed the agents.

"That's curious," Agent Judd remarked, once again shedding the stereotypical tight-lipped decorum of a federal investigator. As the interview progressed, Agent Strickland requested to examine the surveillance videotape of Dr. Abdul and his Iraqi employees. During the viewing, the agents remained transfixed, studying the clan of unkempt laborers as they mundanely hauled trash. When Hussain Al-Hussaini appeared on the screen, the mood shifted from tepid to intense.

Agent Judd abruptly asked, "Can you rewind the tape?" I darted across the room and punched the pause button on the videocassette player, displaying a frozen tight shot of the Iraqi soldier. The agent walked to the television monitor and gazed at the still photograph. No one spoke. The two FBI agents then exchanged an affirmative glance.

Noting their keen interest in the possible suspect, I remarked that Hussain Al-Hussaini fell within the parameters of the FBI's physical profile of John Doe 2.

"We have performed a cursory inquiry into this man's whereabouts for the morning of April 19, and two of his coworkers have shared stories that make his exact location at 9:02 A.M. unaccounted for," I emphasized.

Agent Strickland looked up from his copious note taking, "Please list the witnesses you have interviewed and where they can be contacted." I named Larry, Darby, and Bernie.

"I suggest you speak to Dr. Abdul's secretary, Darby Williams, as soon as possible. She has expressed a desire to move out of town because she fears her employer," I explained.

Before departing, Agent Strickland asked KFOR-TV to provide a courtesy copy of the surveillance videotape of the Middle Eastern subjects. The request impressed me as customary, but what came next stretched beyond routine follow-up. The agent suggested Channel 4's private investigator, who was present at the meeting, take more photographs of the Iraqi immigrants and provide the film to him personally, outside the Oklahoma City headquarters.

After the meeting, I flopped limply into a chair, drained by the three-hour grilling.

"There she is," Melissa said as she pointed to me and ushered Drew into the conference room, "Jayna, what's your take on the FBI's interest level?"

I reached for the television remote and pushed the play button. Hussain Al-Hussaini's presence dominated the center of the expansive TV screen.

"This man, in particular, undoubtedly captivated their attention," I charged, "but an extraordinary request topped the most memorable moments. The FBI, with all its hundreds of agents hunting John Doe 2, wants us to supply additional photos of these Iraqi men. If you ask me, the two agents looked at Hussain Al-Hussaini as if they recognized his face."

Melissa seemed to relish the moment but maintained objectivity. "It all sounds intriguing, but we're still lacking a direct link to the bombing plot."

Drew was drawn to the videotape of Al-Hussaini replaying on the television screen. "That guy looks like a soldier jogging in military formation similar to what I have seen in third world countries. No doubt, he's a soldier. Look at him, he's obviously in good physical shape," he said.

As the video rolled, the camera lens zoomed in more closely, exposing Al-Hussaini's somber raven eyes darting to-and-fro. Drew scrutinized the suspect's skittish behavior, "Notice how he's surveying his surroundings. He is extremely tense and observant, somewhat like he fears he is being watched."

## SUBTLE SIGNS OF SHUTDOWN

Forty-eight hours later, I glanced through the Saturday morning newspaper. Seventeen days after her brutal death, Dr. Abdul's former spouse was officially listed among the Murrah Building casualties for the first time. The medical examiner's report chronicled the macabre story of the forgotten victim. Karen Abdul's remains were delivered to the morgue on April 24, but the cadaver was not identified until the afternoon of May 4, the day I spoke to the FBI.

FBI agents expressed keen interest in Karen's fate while interviewing Bernie Stanton and Darby Williams. The questioning was strenuous, but encouraging nonetheless. Afterwards, I debriefed the witnesses.

"I gave them a list of the Iraqis' names and Social Security numbers. I photocopied the employment records the other day when I was alone in the office," Darby said.

"May I have a copy of that file?" I enthusiastically implored.

"Sorry, it's too late now. I didn't have time to make duplicates," her voice quivered. "I called in sick and Dr. Abdul fired me on the spot. I think he knows the FBI interviewed me yesterday. I'm scared to death."

The list of Dr. Abdul's Middle Eastern employees would inexplicably vanish from the record. Federal prosecutors told McVeigh's attorneys that Darby never turned over the file, but those documents mysteriously materialized, buried in a deluge of discovery documents delivered to the defense team in November 1996. Racked by disbelief, I read the 302s (official form for FBI witness statements) transcribed by the agents who interviewed Darby Williams and me. The information contained in the reports was accurate, but a multitude of glaring omissions gutted our testimonies.

The excising of critical facts effectively neutralized incriminating evidence that was disclosed in our original statements. I had entered the murky world of government-sanctioned suppression and whitewash. In the early days of my investigation, the witnesses and I shared a naïve faith in the FBI to judge the sequence of suspicious activities in the proper context, then implement the Bureau's vast arsenal of surveillance tools to unearth conclusive proof. Such hope proved an ephemeral dream.

On May 8, 1995, just four days after we shared all of our findings with the FBI, the news staff crowded around the satellite monitors, hanging on every word spoken at the latest press conference. FBI spokesman Weldon Kennedy announced to a national audience that the Bureau had pulled the plug on the John Doe 2 tip line. Investigators theorized the dark-haired suspect might have perished in the blast or never existed. I bit my lower lip, choking back a surge of emotion.

"How could this be happening?" I wondered. I had attended the April 27th evidentiary hearing in which McVeigh was bound over for trial. FBI Agent Jon Hersley testified he had interviewed several Oklahoma City witnesses who saw the fair-haired soldier in the company of an unidentified man. How could he simply be erased?

Then it hit me. Did the FBI seemingly abandon the worldwide manhunt based on unproven speculation that McVeigh's accomplice died in the blast? Did investigators believe the shadowy terrorist was unintentionally created in the fanciful imaginations of overeager witnesses? Or, did the nation's preeminent law enforcement agency now know the true identity of John Doe 2? The timeline could not be ignored. Within days of the FBI's viewing the KFOR-TV surveillance videotape of Dr. Abdul's Middle Eastern employees, federal investigators terminated public tips in tracking down a suspect who was still at large.

"The FBI knows John Doe 2 is still alive. I believe they called off the manhunt because they know who this guy is," Drew speculated as I wrestled with the tumultuous news of the day.

Years later, his instincts were validated, in part, when I obtained a confidential memorandum which the FBI's Oklahoma Command Post issued to field offices nationwide, ordering federal agents to "hold Unsub #2 leads in abeyance." The bulletin was disseminated in May 1995 during the same time frame in which the FBI took custody of Channel 4's surveillance footage of the Iraqi soldiers.

Melissa was unfazed by the Bureau's seemingly lackluster interest in the spectral presence of a third terrorist. She had resolved to reject the conventional pack journalism. From that point onward, our investigation into foreign participation moved at a breathless pace. Seasoned investigative reporter Brad Edwards and I scoured downtown businesses and bars, hoping elementary detective work would lead us to witnesses who might have seen Timothy McVeigh, the Ryder truck, or the brown Chevy pickup which carried dark-complexioned foreigners from the bombsite. Were the Middle Eastern men who worked for Salman Properties riding inside that truck? Were they near the Murrah Building when a terrorist bomb obliterated it? Were they savage murderers or innocent captives to circumstance?

During the days and weeks that followed, we invested hundreds of hours interviewing dozens of Oklahomans who claimed to have seen the menacing figure depicted in the artist's rendering of John Doe 2, only to dismiss their testimonies as unreliable. Many of their stories were fraught with inconsistencies, often conflicting with the government's case. Hopes of finding legitimate witnesses quickly dimmed because the FBI convinced the few authentic ones to dodge the press in the best interests of justice. The dead ends seemed infinite.

What was I to do now? Coincidence and suspicion hardly proved guilt beyond a reasonable doubt. After all, what were the odds that I, one inconsequential TV news reporter without high level intelligence sources, had somehow stumbled upon the actual terrorist targeted in the greatest international manhunt in U.S. history? I gave myself a harsh reality check. If these Iraqi men were involved, their arrogance or sheer stupidity defied common sense. They were living and working just thirty blocks north of the bombed out Murrah Building, within arms reach of the FBI. Unfathomable.

Federal authorities had already interrogated and released the group's friend and business associate, Abraham Ahmad. I reasoned if Ahmad were culpable, he would never have been let go. Finally, my desire to further develop the story began to diminish in light of dramatic developments on the national front. The FBI had publicly concluded the Oklahoma City bombing was the work of domestic, not foreign terrorists. The two principal players were in custody and they were Americans. Foremost in my thoughts, I still had not a shred of evidence tying the Iraqi men to either McVeigh or Nichols.

# CHAPTER 7

# BREAKTHROUGH

The Bureau's announcement that John Doe 2 was no longer in the crosshairs of the FBI had effectively planted seeds of doubt, infecting the media like an incurable contagion. The gnawing uncertainty about the existence of a third bomber became a popular theme among press accounts of the burgeoning bombing case. Skepticism engulfed me. I had invested weeks in a fruitless search for a nexus between the Iraqi refugees and the two incarcerated suspects.

"Call Hussain Al-Hussaini and ask where he was the morning of April 19," Melissa suggested.

"But we don't have any evidence linking him to the crime," I objected with incredulity. "Don't you think it's premature to ask him directly about his alibi at this juncture?"

Melissa shrugged, then softly blew a dangling strand of auburn hair from her face. "That's exactly the reason why we should sit down and talk to this guy. We might be overlooking something that eliminates him from any suspicion."

Though reticent about tipping off the target of our investigation, I dutifully dialed Salman Properties. A young woman whom I assumed was Helen Abdul answered the phone. Suddenly, my heart pounded.

"This is Jayna Davis with KFOR-TV. I would like to speak to one of your employees named Hussain Al-Hussaini."

"He's not available," a girlish voice replied. "May I take a message?"

"We would like to question Mr. Al-Hussaini regarding his whereabouts for the morning of the bombing. It is very important I speak to him at the earliest convenience," I insisted.

I hung up the phone realizing one call had effaced our cloak of secrecy. The Iraqi nationals were now aware KFOR-TV was watching, but Al-Hussaini was not eager to face the station's cameras and clear up any misconceptions. He ultimately ignored my request for an interview.

Meanwhile, I produced a broadcast report featuring the felony record, Las Vegas excursions, and deceased ex-wife of the Palestinian real estate magnate, his recent hiring of Iraqi soldiers, and their putative link to the brown Chevy truck seen peeling away from the curb of the doomed federal complex. The story script underwent stringent legal review before editing. The final cut was then shelved, only to be aired in the event federal authorities swarmed Salman Properties. I soon learned the FBI Command Post was not inclined to tip off our news team if such an interrogation had taken place or would ever in the future.

It was now early June, and a month had passed since I handed over Channel 4's dossier to the FBI. I phoned Agent Strickland, hoping to gauge the Bureau's interest level.

"Have you spoken to Jose Gonzales about Hussain Al-Hussaini's alibi for April 19?" I bluntly asked.

A discernible pause followed. "We are tracking all leads."

Before long, the conversation disintegrated into a blind fishing expedition. I posed incisive questions; Agent Strickland offered amorphous, deadpan answers. Then I fired off a statement that registered a pulse.

"My news director, Melissa Klinzing, has advised me to conduct an on camera interview with Al-Hussaini concerning his whereabouts the day of the bombing."

"I would strongly advise against it," he warned.

"Have you detained and questioned Al-Hussaini?"

"No," he answered.

My inflection intensified. "Why not?"

"Because, Ms. Davis, if we were to question Hussain Al-Hussaini at this point, we would be at his mercy," the FBI agent begrudgingly conceded.

A galaxy of possibilities opened in my mind.

"Was Al-Hussaini still under scrutiny, or has the FBI eliminated him as a suspect? If so, what did the feds know that we didn't?" I ruminated.

The only means of soliciting straight answers was to slip through the back door of the FBI Bomb Task Force. The elite group of top federal investigators included a small, tight-knit fraternity of law officers from local and state agencies. A gutsy police detective with inside access offered to help; however, his intrepidity quickly imperiled his career.

"They told me to back off. No more questions about the Channel 4 investigation or I would regret it," the officer nervously disclosed in an urgently arranged meeting.

I was aghast. "You mean your job has been threatened because you simply asked about the status of the FBI's investigation into Dr. Abdul's posse of Iraqi workers?"

The case-hardened detective lowered his eyes, a visual nuance of humiliation and fear. Sensing his vulnerability, I released him from his misguided chivalry.

"This is not your battle anymore. You have a family to support. I would never forgive myself if you were fired. I will always be grateful for what you have done. Walk away."

He nodded affirmatively as he handed me a police report.

"What's this?" I asked.

"It seems the Iraqi with the questionable alibi has a drinking problem."

## ARRESTED AND RELEASED

The thirty–year-old driver slumped over the steering wheel as he slipped into unconsciousness. With an open beer within reach, gear shaft still in drive, motor humming, and headlights illuminating the blackness of night, it was not long before a squad car pulled up. Alcohol fumes drenched the hot summer air as the Oklahoma City police officer opened the driver's side door of the 1986 Cadillac Deville. It took several firm shoves to roust the inebriated motorist from his drunken stupor. Daybreak neared as the Middle Eastern male stumbled from his vehicle, unsteady on his feet. After being frisked for weapons, Hussain Al-Hussaini was placed under arrest outside a seedy bar within walking distance of the bomb site. He was booked into the city jail before dawn on June 3, only a few days after my call to Salman Properties requesting an interview. That call would never be answered.

## COVERT INTERVIEW

Efforts to speak directly to Hussain Al-Hussaini and his Middle Eastern associates were ignored. Educing the underlying truth called for an improvisational approach. The plan was set in motion the afternoon of June 6. Wired with a hidden camera and microphone, Bernie Stanton arrived at the real estate company headquarters. Oppressive heat from the cruel midday sun swept into the office as he entered the foyer unannounced.

"Why have you served me with this eviction notice?" Bernie complained as Dr. Abdul greeted him with subdued hospitality. For the next hour, the Palestinian capitalist puffed on a cigar, artfully side-stepping an inquisition of sorts. The verbal sparring opened with a debate over the contract Bernie made to purchase his house in monthly installments. Dr. Abdul justified his resorting to eviction proceedings in light of Bernie's recent resignation from Salman Properties.

"You changed your attitude after you hired those guys from Iraq," Bernie countered. "Ever since then I felt like I have been discriminated against. You know the Iraqi workers are not equipped to do the job."

"They are laborers. There's no comparison. What you do, they cannot do. They can paint, clean, and haul trash," Dr. Abdul smoothly cajoled the discontented employee.

The discussion abruptly shifted to the bombing. Bernie was particularly perturbed by the careless remarks made by Dr. Abdul's brother, Ahmed Abdul, who occasionally performed work at Salman Properties. "Your brother said to somebody yesterday, 'It doesn't matter how many children got killed in the bombing, they are just like puppies.'" Bernie paused then erupted with indignation, "They were human beings, not puppies."

Dr. Abdul was unfazed by the salacious allegation. "Of course, he's crazy. You know Ahmed, he's a bum."

A slow drip of hostility brewed between the two men. "I have some things I would like to get off my chest. You know that brown Chevy truck they [the FBI] were looking for with the Middle Eastern people?"

"Yes, sure," Dr. Abdul answered.

"Abraham Ahmad was spotted driving that truck at your office before the bombing. And he was also seen in a car like McVeigh's."

"Yeah," the middle-aged businessman agreed as he compulsively wiped perspiration from his brow. The whirl of spinning fans sliced the palpable silence that followed.

"Hum," Bernie sighed as he waited for the tense moment to pass.

"It puzzles you. I know," Dr. Abdul remarked with staid detachment. Bernie had brazenly inferred that both he and Abraham Ahmad could be terrorists, yet the composed Dr. Abdul was neither perturbed nor offended. Moreover, he declined to rebut reported sightings of Ahmad riding in several suspicious vehicles, claiming he had "no idea" the type of cars his friend drove to Salman Properties.

"I don't think Abraham knows McVeigh. Or, if the FBI suspected that he had a relationship with McVeigh or if I know anything about," he stammered, then completed his sentence. "I would be locked up."

"I understand that," Bernie said. "But there's another thing I don't understand. Your ex-wife is missing in the bombing."

"Yes, I know."

"Helen is her only child and she was in need of comforting. Why did you get up and leave for Las Vegas on April 20?" he asked angrily.

"Everybody was asking me not to go. And I was thirty-three percent to go and sixty-six percent not to go. Then next day come. Ten o'clock come and I went to Helen and I tell her not to come to work," Dr. Abdul argued in his own defense. However, his contention contradicted Darby Williams's claim that he arrived at the office early on April 20 and became incensed to find his daughter had not yet reported to work.

"She [Karen Abdul] means a lot to me even though we were divorced. She was my neighbor," he continued. "I was in tears. I wanted to leave that pressure. If I keep it inside then I will explode. That's why I went [to Las Vegas]."

Bernie continued his pointed questions, unmoved by what he perceived to be an emotional ploy. "And another thing that has been on my mind. I do not understand why it took three weeks to report your ex-wife's name to the authorities as being dead or missing."

"Well, as my daughter Helen said, many people in the department where she [Karen Abdul] worked don't want to publicize that. They don't want to mention the names."

The explanation struck Bernie as absurd. "I watched a special on TV two days after the bombing that said officials depended on family members to come forth and report missing people."

Dr. Abdul became flustered. He prattled through a handful of conflicting excuses in which he ultimately blamed his daughter for the blunder.

"I think Helen," he paused, "I don't know if she went to report it." Once again, his account sharply differed with the story related by Helen and her grandmother. Both women told me Dr. Abdul had volunteered to notify the coroner.

"I know that Karen was off work on Wednesdays, and she helped you with taxes on Monday, April 17. So instead of taking off Wednesday, she had to go to work and the building blew up," Bernie snapped with an accusing tone.

"I do not know that she was supposed to go [to work] on Wednesday but she did take off on Monday. She did take off to help me with the taxes," he agreed then began discussing his recent trip to Washington, D.C., to attend the national memorial service for his former spouse and the slain federal employees. Astonishingly, he recounted conversations he purportedly had with two unidentified cabinet level officials who debunked the Middle Eastern connection, personally reassuring him the pursuit for foreign suspects had been abandoned. Remarkably, this incident took place in early May 1995 before the international manhunt for John Doe 2 had crested.

The doctor of psychology took a long draw off his cigar, then coolly opined that the American suspect was incapable of carrying off such a sophisticated attack alone. "Tim McVeigh, I know that he's been locked up. But I would like to know who is the mastermind."

"Right, the money man," Bernie interrupted.

"Yeah, the money man and the engineers and the planners," he hesitated then added, "And the one who targeted that building."

"But in the history of the United States there has never been a militia group who has blown up a building like that," Bernie observed.

"That's true," Dr. Abdul concurred while revealing an unusual knowledge of the militia mindset. "I read a lot of articles about their movement. They think the government of the United States is getting weak. They also think the government is going to be under the control of the army or that the military is going to be under the United Nations command. They don't pay taxes. They resent it."

After sixty minutes of cautiously parsing his words and weighing each response, Dr. Abdul dropped a bombshell. He accused Bernie and Darby of talking to KFOR-TV about the possibility Hussain Al-Hussaini was John Doe 2, a charge Dr. Abdul dispassionately denied. Bernie felt uncomfortable broaching the topic of his cooperation with Channel 4, so he ignored Dr. Abdul's accusation and departed quickly.


## DEAD-BANG CONNECTION

The phone jarred me from a restless sleep. I fumbled in the darkness for the receiver, taking note of the ridiculous hour displayed on the clock. It was 3:00 A.M. on June 7.

"Hello," I whispered in a groggy state of semiconsciousness.

A familiar voice brimming with excitement exclaimed, "We made the connection!" Channel 4's private investigator and reporter Brad Edwards found two eyewitnesses, a bartender and her fiancé, who had independently identified the Iraqi soldier from a photo lineup. Both were confident Hussain Al-Hussaini was the foreign-looking man they observed drinking with Timothy McVeigh in an Oklahoma City nightclub just four days before the bombing. The watershed breakthrough had arrived.

The next morning, I was sitting in the northwest Oklahoma City tavern where the purported sighting took place. The witnesses, Elizabeth Brown and her future husband, Johnny Wilborn, detailed their lengthy, three-hour encounter with a boisterous McVeigh and his soft-spoken, demure comrade.

## Flashback to April 15, 1995

It was early Saturday evening when the scantily-clad dancers strutted onto the stage to entertain the clientele milling about the pool tables. Repulsion washed over Elizabeth. The forty-year-old bartender considered herself an old-fashioned girl, reared by an elderly aunt and uncle who frowned on alcohol and carousing. "My folks would be crushed if they saw me serving drinks in a strip club," she thought, rationalizing that the distasteful duty was only for a short stint. Her fiancé Johnny coaxed her into accepting the temporary assignment as a favor for his pool tournament friend who happened to manage this hole-in-the-wall nightclub. Elizabeth had never tended bar, but the job only required pouring beer from the tap and popping lids off wine coolers.

Soon the cramped, smoke-filled room was teeming with revelers. A wiry, slender-framed customer with a striking military crew cut caught her attention. Before the night shift began, the tavern manager admonished Elizabeth to monitor the dancers. On rare occasions, the girls would lure male clients into the parking lot to engage in prostitution and drugs, illicit activities that could land Elizabeth in jail as the supervisor on the premises. The possibility traumatized the small town girl who had never even received a traffic ticket.

"He looks like a cop with that buzz hair cut," she imagined, apprehensive that the rambunctious patron who was overtly gawking at the dancers could be working undercover.

"Two beers please," the tall stranger said, pointing to his dark-haired companion sitting quietly in the shadows at the end of the bar. As the hours passed, the man ordered a few more beers, each time paying for his taciturn partner's drink, but oddly enough, the two men never conversed. Instead, the olive-complexioned figure with the black, deep-set eyes eerily studied Elizabeth's every move.

"Are you married?" the aloof customer asked with a distinct Middle Eastern accent.

The unexpected overture startled Elizabeth. "Pardon me?" she asked.

"Are you married?" he repeated.

She glanced at her ruggedly handsome fiancé seated nearby then politely replied, "Yes, I am."

The attractive bride-to-be dismissed the flirtatious come-on as harmless flattery. But Elizabeth and Johnny's protracted exposure to the bashful foreigner and his rowdy friend would reshape their future marriage in ways they never would have anticipated. Less than a week later, the first televised footage of the stone-faced Timothy McVeigh debuted from coast to coast.

"That's him, the man in the bar!" Elizabeth shrieked. Johnny shook his head in astonishment. "Unbelievable, it's the same guy you thought could be an undercover cop." Shortly thereafter, three federal investigators entered the nightclub during a routine stop in a citywide canvass of restaurants and taverns. An African American agent with an imposing stature asked Elizabeth's name, address, and phone number and then laid out an array of photographs. The shy witness carefully perused the pictures, several of which featured a boyish, scraggly-haired Timothy McVeigh.

"This man looks like the individual who came into the bar last Saturday, only the person in this photograph is considerably younger," she declared. The expressionless trio listened without posing any questions.

"I instantly recognized the prisoner named Timothy McVeigh when he was shown on TV the other day," Elizabeth added. "But you should know McVeigh bought quite a few beers for another man who looked foreign."

She surveyed the photo spread again and picked up the sketch of the scowling-faced John Doe 2. "He looked somewhat like this drawing. I served him beer over a period of several hours. My fiancé Johnny Wilborn saw him too. At one point, the man asked me if I was married. I remember he had a strange accent."

"What kind of accent?" the lead agent tersely interjected, his interest aroused.

"I grew up in a Hispanic community in Coachella Valley, California. I would definitely rule out a Spanish accent," Elizabeth conjectured. "His voice sounded a lot like the people from Iran or Iraq who were interviewed during Desert Storm. I guess you could say he spoke like they do in the Middle East."

The club manager privately discouraged the dancers on the premises that morning from speaking to the investigating agents. Elizabeth surmised the girls remained tight-lipped about what they might have witnessed because they had no desire to have their criminal records dredged up.

## SCRIPTING THE STORY

Nail-biting interludes of incredulity and exhilaration propelled the afternoon of June 7, 1995. Following my detailed debriefing of the bar witnesses, Melissa phoned the FBI. Our call was routed to Agent James Strickland, who expressed keen interest in our discovery, but somberly conceded he had no authority to act on the lead.

"The investigation was taken out of my hands weeks ago and handed up the chain of command to the Oklahoma Bomb Task Force," the agent confirmed to a roomful of witnesses listening to the conversation on speakerphone. KFOR-TV attorney Robert Nelon, Melissa, reporter Brad Edwards, and I were present to receive the disturbing news.

"I will contact the public information officer, Agent Dan Vogel. He will get back to you with an update."

To our surprise, the return call was patched into Melissa's office without delay.

"We've found two witnesses who independently pegged Al-Hussaini in a photo spread as the man who accompanied McVeigh to a local bar. We're going to run with the story tonight at 6:00 P.M.," Melissa announced.

"Do what you think is the right thing to do," FBI Agent Dan Vogel replied in a flat, unemotional tone.

Nervously digging for any hint that we were about to dive off a cliff, Melissa adopted a softer, more vulnerable approach. "If we're dead wrong about this Iraqi possibly being involved in the bombing, we would sure appreciate a heads up. Or, if our broadcasting the witnesses' testimonies will interfere with the federal investigation, we are prepared to put everything on hold," she entreated.

Once again, Agent Vogel offered the same seemingly scripted response, "Do what you think is the right thing to do." My heart pounded. The most decisive question had yet to be answered: "The FBI has been researching our findings for a month now. Has the Bureau officially ruled out Hussain Al-Hussaini as a suspect?"

A breathless hush permeated the room. All eyes were trained on the telephone. "No, he has not yet been ruled out," the agent hesitantly answered.

After an arduous session of animated debate, the consensus was in. The FBI declined to say we were wrong. We decided we had a moral obligation to report the story. Hundreds of Oklahomans were wounded and lost loved ones in the bloodbath of the monstrous attack. They had a right to know what we knew. KFOR-TV's legal team, spearheaded by Nelon—a nationally renowned broadcast law attorney—painstakingly worked with me to craft the blockbuster story slated to lead the evening news.

Two hours before airtime, a station photographer burst into the newsroom, excitedly waving a videotape. For weeks, Channel 4 had conducted intermittent surveillance of the Iraqi soldier. Finally, in the eleventh hour, we scored the first glimpse of Al-Hussaini's tattoo. I slipped the tape into the edit deck. There it was, located on his upper left arm where the FBI John Doe 2 arrest warrant said it should be. The powerful zoom lens captured the outline of a snake coiled around an anchor. Bernie Stanton's recollection had been confirmed without a moment to spare. The deadline drew near. It was time to cut my audio track and head to the editing booth.

To safeguard the witnesses, management decided to conceal their identities and the location of the establishment where the sighting occurred. We digitally disguised Hussain Al-Hussaini's face because he had not been arrested or charged. At the six o'clock hour, the unnerving story of an alleged terrorist living in our midst reverberated statewide. During a few fleeting moments of television history, my life changed forever.

## Unimpeachable Testimony

The exhaustive FBI investigation failed to produce solid evidence that conflicted with the testimonies of Elizabeth and Johnny. The timeline of McVeigh's movements established that he visited the Junction City, Kansas, body shop shortly before 9:00 A.M. on April 15, prepaying in cash for the rental of the Ryder truck. The five-hour drive to Oklahoma City would place him in town by mid-afternoon, leaving open the opportunity for him and Al-Hussaini to patronize the strip club that evening.

In the spring of 1996, on the eve of the one year bombing anniversary, news leaked that the prosecution planned to call a witness who delivered Chinese food to Timothy McVeigh's Junction City motel room the evening of April 15, 1995. I panicked. If true, such testimony would disprove the story recounted by Elizabeth and Johnny. Thankfully, a reliable source with access to the FBI statements of the restaurant deliveryman assuaged my anxiety. Witness Jeff Davis tainted the government's case, not mine.

I wanted to check out the facts firsthand. In short order, I found myself dashing across a Kansas golf course in a skirt and high heels. An extremely agitated photographer trailed close behind, lugging his heavy equipment.

"Mr. Davis," I shouted, while flagging down a young gentleman preparing to drive the ball down the fairway.

"Who are you?" the shocked golfer grumbled impatiently.

"I'm terribly sorry to interrupt your game, but it is critical I speak with you."

"You're with the press," he stated as my winded colleague lumbered toward us.

Drenched with sweat from the impromptu sprint, I gasped for breath. "My name is Jayna Davis. I'm a reporter with the NBC affiliate in Oklahoma City. I understand you delivered Chinese food to Timothy McVeigh the evening of April 15."

The friendly-faced man with fiery red hair broke into a boyish grin. "Wrong, the man I delivered the order to was not Timothy McVeigh, and he was not the John Doe 2 featured in the composite sketches."

"Would you be willing to state that on camera?" I asked.

"I'd like to help you, but I promised exclusivity to *ABC News*," he replied. The twenty-two-year-old Kansan explained that the network hired freelance sketch artist Jean Boylan to draw the face of the Dreamland guest he had encountered. Boylan's fame soared in the bombing aftermath when she drafted the internationally-circulated profile composite of John Doe 2.

A promise to hold the taped interview until ABC's *World News Tonight* broke the story persuaded Jeff Davis to change his mind. I had just scored the second most exclusive interview.

"When you saw Timothy McVeigh on television, did you recognize him as the man you handed the food order to?" I inquired.

"No, it wasn't him," Jeff insisted, while pointing out the mystery customer he met had collar-length hair, not a military buzz.

The FBI spoke to the restaurant worker on a half dozen occasions. Each time, the pressure to massage his recollection became more apparent. At one point, federal investigators offered Jeff the option to testify that the man who paid eleven dollars for the moo goo gai pan "might have been McVeigh."

"I repeatedly told the FBI there was no such thing as yes or maybe. The answer was no. It was not McVeigh," he emphatically affirmed. But to his amazement, Jeff was summoned to appear before the federal grand jury that indicted the bombers. The witness authenticated the sales receipt for the food order as well as the date and time he delivered it to the motel. But the prosecutors' line of questioning baffled him.

"I was never asked to describe the person I saw."

"Did the FBI pressure you to change your testimony?" I queried.

"It may have bordered on coercion," he asserted, explaining the FBI suggested McVeigh's appearance had "weathered a bit" while in jail.

"I'm sure incarceration has an effect on the human body, but it does not realign facial structure," he waxed indignant. "It does not morph bones into something they were not previously."

Jeff's certitude earned him a subpoena to testify for the defense during the trials of McVeigh and Nichols. While in the crucible of cross-examination, Jeff unflinchingly held fast to his original statement, emphatically denying accusations that he told a Denver hotel bartender and the ABC sketch artist he saw two men in the room, one of which was allegedly McVeigh.

The unshakable witness had ruptured the government's skillfully crafted stratagem to eradicate the lingering notion of additional conspirators. Hence, McVeigh's purported fraternization with the Iraqi national Hussain Al-Hussaini on the evening of April 15 stood. In March 1996, I discovered the defense teams never received documentation of Elizabeth Brown's steadfast identification of Timothy McVeigh with a Middle Eastern companion. More disquieting was the Bureau's decision not to speak to the corroborative witness, Johnny Wilborn. During the federal trials, the attorneys for the bombing defendants roundly criticized federal prosecutors for withholding John Doe 2 witness statements. On June 9, 1995, I interviewed yet another Oklahoman who would meet the same fate, condemned to the graveyard of "nonexistent" witnesses.

# CHAPTER 8

# POSITIVE I.D.

The June 7 broadcast profiling an alleged Iraqi terrorist operating in plain sight triggered a barrage of calls and tips, the majority of which I discounted as conspiratorial nonsense. But one message in a sea of voice mail warranted further attention. The timorous computer programmer trembled as she dialed KFOR-TV, bewildered at the FBI's sudden disinterest in the brown Chevrolet truck. Rachel Sealy had stepped into the path of that speeding pickup at 9:03 A.M., moments after the bomb detonated. The nightmarish image of the driver's icy stare as the truck careened perilously close haunted her thoughts. While viewing the KFOR story, digitized photographs of Hussain Al-Hussaini exposed his distinctive black hair. That two-inch crown of curly locks struck Rachel as menacingly familiar.

Within a few hours of our telephone introduction, the forty-year-old downtown employee sat at a conference table in the Channel 4 studio examining a photo spread of eight Middle Eastern subjects. Under the watchful eye of our camera, she consistently fingered Al-Hussaini as the driver of the elusive brown truck. As the interview progressed, Rachel's brush with death replayed in vivid detail as the clock rewound to the chance moment when the hapless pedestrian came face-to-face with the Middle Eastern motorist.

## Revisiting April 19, 9:03 a.m.

Winded from the brisk walk, Rachel scurried past morning commuters who were congested at a downtown traffic light. No doubt she would be a few minutes tardy to work. Taking a shortcut through the nearby Medallion hotel promised a warm respite from the frosty breeze. A rush of heat thawed the spring chill as she dashed through the revolving glass door. Without warning, an earsplitting explosion reverberated across the lobby, violently convulsing the building from its foundation.

Rachel exited the hotel into a world of blinding smoke, debris, and pandemonium. Blaring sirens and flashing lights whizzed by. Seconds later, the speeding police cruiser screeched to a halt. The officer jumped out of the driver's seat and set off on foot. Rachel watched in stunned disbelief as the patrolman disappeared into an opaque cloud of blackness. A woman brushed past, kicking off her high-heels as she sprinted toward the smoldering federal building. Glistening blankets of glass laced the roadways where rush hour traffic had ground to a standstill.

Rachel slipped through the snarl of stalled vehicles to cross the intersection of Main and Robinson Streets. Suddenly, the deafening roar of a truck engine seized her. Time seemed to shift into slow motion as she stepped off the median. Her head snapped to the right. A brown Chevrolet pickup barreled directly at her. Rachel leapt backwards as the driver glowered at her. His expression of unbridled rage would be indelibly etched in her mind. She clutched her throat and gasped, watching the only moving vehicle vanish from sight. The young woman had eluded death by a split-second reflex.

Later that morning, Rachel gazed upon the ruin and slaughter from her office window. Lines of grief-stricken relatives snaked along the streets surrounding the federal complex, impatiently awaiting news of loved ones, sobbing and embracing one another. The death knell of 9:02 A.M. permeated her innermost soul. Upon arriving home from work, she recoiled at the morbidity of listening to news coverage of the escalating body count. Instead, she escaped into a backyard garden sanctuary. Nurturing the budding blossoms shut out the horror of the day, if only for a moment.

## FBI STATEMENT WIPED

It was early evening when Rachel mustered the emotional strength to watch the news. A reporter standing in the foreground of the towering, wounded structure announced the FBI was feverishly tracking a brown pickup with two Middle Eastern looking suspects.

"Was it the same truck that almost killed me?" she wondered as she dialed 9-1-1. The dispatcher classified Rachel's call as top priority. Within an hour, two federal agents rang the doorbell.

The opening question indicated that in just eight hours, the FBI had already uncovered extraordinary details about the suspects. "Did you see a tattoo on the driver's arm?"

"No," the witness meekly replied while attempting to mask her nervousness. "I recall the driver and the passenger were dressed similarly in long-sleeved, dark blue shirts, so I would not have seen a tattoo."

"Can you describe the subjects in the cab?"

Rachel painted a verbal picture of the driver's scowling face, but admitted her memory of the second man in the cab was limited. "The encounter was so fleeting, I did not get a good look at the passenger. I only had a moment to stare into the driver's eyes, but I will never forget his expression of anger and hate. I have a strong impression that both men inside that truck were Middle Eastern given their olive skin and dark hair. "

The two investigators swapped an affirmative nod, subtly ratifying the story recounted by the shy witness.

"Was there a bug shield on the front of the truck?" one of the FBI agents inquired.

The terrifying image of the approaching truck revisited Rachel with an emotional rush. Her eyes filled with tears. "The pickup was racing toward me so quickly, all I could think about was to get out of the way or get hit. I was in shock. However, I am certain that the truck was painted medium brown with a new finish."

The customarily reserved investigators seemed discernibly enthused with Rachel's testimony, reassuring her that they would be in touch soon. The call never came. Meanwhile, rescuers labored tirelessly to extricate precious human remains from the ashes. But the passage of time proved unmerciful. The odious stench of decaying corpses hung heavily in the downtown air as Rachel repeated her daily trek to work. With every breath the elegant, auburn-haired woman relived the horror of April 19. No matter how fast she sprinted, she could not outrun the unshakable belief she had locked eyes with a cold-blooded terrorist.

On the afternoon of June 9, 1995, Rachel entered the KFOR-TV newsroom to examine a photographic lineup. She realized she had come full circle. The enigmatic stranger had eluded capture, but would never escape her memory. The 10:00 P.M. newscast led with the shocking new evidence that placed the possible Iraqi John Doe 2 at the scene of the crime. I promptly phoned the FBI to report Rachel Sealy's positive I.D. of Hussain Al-Hussaini behind the wheel of the now legendary brown Chevy pickup. Federal agents would eventually interview thousands of people who claimed to have seen a man resembling the John Doe 2 drawing, but investigators audaciously ignored the smoking gun testimony of a witness whom KFOR-TV's legal counsel described as an "attorney's dream." Frighteningly, Rachel's April 19 interview with the two federal agents would be permanently wiped from the investigative archive.

## BACKLASH

Shortly before dawn on June 11, little more than twenty-four hours after Rachel's silhouette interview lit up the airwaves, danger swathed the strip club where Elizabeth Brown was pouring drinks. The hum of a car motor crept in through an open doorway. Elizabeth peered through the rear entrance to investigate. A brown Cadillac with two shadowy figures was parked in plain view. An outdoor security light illuminated the passenger's face as he leaned forward and glared at her with savage malevolence. Panic coursed through Elizabeth's body like a jolt of electricity.

"It's him! The man I saw with McVeigh," Elizabeth shouted inside her head. Fear immobilized her for several frozen moments of sheer terror. She stood captive to his sinister stare, unable to look away from his black, molten eyes. A fellow bartender, Andre La Jeunesse, walked to the cash register.

"Oh my God, it's him. It's him. What does he want? Why is he here?" Elizabeth hysterically cried to Andre. "Shut the door. They might start shooting."

"Calm down and get out of sight," Andre ordered in a southern Cajun drawl. He glanced outside as the brown Cadillac peeled out of the parking lot.

Elizabeth paged me. The numbers 9-1-1 were urgently repeated in succession. I phoned her right away.

"He came back to the bar!" Elizabeth exclaimed.

"Who?" I asked.

"The Middle Eastern man I pegged in Channel 4's pictures."

"Are you sure?" I verified.

"Hell yes!" she shrieked. "How did he recognize the nightclub from the newscast?" Elizabeth crumbled into tears.

"We took extraordinary measures to protect you," I reassured her. "We disguised your face and even altered your voice. The general location of the bar was not even disclosed."

Elizabeth shuddered. "Then we have our answer. This man knew where to find me because he was here with McVeigh."

Traumatized and shaken, Elizabeth resigned on the spot. But she soon realized there was nowhere to hide. The next week, a foul odor greeted her as she entered her apartment. Burglars had rifled through her personal belongings and defecated on the living room floor, but nothing was stolen.

A few days prior to the break-in, Elizabeth's fiancé Johnny Wilborn noticed a foreign looking man skulking about the complex. On several occasions, the dark figure slithered behind the apartment security fence when Johnny emerged to go to work. Three days later, the prowlers struck a second time, leaving behind their signature human excrement yet again. Elizabeth figured the motive was intimidation. The unknown intruders had succeeded in delivering the message. The engaged couple wed in an impromptu ceremony, packed their bags, and moved out-of-state.


## DRIVE-BY SHOOTING

The blistering heat of July 3 enveloped the small Oklahoma City chapel where Elizabeth and Johnny stood before a minister, repeating their marriage vows. That evening, the honeymooners toasted a future free from the memory of Timothy McVeigh's swarthy companion and the tormenting harassment. But while the Wilborns celebrated a new life, the spirit of death invaded the slumber of Darby Williams. She awakened to gunfire rupturing the stillness of night. Bullets ricocheted throughout the house.

Darby instinctively dropped to the floor and crept to the window. Peering through the drapes, she saw nothing but blackness. But her next door neighbor said he watched as the gunman sprinted to a white Nissan pickup and screeched out of her driveway.

When the police arrived, Darby burst into hysteria. "I know who did this. It's my former boss Dr. Abdul."

The officer nodded and continued to take notes.

"I was fired the day after the FBI questioned me about Dr. Abdul's activities before the bombing. He was furious when he found out that I talked to investigators. After that, he refused my rent check. He owns this house, and as my landlord he is trying to evict me," she sobbed.

The officer interviewed a neighbor who claimed gunshots rousted him from bed.

"When I got to the window I saw a dark-skinned male running from the house. He drove away in a white Nissan pickup," the witness recounted.

"Did the man look like Dr. Anwar Abdul?"

"I think it was him, but I'm not sure. It looked like him but I'm not positive," the neighbor equivocated. "But the gunman was driving a white Nissan truck like the pickup I have seen the landlord driving."

The witness later told me he observed two men of Middle Eastern origin break Darby's window with a brick the day before the drive-by shooting. The would-be burglars did not gain entry because the windows were nailed shut. One of the suspects was wearing a ball cap and chewing on a cigar. They reportedly fled the scene in a white Nissan pickup. Darby reported the incident to the police.

On July 6, 1995, Dr. Abdul voluntarily submitted to questioning at the Oklahoma City police headquarters. When asked his whereabouts on the night of July 3, he claimed to be at home sleeping while his white Nissan pickup was parked in the driveway.

"Did you fire your secretary (Darby) shortly after the bombing of the Murrah Building," the detective inquired.

"Yes," Dr. Abdul replied.

"Was she fired because you found out that she talked to federal agents who were inquiring about you?"

"Oh, no sir. She did not talk to the FBI," Dr. Abdul stated resolutely.

"I didn't tell you that it was the FBI," the officer fired back.

FBI Agent James Strickland confirmed for the detective that Darby Williams had, in fact, been interviewed. He then requested a copy of the police report regarding the drive-by shooting. The case was eventually dropped due to "insufficient evidence."

Frantic the next shooting would be deadly, Darby moved out and went underground, registering her phone and utilities in a friend's name. But her efforts to disappear were in vain. Weeks later, she arrived home at her new residence to find the bloody and battered body of her beloved dog dangling from her backyard fence. Terrified by the incident, she had no choice but to relocate again. In August, she entered Oklahoma State District Court to testify that she suspected her former employer was behind the terrorization campaign. The judge granted Darby a permanent protective order against Dr. Anwar Abdul.

# CHAPTER 9

# NO ALIBI

The June 14 newsflash hit with the force of brass knuckles. The headline "FBI Identifies and Clears John Doe 2" monopolized the national wire services. Just two days prior, FBI spokesman Dan Vogel told me that the Bureau was "still trying to identify and locate" the unapprehended bomber, but he clammed up when asked to officially exonerate Hussain Al-Hussaini as a candidate. At that moment, I was clinging to a capsizing life raft amid a sea of confusion.

The government's star witness, a Kansas body shop mechanic who observed the prime suspect leasing the Ryder truck, reportedly backpedaled. The FBI asserted that Tom Kessinger had mistakenly described an innocent Army private as Timothy McVeigh's alleged accomplice, a customer who had patronized the Junction City rental company twenty-four hours after McVeigh's visit. Had the frenzied worldwide manhunt turned out to be a bust? Finding the truth was tantamount to deciphering the Rosetta Stone. When asked if the FBI had withdrawn the suspect sketch, Agent Vogel said the matter was currently under review.

Attorney General Janet Reno also joined in the cacophony of double-speak. The nation's chief cop absolved the Kansas soldier and then issued a cautiously worded statement. "It is very important that we pursue every lead. As the FBI has indicated, it is continuing to investigate whether there was a second individual who participated in the [Ryder] rental."

"So the FBI slams the door on a second suspect, and immediately cracks the steel door open to the possibility of other participants," Melissa postulated while watching the satellite feed of Attorney General Reno's press conference. "I'm not conspiratorial, but the timing cannot be dismissed. Not yet. This announcement comes just one week after we rocked the media with possibly finding John Doe 2."

Our brainstorming session and phone inquiries digging into the origin of the story exposed several kinks in the official line. We learned a Florence, South Carolina, newspaper broke the story weeks earlier. It reported that the FBI had tracked down Fort Riley Private Todd Bunting around May 20 and informed the twenty-three-year-old soldier he was the man erroneously depicted in the sketch. Bunting was questioned, cleared, and released. The newspaper editor said the wire services discounted the piece as just another detention in the massive roundup of John Doe 2 look-alikes and declined to disseminate it statewide. After all, if the FBI deemed Bunting to be the definitive end of the global search, then why not call a press conference in mid-May? Why wait nearly a month to resurrect the story in the wake of KFOR-TV's volcanic discovery?

That evening, Channel 4 launched the newscast with embarrassing questions, uncloaking the FBI's most recent fumble.

"So it would seem that the search for John Doe 2 has come to a screeching halt, or has it?" anchorwoman Linda Cavanaugh asked. "A press release from the Justice Department late this afternoon seems to muddy the waters."

The camera shot switched to Linda's co-anchor Kevin Ogle. "Muddy the waters, indeed. There are quite a few if's surrounding these reports," Kevin announced with authoritative inflection. "The reports actually surfaced in a Florence, South Carolina, newspaper which raises the question—if John Doe 2 really is this soldier from Fort Riley, Kansas, then why didn't the FBI tell us weeks ago when they supposedly identified him? In fact, the FBI still is not saying their John Doe composite is wrong."

The next day, the local CBS affiliate, KWTV, was among several media outlets to backtrack. Reporters statewide scrambled to correct the false spin generated from the FBI's declaration that John Doe 2 had been located and cleared. They collectively conceded it wasn't time to "tear up" the suspect drawing just yet.

I was perplexed by an obvious question that my colleagues in the press were not inclined to ask—why would the FBI publicly debunk witness Tom Kessinger's testimony about John Doe 2, but stop short of withdrawing the composite? Power-packed government records would eventually unearth the reason. I capitalized on a rare opportunity to view a sealed court record which proved federal officials did not rely solely upon the faulty recollection of the Ryder rental shop employee. The FBI sketch artist's notes revealed that Kessinger described McVeigh's coconspirator as "heavy built" weighing no less than "200 pounds." However, just hours after the interview, the Department of Justice filed an arrest warrant for the Oklahoma City bomber that targeted a man of a far different description. Instead, the subject sought in the greatest international manhunt of the 20th century was depicted as "175 to 180 pounds with a medium frame."

Twenty-five pounds lighter was a far cry from the original description of the suspect. The FBI obviously deemed the testimonies of witnesses near the crime scene in Oklahoma City more reliable. One week after the bombing, during Timothy McVeigh's detention hearing, a federal agent characterized the multiple sightings of the dark-haired accomplice as credible.

Moreover, the hydra grew another head in 1997 as the trials for the bombing defendants neared. Tom Kessinger's retraction failed to dissuade the owner of the Ryder rental company, Eldon Elliott, and his secretary, Vicki Beemer. Both held fast to their original statements that a second man accompanied McVeigh.

"I saw another man standing there," Elliott resolutely testified in 1997 before the Denver jury that condemned McVeigh to death. "I walked between the two of them. The second man was a little shorter than me."

During the court recess, reporters asked prosecutor Scott Mendeloff whether the identification of Todd Bunting put to rest speculation about the existence of John Doe 2.

"I don't believe the federal government has ever commented on that," Mendeloff contended. "The indictment charges Timothy McVeigh, Terry Nichols, and persons unknown to the grand jury."

Mendeloff's verbal gymnastics perched the official line squarely on the fence. But behind the microphones and courtroom drama, the furtive campaign to persuade the proprietor of the Kansas rental shop to abjure intensified. During a May 2003 pretrial hearing in Terry Nichols' Oklahoma state murder case, a trembling Eldon Elliott accused FBI agents of trying to convince him he had been confused.

"They wanted me to change my mind that there was a second person there. And I wouldn't change my mind," he stated, steadfastly maintaining that he saw two men.

Even more worrisome was the quagmire presented by law enforcement's finest criminal profiler, Jean Boylan. The feds hired Boylan in late April 1995 to depict John Doe 2 in profile, a drawing which the FBI claimed was based upon "additional witness interviews." The forensic artist who painted with visionary precision faces featured on "most-wanted" posters, such as the abductor of Polly Klaas (a nationally renowned kidnapping case) and the Unabomber, probed the memories of Oklahoma City witnesses to immortalize yet another suspect seen in town prior to the explosion. But much to the chagrin of retired FBI Agent Danny Coulson, the Bureau refused to release the drawing of Timothy McVeigh's swarthy cohort.

Boylan disclosed the embargoed composite to ABC's *World News Tonight* on May 30, 2001. "My conclusion, after having interviewed these witnesses, is that indeed they did see an olive-skinned man, and that in each of these sightings, he was with a man that they were clearly able to identify as Tim McVeigh," Boylan affirmed.


## Media Wars

A federal agent, a veteran county lawman, and three local police detectives, one of whom was among the select few assisting the FBI Bomb Task Force, warned our investigative team to tread softly and brace for the worst. The foreboding rumors leaked from the upper echelons to the rank-and-file—the feds were poised to purge any notion of Middle Eastern involvement. On the evening of June 15, 1995, their prescience transformed into reality as a raging polemic erupted between the local press and KFOR-TV.

Convinced the Todd Bunting story had eliminated McVeigh's reputed collaborator from the crosshairs of the FBI, Hussain Al-Hussaini emerged from anonymity and into the comforting embrace of Oklahoma City's competing media outlets. Eager to discredit Channel 4's reports, sympathetic reporters touted his tale of persecution as a political insurrectionist purportedly jailed for speaking out against Saddam Hussein. His confidential immigration records shattered that claim, but I wouldn't have access to that dossier until much later. Future vindication did nothing to alleviate the pain of the moment. KFOR-TV had been branded an irresponsible purveyor of sensational, biased journalism.

"Hussain says that the Channel 4 reports scared him so much that he stayed in his car for three days because he was afraid to go home," KWTV Channel 9 reporter Dave Balut crowed over the airwaves as he introduced the refugee's interpreter, none other than Abraham Ahmad. Ahmad was the

Jordanian national who was detained temporarily as a potential "material witness" in the wake of the bombing.

"Channel 4 described the man as an Iraqi soldier," the reporter continued. "But Al-Hussaini Hussain says he has nothing to hide because he was not involved in the bombing. He's never met McVeigh and he's never been in a restaurant or bar on NW 10$^{th}$ Street."

Obviously, the Iraqi immigrant was cunning enough to switch his first and last names when introducing himself to the press. Therefore, if KWTV decided to run a criminal background check, his June 3 arrest, in which he was charged with passing out drunk behind the wheel of his car with the engine running, would never have been found. If Dave Balut had discovered the record, then he would have known the Iraqi national was less than forthcoming when he said he had never been in a bar on NW 10$^{th}$ Street. As was mentioned previously, the Oklahoma City police found him unconscious inside his parked Cadillac two blocks east at the intersection of NW 8$^{th}$ and Blackwelder Streets. He was within walking distance of the NW 10$^{th}$ Street pool halls and seedy lounges where Dr. Abdul's secretary claimed she witnessed Al-Hussaini drinking with his cohorts during a followup interview.

"I was working at the time when I hear about the bombing," Ahmad translated for a smiling Al-Hussaini, reposed on the couch, relishing the friendly interview.

"And he can prove it," Reporter Balut boasted. "He does cleanup work for a property management company in northwest Oklahoma City. His time sheet for the day of the bombing confirms he was working. A supervisor verifies it."

The camera panned to a small, framed house on the twenty-two hundred block of NW 31$^{st}$ Street. Dave Balut swaggered along the driveway. "Besides the time sheet, he remembers exactly where he was and what he was doing when he heard the bomb go off. He was painting the inside of this garage."

"I never, even in Iraq, scared like how I scared now," Al-Hussaini whimpered through his translator. His remark bewildered me. A TV station's "false" accusation traumatized him more than the untold "torture" he supposedly suffered at the hands of a murderous regime. If he genuinely feared retaliation by outraged Oklahomans, why did he identify himself on camera as the mystery suspect that KFOR-TV's witnesses pegged as John Doe 2? He dodged the media spotlight three weeks earlier when I called to request an interview. He had ample opportunity then to refute our findings. So why did he step out of the shadows now? Could it be that he perceived the FBI had just pronounced "case closed" in the pursuit of America's most wanted man, John Doe 2?

Channel 9's obsequious coverage capped off with Reporter Dave Balut shaking hands with a grateful Al-Hussaini.

"Hussain says he's been victimized twice. First by KFOR, then by authorities who refuse to clear him officially. Privately, numerous Justice Department employees in Oklahoma City have confirmed the Channel 4 story is wrong, but they say they can't comment because *their bosses in Washington won't let them* [italics added]," Balut announced.

While wrapping up the report, KWTV anchorwoman Jennifer Reynolds posed the question that was begging to be asked, "Dave, why won't the FBI just go ahead and officially clear Hussain?"

"Well, because while they're saying there's no Middle Eastern connection now, the investigation is still ongoing. No telling what they'll turn up later," he confidently asserted.

"Dave, thank you very much," anchorman Kelly Ogle commented. "Dave Balut clearing an Oklahoma City man who had been mistakenly identified as John Doe 2."

## COUNTEROFFENSIVE

The KWTV broadcast set the pace. Like sharks tracking the scent of fresh blood, the local media devoured the story day after day, vilifying our news coverage on KOCO-TV Channel 5, popular morning radio shows, and the pages of the avant-garde weekly magazine, the *Oklahoma Gazette*. Donning the mask of objectivity, reporters unquestioningly propagated Hussain Al-Hussaini's story as gospel truth. The scurrilous reportage had to be addressed head-on in order to squelch the feeding frenzy. Melissa and I strategized our next move in the high-stakes media poker game of one-upmanship.

"I think we start with Channel 9's reporter, Dave Balut, declaring himself the governing authority who has verified Al-Hussaini's alibi and absolved him as a suspect. Meanwhile, the FBI refused to do so," I quipped sardonically, seeking a glimmer of camaraderie in Melissa. But her expression was worrisome.

"Has the Bureau ever issued an official statement clearing him?" she asked.

"No," I replied. "Last week when we spoke to Agent Vogel, he said that Al-Hussaini had not been ruled out."

"Ask Vogel again to go on the record and clear him."

"I'm on it," I replied.

Melissa's mood turned somber. "We have even bigger headaches to deal with. Channel 9 reported Al-Hussaini had a second job at a restaurant. And he was supposedly on NW 31st Street when the bomb went off."

Tension squeezed my stomach. "That's six blocks south of where Bernie Stanton says he saw Al-Hussaini painting a garage after 10:00 A.M.," I explained.

She became discernibly perturbed. "What about this handwritten time sheet that Channel 9 flashed on the screen claiming he was on the job from 8:08 A.M. to 3:30 P.M.?"

"I will connect the dots and report back as soon as possible," I averred. Apprehension seeped from every pore of my being. The exigent task that lay ahead would test my personal courage beyond anything I would ever experience.

## OFFICIAL ABSOLUTION DENIED

I took a deep breath and stared at the telephone on my desk. Repeatedly placing these calls had deteriorated into an exercise in futility, bordering on the comical. Since early May, I had hounded FBI Agents Dan Vogel and James Strickland to clear Hussain Al-Hussaini. Each time, they declined. Local reporters broadcast the Iraqi soldier's impassioned plea for government-sanctioned absolution. I feared the agency would deliver. I was wrong.

"Is the FBI prepared to go on-the-record and officially clear Hussain Al-Hussaini of any suspicion in the bombing?" I asked.

"No, we do not clear. We are not in the business of clearing people," Agent Vogel retorted.

I persisted. "Okay, then can the FBI say if Al-Hussaini has been investigated and ruled out as a suspect?"

"You need to talk to Steve Mullins with the U.S. Attorney's office about that. He's the spokesman for the Department of Justice here in Oklahoma City. See what he has to say," he suggested.

The ensuing inquiries were equally as frustrating. Over the next few weeks, the U.S. Attorney's office dished out the same canned response.

"We have to stick with the same policy that we cannot confirm or deny anybody's status," Spokesman Steve Mullins said.

The manicured explanations had grown tiresome. "But what about the case of Todd Bunting, the Fort Riley private whom Attorney General Janet

Reno personally exonerated in a nationally televised press conference? What about the two drifters from Arizona, Gary Land and Robert Jacks, who were questioned, cleared, and released. I was at the FBI press conference." I hammered with exasperation.

"Those people were cleared through Washington itself," he glibly replied.

"Will Washington not do this? The Hussain Al-Hussaini story has generated local and national attention."

"If you ask Washington to, they might."

The bureaucratic ping-pong ball bounced incessantly between Oklahoma City and Washington. The spokesman for Attorney General Janet Reno, Carl Stern, waited several days before returning my call, then predictably declined comment and referred me back to the Department of Justice in Oklahoma City.

The case of Hussain Al-Hussaini forged the only exception in the bureaucratic rule book. Anytime the press tracked down the names of a few blameless souls snagged in the prodigious roundup of John Doe 2 look-alikes, no matter how ridiculous their potential involvement might have been, the Department of Justice readily lifted the cloud of suspicion. The administrative higher-ups exculpated Kansas soldier Todd Bunting, two oddball transients, Gary Land and Robert Jacks, Oklahoma City resident Kyle Forney, and Army deserter David Iniguez Delgado. When the international wire service quenched the thirsty press with news of a potential bombing conspirator jailed in the Netherlands, General Reno's chief lieutenant, Carl Stern, ardently extinguished the raging rumor mill about fugitive Daniel Speigelman, debunking the story as "untrue."

Assistant U.S. Attorney Steve Mullins told the Oklahoma Associated Press point-blank that Speigelman, the New York smuggler of rare manuscripts, was "not a [bombing] suspect and never had been." Hardly the vacillating Mr. Mullins I implored to answer Al-Hussaini and his claque of reporters who sounded a clarion call for an FBI response. In light of the aggressive vigilance of the Justice Department to rescue innocent citizens caught in the FBI dragnet, it was inconceivable the Iraqi solider would be ignored as to his plight with Channel 4. He was, after all, brought to the FBI's attention, presented on television news accounts, and fingered by solid witnesses. Despite his Arab descent in the age of political correctness run amok and his obtrusive whining for exoneration played before an audience of shell-shocked Oklahomans, the FBI remained mute, refusing to utter even a faint whisper to terminate the media sniping. Unbelievable.

## "YOU'RE THE BABY WITH THE LOADED GUN"

I found myself beating on an unbreakable glass ceiling, so I detoured around the roadblock and contacted Oklahoma's newly-elected senator, James Inhofe. I became closely acquainted with Senator Inhofe while he was still serving in the House of Representatives in the summer of 1994. At the time, I was investigating the untimely death of fellow KFOR-TV journalist Kathy Jones. The beautiful and talented young mother died while shooting a feature story on the thrill of becoming a fighter pilot for a day. Skip Stevens, the man at the helm, billed himself as a former top gun Navy pilot. A dangerous misjudgment in altitude turned an aerial wingover into a fatal nosedive. The horrific moment of impact was memorialized on videotape.

Senator Inhofe, a seasoned pilot himself, offered immeasurable assistance in unsealing military records and Federal Aviation Administration files which laid bare Skip Stevens' sordid past. The "combat" aviator was an imposter. The Navy discharged him from flight training after he nearly flew an A-6 attack bomber off an aircraft carrier into the ocean. The FAA never issued him a civilian commercial pilot's license. The crash could not have been more preventable or more tragic.

Senator Inhofe's sensitivity and responsiveness to Kathy's death engendered a great deal of trust. He seemed to rise above the cesspool of hypocritical, insincere Washington politicians. Therefore, when I became mired in silver-tongued sludge, I reached out to the Oklahoma senator. The veteran lawmaker served on the influential Senate Intelligence Committee. I reasoned his ties to the intelligence community could elicit straight answers about the Bureau's interest in the Iraqi soldier.

Chief of Staff Herb Johnson ordered Senator Inhofe's liaison to the Senate Intelligence Committee to contact the FBI regarding KFOR-TV's investigation. The Bureau dispatched an official to Capitol Hill after two weeks of foot dragging. When asked if the FBI could officially clear Hussain Al-Hussaini as John Doe 2, the agency representative delivered this evasive response: "We cannot comment on a pending investigation."

The refreshingly candid Mr. Johnson, a WWII veteran who served in naval intelligence, confided he had a personal friend who held a key post on the inner sanctum of the FBI Bomb Task Force.

"They call you the baby with the loaded gun," he warned, "And they don't know where you are going to point it next." His unvarnished frankness shouted "watch out"—an unambiguous confirmation that I was on the right track but stepping on big toes.

## SPIN CITY

The mind-numbing journey through the procedural pipeline yielded nothing more than a boilerplate response. The FBI would "neither confirm nor deny" Hussain Al-Hussaini's status as a suspect. Not even Congress could extract an official proclamation. Yet almost simultaneously, the *Daily Oklahoman* printed a polar opposite statement from a local FBI agent.

"The information on Channel 4 is not true," FBI Special Agent Jeffrey Jenkins said at the 55th Annual Newspaper Publishers Association conference in Oklahoma City during a panel discussion regarding the Murrah Building attack. But when KFOR-TV's private investigator and I spoke to the federal agent, he discounted the quotation as misleading and taken out of context.

"That's not what I said," Agent Jenkins stated emphatically. He explained that he never addressed Channel 4's reports about a possible Iraqi suspect, but rather, he publicly debunked rumors that the FBI had been notified ahead of time about a bomb scare. Nonetheless, the *Daily Oklahoman* recklessly reprised the erroneous quote in the years that followed as the only denunciation of KFOR-TV's John Doe 2 investigation from officialdom. Meanwhile, the FBI spokesman for the bombing case, Agent Dan Vogel, refused to comment on our broadcasts, a fact that the newspaper was compelled to recognize, albeit begrudgingly.

The *Oklahoma Gazette,* a free weekly entertainment magazine that packed newsstands at city coffee shops, restaurants, and other business outlets, carelessly parroted Agent Jenkins's quotation without confirming its veracity. However, the media mockery did not cross the threshold of defamation until the summer of 1998 when the *Gazette* published an article entitled, "Liar, Liar." The cover story stemmed from a rash of journalistic prevarications in which several nationally recognized reporters had confessed to printing embellished information, fabricated sources, and outright lies. The *Gazette* reporter, Phil Bacharach, singled out KFOR-TV's expose regarding Hussain Al-Hussaini as Oklahoma's possible "prime example" of the power grab for TV ratings gone mad, implying I had manufactured evidence that implicated the Iraqi national in the crime.

"Federal investigators eventually discredited the [KFOR-TV] story, which remains a favorite of some conspiracy-mongers," Bacharach smattered with vintage tabloid hyperbole. The "journalist" who chided his colleagues for the unpardonable sin of lying had failed to even speak to me before publication. Incensed by the article, I demanded a retraction and even offered Bacharach the opportunity to examine my investigative dossier. He promised to consult with his editor but never called back. The magazine's owner arrogantly ignored a flurry of letters from my lawyer.

In January 2000, I filed a libel lawsuit against the magazine and forced its staff to answer the question it refused upon my initial inquiries: "If an FBI official has given the *Gazette* an on-the-record statement that cleared Hussain Al-Hussaini as a possible suspect in the Oklahoma City bombing, please identify the date and the FBI official." The answer: "No such statements were given."

During his deposition, reporter Phil Bacharach admitted he regretted not interviewing me for the article, conceding he would have been "angry and hurt" if the situation had been reversed. I recoiled at the prospect of lengthy litigation, so I dismissed the case, having already proven my point and achieved a degree of vindication. The lawsuit was also designed to quell the sporadic recycling of erroneous information, setting the record straight about the Iraqi soldier's questionable alibi and inability to elicit absolution from the government.

This much was undisputed: No matter how high profile the mudslinging became between Oklahoma City news organizations, Al-Hussaini had yet to be rescued by an arbitrary exoneration from the FBI. In retrospect, the agency would not have dared to incite the flagship news station into unleashing potentially embarrassing reports which would have obliterated any flimsy basis for absolving Al-Hussaini which federal agents could invent. The Iraqi immigrant's plaintive plea to the FBI to declare him innocent presented a dilemma. He had no plausible alibi. Furthermore, officials on the Oklahoma Bomb Task Force familiar with KFOR-TV's evidence undoubtedly knew it. So the Bureau chose to do nothing, with the exception of sitting silently on the sidelines while the media firestorm burned with ferocity.

## ALIBI COLLAPSES UNDER SCRUTINY

Hussain Al-Hussaini publicly proclaimed to Channels 5 and 9 he was painting a garage at 2241 NW 31$^{st}$ Street when the bomb went off. Bernie Stanton said otherwise, placing the Iraqi handyman at a work site six blocks north at 2220 NW 37$^{th}$ Street, but his alleged arrival occurred sometime after the explosion downtown. However, there was a fifty– to sixty-minute gap in time for which I could not account. Bernie left the job site to retrieve some tools from his house. He departed a few minutes before 9:00 A.M. and returned an hour later to find Hussain Al-Hussaini, Jose Gonzales, and

Mohammed Amir slapping paint on the garage door on NW 37th Street.

Bernie looked at me pensively, contemplating his answer. "The story makes no sense. Dr. Abdul always handed out job assignments at the start of the workday. I've been there since 1987 and have never been assigned to more than one house unless an emergency happened, like a water main break or flooding at one of his properties."

"But Al-Hussaini told the press he was at 2241 NW 31$^{st}$ Street all morning painting the garage," I remarked.

Bernie snickered. "That's exactly my point. I saw Al-Hussaini at the house on NW 37$^{th}$ Street at 10:00 A.M. How can the man be two places at once?" His brow furrowed, then he snapped his fingers. "Besides, the paint color proves he's lying."

"What do you mean?" I asked.

"Take a look at the garage on NW 31$^{st}$ Street. It's white. The garage on NW 37$^{th}$ Street is yellow. When I saw Al-Hussaini the morning of the bombing, he was wearing a dark blue shirt with splatters of yellow, not white, paint. There was not a trace of white paint."

Bernie's observation was intriguing but not quite solid enough to impeach Al-Hussaini's alleged whereabouts. "Who else was working at the location on NW 31$^{st}$ Street on April 19?" I pressed further.

"I think Larry Monroe was assigned to do carpentry work at that house. In fact, I heard from a close friend that Larry is the one who told the Channel 5 reporter that Al-Hussaini was there, but soon afterwards, he realized he was wrong. He was really sorry about the mistake."

I cringed. How was I going to get an on-the-record verification? Larry had burrowed back into the shadows since I spoke to him on April 23. He feared Dr. Abdul would retaliate and fire him.

"Would you be willing to wear a hidden tape recorder and talk to him?" I asked.

"Sure, if it's the only way to get to the bottom of this, count me in."

Bernie pressed the record and pause buttons on a mini-cassette recorder and slipped it into his T-shirt pocket, then headed to Salman Properties. When he arrived, Larry knocked off his construction duties for a brief chat.

The no-nonsense country boy did not mince words. "What did you mean when you said that you were sorry about what you told Channel 5?" Bernie asked.

Larry squinted into the blazing summer sun and wiped a band of sweat dripping from his forehead. "Ah, man, I thought Hussain was with me. He wasn't with me. He wasn't with me," the distraught twenty-four-year-old conceded.

"Who did you tell this to?" Bernie inquired.

Larry hung his head. "Channel 5."

"Did you tell that to the FBI?"

"No, just to Channel 5," Larry moaned regretfully. "The reporter was right there in front of the office with a camera and she started making me feel guilty. See, I asked Hussain right before the reporter walked up. I said, 'Are you sure you were with me?' and he said, 'I don't know. You were there. You know if I was with you or not.'"

Bernie excitedly interjected, "Was he there that morning?"

"I don't think he was," Larry meekly answered. "He wasn't with me. I came close to calling Channel 5 and saying I think I lied to ya'll. I can't say it in any other terms because I didn't mean to. But I think something went wrong, somewhere."

"Hey man, it was a mistake. You didn't mean it," Bernie consoled his tormented coworker.

"I wouldn't deliberately lie to Oklahoma on TV," Larry replied defensively, "And I got to thinking about it. I really got to thinking about it. I was trying to picture Hussain's face at that house and I couldn't picture him. And then I kept asking, asking, and asking. And finally I figured it out. He wasn't with me," his voice trailed off. "He wasn't with me."

Bernie left no room for misunderstanding. "So Hussain wasn't there on NW 31st Street?"

"I was prepping the inside of the brick house on NW 31st for Section 8 Housing approval. He wasn't with me." Larry reiterated.

A retiree living next door to the house in question corroborated Larry's testimony. The former school janitor pulled in his driveway forty-five minutes after the bombing. While unloading groceries from his car, Elvin Devers walked within a few yards of the garage where Al-Hussaini claimed to be painting. The garage door had been torn down during a domestic dispute before the property was vacated. That left Elvin with an unobstructed view inside the garage.

"Was there anybody working inside the garage next door?" I asked while reaching for the microphone.

"No," the elderly gentleman confirmed.

"Did you see any workmen or activity outside of the house?"

"No, as far as I know, there wasn't anybody around." Elvin said as he adjusted his spectacles.

"Do you have a severe vision problem?" I inquired.

"I have difficulty reading with my left eye, but with corrective lenses, I see fine through my right eye," he asserted. He had been granted a driver's license to travel short distances and could distinguish people and objects within twenty feet.

"I am confident I would have been able to see people moving around inside that garage from where I was standing," he claimed.

## FABRICATED EVIDENCE

Al-Hussaini's alibi was unraveling, but several snags remained. KWTV reporter Dave Balut displayed the Iraqi worker's time sheet in a televised report which ostensibly established he was on the job from 8:08 A.M. to 3:30 P.M. on April 19. A supervisor at Salman Properties reportedly verified it. But who? Several company employees confirmed that Dr. Abdul, a Palestinian carrying an Israeli passport, had flown to the Middle East on June 8 for an extended vacation in the West Bank.

"We punched in and out every day with a time clock. We haven't used handwritten time sheets in months," Darby Williams explained, oblivious to Al-Hussaini's television debut.

"When did you start using machine-stamped cards to keep track of your hours?" I asked.

"Dr. Abdul bought this big, stupid, time clock at an auction last fall," she recalled.

"Was that around the same time frame that he hired the Iraqi soldiers in 1994?"

"Yes, that sounds about right," she said.

Bernie Stanton and Larry Monroe also refuted the authenticity of Al-Hussaini's penciled-in work form for April 19. Both men said Dr. Abdul had implemented a new mandate to use machine-stamped cards to calculate weekly paychecks.

"When I tried to write down my work hours, Dr. Abdul insisted I clock in. I watched the Iraqi guys punching their time cards every morning," Bernie said.

"With Dr. Abdul visiting the Middle East, who was the supervisor who authenticated Al-Hussaini's time sheet for Channels 5 and 9?" I queried.

"My best bet is his daughter, Helen. She handles office duties during his out-of-town trips," Bernie speculated. "Do you want me to check out Hussain's time sheet?"

Re-entering the Salman Properties' office with a hidden camera was an audacious move, but it would provide the only means to penetrate the web of subterfuge. Al-Hussaini had ignored my inquiries, so I had no choice.

"If this man really was on the job the hour before the bomb detonated, then he's innocent. Either way, it is my job to find the truth." I somberly replied. The final verdict rested on the legitimacy of his hourly time record. Mercifully, the answer came quickly.

Throughout the surreptitious recording, Helen exuded hostility toward Bernie, her father's ex-employee, and decried the implication that Al-Hussaini was a terrorist. Bernie offered condolences for the death of her mother, Karen Abdul, and respectfully engaged in congenial small talk, but before long an air of tension arose.

"I want to know why everybody lied about their whereabouts for April 19," Bernie brusquely stated.

Helen's temper flared. "Well, I saw them on NW 31$^{st}$ Street. I went over there. I was supposed to go downtown, but my dad told me to get some masking tape to put around the trim so the workers wouldn't mess it up."

Bernie balked at her story. "Were all the Iraqi workers there?"

"All the Iraqis were there," she insisted.

Bernie leaned back in his chair and clasped his hands. "Well, Channel 4 interviewed a neighbor living next door to the work site on NW 31$^{st}$ Street and he said there was nobody working outside that house that morning."

"I was there," Helen smoldered.

"Alright. When I went to work they were painting a garage on NW 37$^{th}$ Street. How could they be two places at the same time?" he sarcastically posited.

Helen dug in her heels. "I have no reason to lie about where they were because I saw them there."

"Larry Monroe told me he was sorry he lied to Channel 5 about seeing Hussain at the job site on NW 31$^{st}$ on April 19. He said flat out that Hussain was not there." Bernie declared with an adversarial tone, "Did you see Larry when you supposedly dropped off the masking tape?"

"I don't know where he (Larry) was that morning," she contended. (Larry Monroe later refuted Helen's claim that she delivered supplies to 2241 NW 31st Street, the house where he was assigned to perform carpentry work on April 19.)

The sinewy laborer removed his ball cap and squared his shoulders. "It seems kind of weird that they would pull off that job to go to work on NW 37$^{th}$ Street," Bernie commented. He was dumbstruck by the suggestion that the Iraqi workers were allegedly dispatched to a second property on April 19. "So was Dr. Abdul on NW 31st Street, too?"

"No, he was here at the office," she contended.

"That's strange. He told me he was down there [N.W. 31st Street] when the bomb went off," Bernie charged.

Helen, looking flustered, replied, "He might have been because, I mean, he might have left right when I got there," she stammered. "I don't know." Dr. Abdul's Jordanian wife was possibly the only witness who could verify his whereabouts during the nine o'clock hour. The company secretary, Darby Williams, notified her employer earlier that she would be arriving shortly before noon on April 19 in order to visit an orthopedic surgeon. But when the bombing occurred, the doctor cancelled her appointment to help with the rescue efforts downtown. Dr. Abdul told Darby to take the rest of the day off.

Bernie, with the zeal of a prosecutor, fired off the climactic charge. "When Hussain and Abraham Ahmad went to Channel 9, they showed the reporter a time sheet, but that wasn't the time sheet that we used. You know we got rid of handwritten time sheets six months ago. Everybody had to punch a time clock."

Helen stared at him blankly. "Yeah, I know."

"And all of a sudden," Bernie continued, "Hussain handed that white sheet of paper to the media. It doesn't make any sense to show a fake one and not show the real one." Bernie alleged.

The young woman bristled. "Why would one of my dad's workers want to blow up a building that my mom worked in?" she snapped while rifling through a large leather satchel spilling over with employee time cards. A staggering admission followed. Helen Abdul confessed she created Al-Hussaini's time sheet to present to the media.

"If I can find it, I will show you," she promised with mounting exasperation. For the next twenty minutes, Bernie patiently waited as Helen examined each card in the stack. She then thumbed through a file box on her desk searching for the April 19 time-stamped card bearing the name Hussain Al-Hussaini. But the search was in vain. Helen insisted she once viewed the time card and could eventually locate it. But years passed, and the document never surfaced, hammering one more nail into the coffin of Al-Hussaini's nonexistent alibi.


## SECOND JOB RUSE?

The ever-widening chasm between truth and fabrication reinvigorated my desiccated will to stay in the fight. Hussain Al-Hussaini's publicly professed alibi had been virtually dismantled with one more hurdle to overcome—his second job. The minimum-wage, unskilled handyman was employed as a restaurant janitor ostensibly to supplement his income at Salman Properties. The spate of television and print news accounts showcased the impecunious immigrant as far too busy and cash poor to be enmeshed in an act of terror. But Al-Hussaini's employment file tarnished his media-generated halo.

Company records indicated that the Iraqi busboy worked as a night custodian during the weekend graveyard shift, Friday through Sunday. He did not work the week of the bombing from April 17 through April 20. In late May, he resigned, then re-applied for his job on June 11, just four days before he spoke to the local press. A week later, on June 19, after having received favorable coverage including his claim of the second job, he reported to duty and promptly quit again.

"I told him to get up and start working because he hadn't been getting the job done to our satisfaction," Al-Hussaini's supervisor explained. "And he said, 'I don't need this job anymore' and walked out the door."

Al-Hussaini's on-the-spot resignation came just four days after he told Channels 5 and 9 he worked a second job doing restaurant cleanup.


## DISSIDENT OR DISCIPLE?

Enjoying his new found status as the cause-celebre, Hussain Al-Hussaini spoon-fed the pliant press his woeful history of imprisonment as a political dissident. His alleged crime involved distributing anti-government literature in leaflet form. The fiendish Saddam Hussein apparently brooked subversion from one of his soldiers and inexplicably spared his life. Instead, a military court supposedly sentenced Hussain Al-Hussaini to thirteen years of incarceration.

A Pentagon source assigned to the Department of Defense Counter Terrorism Directorate howled with laughter upon hearing Hussain Al-Hussaini's "tale." Baghdad was not a democracy like America where protesters passed out fliers on the street corner, exercising their right of free speech. The intelligence expert wryly pointed out that an Iraqi citizen inciting rebellion would be condemned to a "lead breakfast and Saddam would charge the family of the deceased for the bullets" expended in a certain summary execution.

The odyssey woven by the beleaguered "dissenter" became even more outlandish. Al-Hussaini presented a hyperbolic yarn of a prison uprising at the end of the Persian Gulf War in which Allied troops reportedly freed him from eight years of confinement. The fantastic story began when the jailhouse doors swung open. American soldiers purportedly stood by as the liberated inmate escaped the penal compound in a vehicle abandoned by the Iraqi army. Presumably, the panic-stricken Iraqis fled the Allied invasion on foot after leaving behind the keys in the ignitions of their military trucks.

"When the army took off, they just left everything, including their cars, so we just took one of the army cars," claimed Al-Hussaini.

From there, Al-Hussaini raced unmolested to his hometown of Basra, desperate to learn the fate of his family. But when the search proved unfruitful, he surrendered to coalition forces and entered a Saudi Arabian refugee camp straightaway. In 1994, the Iraqi "defector" immigrated to America to find solace in the land of the free.

While cobbling their stories about Al-Hussaini's past travails, local reporters neglected the perfunctory fact-checks that would have exposed the man's contradictory statements. Channel 9 disparaged KFOR-TV's characterization of the possible John Doe 2 as an Iraqi soldier, sensitively depicting him as a refugee seeking political asylum. But in a less guarded moment, Al-Hussaini boasted to the *Oklahoma Gazette* he had, indeed, been conscripted into the Iraqi Republican Guard like "most able bodied male adults." However, the time-tested stories regarding his length of military service fluctuated between three months, six months, and a year.

The disturbing fact remained—only Hussain Al-Hussaini knew the truth. Like the thousands of Iraqi soldiers who surrendered en masse to U.S. and coalition forces during Operation Desert Storm, he had no identification papers or proof of his status as a political prisoner. Many of the eighty-three thousand ex-enemy combatants were repatriated after the war ended. However, a select group refused to return home to Iraq, legitimately fearing persecution or death. The holdouts sought sanctuary at two refugee camps located at Rafha and Al-Artawiyah, Saudi Arabia. Al-Hussaini was housed among the population of former prisoners of war.

Rob Frazier, a U.S. Department of State official stationed at the American embassy in Riyadh from 1991 through 1993, officiated the screening program for asylum applicants. The former Army intelligence officer interviewed hundreds of Iraqi combatants, powerless to distinguish between Saddam's disciples who had mercilessly tortured civilians and those who were legitimate victims of the military's abuse. A steady stream of reports from camp residents further compounded Frazier's quandary. Rumors persisted that the Iraqi regime had dispatched sleeper agents to penetrate the POW population.

"I have long suspected that not every Iraqi there was a refugee," Frazier opined. "I sent cables to the State Department in Washington warning that Iraqi [intelligence] agents had infiltrated the camps."

But the cables outlining Frazier's impotence to adequately background the resettlement candidates went unanswered. Soon Saddam's soldiers, skillfully trained in the art of warfare and weaponry, reached our shores. According to a December 2002 article published by *LA Weekly*, investigative reporter Jim Crogan discovered an influx of six thousand ex-Iraqi combatants had immigrated to the United States in the wake of Gulf War I with only "cursory scrutiny."

"Who knows what we did in backgrounding these people," the former director of the CIA, James Woolsey, told *LA Weekly*. "They should have vetted everyone in a reasonable fashion before they gave them asylum. Instead, as the saying goes, we may have left our most important work undone," he added.

The ex-intelligence chief's acute foresight predicted the law enforcement nightmare to come. Humanitarian deference to the genuine refugees resulted in lax monitoring of the Iraqi settlers. The former POWs blended into a democratic society unfettered. The potential danger of sleeper agents emplaced in the homeland by a foreign power did not make headlines until February 2003 as the nation teetered on the brink of a second Gulf War in the Middle East. The *Washington Times* national security correspondent Bill Gertz disclosed a CIA analysis that prognosticated an "eighty-five percent chance that Saddam would use proxy terrorists to strike [within] the United States" in advance of military operations.

As U.S. forces invaded Iraq in March 2003, the FBI mobilized an army of agents to track down an estimated three thousand illegal Iraqi immigrants classified as missing. The massive sweep was designed to detect and isolate enemy operatives who posed a domestic terrorist threat such as "assassinations, hijackings, and bombings." Astonishingly, the far-reaching initiative ignored the presence of Iraqi Gulf War veterans capable of murderous fury to avenge the overthrow of their president.

One man watched the news coverage of the comprehensive roundup, aware that Iraqi Republican Guardsmen, Saddam's supreme fighting forces, could be living among us. Rob Frazier strongly suspected covert operatives from the distinguished military unit, masquerading as refugees, were deliberately inserted into the Saudi Arabian camps. Once these intelligence agents achieved legal status as immigrants, they could wreak untold destruction from within U.S. borders.

Was Hussain Al-Hussaini the fulfillment of Frazier's darkest apprehensions or simply a wronged man? The Iraqi "defector" later repudiated the

*Oklahoma Gazette* article that claimed he served in the vaunted Republican Guard, accusing the magazine of slipshod reporting. But strident denials could not erase an indelible clue emblazoned on his upper left arm—the snake and anchor tattoo.

Colonel Patrick Lang, a Middle East expert who formerly served as the chief of human intelligence for the Defense Intelligence Agency, determined Hussain Al-Hussaini's military tattoo indicated he was likely a trusted member of Saddam Hussein's Republican Guard before being recruited into the elite Unit 999 of the Estikhabarat, more commonly known as the Iraqi Military Intelligence Service. Headquartered in Salman Pak, southeast of Baghdad, Unit 999 was tasked with "clandestine operations at home and abroad." Several defense and intelligence analysts, with whom I had consulted, concurred with Colonel Lang's conclusions.

## BROADCAST BOMBSHELL

Having completed my homework, I mentally prepared to confront Hussain Al-Hussaini with the explosive new evidence which torpedoed his publicly espoused alibi and claims he had "never been in a bar near NW 10<sup>th</sup> Street." I contacted Salman Properties to request an interview. Al-Hussaini's interpreter, the omnipresent Abraham Ahmad, returned my call. Ahmad said a lawyer advised the Iraqi national not to speak to Channel 4.

The time had arrived to craft our counteroffensive to the media smear campaign. Each keystroke was cathartic. On June 22, KFOR-TV fired a return salvo, a broadcast bombshell that shot gaping holes in Al-Hussaini's alibi. Our aligned enemies offered no response. I welcomed the sublime silence as a weary soldier receiving news of a cease-fire.

The next night, an Oklahoma City policeman, patrolling a vacant lot near NW 10<sup>th</sup> Street, found an inebriated Hussain Al-Hussaini sleeping in the back seat of his car. The right front tire had been blown out. The officer took him into custody for public drunkenness. The arrest occurred less than three weeks after the Iraqi driver was charged with intoxication while in control of a motor vehicle. It would not be the last.

# CHAPTER 10

# COUNTDOWN TO 9:02 A.M.

The strategically leaked story about Tom Kessinger, the confused witness who recanted his testimony, had all the earmarks of a gambit to snuff out public fascination with the ghost of John Doe 2. The third terrorist had been sentenced to death by stealth. As the father of Soviet communism, Nicholai Lenin, preached, "A lie told often enough becomes the truth." The shadowy puppet masters, who called the back channel power plays at the FBI, had embarked on a feat of legerdemain. They were resolved to airbrush Timothy McVeigh's partner-in-crime from the annals of history. A complete 180 from times past, the unspoken rules that governed journalists decreed trust in one's government. But I saw little reason for trust, and inadequately answered questions pushed me to pursue evidence that bucked the prevailing thought.

Screening authentic witnesses from the overzealous ones who were seeking publicity, those who were sincere but sincerely wrong, and those whose testimonies could not be validated through independent sources, was an arduous and exhausting undertaking. Eventually, the heart-wrenching reality of April 19 came into sharp focus through the disturbing recollections of a small cadre of average Oklahomans. The majority of these witnesses were strangers to one another, yet critical details of their stories overlapped with incredible accuracy.

I memorialized their statements on video and audiotape. All willingly signed affidavits to attest to the veracity of their testimonies. Copious interviews with the suspects' relatives, law enforcement officials, and intelligence sources coupled with hundreds of pages of police records, court documents, press accounts, and classified intelligence reports corroborated their stories.

The investigative dossier provided a rare glimpse into the 1995 bombing as recounted by unsuspecting bystanders who witnessed various stages of an Islamic terrorist plot to murder more Americans in a single explosion than the total number of U.S. soldiers who died on the battlefields of the Persian Gulf War. The darkest chapter in 20th century America unfolded through their eyes as the clock ticked closer to 9:02 A.M.

## MORNING DAWNS ON APRIL 19

A purplish haze laced with shades of crimson bathed the downtown skyline as Mike Benton stretched his muscles in the crisp pre-dawn air. His morning jog offered an energizing respite from the hectic schedule of a self-employed executive. Two exercise partners kept him faithful to the daily regimen. Cindy Preston, a young, enterprising businesswoman, and Joan Whitley, an elected county official, joined him for an invigorating jog through the corporate district which encircled the Alfred P. Murrah Building. Afterwards, the chatting friends would enjoy a brisk cool down. Only this morning, something extraordinary disrupted their otherwise mundane routine.

From out of nowhere the sound of pounding footsteps closed in. An oddly-outfitted jogger brushed by within a hairsbreadth of the group. He wore a windbreaker, blue jeans, and red backpack—hardly appropriate running attire.

"Maybe this guy is late for the bus," Joan jokingly remarked as the dark-complexioned man raced past at a breathless pace. "He's hauling so fast you would think he was running for his life."

The mysterious sprinter dashed up NW 5th Street from the federal office complex one block east to Broadway Avenue. As the three joggers rounded the corner, they noticed the winded runner glancing at his wristwatch.

"It looks like he's timing his speed," Mike commented as the Middle Eastern male with the muscular physique spun around to repeat his trek. The dark, stocky figure approached the trio. Mike and Cindy gazed at his face as he sauntered past within an approximate distance of three feet. In less than two hours, a terrorist bomb would carve out a gaping pit of death in the very pavement where they stood before sunrise. And the encounter with the out-of-place jogger would collectively cross their minds.

## "DIRECT ME TO FIFTH AND HARVEY STREETS, PLEASE"

Jesse Pearce gave himself a silent pep talk. "Only eight hours before quitting time." Selling, stocking, and changing tires paid the boyishly handsome father-to-be a decent wage. But the work was grueling, expending every vestige of strength the athletically nimble twenty-five-year-old could muster. Cool spring mornings like April 19 made the backbreaking labor bearable, but it wouldn't be long before the stifling Oklahoma summer would send the mercury rising.

"Customer on site," coworker Brent Martin hollered as a large Ryder truck entered the parking lot of Johnny's Tire Company at the intersection of 10<sup>th</sup> and Hudson Streets.

"Hey man, we just opened for business. My blood is not flowing yet," Jesse groused as he pulled a quarter from his pocket.

"Let's compromise, heads I go, tails you go," he said. Neither man could have envisaged that destiny rested in the simple flip of a coin.

"I suppose I drew the short straw," Jesse chuckled and headed out the door. He sprinted briskly to the rolling moving van, concerned the enormous rear carriage might tear down the shop's monogrammed flags streaming from an aluminum roof. Jesse walked to the driver's side window. His six-foot-one-inch frame enabled him to see inside the cab.

"Good morning sir, what can I do for you?" he asked with gentlemanly charm.

The driver with a flat top haircut greeted him energetically. "I'm sure you can help. Direct me to Fifth and Harvey Streets, please."

"You're not far from it. It's about five blocks south of here," Jesse politely explained.

A raven-haired passenger in a ball cap with exotically foreign features radiated mystery. The man sat rigidly in statuesque silence staring out the front windshield while his garrulous companion conversed with Jesse. The inquisitive motorist quickly descended from the truck and strolled across the parking lot with the young salesman in tow.

COUNTDOWN TO 9:02 A.M. 127

"That large, white building should be a good landmark to lead you where you're going," Jesse volunteered while pointing to a high rise apartment complex which towered above the downtown skyline, situated a stone's throw from the doomed Murrah building. The driver politely thanked him and pulled off the lot, rolling downtown toward infamy. Jesse returned to his morning duties.

## SEVENTEEN MINUTES TO DETONATION

The thirty-seven-year-old dental supply worker drew a long drag on his cigarette and flicked the ashes outside his truck window. On this particular morning, the humdrum of daily jaunts to retrieve his employer's mail presented an unexpected whiff of intrigue. While listening to the humorous joust between his favorite radio disc jockeys, Lance Carmichael espied a possible illicit drug buy transpiring across the street. He was parked outside the downtown post office at the intersection of 5th and Harvey Streets where the nine-story Murrah Building stood.

A large Ryder truck, situated a couple dozen yards to the south, temporarily held his gaze. A slight-framed man with a military buzz cut stood near the truck's rear carriage, exchanging something with a shabbily dressed pedestrian. A dark figure sat motionless in the cab of the moving van. The bill of the man's ball cap shadowed his face; however, Lance could distinguish a rounded nose, pronounced jaw, broad neckline, and muscular shoulders. As the curious on-looker visually scanned the busy intersection, he noticed an eighties vintage Marquis parked two spaces east of the Ryder truck. The old yellow clunker, heavily caked with road dust, brought back memories of Lance's youth to a carefree time when he owned a similar model Mercury Monterey.

His reminiscent thoughts snapped back into the present. "Time to get a move on," he mumbled to himself as he scurried inside the post office, re-emerging minutes later at 8:55 A.M. By then, the men he thought could be drug dealers had vanished. As Lance drove to the nearby stoplight, he noticed the Ryder truck had moved to the front of the federal building. The long-limbed driver exited the truck and jogged northward across 5th Street. Suddenly, a bright flash of reflected sunlight caught his eye, drawing his attention to the darkly tinted rear window of a brown pickup truck parked close to the entrance of the Social Security office. The traffic signal turned green. Lance headed north on Harvey Street, unaware that the landscape in his rearview mirror would disintegrate into a kill zone in less than eight minutes.

## DEADLY EMPLACEMENT

The Social Security office at the Murrah Building was teeming with activity, generating stifling warmth for patrons. Cheryl Hammons immediately secured a place in line and directed her daughters, Daina and Falesha, to fill out the necessary forms. Daina set down the baby carrier that cradled her infant son's eight-pound frame. Little Gabreon's three-year-old sister, Peachlyn, nestled in an adjacent bench, eyeing the crowded room with precocious curiosity. It would not be long before this toddler's vibrancy attracted the interest of nearby strangers. Engaging adults in conversation had become Peachlyn's most creative defense against boredom.

Falesha and Daina stood a few feet away preparing their paperwork. An unexplained, ominous sensation pressed in. Daina resisted an overwhelming urge to pick up her children and run. "This is crazy," she rationalized to herself. "Why do I feel like I should get out of here? This makes no sense whatsoever." In an effort to distract her mind from what she perceived to be imaginary danger, she glanced outside the ground floor lobby windows that spanned the northeast side of the office. A large, yellow moving van piqued her interest.

"Falesha, check out that Ryder truck parked right outside. If he's in a commercial loading zone, you can bet the meter maids will give him a ticket," Daina mused.

Falesha paused to look outside. At that moment, a stocky, dark man with distinctly foreign looking features climbed out of the truck. His thick, black curly hair appeared almost comical, protruding from the underlining of his baseball cap. From her vantage point located just twelve feet away, Daina was able to discern minute details of his appearance.

Daina giggled, "Check him out. He sure looks like he's in a hurry." Falesha lost interest and walked away as Daina watched the man dart to the back of the truck and anxiously survey his surroundings. When he sprung back onto the sidewalk, Daina followed the stranger's nervous stride as he scampered past the windows and swiftly disappeared from view on the northeast side of the building where several witnesses said the brown Chevy truck was parked.

Daina gathered the Social Security forms and crossed the office to where her mother was standing. Cheryl quickly skimmed the documents. "Go back and fill in the empty blanks. We don't want to give them a reason to bump us back in line," she said.

## EYEING THE ESCAPE

The second hand would make seven more revolutions before the terrorist bomb was to explode. The fiendish plot had entered its final phase. As the clock struck 8:55 A.M., Jerry Nance exited the south side of the *Journal Record* building, the historic production center for Oklahoma City's premier business publication. The printing operator decided to slip in a quick break before rolling the presses. The alley where Jerry stood smoking his pipe afforded an unobstructed view of the bustling Murrah Building which lined 5th Street. This morning, however, Jerry felt something was out of place. A dilapidated Mercury Marquis, parked near the south entrance of the *Journal Record* parking lot, interrupted the daily rhythm he knew so well.

"I've never seen this fellow around here before," he mentally noted. Jerry had a photographic memory of the monthly parking lot customers. The yellow road beater coated in dirt simply did not belong. His inquisitive nature compelled him to take a second glance. A dark-skinned male in a ball cap sat behind the wheel, strangely enough, making no attempt to park in a marked space or to exit the vehicle.

"He must be waiting for someone," Jerry thought as he walked to his car which was parked several blocks north. His company dry-cleaned employee uniforms every Wednesday, and he had forgotten to grab his garment sack when he arrived at the office earlier. Minutes later, Jerry entered the *Journal Record* alleyway directly into the path of a speeding Mercury Marquis. The traumatized pedestrian glared at the charging vehicle as it careened perilously close before making a sharp turn eastward. The occupant, whom Jerry had observed earlier, was now sitting in the passenger seat next to a Caucasian driver. The witness perceived the dark-complexioned man to be of Middle Eastern ethnicity. As the car screeched around the corner, the right rear tire bumped over a concrete parking marker, loosening a white license tag that dangled by one bolt. The Marquis escaped downtown racing south on Robinson Street.

## MAD GETAWAY

The clock on the dashboard read 8:59 A.M. as Dan Nelson anxiously weaved in and out of a traffic snarl clogging NW 6th Street. He had a pressing date at the courthouse. The tardy lawyer habitually cut his timing to the wire. Suddenly, an irate motorist plowed past Dan's car and abruptly cut into his lane. The older model, pale yellow sedan caught the attorney's eye as the foreign-looking driver gunned his engine to pass by. The impatient commuter flashed him an irritated glance. Distracted by the late hour, Dan turned south on Robinson and pressed on the gas pedal as he sailed through the yellow light at NW 5th Street, passing the ill-fated Murrah Building. He had traveled just two blocks south of the blast zone when a terrific explosion caused him to lurch forward into the steering wheel.

As Dan listened to police broadcasts which detailed a search for foreign terrorists, he mentally revisited his encounter with the Middle Eastern driver in the yellow sedan, a man so desperate to flee downtown, he willingly violated traffic laws. After becoming aware of Channel 4's investigation into a possible Arab connection in the ensuing weeks, he requested to view the station's surveillance photographs. After meticulous examination, the detail-minded, career jurist picked out one of Hussain Al-Hussaini's Iraqi comrades, identifying him as the visibly edgy man he had witnessed speeding by in the faded yellow car.

## MIDDLE EASTERNER WITH THE DIABOLICAL GRIN

At 9:00 A.M. sharp, the duty-minded employee entered the *Journal Record* basement and resumed running the printing presses. Without warning, an explosive force thrust Jerry Nance to the floor. After navigating his way through blinding debris, the shaken survivor emerged to behold widespread carnage. The parking lot he had traversed just two minutes earlier was now a raging inferno of blazing vehicles.

Jerry dashed to the intersection of 6th and Harvey Streets where he stood paralyzed with disbelief, gaping at the burning Murrah Building. A Middle Eastern looking man standing within arm's reach relished the sight with a diabolical grin. Jerry was aghast. The stranger's inexplicable expression of almost jubilant satisfaction struck the native Oklahoman as highly offensive given the unparalleled suffering and fresh butchery which encircled them.

## DEATH STARE

Billowing plumes of smoke blackened the Oklahoma City horizon. A sudden stillness fell over awestruck motorists and pedestrians traveling the streets which lined a cluster of high-rise buildings. One vehicle was moving at 9:03 A.M. The tires of a brown pickup screeched as the vehicle made a sharp left turn off Main onto Robinson. Rachel Sealy stepped off the grassy median directly in front of the oncoming truck. Instinct thrust her back-wards—a narrow escape from a near fatal collision. The driver glowered at her as he sped by. In the weeks and years that followed, his basilisk death-stare would breathe to life every time Rachel attempted to shut out the wicked memory. She would never doubt her positive identification of Hussain Al-Hussaini as the man behind the wheel of the getaway truck that was targeted in an official FBI all-points bulletin.

## EYEWITNESS AT GROUND ZERO

Tiffany Green grew faint from sheer helplessness. Tears of compassion streaked the paramedic's face. The only way the trapped woman lying a few feet from Tiffany's reach would emerge from the shattered bowels of the unstable Murrah Building was without her right leg. Shock racked the patient's petite frame as the surgeon administered an amnesic. Daina Bradley would feel each agonizing slice during the grisly amputation, but she would not remember the pain. The drug promised to erase her memory of the oper-ation but not the image of the terrorists, who murdered her family, placing their instrument of death.

"It was a Ryder truck!" the frightened survivor shrieked. "It pulled up, a foreign looking man got out, and then before long, everything went black."

Daina was the only victim who lived to tell of John Doe 2 exiting the bomb truck. During the twelve-hour rescue operation to free her from the rubble, she spoke of the enormous yellow moving van parked in front of the building. The witness's revelation was disclosed twenty-four hours prior to the publication of news accounts that the FBI had traced a VIN number from the axle of a Ryder rental truck to a vendor in Junction City, Kansas. Until then, the world's press operated under the assumption that a minivan, not a Ryder truck, transported the explosive cargo.

Daina regained consciousness to learn she and her critically wounded sister lost everyone dear to them in a bloody holocaust. Not long afterwards, she granted the FBI several hospital bedside interviews. Presumably, investi-gators received word of Daina's brush with the bombers from paramedics and firefighters at the bomb site. With painstaking detail, the eyewitness to evil described the "olive-skinned" foreigner who sat in the Ryder passenger seat as the heated international manhunt raged on.

Daina's heartrending loss of her mother, two children, and leg captivated the international media. But despite having granted several prominent press interviews, she feared divulging she had witnessed Timothy McVeigh's bombing accomplice as he stepped out of the Ryder truck. I learned about her testimony from a rescuer who overheard the tormented girl crying out from ground zero. After offering the terrified witness the protection of anonymity, she agreed to view KFOR-TV's photo lineup of the Arab subjects.

"I haven't watched much news," Daina sorrowfully prefaced the interview. "I cannot bear to listen to the constant replay of what happened to me and my family. But I did recognize the face of the John Doe 2 sketch."

"I understand," I replied. Her frail state of health was evidenced by multiple burn scars which marred her tiny arms and neckline.

"My memory is completely gone when it comes to the amputation, but I do remember what happened right before the explosion," she assured me.

"What did you see?"

"I was standing in the building, and I was looking out the window of the Social Security office. I saw the Ryder truck, and I saw the man get out of the Ryder truck."

"Can you describe him?"

"He had an olive complexion, and he had black, curly hair. He was wearing a baseball cap, but his curls were sticking out from his head. It was short in the back, but you could still see the curls in his hair."

"Was he American?"

"No, he was not American," she stressed. "He was foreign. You could tell by his skin and his face, the way his face was." Daina then recounted the suspect's erratic behavior as he crossed the sidewalk and walked behind the Ryder truck.

"He was acting very paranoid. His head moved around very fast. He was looking around like somebody was after him."

I motioned the photographer who was recording our interview to capture a wide angle shot of Daina as she perused the photo lineup of the Middle Eastern men. "Please take your time as you look over these pictures," I instructed.

Her hands trembled slightly as she flipped the pages. After several interminable minutes of quiet concentration, the witness froze. Terror flooded her expressive ebony eyes.

"It was him," Daina proclaimed as she traced her finger around the face of Hussain Al-Hussaini. "The man I saw get out of the truck looked like him."

The enormity of the moment shook me. "Can you describe the similarities?" I asked.

"He has the same olive complexion and same curly black hair. And the same features on his face," Daina quivered.

"Would you testify to that under oath before a grand jury?"

"Yes, I would."

## STAR WITNESS

At 9:02 A.M., the earth heaved and spewed forth a concussive wave that instantly disintegrated the façade of windows that lined the east side of Johnny's Tire store. Jesse Pearce had just entered a rear storeroom that shielded him from the maelstrom of flying glass. He emerged to shrieks of terror. The collapsed ceiling had temporarily entombed a female customer who was frenetically clawing for pockets of air. After rescuing the trapped woman, he dashed downtown to investigate. A Native American man writhed in pain on the sidewalk in front of Jesse. Streaming blood turned his silver-white mane of hair crimson red. The immense force of the explosion had catapulted the mortally wounded man through his office window.

Adrenaline impelled Jesse closer to ground zero. "What happened?" he shouted to a policeman standing in his path.

Snapping the restraints of professional protocol, the traumatized officer bared his humanity. "How the f— should I know?" he bellowed.

The shocked onlooker continued to gravitate toward the epicenter of destruction. Two blocks later, he stopped in breathless horror. A stone rolled over Jesse's heart as he witnessed the life's blood drain from a woman's severed carotid artery. Panic-stricken friends and paramedics tried in vain to plug the fatal gash.

That evening, Jesse drifted into restless sleep, lulled into unconsciousness by the perpetual drone of around-the-clock television coverage. Shortly after daybreak, he was awakened to the latest news bulletins broadcast by ABC's *Good Morning America.*

"As we mentioned, it was a minivan apparently packed with explosives in which the charge was set. The minivan exploded, blew up outside the building, and that's what caused the damage," anchorman Charlie Gibson reported. Hours later, law enforcement corrected the record, publicly stating that a Ryder truck, not a minivan, carried the deadly cargo.

"A Ryder truck!" Jesse exclaimed.

Coworker Brent Martin stiffened. "Unbelievable," he gasped.

The news report struck the men with the force of a fist, dropping their collective jaws. The pair had been boarding up the bomb-ravaged tire store at the time. The presence of death was inescapable. A steady stream of ambulances delivered corpses to the triage unit across the street which served as a processing center for recovered bodies.

"This can't be a coincidence. The building exploded about twenty minutes after those guys in the Ryder truck asked for directions to 5$^{th}$ and Harvey," Jesse recounted as he jotted down the hot-line number for tips. He picked up the receiver and dialed.

The gravity of the moment did not sink in until he heard himself tell the dispatcher, "I believe I may know something that could help you find the people who blew up the Murrah Building. There was a Ryder truck at my place of business yesterday."

The call triggered an instantaneous response. In less than ten minutes, law enforcement swarmed the parking lot of Johnny's Tire Store. Agents from the U.S. Marshals, ATF, FBI, and Oklahoma City police descended upon the two rattled witnesses. John Elvig, an FBI agent headquartered out of Denver, Colorado, took charge of the questioning. For the next thirty minutes, investigators debriefed Jesse and Brent separately, as they scavenged the witnesses' memories to recreate a mental picture of the two Oklahoma City bombers. Brent viewed the Ryder truck through the lobby window of the store, making it impossible to provide a physical description of the vehicle's occupants. However, he corroborated Jesse's story confirming that he, too, witnessed the presence of two men inside the cab.

The Bureau had already traced the axle of the Ryder truck to a rental business in Junction City, Kansas. Jesse's description of the fair-haired driver overlapped with the customer depicted by the owner and employees at Eldon Elliott's body shop. Without a doubt, the government had found their star witness, Jesse Pearce.

On the morning of April 21, the phone roused Jesse and his pregnant wife from sleep.

"Jesse, we have a man in custody that could be the bomber," a robust baritone voice reverberated in his ear. "We're asking you to refrain from watching TV today. If you viewed the suspect prematurely, that would taint your recollection."

"I understand, sir," the former Navy petty officer obediently pledged.

"Be available tomorrow to view a live lineup at the county jail," the FBI agent ordered.

"Yes, sir," he respectfully complied.

Twenty-four hours later, on the evening of April 22, an entourage of federal officials whisked Jesse into the bowels of the Oklahoma County Jail. An expansive two-way mirror separated the witness from a lineup of several men staring straight ahead. Jesse's marine blue eyes scanned the row of nondescript faces. Each subject bore an extraordinary likeness to the fair-haired Timothy McVeigh with a fresh crew cut, tall, lean physique, and discernible military bearing. Soldiers from the nearby army base at Fort Sill, Oklahoma, were chosen for the lineup because of their tightly cropped haircuts. Jesse's gaze fixated on two men in the formation.

"These guys look almost identical. They could be twins," Jesse pondered silently while searching for subtle differences. He had a gut instinct that one of the two was definitely the driver of the Ryder truck.

"These two guys resemble the man who asked for directions to the federal building," he affirmed aloud. "But I'm leaning toward this one in particular. Now that guy definitely looks the same."

The official FBI record of Jesse's identification reflected that the suspect he favored was, in fact, Timothy McVeigh.

The next few days became a frenzied haze of back-to-back interviews with the chief FBI investigators and members of the newly-appointed U.S. prosecution team. The exhaustive questioning focused on harvesting a fertile imprint of McVeigh's accomplice from Jesse's recollection. In late April, the FBI issued a second composite sketch of the suspect donning a ball cap largely due to the tire salesman's testimony. Repeatedly reliving the encounter with McVeigh's companion permanently painted the stoic stranger on the canvas of Jesse's mind—a mental illustration of the third terrorist that government whitewash artists would hope to erase from the public consciousness.

## DRAWING THE MYSTERY JOGGER

Joan Whitley's position as an elected official and highly-placed government connections earned her jogging partners, Mike Benton and Cindy Preston, an immediate audience with federal agents. Mike worked side-by-side with an FBI sketch artist to transfer to paper the freshly inked memory of the haunting stranger. The one-and-one-half-inch halo of ebony curls, coarse olive skin, thick brow, and black, ethnic eyes dominated the portrait of the suspected terrorist. But the drawing would vanish, never to be disclosed to the defense teams.

"I've slept a few nights since the bombing," Mike Benton reminded me before skimming through the photos of Dr. Abdul's Iraqi employees. However, he opined that drafting the FBI drawing engraved a permanent mental image of the breathless jogger. Sitting in a posh downtown office suite, surrounded by snapshots of Mike with high profile politicians, I awaited his answer.

"I believe this is the man I saw," Mike casually asserted while holding a close-up photograph of Hussain Al-Hussaini.

"Can you rate your confidence in your identification of this man on a scale of one to ten?" I asked.

"I would give it an eight or a ten," he averred with businesslike poise and confidence.

That same afternoon, I drove to the upscale business district of Edmond to visit with the second witness, Cindy Preston.

"I looked at his face as he walked by. He came close enough for me to notice his ruddy complexion which I believe had an olive tone," Cindy recalled. "For some reason, the man looked a bit nervous to me. His behavior was odd. It appeared like he was making a trial run from point A to point B," she added as she examined a photo lineup of the Middle Eastern subjects.

The striking blonde with platinum curls patiently studied the sea of faces strewn across her desk. The pictures of Hussain Al-Hussaini elicited a grave expression. After pensive reflection, she pointed to the grainy surveillance photo and declared, "It is highly possible he is the strange man I saw that morning. But I cannot discern from this picture if he has a pitted complexion." This poignant clue would later be confirmed to me face-to-face with the Iraqi soldier himself.

## HAUNTING MEMORIES

For the next three weeks, the reluctant witness shut out the voice inside his head coaxing him to come forward. Lance Carmichael justified his silence with every conceivable excuse. Finally, he could no longer suppress the haunting images of what transpired outside the downtown post office moments before terrorists sabotaged an American federal building. He had seen the Ryder truck, the Oklahoma City bomber, and without a doubt, Timothy McVeigh was not alone. May 11 marked the turning point when Lance pulled off his motorcycle helmet to find a sharp object protruding from the front tire of his bike. A law enforcement pin was embedded in the tread. The guilt-ridden laborer interpreted the discovery as a serendipitous sign to call the FBI.

Agents eagerly recorded the intricate details of his brush with Timothy McVeigh, the disheveled stranger with whom he was conversing at the rear of the Ryder truck, and the stoic passenger sitting inside the cab. After several follow-up interviews and a meeting with a female prosecutor, Lance assumed he would deliver his testimony to the federal grand jury. But that was not to be. Disillusionment engulfed Lance as he watched the June 14 FBI press conference announcing the Todd Bunting snafu, which in actuality, was a cleverly delivered sleight of hand.

"How can they simply erase a mass murderer from existence?" the witness wondered in stunned amazement. The indignant Oklahoman reached out to me to vent his frustration. A microphone to the world offered his only hope to refute the lie.

"I just wanted the victims' families to know that it was not just McVeigh that was involved in this, because I sat there and I saw McVeigh was with another person. The guy was in the Ryder truck," Lance Carmichael stalwartly proclaimed. His televised interview with me was featured in silhouette to ensure his family's safety.

## RESURRECTING THE DEAD

As the August deadline approached for the federal grand jury to hand down the criminal indictment of McVeigh and Nichols, KFOR-TV riveted Oklahomans with exclusive stories resurrecting the corpse of John Doe 2. Jesse Pearce, the witness who directed McVeigh to the federal building from Johnny's Tire Store, stole center stage in our trailblazing coverage.

"Do you have any doubt that you were speaking to Timothy McVeigh the morning of the bombing?" I asked Jesse as the camera zoomed closer.

"No," he answered.

"Do you have any doubt that there was a passenger in the Ryder truck?"

The witness nervously lifted his ball cap as the morning rays washed over his sun-bronzed face. "That's even more certain. I have no doubt. There definitely was a second person. No matter what, I know that there were two people in that vehicle."

Jesse's television debut on Channel 4 thrust the small-town boy from America's heartland into the national spotlight. He exuded a refreshing blend of sincerity and naiveté that earned the confidence of the establishment media including CNN, the *New York Times*, *Denver Post*, *Boston Herald*, and the Associated Press. But inquiring reporters did not know that Jesse had identified Hussain Al-Hussaini as Timothy McVeigh's silent passenger. Because our station disclosed Jesse's face and name, I suggested the most earth-shattering portion of the witness's testimony remain confidential as a precautionary measure.

"That man is very close to the gentleman I saw," Jesse commented after selecting Hussain Al-Hussaini from a photographic lineup.

"Are you saying this individual could be the same man who accompanied McVeigh the morning of April 19 to this tire store?" I queried.

He flashed me a concerned expression, then examined the photo again. "That could very possibly be him," he said somberly. "I didn't get to look at his eyes, but from the profile, which I see right here in this photograph. That could have been the gentleman sitting right next to McVeigh."

I pressed the witness to quantify his level of certainty. "Would you testify to this identification before a grand jury?"

"Oh yes, I would. There would be no doubt in my mind," Jesse vowed. "I'm saying that this gentleman is very close to the person I remember."

He then enumerated the striking similarities between the Ryder truck passenger and Hussain Al-Hussaini, such as an olive complexion, dark hair, light beard growth shadowing the chin and jaw line, and most memorable was the man's uniquely Middle Eastern facial structure.

## "OTHERS UNKNOWN"

Within a matter of weeks, the government's initial fervor over the tire salesman's testimony had plummeted into tepid ambivalence. Phone calls from federal investigators inexplicably stopped. The grand jury summons never arrived. But nonetheless, Jesse's voice resonated with several grand jurors who watched the Channel 4 broadcast of his interview, a perishable television appearance which left an enduring impression. Three days later, on August 10, the panel acknowledged a wider web of intrigue, charging that the bombing defendants acted with "others unknown"—two explosive words that would reshape history. Like flying shrapnel, the phrase "others unknown" shredded the heart of the government's case. Its lifeblood was the theory that Timothy McVeigh single-handedly designed, delivered, and detonated the bomb.

"The indictment alleges that there are unknown coconspirators,"

Assistant U.S. Attorney Joseph Hartzler sheepishly conceded while offering a compulsory, halfhearted pledge to continue the investigation. "Obviously, by implication of the indictment, the grand jury found probable cause to believe that there are others who were involved."

One of those grand jurors confided to me that Jesse Pearce's credibility persuaded his colleagues to recognize a more complex network of participants. On the evening of October 26, 1995, Hoppy Heidelberg caused the best laid plans of the Justice Department to go awry by granting me a tell-all interview on KFOR-TV. The story sent a shock wave through the wire services. For the next twenty-four hours, Channel 4 held the nationwide exclusive with the man who teetered on the legal edge of violating the grand juror's oath of secrecy.

"John Doe 2 is an important player here, and we need to know more about him," Heidelberg said. The Oklahoma horse breeder ruffled influential feathers when lodging a blistering allegation of prosecutorial misconduct in a letter to the federal judge overseeing the grand jury. "The families of the victims deserve to know who all was involved in the bombing, and there appears to be an attempt to protect the identity of certain suspects, namely John Doe 2," he wrote.

The dogged, silver-haired Heidelberg scoffed at the FBI's belief that Fort Riley private Todd Bunting, who patronized the Ryder rental office the day after Timothy McVeigh, had been erroneously identified as a terrorist. He told me privately the photograph of the round-faced, guileless soldier, juxtaposed with the drawing of the menacing suspect, elicited sneers of disbelief from a few of his fellow grand jurors.

"I've seen the photograph of the Fort Riley private, and he bears no resemblance whatsoever to the police sketch of John Doe 2. So I don't believe it," he declared.

"Why don't you consider it plausible that this could be a colossal mix-up?" I asked.

He snickered. "Well, if I were going to perpetrate such a hoax, I would have picked someone who looked more like John Doe 2."

His outburst of anxious laughter belied the seriousness of the charges. The nonconformist juror was unceremoniously dismissed from the panel after presenting a list of witnesses to the judge from whom the grand jury had yet to hear. Each name represented an unwitting bystander who had fortuitously crossed paths with the prospective bomber. Excising this category of testimony rendered it virtually impossible to place Timothy McVeigh at the scene of the crime.

William Dunlap, a passing motorist who sped by the Murrah Building as 9:02 A.M. drew near, reportedly spotted McVeigh as he descended from the Ryder truck. However, Dunlap's statement complicated matters. The witness described a man three to four inches shorter than the American terrorist, and he wavered when asked how confident he was about the identification. Prosecutors scratched the Oklahoma City man from the subpoena list shortly before McVeigh's trial. All other witnesses who observed the bombing defendant within the vicinity of the federal complex saw him in the company of one to three more accomplices. On April 19, providence inducted Jesse Pearce, Lance Carmichael, Daina Bradley, Jerry Nance, Dan Nelson, and Rachel Sealy into that unwanted clique of ordinary citizens who not only beheld the extraordinary, but held the keys to a legitimate indictment of McVeigh's omnipresent accomplice, John Doe 2.

## RECOVERING MCVEIGH'S MISSING PLATE

Inside the crowded courtroom, reporters devoured every morsel of evidence. On the afternoon of April 27, FBI Agent Jon Hersley held the judge's rapt attention as he reenacted the execution of a terrorist's cruel fury and last minute escape through the eyes of Oklahoma City witnesses. Did the government have probable cause to bind over their lead suspect for trial? Jerry Nance had observed a pivotal stage in the bombing plot like the salesman from Johnny's Tire Company, Jesse Pearce. He identified McVeigh as the man driving the Mercury Marquis. Agent Hersley quoted both Jerry and Jesse extensively during the detention hearing of Timothy McVeigh.

The FBI rested comfortably upon Jerry's reliability. Was the Bureau's confidence instinctive or the result of good detective work? The forty–year-old father had provided a clue only a genuine bystander could have known. He described in detail the Mercury Marquis that McVeigh was driving when he was arrested the day of the blast. Jerry Nance's credibility was greatly enhanced by the simple fact that he disclosed his intimate knowledge of the bomber's car before the media broadcast video of the abandoned vehicle. Jerry also independently corroborated Lance Carmichael's recollection of a Marquis layered with thick dust. By the time law enforcement towed McVeigh's car from the shoulder of Interstate 35, torrential spring downpours had washed it clean. Understandably, Jerry's proven trustworthiness enhanced the Bureau's confidence in the witness's sighting of a second man seated at McVeigh's side, prompting initial reports that the Oklahoma City terrorist dropped off his dark-haired accomplice before his traffic arrest near Perry, Oklahoma.

One more tantalizing detail electrified me as I read Jerry Nance's sealed FBI 302. The witness remembered the Marquis's unsecured license tag bore the numbers 119, 116, or 118—a much-desired puzzle piece that snapped perfectly into place. Jerry's fragmented recollection essentially ended the FBI's exhaustive, yet futile hunt for McVeigh's missing license tag. Deductive reasoning led me to believe a KFOR-TV viewer had recovered that very plate.

The historic find surfaced in September 1995 when I produced an investigative story retracing the movements of the Ryder truck from 8:30 A.M. through the fatal nine o'clock hour. With exacting illustrative skill, the KFOR-TV computer graphic artist recreated its deadly trek to 5$^{th}$ and Harvey Streets, bringing to life a visual replay of that calamitous morning through the eyes of the witnesses. The pictorial reenactment highlighted the Mercury Marquis tearing out of the *Journal Record* parking lot with a white license tag swinging precariously by one bolt. That very scene struck a familiar chord with an Oklahoma City viewer.

Betsy Travis worked at a manufacturing plant in Oklahoma City's industrial park, located east of the Interstate 235 service road, the main artery out of town taken by the fleeing terrorist and his dark-haired passenger. The first exit off the highway was NW 23$^{rd}$ Street, located just a few blocks south of Betsy's company headquarters, where a displaced license plate was discovered in the bombing aftermath. On the morning of April 21, Betsy walked onto the loading dock to discover the mysterious tag wedged under the front tires of a stationary semi truck trailer. The witness called the Oklahoma City police who, in turn, referred her to the FBI. However, investigators did not follow up on the tip. She assumed the FBI was uninterested because the media had reported federal officials were searching for a maroon Arizona tag which they suspected McVeigh discarded during his frantic dash from Oklahoma City. The license tag which was recovered on Betsy's company premises was a white Arkansas plate bearing the numbers 811.

Despite the FBI press releases targeting a dark colored plate, Jerry Nance insisted he saw a white tag bearing the numbers 116, 119, or 118. He shared this information with the FBI on April 21, the day McVeigh emerged in shackles from the Noble County Jail. I drew the numbers 811 on my notepad, then sketched how the digits would appear to Jerry Nance if the plate made a complete pendulum swing to the right. There it was. The numbers were reversed, transforming 811 into 118. If the parking lot witness nailed this crucial detail, then he had to be dead on about the second man in McVeigh's car.

"Who owns this plate?" I pondered as I grasped the metal tag in my hands. Two law enforcement sources ran a trace on the license tag's ownership. They delivered the same baffling discovery independently of each other. The Arkansas Department of Motor Vehicles had no record of issuing that particular plate. Both police detectives were stumped. If the plate had been stolen, it would have been listed in the massive database of the National Crime Information Computer until it had been recovered. All the more intrigued, I reached out to a source with a direct channel into the Oklahoma Bomb Task Force.

Within twenty-four hours, the surreptitious computer check on the plate's origins prompted a hostile call from the FBI to my friend inquiring why he was interested in the Arkansas tag bearing the numbers 811. Caught off guard by the agent's overt agitation, he cordially volunteered he was doing a favor for a local reporter.

"Are you referring to reporter Jayna Davis of KFOR-TV?" the federal agent barked.

"Yes, sir," my friend replied. "I did not intend to stir up any trouble. It is my understanding that tracing the ownership of license plates is perfectly legal."

The official did not disclose the reason for his protest, then brusquely cut off the conversation. I could infer from the unnamed agent's temperamental flare up that I had hit a nerve.

My news director, Melissa Klinzing, suggested we track the plate number through a separate database not used by law enforcement. We discovered it had been issued to a grocery store manager living in Fort Smith, Arkansas. Phillip Douglas told me the tag had been stolen from his daughter's car at a local apartment complex in early April. The witness said he reported the theft to the police, but he was unaware the plate had been recovered from an industrial park in Oklahoma City. When I phoned Douglas a few weeks later to check the status of his stolen plate, he demurely requested I not contact him again.

"The FBI visited me after your call and instructed me to refrain from speaking to you or any reporters about the plate. I agreed to honor the request," he said. Obviously, the witness was a patriotic, law-abiding citizen who was intimidated into quiet submission by persuasive federal agents.

I laughed as I hung up the phone. I was the proverbial speed boat launching on a moment's notice. If I found a fresh lead, I simply ran it down, made an on-the-spot judgment, put it on the air or discarded it. In sharp contrast, the FBI was a bureaucratic, lumbering ocean liner, rigidly hamstrung by inefficiencies and compartmentalization. Central command had missed Betsy Travis's report on April 21, five months prior to my stumbling upon the plate. Understandably, the tip was brushed aside as insignificant amidst a surfeit of leads pouring into the agency. In an ironic twist, a local television station would hand the FBI what was likely one of the most coveted pieces of evidence in the doomsday catastrophe of April 19.

## "You've got the plate!"

I briefed Melissa on the Bureau's bumbling antics, clamping down on the owner of the plate and the source who attempted to trace its origins.

"Maybe we're on to something big," she speculated. "Regardless, I suppose it's our duty to give the license tag to the FBI."

I cringed at the suggestion. "For some arcane reason, the FBI has been trying to shut down this lead through back channels. But do you actually expect agents to walk into this television newsroom and retrieve the tag? That's not going to happen." I sardonically predicted.

"We'll see," Melissa smiled, countering my defeatism with her typical zest and optimism. As it turned out, I was wrong.

That evening, Melissa phoned FBI Special Agent Dan Vogel and related the odd chain of events that led Channel 4 to the discarded license plate.

Agent Vogel seemed unimpressed. "What's the number of the tag?" he inquired in a flat tone. After Melissa read off the numbers, the agent promised to check into the matter and report back whether or not the FBI was interested in taking custody of the tag.

Minutes later, the phone buzzed on Melissa's desk.

"Hello," she answered.

"Could you repeat the numbers on the license plate?" Agent Vogel requested. Melissa complied. An unexplained hush lingered in the air.

"Where is the plate?" Agent Vogel asked.

"Well, I'm holding it at this very moment. It's right here on my desk."

Agent Vogel reacted with uncharacteristic surprise. "You've got the plate!" he said exuberantly. He wasted no time coming to the Channel 4 studio to personally take official custody of the mysterious plate. Upon his prompt arrival, he requested I give a detailed statement about who had touched it.

"It would be a lot simpler to list everyone in the newsroom who has not touched it," I quipped. The plate had passed through so many hands, I seriously doubted if latent prints from criminal suspects would have been preserved. In any case, the likelihood of the FBI performing due diligence to retrieve evidence from the license tag was remote.

Despite the Justice Department's public posturing, billing the Oklahoma bomb case as the most comprehensive federal investigation in history, it had failed to perform perfunctory tests to seek matches for more than one thousand fingerprints lifted from motel rooms, documents, the Ryder rental business, and other key areas. If the FBI did, in fact, recover an imprint from the Middle Eastern male Jerry Nance saw riding inside the Mercury Marquis during McVeigh's last minute flight, the findings would remain sealed. And if so, did the same unidentified terrorist remove the stolen Arkansas tag bearing the numbers 811 while beguiling his cohort into believing he was tightening a few loose screws? The forensic clues entombed in the FBI files wield the power to demystify the conundrum. Had the demented, self-professed patriot assumed the role of the perfect dupe who was utterly oblivious to the absence of a license tag as he fled his crime of mass murder—set up to take the fall?

The government dismissed the missing plate as the heartland terrorist's sloppiness. Therein lay yet another contradiction. The twenty-seven-year-old survivalist who carelessly forgot to secure his license tag purportedly possessed the cunning to mastermind a flawlessly executed attack. Eventually, the FBI jettisoned Jerry's sighting of two bombers fleeing together, instead opting for a theory that disintegrated under scrutiny, like a sand castle submerged in the rising tide.

The hypothesis went like this: Timothy McVeigh bragged to Michael Fortier while casing out the target in December 1994 that he planned to place his getaway car a few skips away in the alley behind the YMCA building. He allegedly parked the Mercury Marquis in the designated spot three days before the bombing and propped up a cardboard placard which read, "Do Not Tow." With James Bond panache, the adrenaline-pumped bomber then supposedly sprinted from the Murrah Building to his waiting transportation. He then flamboyantly tossed the key to the Ryder truck out the window as he gassed the engine toward freedom.

The defense assailed the government for "massaging" Fortier's testimony to conveniently bridge any chasm in their premise that a lone executioner carried out the April 19 slaughter. Investigators could not produce even one witness who came across the memorable yellow car stashed behind the

YMCA. While squirming under the prosecutor's vise, Michael Fortier filled in the blank. One can only conjecture that the witness's sudden recall earned brownie points in his quest for a reduced sentence.

To buttress McVeigh's purported claim about the location of the getaway car, the prosecution provided the key to the Ryder truck ignition that was photographed in the debris that littered the YMCA alleyway. There it was, the very key, which had survived the blast in pristine condition, without a trace of fingerprints. Evidently, Timothy McVeigh, composed enough to wipe any vestige of his prints from the key, lacked the presence of mind to ensure his plate was firmly attached.

## LEGAL CATCH-22

Cruel circumstance would test the young woman left motherless and childless from a savage act of terrorism once more. Daina was subpoenaed to testify on behalf of the man who slaughtered her family, Timothy McVeigh. As a brilliant tactician, the bomber's lawyer, Stephen Jones, capitalized on the victim's sighting of the elusive John Doe 2. But a week before taking the stand, Daina torpedoed the defense's strategy when she revealed she saw a second man who resembled McVeigh exiting the driver's side of the cab. Yet remarkably, the dramatic alteration to her original FBI statement did not dissuade the defense from calling her to the witness box.

On May 23, 1997, the tenacious twenty-two-year-old limped on her prosthetic leg into the Denver courtroom to endure with grace verbal blows from both the prosecution and defense. Neither side could risk the jury interpreting her recollection of April 19 as undisputed truth. The suggestion that McVeigh merely acted as a mule who delivered the lethal payload hardly mitigated his guilt. On the other hand, the rebirth of John Doe 2 presented labor pains for federal prosecutors propagating the government-sanctioned scenario that a lone bomber placed and detonated the bomb. Assistant U.S. Attorney Patrick Ryan unleashed an iniquitous assault upon Daina's character. Ryan ripped open her turbulent childhood in which she spent the majority of her formative years institutionalized by the state. The broken young woman had confided to me that parental abuse compelled authorities to take her from her home. Abandoned by her father and separated from her mother, the lonely teenager abused drugs to soothe the aching cavity of rejection.

On April 18, 1995, while cradling her three-month-old son Gabreon, Daina resolved to reconcile rebellion with forgiveness. That afternoon, she reunited with her mother Cheryl, who suggested a trip the next morning to the federal building to obtain her new grandson's Social Security card. Did Daina's dark past shade her perception of the events of April 19? It stretches one's imagination to conceive that a traumatized girl, submerged in freezing water, pinned under fractured concrete, and grappling with the inevitability of losing a limb to ensure her very survival, could have fabricated seeing the dark figure descend from a Ryder truck moments before detonation.

# CHAPTER 11

# FBI EVIDENCE DUMPING

The moment the key entered the front doorknob on the evening of April 25, the tiny west highland terrier's tail spun like a helicopter anticipating the long awaited arrival of her mistress. Virginia King entered the foyer, greeted by a complimentary face washing from her beloved dog Sandy. The overworked middle school teacher grabbed the leash and knelt down to grasp the collar of the frolicking bundle of white fur. Sandy intuitively discerned that in a household with a popular high school boy engrossed in senior year activities, the grown-ups offered the only hope of scoring an afternoon stroll.

"Come on, girl. Let's go," Virginia coaxed as the terrier flounced out the door and charged directly to her favorite haunt. As Sandy explored the secluded area of the northwest Oklahoma City apartment complex where tenants parked their boats and recreational vehicles, a mustard yellow truck pulled in.

"What a hideous, unsightly shade of yellow!" Virginia grimaced. Her eyes tracked the full-size pickup as it moved back and forth until the tailgate angled in squarely against the bordering security fence. After the vehicle parked, Virginia glanced down to monitor Sandy's inquisitive exploration of the property shrubbery. After a few minutes, the fifty-year-old educator felt a surge of uneasiness. The driver turned off the engine but did not exit the truck. She slowly turned to find the stranger's cavernous, onyx eyes staring directly at her, seething with hatred.

The startled woman suppressed an uncontrollable urge to shout aloud, "Who are you?" For ten paralyzing seconds, she gazed at his face. The unwelcome visitor to her neighborhood appeared foreign, most likely Middle Eastern. Shortly cropped raven waves framed his smooth olive skin which blended with the desert sand T-shirt stretched tightly across his broad, muscular shoulders.

His threatening glare transmitted the unspoken message, "Get out and forget what you've seen." Virginia yanked on Sandy's chain and darted across the freshly mowed lawn toward her apartment, her eyes trained on the front door. She dared not look back.

## FBI SEIZES ABANDONED PICKUP

Forty-eight hours later, a security officer inspecting the grounds at Virginia's apartment complex spotted an unfamiliar pickup blocking the dead-end turnaround in the southwest parking lot. Nicholas Migliorato quickly deduced the deserted truck had been stolen, hastily painted, and dumped. An over spray of yellow paint coated the bumpers, tires, and windshield wiper arms. The tailgate, license tag, inspection stickers, molding, and body accents had been stripped. Nicholas lifted the hood to discover brown was the original color of the eighties model, full-size truck which displayed Chevrolet Silverado logos. The guard diligently inspected the engine, dashboard, and doors, searching for a vehicle identification number but to no avail.

Bewildered by the suspicious vehicle, Nicholas contacted the Oklahoma City police. After confirming the make and model of the brown Chevy pickup, the responding officer, Sean Shropshire, alerted the FBI. The abandoned pickup matched the Teletype for a getaway truck that carried Middle Eastern suspects from the bomb site. Without delay, a Bureau supervisor ordered the truck to be impounded. A squad of forensic technicians immediately began processing it for latent fingerprints. But the experts would soon learn this was no garden variety auto theft. The party who pilfered the brown truck had exercised criminal forethought in a painstaking effort to erase any evidence trail.

## CANVASSING FOR WITNESSES

A loud rapping sound startled Joe King as he slipped his key into the ignition. He rolled down his car window to a man in a dark blue windbreaker bearing the bright yellow initials F-B-I. The Bureau had dispatched agents to canvass the apartment complex to find residents who saw the yellow truck on the property.

"Good morning, sir," a youthful looking case agent energetically greeted him as he flashed a laminated identification badge. "If you don't mind, I need to ask you a few questions."

Joe stepped out of the car. Although the forty-nine-year-old salesman was caught off guard by the unexplained presence of a federal officer, Joe's imposing six foot stature and silver white hair exuded equanimity.

"Have you seen this yellow pickup?" the agent inquired as he flipped out a dossier of large glossy photographs.

The witness became circumspect, searching his memory before delivering a measured response. "I do recall a similar ugly yellow truck on the property, but the truck in this picture has a gray tint that does not look familiar." The agent explained that the fingerprint dust used during processing shaded the side panels and cab of the truck with a dark film. The officer's explanation for the slight color difference persuaded Joe to solidly confirm his earlier sighting of the vehicle.

"Where did you see the truck?" the investigator excitedly asked.

"Well, I recall I passed it while driving through the parking lot around April 20. And I believe I saw it again a week later in the rear parking area where residents store their boats."

"How was it parked?"

"It was backed up against the fence over there," Joe said as he pointed to the location.

The agent then introduced himself as FBI Special Agent Jim Ellis from the Dallas FBI headquarters and presented his credentials again.

"Has anybody else in your family observed this truck recently?" he queried.

"Nobody said anything to me," Joe responded, "But my seventeen-year-old son, who is really observant about cars will be home any moment now. If you would like, you can ask him."

Agent Ellis agreed and trailed a few steps behind Joe's lengthy stride toward his apartment. The phone was ringing when he opened the door. It was his wife Virginia calling from work.

"Hello, honey, I'm here speaking to the FBI about an abandoned yellow truck. Did you happen to see that truck parked in the area where we walk Sandy?" he asked.

"How could anyone miss that horrid yellow pickup?" she answered. "I watched the driver pull in. He looked Middle Eastern with a clean shaven, olive complexion. He glared at me in a way that scared the hell out of me."

Upon learning what Virginia had witnessed, Agent Ellis set an appointment to conduct a personal interview. After hanging up the phone, it occurred to Joe that the Bureau would not have dedicated resources from the Dallas FBI office to investigate an auto theft ring in Oklahoma. Before making a career change, he spent ten years as a licensed private investigator, and now his professional instincts detected something much bigger on the law enforcement radar screen.

"Does this truck have anything to do with what happened downtown?" he probed.

"Oh, you mean the bombing," the agent replied.

Joe laughed. "I don't know of anything else that earth-shattering happening in Oklahoma City lately."

The question awakened a sense of somberness which supplanted the agent's naturally buoyant attitude. "Do you remember the all-points bulletin issued on April 19 for two Middle Eastern males speeding away from the Murrah Building in a brown Chevrolet pickup?" he asked emphatically.

"Yeah, I remember," Joe nodded with a seriousness that acknowledged the agent's change in mood.

"Well, this is the truck."

The unforeseen admission sliced the previously ceremonial conversation like a machete.

"How do you know this is that specific truck? This vehicle is yellow, not brown." Joe pointed out.

The young professional, who appeared to be in his early thirties, looked at Joe with childlike enthusiasm. He opened the folder he held in his hands and neatly laid out the photographs on the dining room table. His finger tapped the right bumper of the vehicle in order to clarify his point.

"You see here, there's an over spray of yellow paint," he spoke authoritatively. "Somebody painted this truck in quite a hurry and stripped the VIN numbers, license tag, and model insignia. That's the reason for all this gray fingerprint dust."

"So you're telling me this is the same brown truck seen speeding away from the Oklahoma City bombing?" Joe clarified.

"Yes," he confirmed.

Joe inconspicuously examined the FBI badge hanging around the agent's neck to insure the credentials had not been forged.

"Is this guy legit?" he wondered. Joe was an old hand when it came to dealing with FBI agents from the years he spent working P.I. jobs. They belonged to an exclusive regent of investigators, robotically programmed to convey no emotion and by no means were they permitted to violate the cardinal rule—never disclose the confidential facts of the case. Agent Jim Ellis stood apart from the pack as an anomaly. Joe would not be completely convinced he was truly an FBI agent until he returned a week later to debrief his wife Virginia. During the interview session, she provided the agent a crudely sketched rendering of the driver's menacing face.

Agent Ellis then presented the photographs of the yellow truck. "Do you recognize this vehicle?" he asked.

"Yes. That's the awful yellow pickup I saw while walking our dog Sandy," she answered. The realization sank in as apprehension consumed her. She had come face-to-face with a terrorist.

"Is the FBI interested in the man who abandoned this pickup because it was the brown truck connected to the attack on the federal building?" she trembled.

"Yes, m'am," he answered unhesitatingly. "As you can see this truck was hastily painted yellow."

"Did you find any fingerprints?" Joe casually interjected.

"We lifted several latent prints that have been sent to Washington for analysis," Agent Ellis freely volunteered.


## DÉJÀ VU

Like a crash of thunder rumbling across cloudless skies, the nightmare of April 25 revisited Virginia King out of nowhere. A few months later in July, while crossing the apartment parking lot with Sandy prancing at her heels, an oxidized compact car with dull primer gray paint peeled across her path. Virginia hesitated. The driver stepped on the brakes and slowed dramatically. The two strangers held an evanescent stare for one heart-stopping moment of recognition.

"It's him! The man in the yellow pickup! Why has he come back?" Virginia thought, terror weakening every limb.

Once again, the stranger's malevolent eyes conveyed the unspoken message, "I know who you are, but you don't know me."

This second encounter greatly enhanced her confidence in her original description of the Middle Eastern suspect who dumped the unforgettable yellow pickup. But the aftershock of the traumatizing instant replay left her tremulous. The unidentified terrorist could return without warning, only next time, her life could be imperiled. Joe and Virginia decided it would be best for her to reside with their daughter out-of-state indefinitely. Before leaving Oklahoma, Virginia reviewed Channel 4's photographs of Hussain Al-Hussaini and his Arab confederates.

"I believe this man looks like the man I saw," she proclaimed. Virginia had singled out an Iraqi employee of Dr. Abdul who began working at Salman Properties with Al-Hussaini in the fall of 1994. He was among the self-professed army deserters whom coworkers witnessed lauding Saddam Hussein upon learning that tiny mangled bodies of children had been recovered from the ashes.

"How comfortable are you with your identification of this Iraqi national as the man who drove the yellow pickup?" I asked.

"I'm very comfortable. I believe that is the man I saw."

In the months that followed, Virginia's hopes that the FBI would arrest foreign suspects dimmed. If she were to return home, the possibility that the face of terror could stalk her once more lurked in perpetuity.


## "Your Truck Was Involved in the Bombing"

Luke Conner decided to capitalize on the unseasonably warm temperatures to pamper his lawn and spread fertilizer before the onset of nourishing spring rains. His wife Lori volunteered to lend a hand. The young newlyweds savored their weekend break from pressing work schedules to indulge in the banality of yard work. However, an unannounced visitor would soon disturb the tranquility of that May afternoon. While hauling out the yard equipment, Luke noticed a stranger approaching.

"Hello, sir," a lively voice shouted from across the street. Luke squinted to see through a blinding glare of sunlight. For several seconds he could only distinguish a dark figure wearing a navy blue windbreaker coming toward him. A stocky, medium framed man in his mid-thirties extended his hand to make an introduction.

"My name is Jim Ellis. I'm a special agent with the FBI Dallas headquarters."

"How can I help you?" the twenty-eight-year-old homeowner gingerly asked.

"Are you Luke Conner?"

"Yes, sir."

"Do you own a pickup that was recently stolen?"

"Yes," he replied. "My truck was stolen from my employer's parking lot on December 5, 1994." Luke reported the theft to the Norman Police Department, but he figured it had been stripped of its parts and sold on the black market during the five month interim. He didn't hold out much hope of recovering it. Without comprehensive insurance coverage, he was obligated to continue paying monthly installments on his car loan, making his loss all the more painful.

"I have some good news and bad news for you. The good news is that we found your pickup. The bad news is that your truck was used in the Murrah Building bombing." Agent Ellis bluntly stated.

Luke and Lori looked at each other, dumbstruck. The agent perceived their collective shock and suggested the couple retreat indoors for further questioning. Upon entering their living room, the doorbell rang. Moments later, Lori ushered in a second FBI agent and an officer with the Oklahoma State Bureau of Investigation. The new arrivals exuded a disparate disposition compared to the genial Agent Ellis. They pummeled Luke with questions about his alibi for the morning of April 19. The "good cop, bad cop" routine was definitely in play. During the nerve-racking interrogation, the factory worker, who deeply cherished his quotidian lifestyle, was treated like a potential mass murderer. Thankfully, the trio rapidly sized up the hard-working family man as a random victim of an historic auto theft.

Once the nervousness from the intense questioning subsided, the shocking reality of Luke's predicament set in. "So my truck was the brown Chevy pickup I heard about on the news, the one that carried those Middle Eastern looking guys from the federal building?"

"Yes, we believe your vehicle was possibly connected to the bombing," the Dallas investigator reiterated with the same firmness with which he had previously assured Virginia and Joe King.

"But I don't get how that's even possible," Luke silently speculated. "My truck is a 1983 GMC High Sierra, not a Chevrolet like the vehicle the FBI was tracking."

Before his conversation with the loquacious Agent Ellis concluded, all doubts had been erased. The men behind the heist employed Herculean tactics to render Luke's truck untraceable. Major portions of the engine must have been disassembled in order to obliterate every Vehicle Identification Number, including the confidential, hidden VINs whose locations were known only to the manufacturer. The High Sierra decals and GMC hood ornament had been removed from the vehicle and replaced with a Chevrolet horn button and Silverado emblems to further obscure its identification.

The final measures of disguise involved a new paint job in a popular brown shade frequently associated with later model Chevrolet pickups, complimented by a smoke-colored bug deflector and dark window tinting. The masterful camouflage would deceive even the most discerning eye. Witnesses to the blinding blur of the speeding brown pickup in the bombing aftermath identified a comparatively new Chevrolet Silverado, not an older model GMC Sierra.

With the April 19 mission complete, the truck became a liability. A clean disposal required swift execution of a flawless plan. The terrorists sprayed the truck with a thin layer of cheap yellow paint, stripped the license tag, inspection stickers, and body molding before discarding it at an Oklahoma City apartment complex. They could have exulted in their flawless execution of their plan had it not been for the observant Virginia King, a close-range witness to the brooding countenance of a key player who was caught in the very act of dumping the fabled pickup.

"If there were no Vehicle Identification Numbers, how did you know that the yellow truck belonged to me?" Luke queried.

Agent Ellis explained how a crumbled piece of paper provided the much needed breakthrough. "We discovered an ATM banking slip lodged underneath the seat which led us to the original owner. He told us he sold the truck to you a few months ago."

The Dallas investigator returned the following afternoon to pick up photographs of Luke's truck which depicted its original two-tone tan and brown paint job.

"What do I owe you for the photocopying costs?" Agent Ellis asked.

Luke grinned. "Don't worry about reimbursing me. I'm just grateful I'm going to get my truck back."

The investigator donned a look of genuine disappointment.

"I'm sorry, but the FBI will be unable to return your truck. When we dusted it for fingerprints we used a process known as 'fuming' which involved the release of super glue fumes."

"Okay, but I still don't understand why you cannot return my vehicle."

"The fuming process rendered the truck inoperable. So the Bureau will reimburse you the blue book value of the pickup."


## Hot Truck, Hot Potato

I would not cross paths with Luke and Lori Conner or discover their ownership of the infamous brown pickup until the distant future. Yet in May

1995, our lives intersected unbeknownst to us all, giving rise to the FBI's most shameful act of incompetence or premeditated evidence dumping. On the evening of May 22, KFOR-TV revisited the early days of the investigation and the vigorous pursuit of the Chevy pickup which transported Middle Eastern passengers. I juxtaposed the frenetic police radio dispatches chasing the fleeing truck with the FBI's oblique denials of ever having issued the all-points bulletin.

"I can't comment on this specific incident," FBI spokesman Weldon Kennedy remarked as he sidestepped a reporter's question about the Teletype targeting foreign suspects in the speeding pickup. That was April 20. One month later, when I inquired about the status of the truck, FBI spokesman Dan Vogel confirmed "it had not been ruled out."

The broadcast apparently spawned a tidal wave which would shift the course of the investigation. The phone rang at the Conner residence.

"Mr. Conner, this is FBI Special Agent James Elliott."

"Yes, what can I do for you?" Luke asked.

"We would like to set up an appointment for the FBI to release your truck to you."

Luke was befuddled. "FBI Agent Jim Ellis informed me your agency would pay the blue book value for the truck because the fuming process used to find physical evidence left it inoperable."

Agent Elliott glossed over the comment. "No, sir. We just dusted for fingerprints, but we will reimburse you for any damage caused while processing the vehicle."

A thick coating of powder dust permanently stained the body of the truck. Luke and Lori gulped when they saw the insipid yellow paint job, but they gasped for breath upon examining the condition of the interior. The FBI tore through the cab with the destructive force of an Oklahoma twister. The steering column, seats, door panels, carpeting, sun visors, and seatbelts were slashed, dismantled, or ripped out. The gas cap and battery were removed. The fuel line and wiring to the alternator were severed. The thoroughness of the search underscored the Bureau's rabid focus on the hot truck. But now the FBI exhibited a pressing desire to drop it from the evidence log like a hot potato.

"FBI Agent Jim Ellis led us to believe this truck was tied to the terrorist hit on the Murrah Building," Luke frankly stated.

"No, we've determined it was not connected," Agent Elliott replied.

"Then does the FBI know who stole my truck?"

"No, sir, we do not," the investigator curtly answered. His body language communicated that the line of questioning made him uncomfortable.

Lori was not intimidated. "We understand the VIN numbers on the engine and frame have been chiseled off."

"Yes, whoever stole your pickup really knew what they were doing. They even removed the VIN numbers that only the manufacturer knows about," he admitted.

"Then I expect the FBI to provide some sort of written proof that we own this truck." Lori countered. "Without verification, how are we going to convince an auto service shop to stamp on a new VIN? We could look like car thieves."

The agent became perturbed. He scribbled a short paragraph on a notepad stating the "GMC pickup had been returned" to the Conners without "a license tag or public VIN." His signature was hardly legible, followed by the letters "FBI."

Lori expressed incredulity. "Don't we need something on official FBI letterhead? Anyone could have written this note, even me."

The federal officer discounted her objection. "You shouldn't have any problem. That should be sufficient." Much to the contrary. Lori's prediction was soon fulfilled. No reputable automotive service center would touch the vehicle. Frustration drove the independent-minded bank supervisor to hammer the FBI for official documentation of ownership. Dogged determination compelled the intransigent bureaucracy to capitulate. The letter was belatedly issued, marking the genesis of a damning paper trail.

## On the Record and Without Excuse

A November 5, 2002, confidential FBI letter addressed to a ranking member of the Senate Intelligence Committee yielded a hidden clue which would burst open the enigmatic hunt for the "brown Chevy pickup." The groundbreaking lead surfaced when Senator Arlen Specter issued an obligatory set of cursory questions about a possible Middle East link to the Oklahoma tragedy as a favor for a popular Philadelphia radio host, Michael Smerconish. The sharp-witted lawyer turned on-air talent became fascinated with my case in the fall of 2002. After examining major portions of the voluminous investigative dossier that I had provided to him, Smerconish invited me to come to Washington to give an ad hoc briefing to the legendary Pennsylvania senator. I opened the unprecedented October 10 radio program with a brief overview of the seven-year investigation.

Flanked by two brilliant, nationally acclaimed terrorism experts with intimate knowledge of the case I had compiled, the one-hour live broadcast from Specter's Washington office electrified the Philadelphia airwaves. The presentation included commentary and insightful answers to the senator's questions from Larry Johnson, a former CIA analyst and deputy director of counterterrorism for the U.S. Department of State, and Colonel Patrick Lang, former chief of human intelligence for the Defense Intelligence Agency, who served as a primary consultant on Iraq during the first Persian Gulf War. Both men expressed their supreme confidence in the veracity of the witnesses and corroborating facts which exposed the Middle East's hand in the April 19 massacre.

Their public endorsement of my credibility was highlighted in the September 5, 2002, *Wall Street Journal* article entitled "The Iraq Connection" by senior editorial writer Micah Morrison. The esteemed newspaper put my story at its zenith in a five-thousand word comprehensive analysis of my evidence and the case developed by Middle East expert and best-selling author Laurie Mylroie. Mylroie, an adjunct fellow at the American Enterprise Institute, chronicled compelling proof of Iraqi state sponsorship of the 1993 World Trade Center attack.

The *Wall Street Journal* dedicated months to the critical examination of every facet of my research. I applauded their profound courage in rejecting the conventional wisdom that Oklahoma City was an act of domestic terrorism to objectively consider the sinister indicators that implicated our country's most menacing adversary, Saddam Hussein. The former director of the Central Intelligence Agency, James Woolsey, told the *Journal*, "When the full stories of these two incidents [1993 WTC bombing and the 1995 Oklahoma City bombing] are finally told, those who permitted the investigations to stop short will owe big explanations to these two brave women. And the nation will owe them a debt of gratitude."

Larry Johnson endorsed the former CIA chief's assessment during his interview with investigative journalist Micah Morrison. "Looking at the Jayna Davis material, what's clear is that more than Timothy McVeigh and Terry Nichols were involved," he posited. "Without a doubt, there's a Middle Eastern tie to the Oklahoma City bombing."

America's oldest and most respected newspaper further propelled the mounting coverage from news outlets across the nation such as *WorldNetDaily*, *NewsMax*, the *Indianapolis Star* with columnist James Patterson, *LA Weekly* with investigative journalist Jim Crogan, *Philadelphia Daily News* with columnist and talk show host Michael Smerconish, the *London Evening Standard*, and *Washington Times* columnist Frank Gaffney, whom President

Ronald Reagan nominated to serve as assistant secretary of defense for International Security Policy. I also garnered national exposure on a variety of network news programs including the top rated Fox News Channel's *O'Reilly Factor, On the Record with Greta Van Susteren, The Big Story with John Gibson, Fox News Live,* and CNN's *Moneyline with Lou Dobbs.*

In August 2002, nationally syndicated radio host Glenn Beck broadcast a two-hour probing interview with me and my attorney, David P. Schippers. The former federal prosecutor soared to national prominence in 1998 as the chief investigative counsel who spearheaded the impeachment trial of former President Bill Clinton. The publicity generated invitations to appear on dozens of radio talk shows in the largest broadcast markets.

After a thorough vetting process, respected journalists from across the country readily accepted the possibility of foreign complicity in the 1995 Murrah Building bombing. The wealth of information supporting such a thesis was presented to Senator Arlen Specter in the form of eighty pages of witness affidavits with twenty-three hundred pages of corroborative documentation. In response, one of Specter's chief investigators, Assistant U.S. Attorney Thomas Swanton, hastily cribbed eight questions for the FBI following a closed-door briefing. An insider with the Pennsylvania congressional delegation leaked to me a copy of the Bureau's written response; otherwise, I would have never known it existed. Specter's decision to deny me the opportunity to address the FBI's paltry six-page rebuttal of my massive investigative file bewildered me. In my opinion, the letter was fraught with inaccuracies, falsehoods, and broad brush dismissals of the evidence, including fabricated statements speciously attributed to KFOR-TV's broadcasts and several critical witnesses. Needless to say, I was not wholly surprised given the Bureau's previous track record in dodging pointed questions that it could not adequately answer. On the other hand, I was deeply disillusioned by Senator Specter's willingness to endorse the obvious whitewash.

On March 19, 2003, as the hostilities commenced in Operation Iraqi Freedom to oust Saddam Hussein, the senior senator announced to talk jock Smerconish on WPHT radio in Philadelphia that the "dots did not connect," referencing my multi-year inquiry. He thanked the FBI profusely for its thoroughness in researching the claims set forth in my investigation, but Specter, a former federal prosecutor, was unable to articulate any specific or credible repudiation of the facts. Once again, the gavel had fallen without my being offered an opportunity to present a defense. The reason for such a blind dismissal eluded me and many outraged Philadelphia listeners who flooded my e-mail box with letters of support. Soon afterwards, a pirated copy of the FBI missive fell into my hands and the mystery behind Specter's conduct unraveled. I realized I had been muzzled for good reason. I could dismantle the FBI's discombobulated "refutation" with both hands tied behind my back.

The author of the correspondence, Eleni Kalisch, the FBI's section chief for governmental relations, impudently conceded that Hussain Al-Hussaini had never been interviewed. Arlen Specter, a lawyer renowned as a preeminent legal mind, neglected to question why the Bureau shirked its lawful duty to interrogate the immigrant about his alibi. The FBI, after all, had corralled hundreds of John Doe look-alikes while pursuing additional conspirators, but it refused to even speak to a man whom a plethora of witness affidavits named as Tim McVeigh's principal accomplice. This decision, which was memorialized in the letter to Congress, left the FBI on the record and without excuse.

After all, the sworn statements in Senator Specter's custody identified the Iraqi soldier in the company of McVeigh prior to the bombing at an Oklahoma City dance club. A gas station attendant fingered him as the customer who paid one hundred and twenty dollars cash to fill up a large Ryder truck with diesel fuel on April 18, 1995. Two witnesses named Hussain Al-Hussaini as the dark-haired, olive-skinned male whom they observed timing his run at top speed from the Murrah Building one block east shortly before daybreak on April 19. He was seen climbing into the cab of a Ryder truck that reeked of diesel fuel at a local motel an hour before the explosion. Witnesses indicated that Timothy McVeigh sat behind the wheel of that truck when it pulled off the lot and headed toward downtown.

Furthermore, Al-Hussaini was positively identified sitting in the passenger seat of the Ryder truck next to McVeigh a few blocks north of the Murrah Building at 8:30 A.M., stepping out of that truck at ground zero directly in front of the federal complex moments before the massive fertilizer bomb exploded, and speeding away from downtown in the brown Chevrolet pickup sought by law enforcement.

Five witnesses independently fingered Hussain Al-Hussaini and several of his Middle Eastern associates as frequent visitors to an Oklahoma City motel in the months, weeks, days, and hours leading up to 9:02 A.M., April 19. On numerous occasions the Arab subjects were seen in the company of Timothy McVeigh, and during a few rare instances, associating with Terry Nichols.

The library of witness testimonies also implicated several of the Iraqi soldier's Arab coworkers. Virginia King identified Al-Hussaini's cohort sitting in the driver's seat of the atrocious yellow pickup hours before it was discovered abandoned on her apartment property and towed to the FBI command post. She saw the same man again weeks later as he drove across her path.

To hear from Specter that the "dots did not connect"—after the overabundance of sworn testimonies from credible witnesses I presented to him, after having invested months communicating with his staff, and after the FBI's sham response I was not intended to see—absolutely infuriated me.

## FBI SLIP-UP

An indelible paper trail made any denial of the FBI's possession of the stolen pickup seem ludicrous. I had provided Specter's staff with copies of the apartment security report and police impound record. In my opinion, FBI Section Chief Eleni Kalisch cautiously parsed references to the purported getaway truck in a calculated effort to diminish its value to investigators. Her memorandum to Senator Specter noted that the Bureau issued an all-points bulletin for the brown Chevy pickup with Middle Eastern suspects on "04/19/1995 at 11:56 A.M." However, Ms. Kalisch claimed "no information was found regarding the cancellation of the APB." Such an assertion would obviously preclude the FBI from having to explain why the search was abandoned within hours of the blast. Moreover, the governmental relations section chief explained the Bureau was "aware that this truck was stolen in Norman, Oklahoma, and a known car thief was the suspect." That statement would turn out to be an FBI slip-up.

Apparently, federal authorities had not thoroughly checked their files before responding to Senator Specter in writing. The "Norman car thief" theory contradicted the government's own official version in sworn testimony before the Oklahoma County Grand Jury during its probe into a wider conspiracy. The panel's final report, which was issued on December 30, 1998, summarized the FBI's reason for vacating the pursuit of the mysterious getaway vehicle occupied by foreign suspects:

After the bombing an APB was issued for a brown pickup truck which was reported speeding away from the vicinity of the Alfred P. Murrah Federal Building. Shortly before 9:00 A.M. on April 19, 1995, an employee of the Journal Record Building received a call that one of her children had become ill at school. She got in her brown pickup, matching the description given on the APB, and left the Journal Record parking lot at a high rate of speed.

Unfortunately, the government's imposing presence swayed grand jurors to abdicate their authority to demand a more convincing explanation. The investigative body's official findings categorically ignored the multiple eyewitness accounts of two heavy-set, swarthy, bearded Middle Eastern males seen sprinting toward the pickup before tearing away from the crime scene. The notion that a single Caucasian woman leaving downtown to pick up her ill child would arouse such a depth of suspicion to be mistaken for a major player in a terrorist bombing is questionable at best, but beyond the pale of any plausibility at worst.

## Unearthing Latent Prints

Exasperated with the stiff resistance from federal law enforcement which skirted my inquiries into the notorious yellow pickup, I enlisted the expertise of investigative reporter Jim Crogan, who broke my story in the *LA Weekly* following the infernal terrorist rage of September 11, 2001. Jim presented Ms. Kalisch's private FBI correspondence to *LA Weekly* editor and chief Laurie Ochoa, and editors Alan Mittlestaedt and Howard Blume. Together, the trio devised a clever approach that cracked the Justice Department's monolithic wall of secrecy.

The detective work was elementary but executed with Jim's "Lt. Columbo" style of interviewing. Like Peter Falk's character in the popular television series, Crogan's genteel way of methodically seeping under the target's skin commonly elicited frustrated confessions of truth.

Crogan's quest began with the Oklahoma City Police Department, the agency that took custody of the yellow truck from a northwest Oklahoma City apartment complex on April 27, 1995. Captain Jeffrey Becker confirmed the police report which stated the FBI requested the abandoned vehicle be impounded and examined for fingerprints. The captain's startling disclosure to the *LA Weekly*, during a July 2003 telephone interview, marked the first public admission that three sets of prints were, in fact, discovered.

"One set of prints was found on the driver's side window, a second on the frame of that window, and the last set was found near the driver's side door handle," Crogan said.

The revelation confirmed Joe King's testimony that FBI Agent Jim Ellis claimed several latent prints found on the yellow truck had been shipped to Washington for analysis. Captain Becker told Crogan the Oklahoma City police also ran the prints through a national database but didn't find a match. Immediately afterwards, the FBI seized the truck.

"They picked it up from us," Captain Becker said during his *LA Weekly* interview. "But we never heard anything about where it was stolen or any mention of a suspect. And we never heard back from the FBI on the prints."

## CONFLICTING FACTS FROM THE FBI

The tenacious Jim Crogan wrested from the FBI seven digits that unbolted a storehouse of hidden clues. It was the case number on Luke Conner's December 1994 police report which documented his 1983 GMC High Sierra truck had been snatched from his company parking lot in Norman, Oklahoma. However, the supplemental file made no reference to a "known car thief" as noted in the FBI memo to Senator Specter. More significantly, the record confirmed that the Norman police developed "no suspect information."

The Conner auto larceny case also included a microfilm rendition of an April 18, 1996, letter from the Norman police seeking to close out the investigation. Records Division employee John Spillmeier requested the owner notify the department if his stolen pickup had been recovered.

"I have never seen this letter. If it was sent, then it was lost in the mail," Luke Conner said with sincere surprise. During the interview, he handed me a file folder spilling over with law enforcement reports and auto repair receipts. The letter from the Norman police was not included. Luke's wife, the copious record keeper, also shook her head in disbelief.

"I kept copies of every document in our case because, without proof, we would have been unable to qualify for a reimbursement for damages to our truck," Lori remarked.

I then presented a record which stated that the July 11, 1995, FBI letter confirming the GMC High Sierra had been returned to his custody was hand-delivered to the Norman Police Department by Luke Conner. The couple looked at the incident report dated May 1, 1996, with stark astonishment.

"I never spoke to the Norman police about my truck after I reported it stolen on December 5, 1994," Luke avowed. "I certainly would have remembered walking into the Norman Police Department and handing a detective the FBI letter. That absolutely did not happen."

"Were you ever informed that the police suspected a known car thief?" I inquired.

"No, I never heard a word about the investigation. The officer, who took my report when the truck was stolen, gave me the distinct impression the chances of solving the case were slim to none. The only thing the thieves left behind was shattered glass from the car window."

## CASE CLOSED

Luke and Lori Conner believed that professional protocol required forensic evidence, which was procured during the FBI's exhaustive probe of their recovered vehicle, be shared with the Norman Police Department. They assumed wrong. The police file revealed that the three sets of prints lifted from the driver's side door and window were not disclosed to the detective assigned to the auto theft investigation.

FBI spokesman Gary Johnson confirmed for *LA Weekly* that the Bureau impounded the truck and found prints, but he insisted none matched those on file with the national criminal database. But what about the prints in the immigration dossier of Hussain Al-Hussaini? Witness Rachel Sealy identified him at the wheel of that truck the day of the bombing. Moreover, why was Virginia King never contacted after the FBI officially closed the case and purportedly remanded it back to the Norman Police Department? She could have provided invaluable assistance in leading investigators to the "known car thief" whom the FBI blamed for stealing and dumping the truck. Once again, the Norman police were never notified, the fingerprints were shelved, and the case turned cold. Why? If the Conners were, indeed, victims of a sophisticated auto theft ring, then why were the witnesses, Rachel and Virginia, ignored, and the suspects they pegged from KFOR-TV's surveillance photographs neither arrested nor fingerprinted?

If the criminals purloined the 1983 short bed truck because the black market carried a hot demand for that particular make and model, then why were the parts not stripped at a chop shop and sold off? Instead, the perpetrators possessed the vehicle for four months after swiping it from a Norman business. They exerted untold energy to eradicate all vehicle identification numbers from the engine and frame, then invested money to repair the defective tire hubs that controlled the 4X4 drive. Finally, the car thieves exercised meticulous care to replace all GMC High Sierra emblems with those of a Chevrolet Silverado.

For no rationale the FBI could articulate, the auto thieves decided to dispose of their plunder without pecuniary gain. Curiously, within seven days of a brutal mass murder downtown, the FBI's suspect, the "known car thief" (an individual law enforcement officials have never identified), yanked the license tag and distinguishing body features, slapped on a rush paint job, and strategically deserted the truck where it would obviously be recovered, sooner or later. Without a doubt, the thugs rested confidently in their handiwork, convinced they had wiped out any hint of their presence. Other than a few "untraceable" prints, they were right. It defies all reason that one would steal this truck for any purpose other than to be used in the commission of a crime. That crime, according to four witnesses who spoke to FBI Special Agent Jim Ellis, was the terrorist bombing of the Alfred P. Murrah Building.

## TWISTED LOGIC

Reporter Jim Crogan set out to pose the unsettling questions swirling about the brown Chevy pickup. The FBI's circular, twisted logic shoveled at me for the previous eight years was disgorged in full strength at the already cynical journalist. The Bureau served up a man-size portion of what I had dubbed the "whatever comes out of our mouth is the truth and you will believe it" routine.

The fastidious investigator began with the reported proclamations attributed to Agent Ellis, but *LA Weekly*'s repeated calls to his office went unanswered. Lori Bailey, the spokesperson for the FBI Dallas headquarters, conceded Ellis was assigned at one time to investigate the bombing.

"We had lots of agents chasing down thousands of leads. But I can assure you that if our headquarters told Specter's office the truck was not involved [in the bombing], it was not involved."

Many journalists would have been intimidated by the façade of authority and accepted the wholesale denunciation of the truck's alleged role in the 1995 terrorist attack. Not Crogan. Ever the skeptic, he pressed Bailey to specify the FBI's rationalization for ruling out the brown Chevy pickup and its foreign occupants.

She was stumped. "I don't have that information here. It would be in our case file in Oklahoma City."

The ball bounced back into the court of the Oklahoma City field office and spokesman Gary Johnson. Agent Johnson underestimated the prudence of the inquiring reporter. The conversation quickly evolved into a game of verbal chess.

"Why did FBI Agent Jim Ellis tell several witnesses he believed the brown truck was involved in the bombing?" Crogan asked.

"I don't know what he said. But if he said that, he was wrong," Agent Johnson retorted. "The Bureau is convinced that everyone who was involved in the bombing has been prosecuted," he said as if he were reading the FBI's pre-approved, canned response.

Unmoved by the agent's token dismissal of the evidence, Crogan posed a logical query which inflamed Johnson's ire. "How did the Bureau determine the truck and its passengers were not involved in the bombing if neither the car thief nor the Middle Eastern looking men were found?"

Johnson's patience was running thin after fielding several minutes of Crogan's penetrating questions. "It had no relation. It simply wasn't consistent with our investigation," he snapped.

Taken aback by Johnson's emotionally charged response, Crogan solicited the expert opinion of veteran FBI Agent John Vincent. Before retirement, Vincent had been assigned to perform some investigative work for the Oklahoma City terrorism case. "It sounds like Johnson is saying the truck didn't match up with the scenario of the bombing they were putting together, so the Bureau threw it out. Like any other investigation, they should have followed up on all their leads and let the facts dictate the results."

## No Comment

Innate thoroughness dictated the *LA Weekly* reporter seek the perspective of my attorney David Schippers. The forty-year litigator had become intimately familiar with my investigative research, testing the veracity of the witness testimonies and supporting facts in the fiery crucible of a highly principled federal prosecutor. The no-nonsense Chicagoan became incensed upon reading the FBI's official response to Senator Specter.

"This letter is fraught with lies, omissions, and disinformation," Schippers fumed. "It's the same old story with the FBI. Just cover it up. I don't understand why they [FBI] can't tell the truth. Maybe they just don't know the difference between truth and lies anymore."

When Crogan relayed that Schippers, several witnesses, and I accused the FBI of presenting "lies, omissions, and disinformation" to Congress, FBI Section Chief Eleni Kalisch, the official whose signature appeared on the confidential correspondence, instantly shut down the interview.

"I understand you're asking me about a letter I signed, but I'm not going to speak to you about this," Kalisch said. "You need to go through our press office. They deal with the press. I deal with government officials. That is our protocol and I'm not going to talk to you or any other reporter."

The FBI Washington, D.C., press officer to whom Kalisch referred Crogan promised to arrange an interview, but it never materialized. The reporter found himself wandering through bureaucratic no-man's-land once more when he contacted Specter's top aid, Thomas Swanton.

"I'm wearing two hats: the U.S. Attorney's office and Specter's office, so I need to get any interview approved. I'll call you back if I can talk." Evidently, Swanton couldn't talk. Crogan never heard from him again, and for that matter, neither did I.

# CHAPTER 12

# THE TERRORIST MOTEL

The most profound discovery of the investigation came when I found myself standing on the staging ground where the homegrown terrorist and his Middle Eastern conspirators used an obscure, low-rent motel for clandestine meetings to collaborate in their hellish scheme. The motel was conveniently situated off a major interstate with easy access to downtown. Residents and staff recounted numerous sightings of Hussain Al-Hussaini and his Arab confederates with Timothy McVeigh, and during a few rare instances, Terry Nichols. They witnessed a series of strange events and suspicious liaisons on the motel grounds in the months, weeks, days, and hours leading up to the terrorist strike on America's heartland.

The owner of the Cactus Motel felt duty bound to perpetuate the family owned business which had been handed down from his elderly father. But the Cactus heyday of the 1970s was a bygone era. Criminal elements replaced out-of-state vacationers in station wagons loaded with rowdy kids looking for a clean, affordable room. Despite the dramatic drop in rental rates, improvisation and ingenuity enabled Randy Christian to keep the doors open. He kept his overhead affordable because no job was beneath him. He wore many hats, including that of maintenance man, manager, accountant, and groundskeeper.

Spring of 1995 brought a heartrending divorce. The forty-year-old entrepreneur buried his emotional turmoil in around-the-clock business operations. Shattered by the prospect of his teenage boy enduring the dissolution of his parents' marriage, the loyal father determined an honest work ethic would instill the core values he desired to teach his son. Ironically, the motel owner's professional ardor demanded he spend countless hours on the Cactus property, placing him in the planning epicenter of a cataclysmic worldwide tremor known as the Oklahoma City bombing. Randy and his staff repeatedly and unknowingly interacted with the cast of infiltrators secretly tasked with the importation of Middle East terrorism to U.S. soil.

## Unmistakable Stench

Toolbox in hand, Randy sprinted from the motel office to repair a leaking faucet in room 128. The evening rush hour for customer check-in fast approached as the afternoon of April 18 faded into twilight. The economy-minded owner often opened doors and windows while he worked in vacant rooms in order to save on heating and air-conditioning bills. While sizing up the plumbing parts needed to complete the repair, a gentle wind swept through, flooding the air with noxious fumes. Randy took a deep breath. He discerned the unmistakable stench of diesel fuel. When he walked outdoors to investigate, he observed a large Ryder truck pulling under a cottonwood tree in the recreational vehicle park which occupied the east side of the motel property.

Randy returned to his task momentarily, but the pungent odor grew so overwhelming, he reemerged from the room. At that moment, two men traversed the parking lot from the Ryder truck and strolled along the breezeway where he was standing. Randy would later identify the pair as Timothy McVeigh and Hussain Al-Hussaini. The diplomatic businessman hesitated to admonish them about the truck before inquiring if they were motel guests.

Meanwhile, an irate resident in the Cactus RV campsite phoned the motel lobby to register a complaint about the malodorous van. The desk clerk, Georgia Hammerstein, answered the call.

"A large Ryder truck with an overpowering smell is parked outside my RV. Please get it out of here," the customer implored.

"Yes m'am. We will check it out right away," Georgia tactfully promised. Agitated by the inconvenient interruption, she scurried across the lobby and opened the door. The reek of diesel fuel steamrolled through the office. At that moment, Randy darted through the entryway.

"Did the men in that Ryder truck check into the motel?" he asked.

"Thankfully, they haven't," Georgia replied as her husband Gary limped into the lobby, hobbling on a cane. The putrid smell awakened him from a nap in the next room. The couple often slept on the premises when they split twenty-four hour shifts managing the registration desk. Recovering from an excruciating hip surgery, the forty-eight-year-old army veteran did not have patience to spare.

"Where is that awful smell coming from?" he grumbled.

Randy pointed out the window at the large Ryder truck as the moving van slowly lumbered across the parking lot. The trio watched as it headed north toward the filling station next door.

The incident roused Gary's feisty disposition. "If they come back onto the property, I will tell them to find another motel," he stoutly protested.

Curiosity lured Georgia back to the window. She watched as the moving van parked at the pumps. The driver lifted the gas nozzle, opened the rear compartment door, and climbed inside. She was unable to observe what he did next because a wooden fence surrounding the motel swimming pool blocked her line of sight. A few minutes later, Georgia caught another whiff of the pernicious stench as the Ryder truck returned and drove to the south side of the Cactus property.

"That obnoxious smelling truck is back," Georgia remarked to her husband. She cringed at the thought of having to tell the driver to remove his vehicle, but fortunately, he exited the parking lot without stopping.

## FATAL TOP OFF

Ken Banks lit a cigarette and resumed reading a magazine to kill time and boredom. Working as a clerk at an Oklahoma City gas station was relatively uneventful, with one outstanding exception—Ken had shot an armed robber. With keen perception, he noticed the assailant sliding a handgun under his shirt as he exited his vehicle and headed for the store. Gut instinct told Ken to reach for the loaded weapon hidden under the cash register. He figured he could pull the trigger first or risk becoming another crime statistic. Like a scene out of the Wild West, the observant would-be victim beat the gunman to the draw. Ken fired off a round just as the robber was reaching for his concealed pistol. The bullet shattered the attacker's jaw. The Oklahoma City police agreed that quick thinking saved his life, and the district attorney's office declined to file charges. The criminal survived, but as it turned out, the habitual offender wound up adding a foiled robbery to his rap sheet.

In the years that followed, the forty-year-old attendant settled back into the monotony of his job, still wary of potential danger. Being isolated along a deserted stretch of highway increased the odds he would become a target of yet another random heist. Ken refused to accept those odds. The shooting incident left him forever changed. He scrutinized well-groomed and scroungy customers with equal vigilance. Whenever an unfamiliar face walked through the door, he took careful note of the individual's behavior.

Thirteen years with the same employer enabled the native Oklahoman to become personally acquainted with the regular customers, the majority of whom drove large recreational vehicles, semi tractor trailers, or commercial pickups. Because of the inaccessibility to the nearby interstate, few passing motorists patronized the filling station. On the afternoon of April 18, 1995, one such customer pulled up to the diesel pumps. Ken studied the driver as he descended from a large Ryder truck and disappeared behind the rear carriage. Simultaneously, Georgia Hammerstein witnessed the moving van drive in to the gas station through the office window of the Cactus motel, only a stone's throw away.

"That's odd. I thought the newer model Ryders took unleaded fuel only," Ken contemplated as he leaned forward to get a better look; however, the angle of the truck obstructed his view of the gas pump and the movements of the driver.

A few minutes later, the Middle Eastern looking driver entered the shop and paid one hundred twenty dollars cash for one hundred gallons of diesel fuel. Ken's antennae shot up. The lion's share of the station clientele used charge cards, and nearly all were known to the watchful cashier. Ken inspected the stranger's almost comedic dress, suppressing the compulsion to grin. Thick, black curls stuck out in a perpendicular fashion from his ball cap. Oversized, darkly tinted sunglasses accentuated his large, bulbous nose, giving the olive-complexioned customer a clown-like appearance.

His eyes followed the truck as it rolled through the rear exit and ambled its way across a gravel roadway leading to the adjacent Cactus Motel. Had Ken just witnessed the fatal top off of the lethal liquid required to ignite the combustible compound buried in the cargo hold? Days later, after the bombing, the seemingly ordinary purchase of diesel fuel and the strangely dressed customer plagued Ken's thoughts upon learning a Ryder truck had been converted into the weapon of death.

"That man looks very similar to the truck driver who came in on April 18," the witness declared as he picked out Hussain Al-Hussaini's photograph from a stack of surveillance pictures.

I gauged the store clerk's confidence. "Please rate your level of certainty on a scale of one to ten."

He delivered his answer without flinching. "I'd give it a ten."

"But you said the man's eyes were disguised by sunglasses. How can you be positive?"

"The hair is almost identical, extremely kinky just like that. And his nose was very large. It stood out," he added. "I also remember his height, approximate weight, shape of his face, dark skin, and ethnic look that struck me as Middle Eastern. We rarely see Middle Eastern people in this store."

Ken also recognized a second individual from the photo lineup of Al-Hussaini's coworkers. He recalled seeing the unidentified man whom I had dubbed "chain-smoker" using the gas station pay phones.

"Why would you recall the physical appearance of a man standing at the pay phone? Isn't that a common occurrence?"

"I monitor just about everybody who comes on the lot. I've been robbed before, and I figure my life depends on being very watchful. This guy looked somewhat suspicious to me; so I took a closer look at him. I realized he had come back several times."

Those visits occurred in January and February 1995. During the same time frame, several witnesses observed "chain-smoker" using the pay phone at the nearby Cactus Motel, located just south of the station.

## TIMOTHY MCVEIGH RENTS A ROOM

For thirteen years, Gary Hammerstein juggled a taxing schedule in hotel management. Recurrent graveyard shifts at the Cactus Motel took an unavoidable toll on his family. By late 1994, the protracted separation from his wife and teenage daughters had grown burdensome. The college educated couple decided financial sacrifice afforded the only opportunity to buy more time together. Georgia resigned as dean of a local business academy where she managed the accounting department. The pressure and demanding hours crippled her health. While searching for another teaching position, she decided to fill in part-time for Gary behind the registration desk. Georgia's name topped the duty roster for the evening of April 18.

Shortly after the foul smelling Ryder truck disappeared from the Cactus RV park, Gary kissed his wife good night. He treasured a free evening to dine at home with his girls, Cherie and Jennifer.

Georgia brewed a fresh pot of coffee and filled her mug. Caffeine and cigarettes were the only remedy to combat the inevitable nighttime drowsiness. The bell on the lobby door jingled. Two men entered. A heavy-set Middle Easterner with an unkempt beard ordered a room for the night. His dapper companion with a spit-and-polish military bearing said nothing.

"Fill out this registration card please," Georgia instructed as she sized up the mismatched duo. Both men projected a standoffish posture which made her feel strangely uncomfortable.

"Will that be one room or two?" she inquired.

The sable-haired customer answered with an arresting foreign accent. "We would like one room for tonight only," he stated as he scribbled an illegible signature on the log sheet.

"What will be the method of payment?"

"Cash," he replied, pulling out his billfold. "And I would like to pay in advance."

The transaction transpired quickly because registration at the Cactus Motel required little to no paperwork. The soft underbelly of corruption flourished at the economy motel, opportunely tucked away from the beaten path of a major thoroughfare which offered a convenient drive to the downtown area. The "mom and pop" outfit was not affiliated with a national chain and did not employ modern booking procedures or any computer links in its daily operations. Motel management routinely insisted guests produce photo identification before renting rooms but made a practice of exempting customers who claimed their driver's licenses had been suspended, revoked, or lost.

Fugitives and felons enjoyed anonymity with no surveillance cameras to monitor their arrival and check-in. Criminals who paid with cash, flashed phony identification, and registered under an alias left no trail for law enforcement. Hence, these were the reasons why the terrorist infrastructure, which had been slated to execute the apocalyptic attack of April 19, looked upon the Cactus Motel as a secure haven. They were abundantly aware of the perks of operating incognito.

"You will be staying in Room 105 on the west side of the motel grounds," Georgia announced as she slid the key across the counter to the Arab guest and his American associate. The pair, whom she later identified to be Timothy McVeigh and Hussain Al-Hussaini's fellow Iraqi army "defector" known as Mohammed, returned to their dusty, yellow junker parked outside the office entrance and drove to the back side of the motel.

## MIDDLE EASTERN MECHANIC

Cole O'Brien sauntered onto the motel balcony to stretch out knotted muscles that stiffened his neck and back. Deteriorating health hindered his peripatetic lifestyle traveling state-to-state installing roofs. The forty-four-year-old Tennessean longed for his childhood homestead of Nashville, but the city's manual labor market was competitive and sparse.

Cole and his brother set up temporary housing at the Cactus Motel, expecting to solicit odd jobs from their father's former construction clients in Oklahoma City. But his hopes of negotiating some lucrative contracts soon soured. He had earned only a pittance of pocket money. On the night of April 18, Cole resolved to return to Tennessee within a month if his business prospects did not improve, but for now, he would shrug off his troubles and take an evening walk.

As Cole descended the staircase and entered the ground floor breezeway, he noticed a dilapidated yellow Mercury Marquis. The hood was raised and two men were tinkering with the driver's side door.

"Are you folks having car trouble?" he said. His friendly country twang carried a tacit invitation to banter.

The answer came with marked exasperation. "Yeah, I am working on the door."

"What seems to be the problem?" the curious onlooker asked.

The man, who was stooped over disassembling the door panel, stood up to speak directly to Cole. A unique mist of silver gray tint covered his mustache and coarse, curly hair. His olive skin tone, Middle Eastern facial structure, and accent were equally as striking.

"The door won't lock," the stranger explained with tangible foreign intonation. "And because the lock is jammed, the window won't roll up and down."

The second individual, who was wearing an American flag T-shirt, delivered a look of nonchalance. The amiable southerner perceived that this particular motel customer, whom Cole later determined to be Timothy McVeigh, had no interest in idle chat.

A dark blue Caprice pulled up, interrupting the uncomfortable silence that befell the conversation. A spindly African American male with shoulder length waves stepped out of the decades-old jalopy and greeted the Middle Eastern man. Their aloof body language and soft murmurs communicated a need for privacy. Cole continued walking to avoid the appearance of eavesdropping.

"Excuse me," a voice cried out. Cole glanced back. The Middle Easterner hoisted a metal toolbox and placed it on the backseat floorboard of the Mercury Marquis.

"This door doesn't lock. Do you suppose it would be safe to leave the toolbox in the car or would someone steal it?" the slender built foreigner inquired.

"I don't reckon you have anything to worry about," Cole remarked. "I've lived at the Cactus for the past few months, and I haven't had anything stolen."

Cole's assurance mollified the visitor's concerns. The Middle Eastern man slammed the door of the Marquis and joined his black companion who was then waiting in the blue Caprice. As the vehicle rolled through the motel exit, McVeigh discreetly retreated into room 105.

In the coming days, Cole would relive the laconic verbal exchange with the nameless Middle Easterner and his quiet friend with the all-American appeal. Eventually, the witness would view KFOR-TV's photo spread and finger yet another one of Hussain Al-Hussaini's coworkers as McVeigh's Middle Eastern mechanic. Cole would find out years later, during the trial of Timothy McVeigh, authorities recovered a toolbox from the Marquis after his arrest near Perry, Oklahoma.

## UNDER THE COVER OF DARKNESS

Cole stared at the digital clock on the nightstand. The stroke of midnight had come and gone, and still, slumber eluded him. He thought some fresh air might cure the bout of insomnia. He ambled onto the dimly lit balcony outside room 203 and leaned against the guardrail. He heard a door shut followed by heavy footsteps. His eyes rapidly scanned the parking lot below. A brawny figure slithering under the cover of darkness walked briskly toward a 1990s model, four-door Honda. The security lights illuminated the black bearded man as he approached his vehicle. Cole leaned forward and squinted to ensure his vision had not deceived him. The strapping, potbellied stranger, whom I later learned from inside sources went by the first name "Mohammed," carried two firearms, a shotgun and a semi-automatic pistol, one in each hand. After placing the weapons in the back seat, he paused to speak to someone obscured by shadows. The distressed witness stood motionless, hoping the unsuspecting foreigner and his confrere would not detect his presence.

The waning hours of the night continued to plague Cole with restless sleep. The sound of a starting engine awakened him several times. Sleep deprived and agitated by the intrusion, Cole stumbled to the window to investigate. The distant rumble of a motor drew his attention to a large yellow car parked near the motel dumpster. He assumed the vehicle was the same Mercury Marquis that the Middle Eastern visitor and motel guest from room 105 tried to repair. He collapsed into bed and dozed off. Six hours later, a thunderous explosion jolted him to consciousness and the stark reality that he witnessed the brokers of terror execute last minute preparations.

As the bombing case unfolded, Cole instantly recognized television footage of Timothy McVeigh and the Mercury Marquis, but the absence of Middle Eastern suspects mystified and frightened him. He was equally as bewildered to view KFOR-TV's photographs of Hussain Al-Hussaini's inner circle of confidants. He testified to observing several of the Iraqi ex-enemy combatants at the Cactus Motel. One of the Arab subjects habitually used the motel pay phones.

Cole also paused on the photograph of Mohammed, the same Middle Eastern male whom the motel clerk, Georgia Hammerstein, independently named as the guest who checked in to room 105 with Timothy McVeigh. He noted that Mohammed's thick curly hair, dark beard, and portly physique bore a strong resemblance to the individual he watched load weapons into a vehicle parked near McVeigh's room.

"I'm pretty sure he was the man walking from the direction of room 105 carrying a shotgun and large pistol. But I hesitate to say I'm one hundred percent certain because I was standing on the second level balcony," Cole clarified.

However, the witness exhibited no compunction when pegging Al-Hussaini's Jordanian work associate as the Middle Eastern mechanic with whom he discussed the faulty door lock on the Mercury Marquis.

"That's the man I spoke to on April 18 and I'm one hundred percent positive that is the man," he asserted. With the same veracious intensity, he recounted Timothy McVeigh's blasé disinterest that threw cold water on his attempt to strike up a conversation with the two men.

## "THEY'RE GOING TO BLOW UP THE BUILDING!"

Living on premises as the resident handyman offered the benefit of free rent with one inconvenient drawback. David Elmore remained on call for the proverbial twenty-four/seven. No matter what the crisis, from clogged plumbing to malfunctioning heaters, the thirty-seven-year-old father answered the page for help. The April 18 night shift ended with a hysterical outburst from a motel resident, capping off an already trying day.

"They're going to blow up the building!" Larry Miller ranted.

David was unimpressed. "Larry, what are you belly aching about now?"

"They're going to blow up the building!" the trembling man repeated with slurred speech. David detected the heavy odor of liquor. Reputed as the town drunk in the microcosm of the Cactus Motel, Larry Miller imbibed alcohol to anesthetize the emptiness brought on by the recent separation from his wife.

"Where did you hear such a crazy thing? No one is going to blow up a building." David balked.

"Never mind," Larry muttered and vanished behind the door of his motel room. The two men had shared a few inebriated moments drinking beers in the evening, but David's wife, Rosanna, frowned upon the relationship. She recoiled from Larry's right-wing extremism and deep-seated hatred of the federal government. The middle-aged migrant worker from Arkansas claimed he served in the U.S. Army and received training in demolitions. In the spring of 1995, he openly expressed to the Elmores his intention to join the militia movement.

Rosanna recalled that Larry had stockpiled foot-long metal pipes, gunpowder, and spools of cord and metal wire. During a visit to her nefarious neighbor's motel room, her three-year-old son accidentally spilled a container of gunpowder. Needless to say, the horrified mother put a moratorium on further socializing with him. David recounted a disconcerting moment when Larry pulled out a homemade pipe bomb from a shoebox stashed in his closet.

"I'm going to set this thing off one of these days," he vaunted. David discounted Larry's boast as empty bluster from a drunken blowhard. He was accustomed to dismissing the serial distortion and violent rhetoric spouted by his neighbor.

In early January 1995, Larry issued the same warning to Cactus owner Randy Christian. The emotionally unstable guest used similar language, claiming that someone planned to "blow it up." When Randy insisted he disclose the identity of the would-be bombers and the alleged target, Larry clammed up. Randy summarily disregarded the comment. A temporary motel clerk previously complained that Larry set off a small pipe bomb in the Cactus parking lot, but overall, Randy considered the rabble-rousing guest a harmless braggart.

Two months later, in March, Larry reiterated his alarming portent, but on this occasion, Randy sensed an all-consuming fear.

"They are going to blow it up!" Larry exclaimed.

"Blow up what?" Randy inquired.

"I don't know," he insisted. "I just know they are going to do it. You have to do something!"

"Who are these guys?" the perplexed and annoyed owner asked.

"I'll find out and get back to you," he vowed. Randy decided not to wait for Larry to deliver an answer. He notified the Bureau of Alcohol, Tobacco, and Firearms. He spoke to a female receptionist and disclosed that Cactus Motel guest Larry Miller warned that some unknown perpetrators planned to possibly bomb a building. A few days later, two plainclothes agents, whom Randy assumed were from the ATF, came to the motel, handcuffed Larry, searched his room, and then released him. The ATF agents told the motel staff when Randy was not present that if Larry Miller caused any more trouble, they were to report it to the Bureau.

## DISQUIETING REFLECTION

The breaking news of the April 19 slaughter sent Larry Miller underground. The two-year resident of the Cactus Motel vanished without notice or a forwarding address. His unexplained departure stunned Randy and David alike. The Arkansan abandoned an inventory of personal items including clothing, trade tools, and a stereo. Larry would never be heard from again, but his prediction uttered on the eve of April 19 would echo in David Elmore's thoughts.

Unaware of Randy's previous call a month earlier to the ATF, David mulled over his missteps. He would be forever haunted by his callous failure to seriously explore Larry's fatidic statements and decision not to contact law enforcement. Disquieting reflection brought to mind the evening of April 16 when Larry invited David and his wife Rosanna to share a nightcap. They heard spirited conversation upon entering Larry's motel room, but the couple's presence caused the chattering voices to abruptly fall silent. Three unfamiliar faces glowered at the Elmores. Two of the men were of Middle Eastern origin; the third was a wiry framed Caucasian with glasses and bland, unremarkable features. Both witnesses later testified the nondescript white male was very likely bombing convict Terry Nichols.

Their penetrating stares flustered Rosanna, a naturally bashful woman. She politely excused herself and quickly departed. David remained a short time longer, affording him extended exposure to the mysterious foreigners, one of whom he comfortably picked out of a photo lineup of Al-Hussaini's former army buddies. David recalled seeing the Iraqi soldier known as "Majid" earlier that Easter Sunday slumped over asleep in the front seat of the Mercury Marquis. As he peered inside the driver's side window, he recognized the man's face as someone he had seen at the motel on several occasions in recent months. David reported the incident to motel management because the owner strictly prohibited Cactus customers and their visitors from napping in vehicles.

During a separate interview, Randy Christian unknowingly provided corroborative testimony. During the same general time frame in which David witnessed Majid sleeping in the distinctive yellow Marquis, Randy watched it drive onto the premises. A diminutive Arab man, who was not featured in KFOR-TV's surveillance shots, exited the driver's side and checked in. He paid cash for double occupancy in room 105 and registered under the name "Hotaday." Randy remembered this guest in particular because he had asked to borrow a screwdriver and pair of pliers to repair the Marquis. The request perturbed him because he frowned upon his clientele performing car maintenance in the motel parking lot. As a result, Randy was attentive to the yellow Mercury. Sometime on April 17, he saw Majid, the man David Elmore encountered the previous day, walking away from the Marquis which was parked near the trash dumpster on the west end of the grounds.

## PRELUDE TO THE FATAL FINALE

The foreboding signs which unfolded on the Cactus stage in the days leading up to April 19 paled in comparison to the events which transpired in the concluding hour that dreadful morning. The prelude to the fatal finale played out like a well-orchestrated ballet of death. Each actor performed his role with macabre zeal and precision.

The workday began at 7:30 A.M. as David opened his motel door to a chilly gust of wind. Diesel fumes flooded the air and penetrated his sinuses, causing a sudden wave of nausea.

"Do you smell that odor of diesel fuel?" David said to his wife Rosanna, who was preparing breakfast for their toddler son. The former oil field worker could instantly distinguish the smell of diesel.

"Who could miss that overpowering stench?" Rosanna answered rhetorically.

David surveyed the grounds and isolated the obvious culprit—a large yellow Ryder truck located a few feet from the garbage bin. He slowly circled the vehicle, searching for possible sources of a diesel leak, but failed to find any. What he did discover puzzled him. The label above the gas cap read, "Unleaded Fuel Only."

David visually canvassed the area surrounding the rear carriage of the truck and noticed a detached Arizona license plate lying on the ground. He picked up the tag and tossed it into the trash receptacle along with other debris he had collected. At that moment, Randy Christian drove onto the Cactus property. The potent odor swiftly seeped into the ventilation system of his pickup.

"What is the source of that noxious stench of fuel?" Randy shouted to David as he rolled down his truck window.

"There's no doubt it's coming from that Ryder truck parked near the dumpster," he replied.

"Did you find any leaks?"

"No, I've walked around it twice and checked it out. There are no diesel spills," he answered. "Believe it or not, the gas cap says the truck takes unleaded fuel."

"That's strange," Randy remarked.

"No kidding," David laughed. He leaned forward and tapped on the roof of his employer's pickup. "Well, I have a few tasks to finish up before I report to the office for the list of things you need done today."

"I'll see you in a few minutes," the owner said as he glanced through the windshield at several men walking from the vicinity of a ground level room toward the Ryder truck. As he continued his daily drive around the motel to inspect for maintenance problems, he noticed a brown sport utility vehicle. The SUV caught his eye because the socioeconomic class of customers who stayed at the Cactus rarely drove expensive, late-model vehicles.

Meanwhile, David dashed up the staircase to the second level to resume his repair work, but the activities of the people associated with the foul-smelling truck distracted him. He later testified he paid close attention as Timothy McVeigh climbed into the driver's seat. The Middle Eastern male whom David witnessed stepping into the cab with the Oklahoma City bomber was the Iraqi national named Mohammed, the same man the desk clerk said paid cash for room 105 on April 18.

"Timothy McVeigh and the curly-haired Middle Eastern guy noticed me watching them. They stopped and spoke to each other, then glared at me." David recounted during an interview. "They were looking directly at me to intimidate me. There's no doubt in my mind."

The morning of April 19 marked one of several sightings of Mohammed, McVeigh's heavy-set partner, at the Cactus Motel. During one such occasion, David saw him driving a 1960s pickup with a distinctive stepside bed. Cole O'Brien also noticed a similar looking vehicle parked on the west side of the Cactus on April 18, the night he witnessed Mohammed toting weapons from the general direction of Timothy McVeigh's room.

## CONVOY TO CARNAGE

Randy arrived at the office to find Gary Hammerstein busily answering the motel switchboard. Anticipating the customary flow of guests for morning check-out, he slipped behind the registration desk to lend a hand. The door chimed, and David entered to retrieve his duty assignment. The clattery drone of a motor trailed behind him. Randy gazed outside the north window, as the odoriferous Ryder truck he noticed earlier rolled to a stop.

The gangly driver sprinted to the lobby, brushed past David, and placed the room key on the front desk. The owner smiled and purposely made eye contact with the hurried customer, but he ignored the thankful gesture. The man's cropped military coiffure and subtle intensity reminded Randy of a cop working undercover. Within forty-eight hours, he would be shocked to learn otherwise. Both David and Randy would discover they came within inches of the Oklahoma City bomber, Timothy McVeigh.

Randy became engrossed in the methodical repositioning taking place in plain view. He watched as Mohammed, the burly Arab with a scraggly beard, exited the passenger seat of the Ryder truck and darted around the rear carriage to meet McVeigh. The two men spoke briefly as McVeigh climbed inside the truck cab and assumed his designated post at the wheel. Mohammed then trotted in front of the Ryder to the east side of the office where he jumped into the same brown SUV which Randy spotted minutes earlier parked at the rear of the property. Simultaneously, a third member of the execution team emerged on the scene. With a dexterous stride, the woolly-headed Middle Easterner rounded the east corner of the office and leaped into the passenger side of the Ryder truck.

The feverish transfer of men and vehicles instantly grabbed Gary's attention. "What's going on out there? These guys are moving so fast and furious, you would think they were participating in a military exercise."

"No kidding," Randy affirmed as he continued to monitor the commotion outside.

While stuffing his dense, black curls under a ball cap, the Ryder truck passenger noticed Randy's fixed gape. He turned and fired off an evocative stare at the motel owner. An unquenchable rage churned within the dark stranger, conveying a raw feeling of hatred—an expression unlike Randy had ever seen. Without hesitation, the witness fingered Hussain Al-Hussaini from KFOR-TV's photo spread. He was the man Randy watched depart his motel at 7:50 A.M. on April 19, seated next to the terror network's hand-picked lackey, Timothy McVeigh.

Randy watched as the brown sport utility vehicle, which bore a strong resemblance to the Chevrolet Blazer that would be targeted later that morning in an official Teletype issued by the Oklahoma Highway Patrol, and yellow Mercury Marquis, the car in which McVeigh would be captured, tailed the Ryder truck as the convoy to carnage merged onto the interstate bound for downtown Oklahoma City.

## RALLY POINT

Seventy-two minutes later, a monstrous explosion at $5^{th}$ and Harvey Streets jarred the earth's crust, sending tremors citywide. The Cactus Motel rested on the fault line of the ground-shaking gyration.

"What was that?" Randy shouted to maintenance employee Richard Parnell. The two men stood immobile on the motel breezeway for a moment exploring the source of the thunderous crash from the eastern horizon.

"Do you think a gas main exploded downtown?" Randy postulated.

"No, sir, that explosion bore the distinct signature of a military ordnance," Richard said assuredly. Navigating the combat zones of the Vietnam War had fine-tuned the former Marine's battlefield perception. "Experience tells me that was most definitely a bomb."

Suddenly, a brown sport utility vehicle, which Randy believed was the same SUV that trailed the Ryder moving van that morning, screeched off the highway service road and plunged through a grassy ravine lining the back side of the Cactus. The truck stopped near a drainage ditch and two men jumped out. Randy watched as they scurried to the west side of the vehicle and momentarily disappeared from sight. When they reemerged, the passenger tossed a white object into the field while the driver squatted down near the rear bumper. Their well-timed actions appeared rehearsed as if they were carrying out a drill. Shortly thereafter, the brown SUV backed up, zipped through the Cactus recreational vehicle park, and sped back to the freeway at approximately 9:30 A.M.

In the spring of 1996, Randy was using a backhoe to clear away weeds and plant trees in the grasslands surrounding the Cactus. The excavation unearthed several items in the general vicinity where the brown sport utility vehicle had screeched to a halt the morning of the bombing. Groundskeeper Richard Parnell picked up an expired Arizona license plate which had been thinly veiled by a layer of Oklahoma red clay. Employee David Elmore found a ball cap while Randy reached down to retrieve a white T-shirt bearing an American flag emblem which was heavily stained with motor oil. Cole O'Brien had previously described the same design on the shirt worn by Timothy McVeigh while he and the Middle Eastern mechanic repaired the Mercury Marquis the evening of April 18.

Concerned that the T-shirt, plate, and cap that had been stashed in the adjoining ravine might harbor physical ties to the Middle Eastern collaborators, Randy Christian dutifully notified the FBI. Once again, no one would listen. He confronted the same lackadaisical attitude he had elicited when reporting Timothy McVeigh's frequent visits to his motel.

## Suspicious SUV

On the afternoon of April 19, five hours after Randy and Richard watched the suspicious SUV tear off the Cactus grounds and disappear into expressway traffic, the Oklahoma Highway Patrol issued an all-points bulletin for a brown Chevrolet Blazer, not to be confused with a second APB for a brown Chevrolet pickup which had been targeted by the FBI. The official Teletype that was disseminated by the Oklahoma Highway Patrol identified several Middle Eastern occupants who were considered possible bombing suspects. The Blazer bore a license tag which was originally issued to a Chevrolet Cavalier that a New York man of Pakistani descent rented from the Dallas/Fort Worth International Airport.

Media accounts indicated a trooper came across the brown Blazer driving through Oklahoma City an hour before the blast. Several Arab men asked the officer for directions. After the Murrah Building attack, the FBI disseminated an APB for a brown Chevy pickup with Middle Eastern men. Because the manhunt focused on foreign terrorists, the patrolman decided it would be prudent to trace the license tag number which he had routinely jotted down during the courtesy traffic stop. Alas, he discovered the plate did not belong to the brown SUV, but rather, it had been switched from a leased Chevy Cavalier owned by National Car Rental. The Oklahoma Highway Patrol issued an APB forthwith.

Within twenty-four hours, the FBI tracked down the Pakistanis associated with the Cavalier and Blazer. Following extensive interrogation, the men were released. However, the FBI reports, which documented interviews with two Arab detainees, were withheld from legal counsel representing Timothy McVeigh and Terry Nichols. In the summer of 2001, the Bureau confessed the records had been "unintentionally" excised from the discovery materials submitted to the defense.

## BLINDED TO THE VISIBLE ENEMY

The untold human loss of April 19 inflicted a permanent ache that clawed at the hearts of the Cactus Motel witnesses. Randy Christian, David and Rosanna Elmore, Gary and Georgia Hammerstein, Cole O'Brien, Richard Parnell, and gas station attendant Ken Banks were forever united in the torment of inconsolable regret. They contemplated the imponderable question—did the frequent sightings of Timothy McVeigh, his Islamic handlers, and the Ryder truck that reeked of diesel fuel warrant a louder cry to law enforcement? Randy contacted the ATF in March 1995 when a petrified Larry Miller screamed aloud that someone was going to blow up a building, but the ensuing federal investigation yielded no action.

During the post April 19 era of mourning and haunting reminiscence, the Cactus Motel witnesses grappled with the poignant revelation they had encountered more, much more. The eccentric smells, strange liaisons between the American terrorist and his foreign henchmen, and the sepulchral caravan to the federal building would not eclipse the most damning tip-offs that went unheeded. The planning for the bomb design and several test runs unfolded before their eyes virtually undetected. Now hindsight remembrance redefined mundane occurrences as murderous intentions. They had been blinded to the visible enemy.

McVeigh's posse of Middle Eastern pals routinely rented rooms at the motel in late 1994 and early 1995. Oftentimes, they purchased snacks from the lobby store and gravitated to the public pay phones outside the office. Superficially, their behavior appeared innocuous, but occasionally, their activities bordered on the bizarre. One prime example took place in mid-February 1995 when manager Gary Hammerstein patrolled the perimeter of the Cactus RV park conducting a routine security check. An oversized yellow Ryder moving van blocked the south end of the motel office building. As he strode past, a clanking noise rattled the cargo hold, beckoning him closer. The inquisitive witness snooped inside the open rear door where an athletically built Middle Eastern male busily rearranged blue fifty-five gallon drums.

"Nice day," Gary hollered in a brisk lively fashion, but the stone-faced foreigner ignored the amiable overture. Instead, he answered with an intimidating stare. Uneasy with the impertinent response, Gary resumed walking. He would later select that same man from KFOR-TV's library of photographs. The suspect happened to be the individual whom Virginia King stated drove to her apartment complex to purposely abandon a stolen pickup that FBI Agent Jim Ellis theorized carried Middle Eastern bombers from the burning building.

An intriguing clue arrived on the heels of Gary's encounter with the Arab man moving large drums inside the Ryder truck. A motel maid complained several bags of fertilizer frustrated her efforts to thoroughly clean a customer's room. Employee Richard Parnell also overheard the cleaning woman's allegation. Gary deemed the charge so preposterous he personally investigated the motel room, and oddly enough, discovered the grievance was true. During my interview with Gary in the fall of 1995, he could not recall the name of the guest who stacked fertilizer in the room. The incident was memorable because it involved a key ingredient used in the Murrah Building bomb.

The goings-on at the Cactus would become even more peculiar in the weeks that lay ahead. As the winter thawed into springtime, the motel owner, staff, and guests shared numerous run-ins with Middle Eastern men loitering around a moving van packed with fifty-five gallon drums that leaked lingering puddles of diesel fuel on the gravel parking lot. The 1980s broken-down white truck with a soiled undercarriage summoned the attention of even the most oblivious bystander. Gary remembered an incident when a Hispanic customer with a Texas driver's license registered for a room. Meanwhile, two unidentified passengers of Arab origin waited silently in the cab of the white truck. Not long afterwards, he watched the van sputter and die on the Cactus premises. The group of foreign occupants worked feverishly for an extended period to restart the engine. Eventually, they succeeded.

"How could you miss that dilapidated old moving van? It had no labels. It definitely was not a rental," Randy Christian ardently emphasized. "I recall one incident when a brown pickup backed up to the van and some Arab guys unloaded several items into the rear carriage where large blue barrels were stored. This kind of activity occurred on at least three separate occasions."

The recollection distressed Randy. He believed wholeheartedly he had naïvely watched as the April 19 executioners honed their lethal craft. Often, he was standing at too great a distance to identify the men associated with the mechanically unsound truck with one extraordinary exception. In late March 1995, the white moving van rolled into the Cactus and parked on the northern edge of the entrance. At that moment, heavy fumes overcame Randy and Richard Parnell as they walked past the lobby doorway.

"That smells like diesel fuel. Do you suppose the gas station next door is responsible?" Randy asked.

Richard pointed toward the motel swimming pool. "It's coming from that white truck."

The pair walked over to the vacant van to investigate. At that moment, a man whom Randy subsequently identified as Hussain Al-Hussaini jogged around the front grill.

"We weren't bothering your truck. We were just wondering why it smelled so bad of diesel," Randy politely commented.

Randy said Al-Hussaini replied in broken English, "I move truck now."

Randy studied the man's face in KFOR-TV's photo lineup with instant recall. He testified to several sightings of the Iraqi solider at the Cactus in the fall of 1994 and spring of 1995. Randy contended the most recent encounter took place in March 1995 when he saw Al-Hussaini get out of the older model white moving van and enter the lobby.

## BUNGLED TEST RUN?

One nippy spring morning, Randy came across the shabby white truck once again while making his usual rounds of the motel perimeter. A group of Arab men crowded around the disabled vehicle. An unidentified Caucasian driver repeatedly turned the ignition, but the engine coughed and spit, refusing to start. Randy drove back to the motel office. After several minutes, the vehicle rumbled to the exit. An Arab man wearing a blue jogging suit and sporty headband hopped out and dashed toward the lobby entrance. Randy stepped forward and courteously opened the east door.

The guest dropped the room key on the registration desk and promptly departed. Randy glanced out the doorway as a thick bearded man in coveralls exited the passenger side of the cab. While the Middle Easterner who returned the room key was not featured in KFOR-TV's photographs of Al-Hussaini's Iraqi comrades, Randy did identify from the photo lineup the second individual—the black-haired male in the coveralls—as Mohammed, McVeigh's partner whom motel clerk Georgia Hammerstein and guest Cole

O'Brien witnessed at the Cactus on April 18. Randy and Cactus employee David Elmore saw the same man the next morning, one hour before the bomb detonated.

After the broken down moving van limped off the Cactus property that frosty morning, Randy traveled downtown to buy air-conditioning coil cleaner. While driving eastbound on the interstate, he passed the white truck, which had stalled on the center median. A brown pickup was parked close by, apparently offering assistance to the stranded Middle Easterners. Randy completed his errands and doubled back to the same location. By that time, a wrecker service had been called to the scene.

In the wake of the terrorist truck bombing, the events of that baleful day flashed back to Randy's remembrance. Was an explosive tinderbox encased within, rigged to detonate if the truck motor had not failed before reaching an unknown target? Or, had Randy witnessed a bungled test run that foretold the annihilation that loomed in the not so distant future?

## COMMANDEERING THE MOTEL LOGS

The FBI cast a far-reaching net to track the movements of the prime suspects in custody, Timothy McVeigh and Terry Nichols. Truckloads of registration logs were confiscated from Oklahoma City hotels and lodges. Given its straight-line access to downtown, the feds swiftly descended upon the Cactus as a potential McVeigh hideout. An ATF agent unexpectedly walked into the motel office and requested the registration logs dated December 1994 through April 1995.

Gary Hammerstein's bachelor's degree in accounting and hotel management taught the tough-minded supervisor the cardinal rule not to relinquish original records.

"We would be more than glad to oblige, but we will provide photocopies only. Turning over the originals would require a court order," he stipulated. The agent became annoyed, spun around, and walked out, stating he would be back later.

When the shift changed that afternoon, his wife Georgia took over the registration desk. A satellite television repairman called in and asked to speak to the owner. Georgia hollered to her husband who was resting in the adjoining bedroom to notify Randy he had a caller holding on the line. Moments later, Randy entered the lobby.

"What's wrong with the motel's satellite TV service?" Gary inquired.

Randy looked quizzical. "Nothing, why do you ask?"

"The call that came in earlier was from a man claiming to be a TV repairman."

"What are you talking about?" Randy replied. "The man on the phone was an ATF agent who set an appointment with me to retrieve the motel logs for the bombing investigation."

"That same guy came in this morning and asked for the originals, but I agreed to turn over photocopies only. He did not take me up on the offer," Gary said in a gruff tone.

When the federal investigator returned that same day, Randy heeded Gary's advice and adeptly dodged the request.

"I would be happy to cooperate and photocopy my records for you, but I want to maintain custody of the original logs," he said.

"In that case, I would prefer to take the documents with me and pay the expense for photocopying," the agent imperiously suggested. But the owner remained intransigent. Randy declined once more to surrender the files.

"I can save you time and trouble. I will do the job right here and now," he said tactfully as he stacked five months of motel logs on the photocopier and pressed the start button. The task seemed interminable, but it afforded Randy a chance to placate the worrisome feeling that the incarcerated suspect had converted the Cactus into a nerve center of operations. Contrary to his character, the naturally tactful man broached the topic directly. "You could really put my mind at ease if you could tell me if you know where Timothy McVeigh stayed the night before the bombing. I know this may sound crazy, but I watched him come into this office on April 19 and place a room key on the counter. That was about an hour before the bombing."

The federal officer shrugged, but astonishingly, he offered no comment, posed no questions, and requested no interviews with staff members who could substantiate the claim. In short, the federal investigator displayed not a flicker of interest in Randy's bombshell statement and knowingly left a groundbreaking lead on the table unexplored.

Two federal trials and the nation's most exhaustive criminal investigation, which included seven hundred field agents, failed to produce documentation establishing McVeigh's whereabouts for the night of April 18 and the early morning of April 19. The prosecution scratched the only witness who could have filled in the time gap. Gas station attendant Fred Skrdla told investigators he sold fuel to McVeigh between 1:00 A.M. and 3:00 A.M. on April 18. The twenty-four hour truck stop was located on Interstate 35 in northern Oklahoma near the town of Billings.

The defense handily impeached the witness's credibility upon filing Skrdla's medical records which stemmed from a previous worker's compensation claim. The report revealed Skrdla suffered episodes of blurred vision. On May 12, 1997, the *Daily Oklahoman* quoted unnamed federal sources who expressed reticence about putting the cashier on the stand because his testimony "could not be corroborated by other evidence." Evidently, McVeigh paid cash for the gas, therefore there was no credit card receipt to prove Skrdla's claim.

The government presented a case that hinged exclusively upon circumstantial evidence. Not one eyewitness placed the American terrorist in the state, city, or near the crime scene in the final hours leading up to the bone-shattering explosion. Meanwhile, four Oklahomans who completed the timeline and fingered McVeigh at the Cactus Motel surrounded by men of Arab extraction were conspicuously ignored. But more telling, the paper trail that validated or disproved their claims would disappear.

## BACKDOOR SEIZURE

Stumped by the ATF agent's lethargic response to his allegation that McVeigh spent the night at the Cactus, Randy pressed the officer in a subsequent phone conversation for an explanation.

"We are collecting motel logs citywide and we intend to cross reference the records," the investigator stated authoritatively. The evasive, essentially meaningless answer boggled the witness all the more. Where could he turn now? In a galling move, the feds had snubbed his declaration that the Oklahoma City bomber checked in to the Cactus Motel. In the weeks that followed, the press reported that Timothy McVeigh used the alias "Bob Kling" to rent the bomb truck. According to Randy, that name appeared several times on the original sign-in sheets that he kept, but he would not possess the evidence for long.

On May 26, 1995, Randy arrived at the Cactus to find his father, Gene, handing the registration logs to ATF Agent Doug Moore. Obviously, Randy's decision to withhold the original paperwork presented a nettlesome quandary. The wily agent played upon the gullibility of the retiree to execute a backdoor seizure. At that point, it was too late to intervene. Randy's father had legal authority as co-owner of the Cactus to deliver the documents. Unfortunately, Randy had not yet photocopied an extra set of the files. The originals would disappear into the abyss of missing evidence.

## "Tampered Records"

Though unrelenting in his quest, Randy Christian's efforts to recover the original Cactus logs proved fruitless. The FBI predictably rejected his Freedom of Information Act requests for the documents, stating such a release "could reasonably be expected to interfere with law enforcement proceedings." Randy and his team of employees clung to the belief that the 1995 sign-in sheets held hostage by the government yielded their vindication. But given the monolithic wall of resistance, hope for their return soon caved into defeatism.

No one expected the call that came through the Cactus switchboard in the spring of 2000. An FBI representative notified Randy that the Department of Justice had scheduled the return of all motel and hotel logs sequestered in the bombing case. But when Randy showed up to collect, he slammed into yet another roadblock. The FBI released photocopies of the registration logs for March and April 1995, but not the originals. Moreover, the agency withheld three months of files which included the sign-in reports extending from December 1994 through February 1995—documents which were critical to establish the presence of additional conspirators at the motel.

The disheartened witness registered his complaint with a female FBI clerk who appeared baffled upon learning the original Cactus logs had not been provided. She also made a notation that the bulk of the motel documents the ATF confiscated in May 1995 were still missing. But despite the conspicuous fact that the Cactus Motel was arguably the only business among hundreds denied the return of original records, the FBI vault remained sealed shut. Randy's petition was denied once again.

The photocopy of the customer register for the evening of April 18, 1995, crushed Randy's spirit and his employees alike. The room where motel employee Georgia Hammerstein and guest Cole O'Brien testified Timothy McVeigh stayed was shown to be vacant on the night in question. Both witnesses claimed the bomber stayed in room 105, but the entry for the guest's name was blank.

"These are tampered records," Gary Hammerstein firmly stated as he scrutinized the motel log sheet. "I believe the customer's name that was written down next to room 105 the evening of April 18 was redacted before this photocopy was made, and I can prove it."

I had become familiar with the accountant's exacting, analytical nature during the five year interim. While he was initially reluctant to speak with me, given the FBI's shameless disregard for Middle Eastern complicity, a sense of patriotism impelled the former Army serviceman to open up.

"I calculate the room occupancy every day, and if room 105 was vacant, then the rate would have been ninety-three percent, not ninety-five percent as I noted on the bottom of the page."

"Can you verify that this is your handwriting?" I queried.

"Absolutely, this is my handwriting," he certified as he pointed to the notation. "I verified the Cactus Motel had an occupancy rate of ninety-five percent on the eve of the bombing. That means room 105 had to be occupied. I will testify to it under oath if necessary. I believe the name on room 105 was blotted out before this photocopy was made."

"I agree," Georgia interjected. "Since 1995, I have steadfastly maintained that I assigned the Middle Eastern man and Timothy McVeigh to room 105 when they checked in together. I'm positive there was a Middle Eastern surname on that blank line. For that matter, I strongly believe the logs that the FBI refused to return are replete with foreign aliases of the Arab men who hung out with McVeigh."

I bandied about the possibility Gary might have erred in his estimate. But he insisted the mathematical equation used to factor the occupancy rate is too complex not to double check.

"As a matter of habit, I verify the calculation and do the math twice," he affirmed. Gary explained how he first subtracted the number of rooms that were out of order for maintenance. On April 18, fifty-eight units were available to rent. He then deducted the number of vacancies, which at the time, totaled three. Therefore, he had fifty-five rooms rented out of fifty-eight which equaled a ninety-five percent occupancy rate. If the guest register was, indeed, doctored to reflect a vacancy in room 105, then whoever performed the task was ignorant as to the adjustment needed to reflect the occupancy was ninety-three percent. The fact that Gary had an in-house formula that was unknown to the FBI made the supposition the record had been doctored all the more probable.

## FBI "FIB"

While the evidence suggesting the FBI falsified the Cactus Motel log for April 18 seemed persuasive, the crime of obstructing justice had not been established beyond a reasonable doubt. The original sign-in sheet yields the undeniable truth, and the FBI retains custody of that record, as well as months of registration sheets for which it refused to furnish the owner with photocopies. The Bureau's suppression of any linkage between McVeigh, his

Iraqi counterparts, and the Cactus Motel crossed the line of credulity in the fall of 2002.

After Senator Arlen Specter requested I turn over the massive investigative file indicating foreign involvement in the April 19 terrorist attack, the FBI alleged to the senator in writing that Randy Christian admitted to federal agents he had "destroyed" the registration record for April 18.

"That's an outright lie!" the livid motel owner proclaimed. "Sure, it was Cactus policy to dispose of daily sign-in sheets after a certain time period, or we would be swimming in paperwork. But I have several witnesses to the undisputed fact the ATF collected the records for December 1994 through April 1995."

This time, the FBI's written words laid a trap from which it could not escape. It was a classic case of the left hand not knowing what the right hand had done. The Bureau claimed it could not produce the original log sheet dated April 18 because the owner purportedly "destroyed" it; so how could the FBI return to Randy Christian in 2000 a photocopy of that very same record if authorities never confiscated it in the first place? In short, the Bureau returned a photocopy of a record that it claimed did not exist.

## "Falsified Statements"

Disillusionment permeated Randy's soul. He wondered if the FBI was engaged in a premeditated effort to deep-six evidence that suggested the Cactus may have served as a logistical base for planning the Murrah Building bombing. After the ATF agent retrieved his business records in late April, he placed several calls to the FBI, but to no avail. In the fall of 1995, Randy recounted his recurrent exposure to Timothy McVeigh in the presence of foreign suspects to a childhood friend who happened to be a local attorney. Appalled by the FBI's refusal to take an official statement from the proprietor of the Cactus Motel, the lawyer relayed the story to a retired federal judge who, in turn, contacted a lead prosecutor assigned to the pending criminal trial. Lo and behold, two investigators knocked on Randy Christian's door, but these men were no rank-and-file agents. They held influential positions with the Oklahoma Bomb Task Force. Randy soon learned the FBI exhibited no desire to verify the truth, but rather to discredit and pervert the facts.

"The FBI has quoted me inaccurately," Randy smoldered. Shock besieged him as he reviewed leaked copies of the written reports documenting his fall

1995 and winter 1996 interviews with the FBI. The Bureau had denied his requests to obtain these reports. "They have twisted my words. These records definitely contain falsified statements."

"Did the FBI use recording equipment to memorialize your testimony?" I asked.

"No, they only took handwritten notes," he answered. Ordinarily, sorting out the truth would have come down to Randy's word versus that of the FBI's. But federal officials did not anticipate being held accountable by my meticulosity. While vetting Randy's credibility, I recorded his lengthy testimony on audiotape, thoroughly debriefing him shortly after his taxing, and at times, grueling FBI interrogations. He would exit the FBI building after hours of questioning and report directly to me all that was said and asked.

Repeated sightings of Timothy McVeigh associating with his Middle Eastern band of brothers, the debilitated white moving van stacked with fifty-five gallon drums, recurrent smell and spills of diesel fuel, the famed Mercury Marquis, the targeted brown SUV, the malodorous Ryder truck rolling across the parking lot the evening of April 18, and motel resident Larry Miller's ominous caution to beware of an impending plot to blow up a building were all independently corroborated. Substantiation came from one or more staff members, motel guests, and the nearby gas station attendant. More significantly, the sinister happenings that implied an Iraqi/domestic conspiracy had been carried out at the crime-ridden lodge did not contradict the government's timeline documenting the movements of Terry Nichols and Timothy McVeigh.

At no time during the months of my interviews with Randy Christian did he equivocate, embellish, or recant. According to the FBI, he was guilty of all three acts. But by then, I had grown tragically accustomed to such artful tactics. The federal records I reviewed through impeccable sources established the FBI's pattern of demonstrably changing critical elements of my witnesses' statements or, equally disturbing, removing the written reports from the archive altogether. Subsequent investigation of these occurrences provided proof that several key witness reports were simply not turned over to the defense attorneys. The FBI claimed they didn't exist.

Through the handwritten documentation of witness interviews, it was all too apparent the FBI had at its disposal a built-in plausible deniability of any malicious intent. If what the witness said contradicted the lone bomber theory, the agents could simply twist, distort, or manipulate written reports classified as 302s. While I believe unquestioningly in the honest work ethic of the majority of federal officers, the Bureau's regulations conveniently banned voice recorded interviews, leaving an open door for abuse by a corrupt few. The Randy Christian 302 marked the most egregious example of witness statement tampering I would encounter.

The FBI fallaciously set forth in its November 2002 letter to Senator Arlen Specter that Randy had recanted his claim he witnessed the Oklahoma City bomber drive off the Cactus motel property in a Ryder truck the morning of April 19. According to FBI Section Chief Eleni Kalisch, he confessed he had mistakenly identified an unmarked, mechanically unsound white moving van for the large yellow rental truck. The "false" admission had been recorded in an FBI 302.

"This is an out-and-out lie. I never said that to the FBI," Randy charged with controlled anger. "I made it perfectly clear that on the morning of April 19, I witnessed Timothy McVeigh return a room key and drive out of the Cactus parking lot in a large yellow Ryder truck with a Middle Eastern male by his side. The Mercury Marquis and the brown SUV followed the truck out. Middle Eastern men were inside those vehicles."

"Why did the FBI claim the media and a coworker convinced you the Ryder truck had not been on your motel property the morning of the bombing?" I inquired. "The written 302s allege that you conceded you had been mistaken and that the Ryder truck was never there."

"This is a blatant lie. I never said anything remotely like that," he steadfastly maintained. "The FBI has twisted my words in its reports. I did tell several agents I saw foreign men at the Cactus riding in a broken-down white moving van that reeked of diesel fuel and contained large blue barrels. I said the engine on that dilapidated van died several times in the motel parking lot in the months and weeks prior to the Murrah Building bombing. I never said it was on site the morning of April 19."

"Did the FBI conduct any follow up interviews with your employees and guests in an effort to prove or disprove your claims?" I asked.

"No. I waited for them to arrive. My staff and guests had volunteered full cooperation, but the FBI did not accept my invitation to conduct interviews," he said with exasperation.

Gary and Georgia Hammerstein, Cole O'Brien, Richard Parnell, and Ken Banks awaited calls from the FBI. They never came. Maintenance employee David Elmore's circumstances were more complex. He had failed to pay several years of federal income taxes and had a criminal record that included charges of driving while intoxicated and possession of marijuana. He justifiably feared he would be considered a possible material witness who failed to issue a prior warning—the same charge that led to Michael Fortier's incarceration. After all, Larry Miller's portentous mention to David of a bombing conspiracy and his brief meeting with Terry Nichols and the Middle Eastern men the night of April 16, 1995, could have easily been mis-construed. David's wife Rosanna confided to me that her husband wrestled with the torment of not coming forward immediately.

Finally, in November 1995, David's conscience crumbled under the strain of silence. He phoned the FBI and set an appointment with an agent to give his statement. When he arrived at the FBI headquarters in Oklahoma City, he was asked to wait. A staggering three hours passed and no one acknowledged his presence or spoke to him. He informed the receptionist he was leaving, but she persuaded him to stay awhile longer. His patience was in vain. The FBI had no intention of creating a 302 which would have doc-umented testimony that validated the claims of Cactus motel owner Randy Christian.

Ironically, on that very afternoon, while David sat in the lobby, three FBI agents questioned Randy in the inner chambers. They had placed a polygraph machine on the conference table an arm's length from where the witness was seated.

"I told them I could identify the Middle Eastern suspects who were at the motel with Timothy McVeigh," Randy declared. "I said I would gladly sub-mit to the lie detector test and state for the record the men I saw colluding with McVeigh were featured in KFOR-TV's surveillance photographs. They never hooked me up to the polygraph machine, and I have no idea why."

Randy described the nine-hour marathon as nothing less than a hostile interrogation. He was offered no food, drink, or restroom breaks.

"The agents were clearly not the least bit interested in the facts. I spent the entire time refuting false statements they attributed to me. It was totally exhausting and quite ridiculous."

CHAPTER 13

# THE INSIDER

On June 7, 1995, KFOR-TV led the evening news with a landmark story featuring an unconventional partnership between a Desert Storm Bradley gunner and an ex-enemy combatant who once took up arms in defense of the barbarous Saddam Hussein. Rita Edwards, an Oklahoma City nurse, watched the broadcast in stunned disbelief. She was seated in a room filled with the very men Channel 4 had been investigating. When the disguised photographs of the unnamed Middle Eastern suspect appeared on the screen, one of the Iraqi spectators exclaimed, "That's Hussain, he's got my shirt on."

That evening, Rita and the Iraqis visited a local nightclub. An inebriated Hussain Al-Hussaini turned hostile, throwing his ball cap into the air, barking proudly into the night sky, "Jayna Davis, come and get me! Jayna Davis, come and get me!"

The witness shrugged off the news report implicating Al-Hussaini as sensational journalism. She refused to entertain the notion she blindly ventured inside the nucleus of a terrorist cell. It was an affront to her sensibilities. After all, Rita considered herself an educated professional. Surely she would have detected the red flags. She had been socializing with these Arab immigrants for months. Her niece, Stacy McBride, was the live-in paramour of Majid Ajaj, a self-professed "deserter" from the Iraqi army.

But with the passage of time, nagging doubts tugged at Rita's conscience. Sinister implications began to overshadow seemingly benign events and conversations. She learned the FBI had interrogated Stacy and her boyfriend Majid about Al-Hussaini's alibi for the morning of April 19. Shaken by the interview, a hysterical Majid confided to Rita he was concerned federal investigators would discover his outstanding arrest warrant for failing to show up in court after being charged with driving while intoxicated in Hutchinson, Kansas—a town just south of McPherson where the Denver jury determined bombing suspect Terry Nichols purchased the ammonium nitrate fertilizer used to construct the Murrah Building bomb. A law enforcement source confirmed Majid's Kansas arrest, but when I requested a copy of the driving citation from municipal officials, the record had been expunged for reasons unknown.

As Rita became more reflective, perplexing questions left her all the more suspicious. "Were Al-Hussaini and his Iraqi friends truly 'dissidents' or were they just posing as enemies of the state to gain political asylum in the U.S.?" she pondered. Rita could not understand why they never openly condemned Saddam, yet they had spun sensational, far-fetched tales of harrowing escapes from the Iraqi dictator's death squads. More curious, the band of ex-soldiers harbored unabashed, deep-seated hatred against the United States, the country which had granted them safe haven and taxpayer monies for resettlement.

After contacting me, the troubled witness unburdened herself, disclosing secrets only an insider would know. Flashing back to the fall of 1994, Rita described the influx of Hussain Al-Hussaini and his Iraqi confederates who sought employment doing janitorial and menial fix-it duties at Dr. Anwar Abdul's property management company. She was deeply puzzled by their unexplained source of funding. The minimum wage laborers mysteriously afforded frequent forays to Chicago, Dallas, and other metropolitan areas where terror networks thrived. They engaged in auto insurance scams that netted illicit proceeds which were purportedly wired to "distressed" family members residing in the Middle East.

One particularly disturbing memory took center stage. Rita contemplated why Al-Hussaini and his dapper Iraqi escort from Boston, Abu Mahmud, requested a tour of downtown Oklahoma City six months before the terrorist attack. She recalled how the pair sat silently in the back seat as she played the role of the unquestioning chauffeur.

"This guy Abu stood out in the crowd. He was well-dressed and spoke English flawlessly. If you talked to him on the telephone, you would not detect a Middle Eastern accent," she noted. "But I never figured out why they wanted to tour downtown. When I joked about the preposterous suggestion to go sightseeing in Oklahoma City's business district, both Abu and Hussain didn't see the humor. When they glared at me, I decided it was best to oblige."

After Channel 4's June 1995 broadcasts, Rita bluntly confronted Al-Hussaini about the downtown excursion, but the Iraqi expatriate feigned a language barrier.

"I was flabbergasted." The animated blonde with expressive blue eyes grew circumspect. "I had been conversing with Hussain for months, and suddenly, he couldn't comprehend English. I have no doubt he understood what I said about Abu and the drive near the Murrah Building, but I perceived the strong hint to drop the subject."

In the fall of 1994, the cosmopolitan Bostonian escorted Al-Hussaini to Oklahoma City, sought interim employment with Dr. Abdul, and slept on the living room floor of Stacy and Majid's apartment. In the days leading up to the bombing, Abu Mahmud vanished from Oklahoma and presumably returned to his entrepreneurial ventures on the East Coast.

Rita soon discovered the very mention of his name among the gang of Iraqi comrades elicited menacing stares and the unspoken message to forget she ever met the Boston traveler. But the memory came crashing back on "Black Tuesday" as Al-Qaeda's crazed pilots slammed jetliners into the majestic Twin Towers. She would discover Mahmud's and Al-Hussaini's ties to Boston Logan International Airport, the point of origin for two of the hijacked flights. But the revelations would not stop there. The unwitting insider confronted the daunting prospect that fate had destined her to unearth the nexus between 4-19 and 9-11—the greatest acts of terror on U.S. soil.

CHAPTER 14

# DEATH THREAT

In the summer of 1996, a cryptic phone call beckoned me inside shady business transactions and clandestine activities at a foreign-owned automotive garage opportunely situated a short drive from the bomb site. The two minute telephone conversation with a woman who insisted she remain anonymous caused me to seriously consider the possibility that the Ryder truck bomb was constructed locally, contesting the government's unconvincing theory that McVeigh and Nichols mixed the lethal concoction at a Kansas state park in plain sight of passing motorists and campers.

"Have you looked into the auto repair shop near the Murrah Building?" an unidentified female, who sounded like a heavy smoker, whispered over the line.

"Who is this? How did you get this number?" I said with unmistakable agitation. I was not accustomed to receiving story tips on my unlisted home phone number and had grown impatient with paranoid, wannabe informants who wasted my time with wacky leads.

"I don't feel comfortable giving my name. However, I will tell you that I am the girlfriend of Carlos Perez. He worked at a garage called International Auto Mechanics. Two months before the federal building blew up, his Iranian boss laid off all the mechanics."

"I don't get your point." I bluntly stated.

"I have a friend, Darby Williams," the woman volunteered in an obvious effort to show bona fides. "She's the secretary at Salman Properties. She told me about Channel 4's investigation into the Iraqi men who work there. Darby gave me your phone number."

"So what does that have to do with the garage you mentioned?" I inquired.

Exasperated with my terse attitude, the mysterious caller drew in a deep breath. "The Iraqi soldiers had been seen hanging out at the garage," she said firmly as her volume grew louder. "There were also some strange things going on down there in February 1995. My boyfriend Carlos noticed a sudden increase in overseas calls to the shop from London and Iran. The owner, Ali Kamel, stacked the parking lot with old junkers he bought at an auto auction to make it look like he had a pretty good business. But then for no reason, he sent his employees packing and shut everything down. Then after the big boom downtown, he rehired the same guys. Explain that!"

"Your story sounds compelling, but I will have to speak to Carlos Perez personally to confirm what you have told me."

Her voice quivered. "I'm sorry, but that's not possible. Carlos is an illegal alien. He fears he could end up deported, or even worse, if he's caught snooping around, he could wind up dead."

## ACTIVATED SLEEPER AGENT?

Skeptical but intrigued, I decided to check things out. A few initial phone calls quickly determined that International Auto Mechanics had been operating under the radar screen for approximately five years. Owner Ali Kamel decided his business was exempt from the required city and state permits, but then again, the notoriously unscrupulous businessman exhibited a penchant for breaking the rules. Kamel had been named as a defendant in several civil lawsuits which accused the Iranian immigrant of swindling former partners in retail enterprises that included a fast food restaurant and donut shop. The obligatory due diligence would understandably put a damper on attracting future investors.

But while the unsavory Kamel could be viewed as a loose cannon, if indeed he was a sleeper agent who had been activated for a forthcoming operation, his past nefarious business dealings would be overlooked. He provided ideal logistical support as the proprietor of an auto garage conveniently located sixteen blocks north of the intended target that would conceal the surreptitious construction of the truck bomb and on-the-spot spray painting of the getaway vehicle, the brown Chevrolet pickup. So it was not surprising to learn that two Pakistani nationals, Rizwan Sidiqqi and Adnon Khan, appeared on the scene in November 1994, as the strike date neared, and offered Kamel $25,000 cash to purchase the garage in spite of his scandalous reputation. I speculated that Sidiqqi and Khan possibly served as handlers dispatched to take control of International Auto Mechanics, change the company name, and legitimize the business by registering with the proper government agencies, thereby deflecting unwanted attention.

I began my research with Bernie Stanton, the former company foreman at Salman Properties. Bernie expressed instant familiarity with International Auto Mechanics. He drove by regularly on his way to his ex-wife's residence to pick up his child for weekly visitations. His daughter had to be home in time to catch the school bus, therefore, Bernie's commute took place in the early morning hours. On several occasions in the spring of 1995, he breezed past the garage and casually observed his Iraqi coworkers, Majid Al-Saad and Jaffar Halima, standing in the parking lot outside the aging brick edifice.

"I just assumed they were moonlighting, trying to earn some extra cash. Maybe they were learning auto repair or just offering to clean-up the garage," Bernie speculated.

## CLASSIC COVER OR BUSINESS BLUNDER?

From there I combed the neighborhood. Nothing slipped by Leon Rhodes, a nosey elderly gentleman eking by on a disability pension. Perched under the shade of his front porch, Leon kept a watchful eye on the garage which was situated in his direct line of sight just a few hundred feet across a two-lane roadway.

"Yep, I reckon things slowed down over there in February or March. I almost felt sorry for the foreign fellow, Ali, who ran things. I figured his business had dried up all of a sudden like," Leon said with a slight lisp due to a few missing teeth.

"Did you notice any customers coming or going during those months?" I asked.

"Nope, but it was kind of curious. I couldn't figure out why the parking lot was always chocked full of cars."

"Did you see different vehicles everyday?"

"Nope, I remember thinking those are the same clunkers I saw there for weeks, but eventually that old boy got his business off the ground again."

"Was that before or after April of 1995?"

"It was getting much warmer during those days, so I would guess it was sometime in late April or May."

"So the place was closed for business on April 19, the day of the bombing?"

"Yep, but I do recall seeing the owner, Ali, pop in and out that day," Leon said as he paused to reflect. "I remember after that awful bombing downtown, things got strangely quiet over there for a few hours."

I studied the aging brick edifice with the opaque, spray-painted windows. The dust-caked garage door entrances were sealed shut. Motorists whizzed by during the height of the business week, but none turned in for service or a tune-up. The parking lot remained eerily still. More than a year had passed since the bombing, and the clientele at International Auto Mechanics had dwindled to anemic levels.


## Ambush Interview

On the afternoon of July 7, 1996, I surveyed the garage hoping to find signs of life. I planned to slip inside posing as a prospective customer to explore the interior. I arrived to find Ali Kamel scampering from the shadows of the garage to his car. He hoisted a box overstuffed with papers into the back seat of a dilapidated 1983 Pontiac Grand Prix. I dashed to Kamel's side.

"Are you Ali Kamel?" I asked as I lifted my handheld tape recorder.

"Yes." Kamel answered. He inched backward toward his driver's seat.

"My name is Jayna Davis. I am a reporter with KFOR-TV. Do you own this garage?"

He raised his eyebrows and stared at me intently. "Yes."

"How long have you owned it?

"A long time," the shabbily dressed man with dark, sallow eyes answered.

"How many years?"

"I used to own it," he stammered. "But now I do not own it."

"Were you open for business in April 1995?" I casually inquired. My question elicited an abrupt change in Kamel's demeanor. At first, he appeared gracious as he assessed the purpose for my inquiry. But by now, he had become visibly edgy and surly.

"No, I wasn't here in 1995. At that time, I was in Iran," he retorted.

I took another stab at breaking through the stalemate and posed the question more precisely.

"Did you own this business in April 1995?

Kamel's forehead furrowed as he nervously stroked his unkempt beard. "If somebody walk in and ask if you own this building, what does that mean?" he muttered as he waved his hand signaling me to back off. "I don't want to talk to you anymore."

Kamel mumbled several inaudible comments as he ducked behind the wheel of his car and cranked the engine, drowning out my rapid-fire questions. I jotted down his license tag number as he pulled away. The plate traced back to a "Myrna Morrissey" at a fictitious Oklahoma City address.

Though my ambush interview with Kamel netted scant information, one conspicuous inconsistency came to light. The Iranian native insisted he was out of the country when the bombing occurred. But two witnesses impeached his statement. The ever-present busybody from across the street, Leon Rhodes, confidently asserted he watched Kamel enter International Auto Mechanics on April 19. Moreover, Kamel's former business partner in the failed renovation of a fast food restaurant, Tim Rains, expressed the distinct impression Kamel was in town that day. He and his wife Thelma recounted when Kamel phoned their home unexpectedly in late April, claiming he had just arrived in Oklahoma on a flight from Iran. He demanded Rains pick him at the airport, but when Rains arrived, Kamel was nowhere to be found. The annoyed chauffeur requested airport personnel page the missing passenger, but there was no response.

The even-tempered retiree seized the moment to vent some pent up frustration. "I wouldn't put it past Kamel to stage an airport pickup to convince me he traveled home to Iran for a visit. We had a contractual agreement to remodel a restaurant, but when the deal went south, this guy had a bad habit of making himself scarce whenever I demanded answers," Rains sniped. He then handed me a copy of a $2,500 bounced check Kamel wrote to him as a partial down payment in the doomed eatery venture.

When Rains inquired about the airport debacle, Kamel seemed rattled and offered a rambling, "nonsensical" excuse for the miscommunication. "I frankly believe he was trying to use me as an alibi to establish that he flew in from an overseas trip after the bombing, but I just don't get why he went to all that trouble," he postulated.

## SHADY SALES TRANSACTION

State filings showed that Kamel transferred ownership of International Auto Mechanics to Rizwan Sidiqqi in the fall of 1994, but the corporate status of the new company fell inactive the following June. But while the time frame surrounding the bombing could have been purely coincidental, I could not reconcile the money factor. Kamel's ex-associate, Tim Rains, was acquainted with Adnon Khan and leased an apartment to Rizwan Sidiqqi. He claimed to have firsthand knowledge of the peculiar transaction surrounding the sale of the garage.

Rains's disclosure left me contemplating the limited financial resources available to Sidiqqi, a full-time college student, and his partner Adnon Khan, a New York taxi cab driver who had temporarily set up residence in Oklahoma for the sole purpose of acquiring Kamel's garage. I could not help but question how they scraped together the start-up capital to launch a new business—and a risky one at that. According to the owner of the building where International Auto Mechanics was housed, Sidiqqi, unlike Kamel, prepaid the lease on the garage through August 1995. So why did job dismissals come down in February, and the business become stagnant without any outward effort to solicit new customers? The answers would further solidify my theory that something in this equation was amiss.

On the evening of July 14, 1996, my husband Drew and I showed up at Sidiqqi's apartment. When the doorbell chimed, someone parted the blinds and spied at us through window, but no one answered. We departed soon afterwards, but came back some time later. We returned to find the front door slightly ajar and the trunk of Sidiqqi's car propped open.

"Hey Jayna, check out the personalized license plate. Do you think we have located the right guy?" Drew laughed as he pointed to a rear tag bearing the name "Rizwan."

A silhouette crossed over the light streaming from inside. I darted toward the front porch and lightly tapped on the door. A gargantuan man, towering nearly six-feet-seven-inches, wearing a black pajama-type ensemble, stepped outside to greet us. Disarmingly polite, Rizwan Sidiqqi invited us into his home. I immediately discerned Sidiqqi was far more urbane than the skittish Kamel.

"Your landlord, Tim Rains, tells me that you purchased International Auto Mechanics from Ali Kamel in September 1994."

"Yes, that is correct," he stated. "At first we paid him [Ali Kamel] like half the money for buying the business. But after that, we did not pay because business was not going good, so we had to give it [the business] back to him [Kamel]."

Sidiqqi did not betray a glimmer of curiosity about why a local reporter would be prying into the demise of his automotive repair shop. He conspicuously declined to ask me the news value of the story, but he did make it abundantly clear the investment went belly-up.

"Did you and your partner, Adnon Khan, invest a lot of money?"

"Yeah," Sidiqqi replied. "Twenty-five thousand dollars, and it's hard for a student to raise that kind of money."

"May I examine your sales contract?"

"Adnon has everything."

"When you purchased the garage from Ali Kamel, did you have the impression he was an honest businessman?"

The Pakistani expatriate looked at me nervously, then seized the opportunity to impugn Kamel and validate the untimely failure of the garage. He scurrilously charged the former owner duped him into believing the business generated a viable commercial clientele by stacking the parking lot with broken down vehicles. I would later learn such a ruse was a well-established modus operandi of terrorist organizations for money laundering operations through shell companies.

"He (Kamel) borrowed fifteen, twenty, twenty-five cars from his friends and he was telling me, we, they were his customers' cars, and in fact, they were not." I found it incredulous that the intellectually gifted student, who was working toward a degree in both computer science and international business, would fall prey to such a transparent scam.

"My research indicates that you laid off your staff and closed the doors a few months later in February 1995. What precipitated that decision?" I asked.

"It was because of the bad reputation of Ali as well as the location. We had real bad crime at the shop." He did not elaborate further. At that point, his explanations only augmented my misgivings about his veracity.

Sidiqqi said the financial bind forced him to stop paying rent on the building when he handed out pink slips in February 1995. That was a lie. I had already confirmed with the owner the lease had been prepaid for another six months through August. Why would he subsequently swallow a $25,000 loss and hand the keys to the unprofitable enterprise back to Kamel? Why would he acquire an illegitimate repair shop that both he and Khan knew lacked the mandated operating permits? Without a doubt, the warning signs had been posted.

I wanted to pose this string of queries directly to the unseen partner, Adnon Khan, but Sidiqqi adeptly sidestepped my request.

"He's probably going to New York because he's working there. He's a taxicab driver. But if you can get a hold of him before Tuesday, he knows a lot of stuff about Ali [Kamel]."

## New York by Tuesday

Given Sidiqqi's reticence about arranging an interview, I decided to consult the Oklahoma City phone directory. To my surprise, Adnon Khan was listed. I surmised a frontal approach might elicit the same lockdown I received from Ali Kamel, so I opted for a more subtle tactic. I enlisted the talent of my husband Drew, a trained U.S. Army linguist, who had a knack for mimicking foreign accents. With that untapped skill in mind, we devised an audacious ruse that bordered on outlandish. But somehow, we pulled it off.

Posing as a friend named "Mohammed," Drew called Khan and spoke to him with a contrived Middle Eastern accent.

"I hear that you are leaving on Tuesday to return to New York," Drew suggested as I pressed my ear close to the mobile phone and feverishly jotted down notes.

"Yes. This is true," Adnon confirmed, oblivious to the imposter on the other end of the line.

"I need number to reach you," Drew stated firmly. The Middle Easterner quickly obliged, and after placing him on hold for a moment, returned to the phone and dictated a number in Queens where he would be residing.

"Where do you work in New York? Maybe I contact you if I come to town." Drew proposed.

"I work ordinary job," Adnon responded glibly.

"I know, but I hear you going to drive taxicab. I need your work number."

"I work ordinary job, you know that," Khan's impatience sent the tacit message he was unfamiliar with the taxicab story. Obviously, he had forgotten that he told Sidiqqi's landlord, Tim Rains, that he moved to New York after the 1995 bombing to drive a cab.

"I know you work ordinary job, but I . . ." Drew continued, but by then, Adnon had detected the man to whom he was speaking was not his friend.

"Which Mohammed is this?" he interrupted.

Drew flashed an uncomfortable expression my way, then improvised.

"As I told you before…" click, he ended the call and bailed out before the conversation deteriorated further.

I grabbed the phone and immediately dialed the Queens, New York residence, desperately hoping Adnon had not called ahead to warn his friends that he had been conned into compromising the phone number. Swift action paid dividends.

"Hello," a stout voice penetrated the earpiece.

"This is Mohammed, I want to speak to Adnon," Drew ad-libbed.

"He will be here on Tuesday," the man replied with an Arabic inflection.

"I need to reach Adnon at work. Do you have his number where he drive taxicab?"

"You mean Sabah," the Middle Easterner stated emphatically.

"No, I am calling for Adnon Khan," Drew insisted, not realizing that "Adnon" was apparently an alias for "Sabah."

A sharp order shot back. "You call back Tuesday and talk to Sabah."

Drew shrugged as he sank deeper in the quick sand. "Who is Sabah?"

"You don't know who Sabah is?"

"No."

"Who is this?" the stranger bellowed.

Drew immediately reverted to the impromptu fallback plan. "As I told you before . . ." click, the line went dead.


## Death Threat

In a relatively short time span, three people informed me that Adnon "Sabah" Khan planned to arrive in New York City on Tuesday. Tim Rains, Rizwan Sidiqqi, and Adnon himself all noted the date of his return to his home state was July 16, 1996. Distracted by the challenge to get inside the garage to steal a look around, I disregarded the factoid regarding Khan's travel itinerary as frivolous. My attention would be redirected to the jet set New York cabbie soon enough.

The next morning, at 1:17 A.M. on July 16, the phone rang, piercing the darkness. As I awakened from deep slumber, my answering machine picked up.

"It is very urgent I reach Jayna Davis," a guttural voice with an unmistakable foreign accent spoke into the dead of night. "Jayna, you must wake up to answer this phone call."

My heart pounded. In my disoriented state floating between sleep and consciousness, I felt like the man on the phone was standing in my room.

Then I heard the line disconnect followed by dial tone. While trying to assess what just happened, the phone rang again. I froze. The answering machine recorded the message.

"Jayna, don't try to run away. Jayna, you can't get away. You're not going to get away with this," the unidentified caller threatened. "Okay. See you in hell!"

A trusted police source tracked the origin of the call, but the trail of clues quickly vaporized. The number that registered on my caller I.D. originated from a prepaid cell phone which was purchased under an alias with no address or employment information.

Ten months later, after residing in the United States for more than a decade, Ali Kamel liquidated his assets, sold his donut shop, and returned to Iran. Simultaneously, Kamel's Oklahoma City lawyer closed his practice, resigned from the state bar, and left Oklahoma. Shortly after his unexplained exodus, he faced disciplinary proceedings for moving out of state without giving proper notice to several clients. The vanishing attorney could not be located to resolve pending cases because he left no forwarding address. He opened a new law firm years later in North Carolina.

CHAPTER 15

# CIVIL WEAPON

Airing one investigative expose after another, KFOR-TV obliquely alluded to the possibility of foreign state sponsorship in the April 19 act of terror. From the tire store employee who gave Timothy McVeigh directions to the intersection of 5th and Harvey Streets to the young mother standing at ground zero cradling her newborn son, the eyewitness sightings consistently overlapped—the Caucasian driver was accompanied by a Middle Eastern male.

The August 1995 indictment of the Oklahoma City bombers punctuated Channel 4's provocative reporting. The federal grand jury determined McVeigh and Nichols acted with "others unknown." But Hussain Al-Hussaini was not waiting for the feds to show up on his doorstep seeking an explanation for KFOR-TV's witness identifications placing him in the blast zone. Instead, he fired the first shot in an orchestrated offensive to silence and discredit my reporting. He and his Middle Eastern cohorts scored a public relations coup by retaining nationally acclaimed Tulsa lawyer, Gary Richardson. Flanked by his team of high-profile attorneys, Hussain Al-Hussaini called a citywide press conference on August 24, 1995, to announce he had filed a multi-million dollar libel lawsuit in state court against KFOR-TV, naming me personally as a defendant.

"The identification of our client as John Doe 2, the way that the investigation was conducted by this television station, not only shows malice but an absolute disregard for this man's integrity as a human being," co-counsel William Donovan impugned with melodramatic indignation. "It's one of the most horrendous cases we've seen."

But Donovan would not litigate the lawsuit. He soon found himself embroiled in a disbarment investigation for allegations of misappropriating $86,000 from a client trust account. To avoid disciplinary proceedings, Donovan voluntarily surrendered his law license and resigned from the Oklahoma Bar Association.

## HIGH-PROFILE LYNCHING

The press ceaselessly pilloried the station and me in what quickly became the most highly publicized defamation case in Oklahoma history. It didn't seem to matter what the facts were or that in producing the broadcast reports I had independently corroborated the witnesses' stories and consulted the station's legal counsel throughout every phase of the investigation. As a precautionary measure, KFOR-TV's attorney Robert Nelon and news director Melissa Klinzing were even present during a telephone conference call in which FBI Special Agent Dan Vogel admitted that Hussain Al-Hussaini "had not yet been ruled out" as a possible suspect.

Regardless of its merits, the lawsuit had achieved its purpose, which was to shut down any further broadcasts. As a result, the majority of the evidence that I believed implicated Al-Hussaini in the terrorist attack would never reach the public airwaves. Eyewitnesses had identified the Iraqi expatriate fraternizing with Timothy McVeigh prior to the bombing at an Oklahoma City tavern and also a local motel, riding in the passenger seat of the Ryder truck the morning of April 19, exiting that truck onto the north sidewalk which lined the entrance to the Murrah Building, and racing away from the shattered and burning remains of the Murrah Building in a brown pickup flagged by law enforcement. Yet the FBI remained impervious, refusing to question the possible Iraqi John Doe.

I would eventually pose the questions the feds declined to ask. The disquieting answers that poured forth from the man accused of merciless terror would ultimately cause the civil weapon he aimed at me to backfire.

## LEGAL VINDICATION

Before long, Hussain Al-Hussaini's legal strategy to stall, silence, and subvert became apparent. Two years passed and he still had not offered any evidence or witness statements which refuted Channel 4's stories or established his innocence. In April 1997, the plaintiff voluntarily dismissed his libel complaint just twenty-four hours before an Oklahoma state district judge was slated to rule on KFOR-TV's meticulously documented motion for dismissal. Six months later, in September 1997, the Oklahoma County Grand Jury investigating the prospect of unknown conspirators in the bombing subpoenaed me to testify. One day following my publicized appearance before the panel, Al-Hussaini re-filed his libel lawsuit—this time in *federal* court.

Two years later, on November 17, 1999, U.S. District Judge Timothy Leonard delivered sweeping vindication, dismissing the case in a ruling which upheld as "undisputed" all fifty statements of fact and opinion that KFOR-TV set forth implicating the plaintiff in the bombing. Most notably, Al-Hussaini had failed after four years of litigation and two separate lawsuits to produce even one witness affidavit verifying his alibi, leaving the witness testimonies which discredited his whereabouts for the morning of April 19 unchallenged.

Al-Hussaini's arrogant abuse of the civil justice system multiplied with each resounding defeat. The Iraqi national appealed the trial court decision to the Tenth Circuit Court of Appeals. On September 10, 2001, the eve of the apocalyptic Islamic terrorist strikes on the World Trade Center and Pentagon, oral arguments in favor of granting the Iraqi national his right to a jury trial were presented by his attorneys to the Denver appellate court.

The final chapter in the eight-year legal saga would not be written for another eighteen months. March 26, 2003, marked the day of deliverance. The three judge panel handed down a stinging rebuke of Al-Hussaini's pattern of legal foot-dragging and delays. More importantly, they reached a unanimous across-the-board affirmation of the evidence I had presented which painted a portrait of guilt, stating KFOR-TV had not "recklessly disregarded the truth."

## DODGING THE SUBPOENA

As in the three-judge panel ruling issued by the Tenth Circuit Court of Appeals, when Al-Hussaini resurrected the defamation lawsuit in federal court, he employed similar stall tactics to those in his aborted state suit. From its filing, a year passed while the case languished. There were no scheduled depositions, hearings, or a trial date. In the summer of 1998, my attorneys decided to ripple the waters. They issued several subpoenas ordering the plaintiff to appear in Oklahoma for a deposition. Each time the summons was ignored. Al-Hussaini also stonewalled repeated discovery requests for immigration and medical records.

In July 1998, Judge Leonard intervened and ended the stalemate. Finally, after months of legal wrangling, Al-Hussaini's attorneys begrudgingly released hundreds of pages of psychiatric records in which the Iraqi immigrant claimed to be experiencing mental delusions, depression, and suicidal thoughts. The documents told a chilling story.

In October 1997, Hussain Al-Hussaini committed himself to a psychiatric hospital in Boston complaining of sleeplessness, nightmares, auditory hallucinations, and terrifying flashbacks. His doctors attributed his heavy drinking and emotional breakdown to a condition known as Post Traumatic Stress Disorder (PTSD), speculating that years of torture in an Iraqi prison triggered the "chronically delayed" onset of symptoms. But the self-professed Iraqi dissident was not able to produce the paperwork necessary to legally substantiate his claims of imprisonment.

The timing of Al-Hussaini's hospitalization intrigued me. He entered the facility for in-patient treatment two full years after Channel 4 broadcast the reports which he contended had falsely depicted him as a terrorist and inflicted emotional distress. Did he check into the mental health facility to console "trauma" suffered as a result of KFOR-TV's stories? Was he reliving agonizing torment suffered in Saddam's death chambers? Or, did a hidden agenda drive him to seek help?

The patient privately lamented to his doctors he was suffering extreme apprehension about the prospect of being subpoenaed before the Oklahoma County Grand Jury, claiming he was emotionally unfit to travel to Oklahoma to testify. What Al-Hussaini did not tell his doctors was that the panel was exploring lingering questions revolving around the legendary John Doe 2 and had subpoenaed me to testify just two weeks prior to his hospitalization.

On December 22, 1997, he pled with Dr. Frank Kahr to write a letter exempting him from being questioned by the panel. I wondered if he had become inordinately apprehensive about a grand jury inquiry because the FBI denied his public requests to officially clear him. The following entry was excerpted from Al-Hussaini's medical file:

Hussain and his girlfriend expressed concerns that he may be subpoenaed for a grand jury investigation in Oklahoma. I agreed with him that he is not ready to go to Oklahoma, and said that if he receives a subpoena, I will write a letter to support his not traveling there. He will be faxing the correspondence he has received so far to me and we will respond accordingly.

Dr. Kahr did, in fact, subsequently author a missive to the Oklahoma County district attorney asserting Al-Hussaini's psychiatric condition was such that he would "not authorize medical clearance for him to travel to Oklahoma City and testify in the Grand Jury proceeding."

During his deposition in his KFOR-TV lawsuit, Al-Hussaini denied the Oklahoma County Grand Jury or district attorney had requested he appear for questioning. However, his claim turned out to be patently false. In the eleventh hour, my attorney, Daniel Woska, discovered Dr. Kahr's letter attached to a plaintiff's brief which had been hastily filed during the heat of our depositions. Quite frankly, it was a miracle the exhibit was discovered given the tremendous time crunch under which my lawyers were operating, frantically sifting through mountains of medical records and immigration documents which were not released until the last minute.

## DAMNING DOSSIER

The comprehensive medical dossier yielded damning clues into the troubled mind of the ex-Iraqi serviceman. Haunting images of lifeless bombing victims pervaded his thoughts. He fantasized about making a bomb and confessed his paranoia that the police might arrest him when the darkness of night descended, compelling him to sleep in his girlfriend's car to avoid capture. Medical records of his fall 1997 therapy at a psychiatric clinic include the following notations by his attending physicians:

- Patient called this center this morning to say he was despondent. He also said he had been drinking vodka and had thoughts about making a bomb, although he did not know how to do this.

- Patient reported he was feeling distressed and was feeling like "making a bomb" and doing something "very bad" and this was the reason he asked to be hospitalized. Patient reports his medication is causing him to have angry outbursts at work, etc.

- Sometimes after his girlfriend has fallen asleep, he'll take the car keys and sleep in her car, to avoid the police if they come to the house. He drinks partly to stop thinking about these issues.

- He did not tell us the extent of his paranoia, i.e., he would sometimes sleep in his girlfriend's car to avoid "being taken away."

- Patient admits to auditory hallucinations. Voices say "I'm John Doe #2." States he hears voices of bombing victims and hears Timothy McVeigh all the time.

- He still hears voices on the train home from work, and "sees" people from the Oklahoma bombing on the train.

- [He] believes people on the train are talking about him, thinks he "sees" people from the Oklahoma City bombing on the train.

- Patient states that he is still hearing voices occasionally, voices that tell him he should die.

The experts who treated Al-Hussaini's delusional episodes surmised the psychological malady known as PTSD produced recurrent dark visions, fits of anger, "crying," and "fearfulness." Meanwhile, KFOR-TV's lawyers conducted an independent psychiatric evaluation in which our expert concluded the distraught patient was manifesting the classic "symptoms of guilt," not PTSD.

## DAUNTING DEPOSITION

My attorneys would eventually address the probability of Al-Hussaini's complicity in a white knuckle confrontation with the Iraqi soldier. In October 1998, after it became abundantly clear the plaintiff must comply with the presiding judge's order to appear for a deposition or risk an almost certain dismissal of his lawsuit, Al-Hussaini showed up in Oklahoma City. Much to my legal team's surprise, he broke down under intense questioning. Visibly shaken, he described an auditory hallucination in which a voice he believed to be Timothy McVeigh's said to him, "Why should I be executed, executed by myself? I want you to be executed with me."

Al-Hussaini's focus drifted into a trancelike gaze. "He [McVeigh] said you have to die."

When presented with the macabre statements he made to his psychiatrists, Al-Hussaini confessed he had been prescribed anti-psychotic medication to control his auditory and visual hallucinations. He said he was haunted by the image of a "lady who lost her two babies" and could see her face in his mind's eye and hear her voice. Curiously, he said both the grief-stricken mother and bombing convict Timothy McVeigh spoke to him in English, a language in which he professed little proficiency.

The most riveting moment in the eight-day deposition arrived when the Arab émigré reluctantly admitted he heard voices inside his head that whispered, "You are John Doe 2."

In that breathtaking moment, the room filled with an eerie, palpable silence. I grappled with the enormity of the ramifications. I determined that even if he was telling the truth about his unstable state of mind, he could not have imagined himself to be a bloodthirsty terrorist after viewing several brief television news broadcasts in which his identity and name were painstakingly concealed.

Damning questions began to flood my mind. Why did Al-Hussaini dream about making bombs, hide from the police, cower from the ghoulish images of those who perished on April 19, and evade being interviewed by the grand jury? Was he a lunatic or was the explanation much simpler? Could it be he was burdened by inexorable guilt because he *was* John Doe 2?

## UNWITTING CONFESSION

Oddly enough, Hussain Al-Hussaini himself unraveled the mystery. During eight days of what amounted to be grilling sessions by KFOR-TV's attorneys, the truth slowly emerged from the man's own lips. In statements that would seem innocuous to the casual observer, Al-Hussaini unwittingly confessed to incriminating details known only to the eyewitnesses and the diffident customer whom they observed socializing with Timothy McVeigh at a sleazy Oklahoma City dance club on April 15, 1995.

My attorneys and I were astounded when Al-Hussaini enthusiastically admitted he had, in fact, visited the bar in question following KFOR-TV's June 1995 newscast. He explained a friend drove him to the rear entrance of the nightclub and parked. Al-Hussaini said he then leaned forward in the passenger seat and peered inside the establishment through an open door, but he claimed he did not enter. His testimony mirrored the story recounted by bartender Elizabeth Brown. In June 1995, she shared her terrifying second encounter with the possible suspect who glowered menacingly at her. Most incriminating was the undisputed fact that KFOR-TV never publicly disclosed that portion of the witness's testimony. The station's lawyers were the only parties who were privy to the information.

Al-Hussaini was then shown the June 7, 1995, broadcast in its entirety. At the end of the story, Channel 4's legal counsel challenged the plaintiff to point out how he determined the location of the bar from the news report. Al-Hussaini floundered for an answer—an answer he didn't have. KFOR-TV had chosen not to broadcast outside footage of the establishment and did not disclose the name or address of the business. Therefore, there was no reasonable explanation as to how Al-Hussaini could have returned to that location unless he was, indeed, the mysterious man who accompanied the Oklahoma City terrorist Timothy McVeigh.

## PUBLIC PROPAGANDA, NO PROOF

The protracted litigation turned into a slow bloodletting campaign. Al-Hussaini and his legal interlocutors summoned the press microphones and unleashed scurrilous charges of journalistic malfeasance. Meanwhile, I stood by mute, powerless to respond. KFOR-TV's lawyers issued strict guidelines to sort out the facts in court, not on the evening news. Three years had passed before Al-Hussaini's baseless public assault against my professional conduct would be exposed as public propaganda with no proof.

Lead counsel Gary Richardson touted himself as the "top gun libel law attorney in the American Southwest" with several favorable multi-million dollar judgments against television networks under his belt. During the August 24, 1995, press conference, it became painfully obvious Richardson had performed little to no research on his client's hyperbolic accusations.

"There's unbelievable harassment by Channel 4, parking in a position when he couldn't even leave his home in his car, following him, intimidating him, harassing him," Richardson excoriated with animated bravado. "They are trying to interview this man without an interpreter. They [KFOR-TV] put a lot of pressure on him. They encountered him time and again. [They] attempted to stick a microphone in his face and talk with him. He can hardly even understand English."

Hussain Al-Hussaini's interpreter and Palestinian employer, Dr. Anwar

Abdul, joined in the carping session. I assumed Richardson was unaware Dr. Abdul was a convicted felon who had been imprisoned for insurance fraud schemes and previously suspected by the FBI as having ties to the Palestinian Liberation Organization.

"His life is in danger. He can't leave his house without somebody accompanying him. When he attempted to go and buy some food from the grocery store, some people chase him, spit on his face, and beat him up, so he had to run for his life," Dr. Abdul stated in an effort to elicit sympathy from a roomful of attentive reporters.

Al-Hussaini did not report the alleged harassment and hate crimes to the police. While being deposed three years later, the "downtrodden" Iraqi suffered a bout of amnesia. When compelled to delineate the previous charges of public retaliation and physical abuse, Al-Hussaini could only recall two verbal exchanges in which strangers treated him with disrespect. During the first incident, he claimed a customer at a local grocery store recognized him from television broadcasts and blurted out a derogatory name. Al-Hussaini became frightened and ran out of the store, but the would-be attacker did not pursue him. The second clash with the public purportedly occurred while Al-Hussaini was manicuring a lawn at one of Dr. Abdul's properties. Several tenants whom he could not identify hurled insults at him. He provided no witnesses to corroborate his testimony, even though the suspects would have resided in his employer's rental houses.

Most unbelievable was the Iraqi soldier's failure to recall any specific incident in which he was chased, spit on, or physically assaulted as Dr. Abdul avouched during the 1995 news conference. For that matter, he could not recount one incident in which I blocked his driveway, foisted a microphone in his face, and forced him to speak to me without the benefit of an interpreter as his lawyer, Gary Richardson, wildly asserted. However, Al-Hussaini did recall a legitimate incident in which an unmarked Channel 4 news van followed him from a distance. That afternoon, a KFOR-TV photographer recorded video of the telling tattoo on his upper left arm.

A confidential witness who socialized with Hussain Al-Hussaini and his Iraqi comrades further disputed his testimony. In a detailed affidavit, the Oklahoma City nurse confirmed Al-Hussaini "never mentioned he was the target of public scorn or insults as a result of KFOR-TV's broadcasts."

The manic attempt to garner public sympathy tipped the scales of credulity when Dr. Abdul accused unnamed Channel 4 employees of stealing Al-Hussaini's immigration records.

"He is not doing anything, just sitting at home, and as I mentioned to you, he [is] trying to figure out what is happening to him, and he is trying to seek employment and the people rejected him up front," the Palestinian ex-convict avowed. "He can't do anything. They [KFOR-TV] stole his papers too, and he couldn't get any identification or get anything to prove his identity also."

During questioning in the civil lawsuit, Al-Hussaini parroted the original accusation, stopping short of naming Channel 4 as the responsible party, yet the insinuation of criminal guilt was crystal clear. He described two suspects riding in a green Plymouth circling his house in the dead of night. The next morning, he awoke to find his "paperwork" missing from the trunk of his car.

"My car broken [into] at night. [These] things happen at night, and then the next morning [is] when Channel 4 called the office [Salman Properties]. They want to talk to me," Al-Hussaini said as he acknowledged declining my request for an interview.

The intimation that Channel 4 stole his personal documents struck me as the proverbial grasping at straws. Even if an unknown burglar absconded with his immigration records, why did he not contact the Immigration Naturalization Service and obtain a computer generated duplicate? He publicly harped on the theft of his identification cards as the reason for not finding employment in the wake of KFOR-TV's stories. How then did he access the voluminous immigration file that the court ordered he remit to the news station's legal team? Once again, outrageous statements had boxed him into a corner with no wiggle room.

## SHATTERED ALIBI

The 1995 news conference laid the groundwork to impeach the heart of Hussain Al-Hussaini's declaration of innocence—his alibi. A fair-minded journalist from the crowd requested Hussain Al-Hussaini specify his whereabouts when the terrorist bomb detonated. Astonishingly, his attorney Gary Richardson interjected, "I'm going to stop them on giving his [Al-Hussaini's] exact location."

Richardson's client had previously apprised the Oklahoma City press that he was painting a garage at 2241 NW 31st Street at the critical hour. However, a June 1995 KFOR-TV expose shattered the cornerstone of the Iraqi handyman's publicly espoused alibi. Next door neighbor Elvin Devers adamantly insisted he saw no one working inside or outside the garage at the house in question. Furthermore, Al-Hussaini's coworkers lambasted his story, asserting he had been assigned to a different job site six blocks north at 2220 NW 37$^{th}$ Street, but did not arrive until well after the bombing.

Fellow Salman Properties employee Bernie Stanton performed construction tasks that day at the same NW 37$^{th}$ Street location but left temporarily to collect some tools. He pulled out of the driveway just a few minutes shy of the explosion downtown. An hour later, he returned to see Al-Hussaini "slapping paint" on the garage door alongside Mexican national Jose Gonzales and Iraqi associate Mohammed Amir. Where was Al-Hussaini between 9:00 A.M. and 10:00 A.M.? The answer would indict or exonerate.

Confronted with the damaging broadcast report and sealed court evidence, Al-Hussaini came to the deposition table in 1998 and offered the memory lapse defense. He recalled painting a garage the morning of April 19 but could not remember the specific address. What came next left me dumbstruck. Al-Hussaini said he never told the media he was at 2241 NW 31$^{st}$ Street when the bomb detonated. He then brazenly accused KWTV reporter Dave Balut of slipshod journalism by placing him at the incorrect house.

"When I see the guy [reporter Dave Balut] from the TV, working in the TV, he talking about me, he said I'm working in this house that day of the bomb, but that's wrong. Not this house I work in. Another house, another site. I know where it is, but I can't remember what address," Al-Hussaini testified.

Assuming the friendly media did get his alibi wrong, Al-Hussaini chose not to correct the supposed error with KWTV, KOCO-TV, or the *Oklahoma Gazette*. I had no doubt his lawyers discerned his deleterious about-face. Al-Hussaini's waffling alibi elucidated attorney Gary Richardson's urgent need to shut down reporters' questions regarding his client's whereabouts.

Three years later, during his deposition, the Iraqi plaintiff was still unable to pinpoint his precise whereabouts when the horrendous crime occurred, a terrorist slaughter in which he had been implicated. Appearing cooperative, he provided a general description of the house and detached garage where he claimed to be working. My attorneys and I found the gesture laughable. How were we to determine the address? White siding and green trim hardly distinguished any home in the depressed section of town replete with countless single story rental units that looked virtually alike. Why would Al-Hussaini fail to obtain Dr. Anwar Abdul's bookkeeping records of his April 19 job assignment? The answer was no mystery.

By that point, Al-Hussaini's legal team had discovered through confidential KFOR-TV defense filings that Dr. Abdul told Bernie Stanton in a hidden camera interview that Al-Hussaini was working at 2241 NW 31st

Street. But as the litigation entered its third year, the record reflected the fact that not one Iraqi colleague was willing to sign an affidavit corroborating Al-Hussaini's presence at the work site. The testimony of coworker Larry Monroe presented another insurmountable hurdle. In a surreptitiously recorded interview, the crestfallen witness confessed he had mistakenly informed the local press that Al-Hussaini was working with him on NW 31st Street that morning.

"Ah, man, I thought Hussain was with me. He wasn't with me. He wasn't with me," Larry confirmed as his voice cracked with emotion.

As the questioning intensified in Al-Hussaini's deposition, a telltale clue came to light. The plaintiff recalled that Jose, Mohammed, and Bernie had been dispatched to the same rental property the morning of April 19. Such a disclosure amounted to a confession that he was indeed working at 2220 NW 37$^{th}$ as Bernie Stanton had testified to the FBI and on KFOR-TV's airwaves years earlier. Clocking the Iraqi soldier's exact time of arrival called for minute by minute reconstruction. The process began with Bernie's departure from the job site at approximately 8:57 A.M. and extended through his return shortly past 10:00 A.M. when he first witnessed Al-Hussaini on the property. Attorney Robert Nelon's masterful sequencing of carefully prepared questions guided the plaintiff into a crucial admission, popping the latch on Al-Hussaini's lockbox of secrets. The lost hour between 9:00 A.M. and 10:00 A.M. had been disinterred.

Q: "What time did you get to this house [2220 NW 37th Street] on April 19 to start work?"

Al-Hussaini: "About 8:30 A.M., 8:20 A.M."

Q: "Did you have to go by Dr. Anwar Abdul's [pseudonym] office to get your job assignment?"

Al-Hussaini: "Yes."

Q: "Did you drive to this house yourself?"

Al-Hussaini: "Yes. I took Jose Gonzales [pseudonym] and Mohammed Amir [pseudonym] and I drove the car, in my car."

Q: "Was Bernie Stanton [pseudonym] at the house when you got there that morning?"

Al-Hussaini: "No. He come at 10:00 A.M."

Bernie Stanton flatly disputed Al-Hussaini's testimony. When Bernie pulled up to the job site at 8:30 A.M., he noticed the garage and interior of the house were empty. Thirty minutes later, as 9:00 A.M. approached, Bernie jumped into his pickup to return home to retrieve some construction equipment. Al-Hussaini and his carpool companions, Jose Gonzales and Mohammed Amir, had not yet shown up.

From there, Al-Hussaini found himself increasingly squeezed into yet another tight spot. In a secretly recorded conversation, Mexican coworker Jose Gonzales admitted to Bernie that he was unsure when he and Al-Hussaini drove up to the house at 2220 NW 37$^{th}$ Street. He eventually guessed the pair's time of arrival at 9:30 A.M., more than an hour later than Al-Hussaini's estimate. More significantly, Al-Hussaini's only alibi witness had obliterated his claim that he reported to work prior to the bombing.

Al-Hussaini's April 19 time card, or lack thereof, further undermined his already dubious alibi. He acknowledged to KFOR-TV's lawyers that the owner of Salman Properties, Dr. Anwar Abdul, tabulated employee work hours with handwritten time sheets. But shortly after Al-Hussaini and his Iraqi associates were hired in November 1994, Dr. Abdul instituted a time clock to tabulate payroll. Henceforth, workers punched time cards to document the beginning and end of their work shifts.

With perceptible reticence, Al-Hussaini admitted he no longer possessed his Salman Properties time record for April 19. Moreover, he contended his memory was a bit foggy on whether or not the time card that was presented to the local media in 1995 was typewritten, computer generated, handwritten, or machine stamped. According to a hidden camera interview, Dr. Abdul's daughter, Helen, confessed to Bernie Stanton she fabricated Al-Hussaini's handwritten time sheet because his machine stamped card for the day of the bombing could not be found. When confronted with the allegation that Helen gave the press a falsified time sheet, Al-Hussaini coyly slipped into a state of confusion and forgetfulness.

> Q: "Were you present when Helen Abdul [pseudonym] gave Dave Balut [KWTV reporter] the time sheet?"
> Al-Hussaini: "Yes."
> Q: "Did you ask Helen to give him a time sheet showing where you were that day on April 19?"
> Al-Hussaini: "Yes."
> Q: "Where did Helen get the time sheet that she showed to Dave Balut?"
> Al-Hussaini: "I can't remember. I don't know how. She works in the office. She knows everything."
> Q: "Do you know whether Helen made up a time sheet to give to Dave Balut?

Al-Hussaini: "She made a copy of the time card."

Q: "A Xerox copy on a machine?"

Al-Hussaini: "Okay. All right. The time was on the computer. She gave him a printout from a computer."

Q: "Was the information in the computer based on time cards you had punched in on?"

Al-Hussaini: "I don't know. Okay. I don't recall if it was a typewriter or computer, but she [Helen Abdul] just typed something, and she gave him [reporter Dave Balut] a copy of—it was supposed to be the time—time sheet or . . ."

Q: "So it may have been a typewriter rather than a computer that she used to make the time sheet?"

Al-Hussaini: "I don't know."

Salman Properties employees Bernie Stanton and Darby Williams confirmed that the company owner did not use handwritten, typed, or computer tabulated time sheets, only machine punched cards. From the fabricated, missing time record to the discredited claim that Al-Hussaini reported to the job site before the Murrah Building attack, the opening on his escape hatch had narrowed dramatically. The "I don't know" fallback excuse and wonted forgetfulness ensnared him in a morass from which there was no way out. Hussain Al-Hussaini failed to present a provable alibi.

## No Clearance

Incredulity reached new heights when the Iraqi national pleaded through the media in June 1995 for the FBI to officially clear him as a bombing suspect, but the Department of Justice spoke not a word in his defense. Local reporters interpreted the FBI's silence as tacit absolution as they blindly defended the "persecuted" Iraqi's proclamation of innocence. With a smug countenance, lawyer Gary Richardson, who formerly held the prestigious title of assistant U.S. attorney, exulted that the FBI assured him Al-Hussaini "was never a suspect." In deposition, the stoic KFOR-TV lawyer, Robert Nelon, adopted a uniquely predatory stance as he thoroughly dismantled Richardson's boast.

Q: "Is it your belief that at some point in time, the FBI cleared you of suspicion in the Oklahoma City bombing?"

Al-Hussaini: "The FBI never approached me or even asked me if I am a suspect or if I am John Doe 2."

Q: "Did anyone from the FBI or other police authorities ever tell you that they did *not* believe that you were John Doe 2?"

Al-Hussaini: "No."

Q: "To your knowledge, has any official agency of the United States government cleared you as a suspect in the Oklahoma City bombing?"

Al-Hussaini: "Again please."

The Interpreter: "That includes the officials, like FBI, something like that?"

Mr. Nelon: "FBI, whoever."

Al-Hussaini: "No."


I exhausted all legal channels seeking on-the-record commentary regarding Al-Hussaini's status as a suspect. In addition to prompting an official inquiry to the Bureau through the Senate Intelligence Committee, I repeatedly pounded at the door of the FBI and U.S. Attorney's office in Oklahoma City, the Department of Justice in Washington, D.C., and the office of former Attorney General Janet Reno. But after eight years of litigation, the man who sued me for libel was left with no official clearance. The DOJ willingly cleaned the slate of suspicion for dozens of John Doe 2 look-alikes named in widely publicized cases, but for reasons unknown, the FBI denied Hussain Al-Hussaini the same courtesy.


## DELIBERATE DECEPTION

The summer of 1995 through the fall of 1996 marked a year of living dangerously for the Iraqi immigrant as he dodged one arrest warrant after the next. The charges ranged from misdemeanor traffic violations to driving while intoxicated and public drunkenness. Missed court appearances and failure to pay the fines led to a suspended driver's license and several bench warrants to apprehend him. Strangely enough, Al-Hussaini's rash of run-ins with the law frequently coincided with KFOR-TV's discovery of new evidence which pointed the finger of suspicion in his direction.

As night slinked closer to daylight on June 3, 1995, the Oklahoma City police found Al-Hussaini passed out cold behind the wheel of his brown Cadillac, headlights and motor still running. As previously mentioned, the incident report registered his blood alcohol level at nearly twice the legal limit.

Was it just happenstance that the intoxicated driver parked his Cadillac within a few yards of Brian's Bar, a seedy pool hall where a bartender reputedly served beer to Timothy McVeigh in early April 1995? Earlier that same night, I had been interviewing patrons in Brian's Bar trying to determine if McVeigh had been seen there in the company of Al-Hussaini and his Iraqi friends.

> Q: "You've testified that you didn't know that Jayna Davis had been at Brian's Bar on June 3, 1995. So was the fact that she had been interviewing witnesses and the fact that you were passed out in your car some five hundred feet away from that bar was just purely coincidental?"
>
> Al-Hussaini: "Yes, it was coincidental because I was surprised by this information."

Al-Hussaini testified he was not only ignorant of my close proximity to the location of his arrest, but that he had never heard of Brian's Bar. Even more mind-boggling was his inability to recall where officers apprehended him, even though the police report placed on the table in front of him plainly stated that his vehicle was parked at the intersection of NW 8$^{th}$ and Blackwelder Streets. Clearly such an admission would impugn his 1995 claim to the Oklahoma media that KFOR-TV erroneously reported that he had been seen in the general vicinity of a bar on NW 10$^{th}$ Street, just two blocks away. Furthermore, coworker Darby Williams said she had personally accompanied Al-Hussaini and her fellow Iraqi work associates to a nearby night club on several occasions.

The repeat offender attributed the uncanny timing of a subsequent arrest to chance as well. On June 24, 1995, within forty-eight hours of Channel 4's story which punctured the potential suspect's alibi, Al-Hussaini said he feared spending the night at home. So he drove to a vacant lot, deflated the air from his front tire to make it appear as though his vehicle was disabled, crawled into the back seat, and fell asleep. But he adamantly insisted he was not intoxicated. Law enforcement offered a far less sanitized version of events. According to the arrest report, the inebriated Iraqi awoke to charges of public drunkenness. Attorney Dan Woska elicited a rare acknowledgment that Channel 4's public assault on his alleged whereabouts for the morning of April 19 contributed to his paranoia and subsequent arrest.

> Q: "If you had seen the June 22 [KFOR-TV] report and a witness or witnesses disputed your alibi, would that have had any impact on your decision to sleep in your car that night?"

Al-Hussaini: "That's not the main reason as far as witnesses saying that I
wasn't at work at the time of the explosion. That wasn't a main reason
for sleeping in my car."

Q: "But could it have been one of the reasons?"

Al-Hussaini: "It's possible."

Al-Hussaini had previously confessed that he sometimes slept in his car
to avoid being arrested. He seriously considered the possibility that authorities would believe KFOR-TV's investigation and suspect him of involvement in the bombing. However, that fleeting moment of candor was quickly
overshadowed by a brazen attempt at deliberate deception.

"Other than the two times when you were arrested for being drunk and
asleep in your car, had you ever been arrested in the United States?" Attorney
Jon Epstein asked.

With cool assurance, Al-Hussaini replied, "No." Was his answer a memory lapse or straight-out lie? Either way, his sworn testimony turned out to
be false.

When I learned the former Oklahoma City resident had relocated to
Dallas, Texas, I figured his atrocious driving record warranted a check for
out-of-state violations. The search scored an instant hit. On February 14,
1996, an Irving police officer noticed Al-Hussaini's car weaving on the roadway and pulled him over. The patrolman detected the strong odor of alcohol, slurred speech, and loss of balance. During the field sobriety test,
Al-Hussaini urinated on himself. The officer immediately took him into custody for driving while intoxicated (DWI), but the prisoner quickly became
surly and uncooperative.

"I asked the defendant [Hussain Al-Hussaini] for his name, and he
refused to tell me. He told me that I could check the computer if I wanted to
know what his name was," officer Mont Vincent wrote in the arrest report.
"At the jail, the defendant finally started crying and told me what his name
was and we were able to find the driver's license number on computer."

Officer Vincent had no idea that the man handcuffed before him had
lied about his identity. At the time, Al-Hussaini knew he was in quite a jam.
He was the target of several Oklahoma arrest warrants and had never been
issued a Texas driver's license. So instead of coming clean, he compounded
his crime and gave law enforcement his roommate's name and birth date. A
resourceful police detective would not discover the ruse until months later.
In a bold disregard for the law, Al-Hussaini failed to show up to court to
address the charges. A bench warrant was subsequently issued for his arrest.

Two years later, during the deposition, my attorney, Steve Martin, reminded the plaintiff that he had previously testified he did not qualify for a Texas driving permit because his Oklahoma license had been suspended. More importantly, he stated for the record that he had never been arrested outside Oklahoma borders. The cunning lawyer then whipped out the Irving, Texas, DWI record and demanded an explanation for his blatant misstatement. But the intransigent plaintiff eyed the KFOR-TV legal team defiantly, inviting a contentious parley in lieu of surrender.

"I think the information here is wrong," Al-Hussaini stated as he and his lawyer, who had obviously been caught off-guard, examined the police report.

"I want to know if he is the Hussain Hashem Al-Hussaini that is referenced in this document," Steve countered while pointing to the arrest record.

"My birth date and my name are correct," Al-Hussaini conceded.

"Right. But the Hussain Hashem Al-Hussaini in here was arrested for driving while intoxicated in Texas, and you had disputed that that was you."

"I can't remember. I need time because I . . . now my head messed up," Al-Hussaini said with a flushed face.

After an hour-long adjournment and some "recollecting," Al-Hussaini returned with flawless remembrance of the Texas arrest.

## TALE OF WOE

With extraordinary frequency, Hussain Al-Hussaini's sworn testimony contradicted his on-the-record comments to the media. His heartrending stories of persecution and imprisonment under the villainous leadership of Saddam Hussein collapsed as my lawyers placed before him his immigration records that exposed glaring inconsistencies in his personal history. The documents refuted his claims of having been convicted of distributing anti-government propaganda.

Al-Hussaini could not explain why he failed to tell his intake officer at the International Rescue Committee upon entering the United States in 1994 that he had served eight years behind bars as an outspoken dissenter. How could such a pertinent fact slip his mind? After all, imprisonment was central to his application for political asylum. But according to Al-Hussaini's immigration file, the years of "confinement" and "torture" he supposedly endured in an Iraqi jail cell were actually spent working as a calligrapher for an Arabic advertising institute.

He attributed his skillful penmanship to the patient teaching of his father, Hashim Jassem Shamkhy Al-Hussaini, a professor of calligraphy who taught at an art school or university in Baghdad; however, the name of the institution escaped him. Oddly enough, he said his father never served in the Iraqi military but could not provide the reasons for the waiver. He described growing up as a child in the Islamic faith, yet he ardently clarified that his family was not "fanatical" about religion.

Al-Hussaini depicted his deceased mother as a mild-mannered, illiterate woman who reportedly shied away from the political rebellion espoused by her husband and daughter. Hashim Jassem Al-Hussaini was reputedly a Communist and vociferous critic of Saddam's ruling Baath party. His political activism allegedly led to the arrest of the entire Al-Hussaini family on May 15, 1981. A year later, Al-Hussaini and his brothers were summoned to the directorate of security in Basra and informed that the Iraqi government "executed" his father and confiscated his financial assets.

The director of the Congressional Task Force on Terrorism and Unconventional Warfare, Yossef Bodansky, debunked Al-Hussaini's anecdote about his father's ill fortune. He noted that in the late 1970s, after Saddam Hussein entered a treaty with the former Soviet Union to supply weaponry to sustain Iraq's war against Iran, the Iraqi despot declared a moratorium on executing Communists.

"It was very highly unlikely that Al-Hussaini's father was a professor of calligraphy and a Communist," Bodansky said. His refutation was rooted in the cultural discord which fractured the Shiite Muslim population in southern Iraq when a faction of Shiites joined the Communist party. During the ensuing political upheaval, those who subscribed to Communist beliefs abandoned the traditional Shiite arts, such as calligraphy. Therefore, it would be virtually unheard of for a devout Shiite Communist like Hashim Jassem Al-Hussaini to earn a living as a professor of calligraphy.

Although the former soldier attributed his grievous suffering at the hands of the despotic government to his father's longstanding dissension, he chose to conceal that relevant fact while spinning his tale of woe to local reporters. My attorneys grilled him for an explanation.

Q: "Did you tell the Oklahoma press that your father had been executed
    by the Iraqi regime?"
Al-Hussaini: "I don't think so."
Q: "Okay. Or that your mother had died while you were in prison?"
Al-Hussaini: "I probably didn't say [anything] about those things because

I was afraid maybe the followers of Saddam are going to see this information in the papers and know where I am. I was afraid."

Q: "You mean his followers that are in this country?"

Al-Hussaini: "I don't know where, but I was afraid of that. I mean, anywhere. I don't know."

Q: "Why were you afraid?"

Al-Hussaini: "Because that was the first time for me to talk to the public . . . to the press."

Q: "Well, I understand. That's my point. I mean, your picture is in the article [the *Oklahoma Gazette*] and your name. So I don't know. I'm not following why you would be afraid to share that specific information when your identity is disclosed in this article."

Al-Hussaini: "I don't know why. I don't remember why."

Sitting just feet away from this man, staring into his black, presaging eyes, the irony of the situation permeated me. The legal weapon which Al-Hussaini wielded against me had become the sword upon which he had fallen. By November 1998, I had legally acquired a virtual library of immigration records, psychiatric evaluations, and criminal arrest reports, which laid bare key signs that the Iraqi expatriate had likely fabricated his background as a refugee who sought political asylum. Instead, the man who lurked beneath the facade of deception possibly served as a devoted member of Saddam Hussein's prized military unit, the Republican Guard. Was he a foreign agent of terror dispatched to our shores to exact Saddam's vengeance on the United States for the Persian Gulf War—a battle which left the megalomaniac scarred by humiliating defeat? During the remainder of the deposition, KFOR-TV's legal counsel fought vigorously to expose Hussain Al-Hussaini's true identity.

## PRISONER OR PREVARICATOR?

Throughout the eight days of testimony, Al-Hussaini relied heavily upon his handwritten notes neatly printed in Arabic to remember names, ages, and the fate of family members, as well as life-changing events such as his level of education, financial hardships as a child, date of enrollment in the military, base of infantry training, and of course, it goes without mentioning, the supposed criminal charges that led to his brutal imprisonment. Inexplicably, the former "inmate" could not recite the date of his long awaited liberation;

thus, he jotted down a few reminders. At one point, attorney Robert Nelon asked Al-Hussaini through an interpreter if he was tortured while awaiting trial by a military tribunal. Stunningly, his recollection faltered.

"What about during the time he [Al-Hussaini] was in a holding cell in Baghdad awaiting trial, was he tortured there?" Nelon asked. Instead of waiting for his interpreter to translate his answer, Al-Hussaini promptly delivered a definite "no."

Perplexed by the denial, Nelon paused to scan the English translation of Al-Hussaini's personal history. The document clearly stated that upon his arrest, he was "forced to confess by all sorts of torture." Iraqi officials allegedly ordered the political prisoner to sign a blank sheet of paper after which they "filled in the accusations against" him.

Reviewing his "crib" sheet refreshed Al-Hussaini's memory. "All right. In the beginning when they tortured me, after I signed this [blank sheet of paper], they stopped torturing me," he proclaimed but neglected to say why he required notes to remember when and under what circumstances he was physically tormented.

According to his two page journal, the alleged methods of torture included hanging by his right leg while his "left leg was attached to a gas [butane] container," in addition to being "detained in a restroom for several days." One would think that years of harrowing confinement would be unforgettable, but it seemed those nightmarish memories had faded from his instant recall.

As the deposition progressed, the reasons for Al-Hussaini's second arrest in 1985, after having served a year in prison as a teenager, evolved. This time he purportedly committed seditious acts while he was enlisted in the Iraq Air Defense. Initially, Al-Hussaini explained that he "used to talk about Saddam Hussein, that he is not a very nice guy." When Nelon inquired if he ever openly called Saddam a "dictator," Al-Hussaini immediately corrected the record.

"I didn't say dictator. He wasn't a nice guy," he stipulated. The megalomaniac who presumably ordered the murder of his father and the torture of him personally as well as that of his family members was innocuously referred to as "not a nice guy."

But as the stilted interviewee, who feigned an inability to understand English, warmed up to the questioning, his story was altered again. On this occasion, he attributed his years of captivity to a refusal to sign a billboard in honor of Saddam's birthday. But moments later, that account underwent surgical nips and tucks.

"I could not do it [sign the billboard] because I wasn't feeling good, not that I refused," he stated. "They [Iraqi military authorities] assumed that I wasn't really sick when I said I couldn't do the work, the art work."

At the end of the day, Al-Hussaini settled on yet another set of circumstances that apparently landed him in prison in April 1985. This time he contended that the starving, impoverished condition of the Iraqi people incensed him while watching military partygoers gorging on a celebratory meal commemorating the Iraqi president's birthday. Letting down his guard, he reportedly uttered a derogatory remark in confidence to a friend, Corporal Hassen Ali. The next day, Ali reportedly turned over an audio cassette of the secretly recorded conversation to authorities and Al-Hussaini was summarily arrested, tried by a military court, and sentenced to serve thirteen years.

"During Saddam Hussein's birthday, they were having a big feast and everybody was eating," Al-Hussaini explained through an interpreter. "It bothered me that a lot of [Iraqi] people were hungry and all those big guys [were] eating."

Middle East expert Colonel Patrick Lang dismissed Al-Hussaini's rendition of the starving population as absolute "non-sense." From 1985 through 1992, Colonel Lang served as a Defense Intelligence officer for the Middle East, South Asia, and terrorism. In 1992, he assumed the directorship of the Human Intelligence Collection division of the Defense Intelligence Agency. During the Iran/Iraq war and Operation Desert Storm, the military intelligence chief acted as principal advisor regarding Middle Eastern Affairs to the secretary of defense, chairman of Joint Staff, and president of the United States. He traveled to Iraq during the 1980s for extended visits, the same time frame in which the "embattled" soldier broiled with resentment over purported nationwide famine.

"This would have been before the Gulf War that Al-Hussaini was talking about people starving in Iraq. Nobody was starving in Iraq. I was there quite often and people were not starving. There were never food shortages," Colonel Lang upbraided, drawing upon his wealth of firsthand knowledge of the Iraqi culture and history. "Before the war, I remember going to restaurants in Baghdad where there were tremendous parties, big feasting with people singing and dancing on tables. They were having a good time."

The tales grew taller as the perpetually vacillating litigant proceeded to brag about his publicly espoused hatred for the Iraqi army and refusal to follow orders during his short stint in the military; however, such open defiance did not earn him a prison term. Instead, Al-Hussaini claimed the understated derogatory remark, "He [Saddam] was not a nice guy," consigned him to a jail cell.

Perceiving the collective disbelief of six attorneys aligned on the opposing side of the table, the fidgety plaintiff floated the fourth rendition of his story. Al-Hussaini asserted that after his arrest for making the tape-recorded comment, Iraqi authorities charged him with producing subversive materials. When asked specifically about the content of the leaflets he authored, he suffered a memory lapse, unable to recall the text that robbed him of his freedom and imperiled his life.

> Al-Hussaini: "There wasn't a word or two or three. It was an article and I don't remember the whole article."
>
> Q: "Okay, would you agree with me that people over in Iraq who distributed anti-Saddam literature often were put to death, right?"
>
> Al-Hussaini: "Some people get executed, some people do not."
>
> Q: "Right. And if I understood you correctly, just to run through it real quick, your father was put in prison for being a Communist, your sister who was in the university where he taught was also imprisoned, you were imprisoned, you ultimately were put in prison again because of the audiotape of you making anti-Saddam comments, I mean, derogatory comments, whatever. And I believe you said you also refused to sign a billboard in honor of Saddam's birthday and you issued these pamphlets. As I'm listening to you, it just sounds like there was more than enough justification for Saddam to have put you to death. And the reason I'm asking this—why do you think you weren't put to death? I mean, it just sounds like there were a whole host of things that happened. I'm just curious if you have kind of a conclusion on why that didn't happen to you."
>
> Al-Hussaini: "Because I was lucky."

"He [Al-Hussaini] kept saying that he was lucky. That's all nonsense. They would have shot this guy in a heartbeat as a dangerous subversive," Colonel Lang scoffed.

Intelligence and defense experts who comprehensively reviewed Hussain Al-Hussaini's deposition and immigration file categorically dismissed as "absurd and concocted" the ex-soldier's stories of participating in treasonous activities while donning the military uniform. Moreover, analysts detected hints of deception stemming from the fantastic circumstances which led to the convict's release. At times, the plaintiff's spontaneous rendition of events teetered on the chimerical.

According to Al-Hussaini, the prison population at Rumaila where he claimed to be housed was unaware that Saddam Hussein had invaded Kuwait in August 1990 and within five months had entered into war against the United States and coalition forces. He attributed the steady "two-month" pounding of military ordnance outside his jail cell to the Iran/Iraq war.

> Q: "You could not hear the sounds of any battle between military units when you were in prison?"
>
> Al-Hussaini: "When the American Army or Allies went into Basra, that's when we heard the explosions and the fireworks. But we didn't know who it was. We heard the explosions, but we didn't know what [it] was. We expected that the war with Iran was where those explosions came from."

Al-Hussaini's response contradicted historical fact. To begin, Iraq's long-standing conflict with Iran had ended years earlier in the late 1980s, but more far-fetched was his assumption that the booming battlefield artillery closing in on the Rumaila detention facility originated from Basra.

"American troops never entered Basra. We stopped well short of there, well short of Basra," Colonel Lang affirmed.

From there, his story sank more deeply into the implausible. Al-Hussaini claimed the correctional guards stationed at the Rumaila penal institution deserted the facility forty-eight hours prior to the arrival of American soldiers.

> Q: "At some point in time did you become aware that the guards had left the prison sometime before the Allied troops arrived?"
>
> Al-Hussaini: "We didn't know until the time they broke in the prison."
>
> Q: "Did you continue to receive food each day from the guards until the Allied soldiers arrived?"
>
> Al-Hussaini: "There was two days we didn't eat. Until the time they broke into the prison, it was about two days."

Unbelievably, the oppressed captives walked free without being debriefed or detained as potential prisoners of war. The invading forces made no inquiry into the inmates' identities or criminal histories. Instead, they opened the security gates and everyone went his "own way."

> Q: "Did the Allied troops ask you any questions or seek any information from you when you were released?"

Al-Hussaini: "I don't recall them asking me any questions in the prison. I was very happy, and I just wanted to get out."

Q: "Did any of the American or Kuwaiti soldiers ask you questions, interrogate you about why you had been in prison?"

Al-Hussaini: "No, they didn't ask us why we were there; they just said go ahead, get out, you know; so we did."

According to the scenario Al-Hussaini painted, he would have had access to his prison file to validate future claims of torture and imprisonment when applying for political asylum. But that paperwork would be forever lost as the "condemned" man made a clean getaway and headed to his hometown of Basra. Transportation would not present a problem. He simply jumped into a mechanically sound army Jeep that had been conveniently abandoned by fleeing Iraqi military units.

Further, we were led to believe that upon arriving in Basra, he searched for lost family members but could only locate his uncle. After two months, the Iraqi army returned. Al-Hussaini took up arms against his countrymen. An intense, week-long firefight ensued. He escaped unscathed and journeyed to Al Safwan where he surrendered to U.N. troops, professing to be an embattled dissenter.

Shortly after his legendary prison caper, Al-Hussaini learned of his mother's death. But Rita Edwards, a female acquaintance who often conversed with the Iraqi national following his 1994 move to Oklahoma City, challenged his veracity. The witness testified that Al-Hussaini expressed brokenheartedness over being separated from his mother not by death, but by distance. She apparently still resided in Iraq. The bereaved son also failed to mention that Saddam Hussein had ordered his father's execution.

## MAN OF MIRRORS

As my attorney Steve Martin so aptly put it, "Hussain Al-Hussaini contradicted himself every time he was asked the same question more than once."

Steve's observation bore a direct application to the Iraqi immigrant's previous military service. Al-Hussaini's obtrusive inconsistencies when discussing the subject reinforced his emerging persona as a man of mirrors. In June 1995, he told KWTV reporter Dave Balut that he was a political "refugee," not a former soldier who fought in Saddam Hussein's army. However, that storyline underwent radical modification when he spoke to the *Oklahoma Gazette* reporter George Lang. On this occasion, Al-Hussaini admitted he was conscripted into the Iraqi army and served six months before his being apprehended as a political revolutionary. In a subsequent interview with the *Oklahoma Gazette*, Al-Hussaini revealed he had earned an esteemed post with Saddam's elite Republican Guard.

Two years later, in October 1997, Al-Hussaini informed his Boston psychiatrists that just three months after being drafted into the army, he was tried and convicted as a traitor. In 1998, when confronted by a team of razor-sharp legal minds, he spontaneously extended his military career to a full year. As the story goes, Al-Hussaini "voluntarily" enlisted with the Iraqi Air Defense, not the army, upon turning eighteen before he faced mandatory service. But incredibly, he was unable to specify his rank or identify the military unit to which he was assigned. He offered limited, often nonsensical information about being stationed at the "infantry" training center in "Al-Kut" where he was forbidden to undergo any weapons training. However, he reported to sentry duty without having been issued a gun.

Q: "What kind of training did you receive in the Iraqi Air Defense?"

Al-Hussaini: "I was in the Air Defense for a short time, for only one year, so I didn't have time to be trained on anything specific."

Q: "Where were you assigned? Where were you stationed in the Air Defense?"

Al-Hussaini: "In the city of [Al] Kut."

Q: "Did your unit have a number or other description by which it was known?"

Al-Hussaini: "Central training for infantry."

Q: "What was your job with this unit?"

Al-Hussaini: "I did guard duty."

Q: "What was your rank?"

Al-Hussaini: "As a soldier."

Q: "Why did you serve only one year?"

Al-Hussaini: "Because they put me back in jail and convicted me for thirteen years in jail."

Q: "While you were in the Iraqi Air Defense, were you taught how to use weapons of any kind?"

Al-Hussaini: "No, in my case, I wasn't. They did not let me train on any weapons."

Q: "Did you carry a weapon on guard duty?"

Al-Hussaini: "No."

The soldier defensively interjected that the majority of his job assignments involved cleaning and construction, nullifying the necessity for a firearm.

The lawyers' trenchant queries laid bare irreconcilable discrepancies in Al-Hussaini's answers. When presented a chart of military insignia associated with the Iraqi Army, Air Defense, and Navy, Al-Hussaini grudgingly pointed to the rank of army officers (1st and 2nd lieutenant) as familiar but failed to identify the insignia associated with the Air Defense, the branch of the Iraqi military in which he ostensibly served.

## TATTOOS, TELLING CLUES

It seemed reasonable to me that an authentic diehard rebel with a deep-rooted aversion for his country's president would have no difficulty recalling every detail of compulsory military service. But in Al-Hussaini's case, recurrent memory lapses hampered his ability to deliver consistent testimony. Was Hussain Al-Hussaini a citizen refugee or an ex-soldier once assigned to the Iraqi Republican Guard, Air Defense, or rank-and-file army infantry unit? Was he conscripted or did he voluntarily enlist? Was his term of service three months, six months, or one year?

"He clearly is not a refugee," Colonel Lang remarked after reviewing Al-Hussaini's deposition and INS file. He postulated Al-Hussaini's personal background was devised as a clever means to facilitate his infiltration into the United States as a false defector and an Iraqi intelligence agent. Like several defense and intelligence experts I had consulted, the ex-military intelligence chief lampooned as "complete nonsense" the Iraqi's claims of having been an enemy of the regime whose luck rescued him from certain death.

"His story about how he was an oppressed guy in the [Iraqi] Air Defense and that they didn't let him have a gun, and that he escaped from prison, none of that fits with his tattoo," Colonel Lang observed.

While Al-Hussaini later denied having informed the *Oklahoma Gazette* he was a Republican Guardsman, his tattoos told a much different story, yielding telling clues into his past. Former Defense Department analyst and war planner, retired U.S. Army Major Lin Todd, assisted Colonel Lang's examination of Al-Hussaini's tattoos—a snake and anchor positioned on his upper left arm and the name "Adnan" scrolled across his hand.

"It's a worldwide phenomenon. In military units, enlisted men usually at some point get tattoos," Colonel Lang commented. "Our conclusion would be that this guy [Al-Hussaini] had been a member of either the Special Troops Division of Iraqi Military Intelligence or the Adnan Division of the Republican Guard."

Al-Hussaini vehemently denied any such connection. He said he tattooed himself while interned at a Saudi Arabian refugee camp. Several intelligence experts rejected the notion as farcical given the simple fact that tattoo needles and ink were not freely dispensed to camp residents. Furthermore, Al-Hussaini alleged he chose the snake and anchor design at random while the name Adnan honored the memory of his younger brother from whom he was separated during imprisonment. But strangely enough, the trained Arabic calligrapher stenciled his brother's name in English, not his native language. KFOR-TV's attorneys found that fact quite intriguing.

> Q: "Now, you did this [Adnan tattoo] while you were in a Saudi Arabian camp?
> Al-Hussaini: "Right."
> Q: "Had you been taught English back in school?"
> Al-Hussaini: "In the fifth, fifth grade, we had to learn the alphabet at least, not more than that. We had to have at least, learn the English alphabet."
> Q: "Was it normal for you and Adnan to write each other's names in English?"
> Al-Hussaini: "No, but since I lost my brother, I just want to write it in English. I just like to write it in English."

Colonel Lang speculated Al-Hussaini's motives were more duplicitous. "This is a guy who tattoos his unit name on his hand. I mean why the hell would he tattoo his brother's name on his hand? He tattooed the word [Adnan] in English just to thumb his nose at us because that's his unit's name."

The veteran defense intelligence expert hypothesized that Al-Hussaini likely moved "higher up the [military] food chain" to Unit 999 of the Estikhabarat, more commonly referred to as the Iraqi Intelligence Service. If true, the self-declared refugee and subversive was, in reality, an enemy intelligence agent who infiltrated U.S. borders with his fellow Islamic mercenaries to execute the bombing of an American federal building.

# CHAPTER 16

# THE FARMER MEETS THE TERRORIST

Tracking Timothy McVeigh's footprints in the Middle Eastern plot came with relative ease compared to unscrambling the rubic's cube enveloping his crafty accomplice, Terry Nichols. The seemingly devoted husband and father premeditatedly established his alibi, and for the most part, prudently avoided conspicuous contact with the Oklahoma City gang of Iraqi soldiers. During Nichols's 1997 Denver federal trial, the defense convincingly portrayed the bespectacled terrorist as an unwilling dupe who became too deeply entangled to escape McVeigh's web of control, a characterization that dramatically gutted the guilty verdict.

In a bold and unexpected move, the Denver jury convicted the defendant, whom it looked upon as McVeigh's craven subordinate, of conspiracy and involuntary manslaughter, not murder. Sentencing deliberations quickly reached an impasse. The jury deadlocked while debating if Nichols's degree of culpability warranted execution. Instead, the federal judge condemned him to life behind bars without the possibility of parole. How did a terrorist collaborator in the slaughter of one-hundred-seventy-one innocents cheat death? Malice and motive. Both factor into the criminal equation and both were absent from the prosecution's case. Apart from his vitriolic anti-establishment animus and burning resentment over the FBI's catastrophe at the Branch Davidian compound near Waco, Texas, several jurors openly complained the government presented no salient reason justifying Nichols's readiness to exact insane vengeance.

Ironically, federal prosecutors were unwittingly transformed into the defendant's most effectual courtroom ally. Whether intentional or not, verdict-swaying facts which exposed Nichols's malicious intent were expunged from the record. While apprised of the bomber's travels to the Philippines for a mail-order bride, jurors remained ignorant of the more sinister motives behind his South Pacific forays. They would hear not a whisper about the secret life of the small-time Kansas farmer—a man of modest means who spared no expense to visit the breeding ground for Islamic fundamentalism. Nichols's alleged liaisons with international terror brokers would never enter the courtroom trial, tantalizing evidence which came to light following a private gathering in Washington, D.C., one which I presumed would yield nothing. Who could have predicted the groundbreaking sequence of events? Certainly not I.

## WASHINGTON RENDEZVOUS

The pivotal March 1996 meeting in the nation's capitol came about under a unique set of circumstances. Twenty-four hours after KFOR-TV broadcast its June 1995 expose about Hussain Al-Hussaini's identification as McVeigh's mystery companion, a highly placed Pentagon official contacted me about the story. In light of my journalistic pledge to ensure his anonymity as a confidential source, I will refer to the gentleman as Thomas Black.

Mr. Black introduced himself as a soon to be retired Foreign Service officer with the U.S. Department of State assigned to the U.S. Department of Defense, Counter Terrorism Directorate, Special Operations/Low Intensity Conflict (SOLIC). Our news operation retained the acknowledged terrorism expert for a brief stint to facilitate Channel 4's probe into primary suspect Terry Nichols's purported ties to Islamic extremists in the Philippine Islands.

Mr. Black's intelligence source in Manila, Dr. Oscar P. Coronel, served as chief of the Intelligence Division for the Philippines Bureau of Immigration. The intelligence director commissioned field agents (most likely Philippine National Police officers) to research early leads that Nichols affiliated with terrorists headquartered in Cebu City. The investigation, according to Black's memorandum, was considered "strictly off the books."

He sternly warned me that the findings were not to be officially disclosed to U.S. authorities. Consequently, Black concealed Dr. Coronel's identity in phone conversations and written correspondence with me.

In early March 1996, KFOR-TV received a handwritten summary of Dr. Coronel's preliminary investigative file in which his name, official title, and Philippine government letterhead had been redacted. My news director Melissa Klinzing and I knew him only as a Filipino official in whom Black placed "the highest levels of credibility and confidence."

A few weeks later, KFOR-TV attorney Robert Nelon and I flew to Washington, D.C., to meet Black. Frustrated by his clandestine tactics, I insisted the Foreign Service officer hand over the original Philippine dossier and disclose the identity of the unnamed overseas source. Quite reluctantly, Black acquiesced, knowing that if he refused to cooperate, his consulting contract with Channel 4 would be terminated.

Dr. Coronel's interim notations, though fragmentary, provided fascinating fresh clues linking the Kansas farmer to international terrorists. The "aliens" with whom Nichols associated were "Pakistanis, Abu Sayaf [sic], Arab Nationals, Iran and other Middle East terrorist[s]." Initial surveillance revealed that Nichols's group consisted of "professionals in terrorism activities" financed from abroad. They rented a large apartment posing as wealthy tourists, maintained a "good safe house in Cebu City," and moved about with the "utmost care to avoid detection by law enforcement." Dr. Coronel advised Black that his field investigators "were proceeding with extreme caution and sensitivity in developing an informant base because, after all, these people are terrorists."

The intelligence that poured forth from the Philippine pipeline fueled suspicions of foreign hegemony in the Murrah Building plot, but the information was virtually useless. I had no way to corroborate the implication that Middle Eastern handlers recruited Nichols; the raw data was, therefore, disqualified for broadcast. Black assured me a more conclusive report with verifiable documentation would be forthcoming, but months passed and still no report.

The excuses regarding the delays grew tiresome. Finally, I dropped indubitable hints that Channel 4 management speculated the report might have been fabricated. With obvious angst, Black explained that the U.S. government had unexpectedly intervened. He said a "legal attaché from the Tokyo embassy" accompanied by another unidentified official emphatically warned Dr. Coronel to cease funneling intelligence information to KFOR-TV.

The subject matter was far too compelling to abandon, but developing the story was undoubtedly beyond my grasp. Our tight local news budget fell woefully short of bankrolling an overseas investigation in a third world country, so I decided to improvise. During a confidential meeting in Washington, D.C., I introduced Thomas Black to Timothy McVeigh's chief legal counsel, Stephen Jones, and sprung my impromptu plan.

I suggested that Jones, with inexhaustible government reserves at his disposal, incur the travel expense to the Philippines to research Dr. Coronel's "off the books" investigation. I volunteered Black to act as the intermediary, thrusting him into the unenviable position of having to produce a "live" source. For all I knew, Dr. Coronel did not exist. Black had spurned my requests to correspond with his Filipino contact. The Pentagon insider's stilted body language communicated that he was less than enthused with my spontaneous proposal, but reluctantly agreed to schedule the meeting.

## CHAIN REACTION

Several years passed before I learned of the chain reaction set in motion by the March 1996 Washington rendezvous and my unrehearsed strategy to put Stephen Jones in touch with the Filipino official. In his book *Others Unknown*, Jones chronicled the political backlash and intelligence bonanza which came about as a result of his Philippine liaison with the immigration intelligence chief. However, he chose to protect the anonymity of his Washington source (Thomas Black) who "arranged entrée with an official [Dr. Oscar Coronel] high up in a very key Philippines ministry."

Although originally reluctant and uncooperative, Dr. Coronel eventually allied himself with Jones in retaliation for a tongue-lashing by an "FBI attaché from Tokyo and a Justice Department lawyer." The irate U.S. officials admonished the Bureau of Immigration director to sever communication with McVeigh's defense lawyers. According to Black, the scolding applied to KFOR-TV as well; hence, Coronel's long awaited final report never arrived. Instead, the Philippine intelligence minister, incensed by the official chastisement from U.S. envoys, unlocked the prison door to Edwin Angeles, a terrorist who turned police informant. The McVeigh camp would be granted rare access to the interrogation chamber of the only man with intimate knowledge of Terry Nichols's direct contact with the world's most prolific and diabolical bomb maker, Ramzi Yousef.

## THE FARMER, THE BOMB MAKER, AND BIN LADEN

Edwin Angeles co-founded and commanded the Abu Sayyaf Group, a Filipino separatist movement classified as the "largest and most violent insurgency based in the Philippines" with an "international reach" of terror. Ransom demands for kidnapped U.S. tourists and missionaries, which at times resulted in murder, only netted a shoestring budget until the fledging organization attracted a global paymaster.

In his epic terrorism study, *1000 Years for Revenge*, Emmy Award-winning investigative journalist Peter Lance tracked Abu Sayyaf's funding to archterrorist Osama bin Laden. Lance reported that in 1988, bin Laden dispatched his "brother-in-law Mohammed Jamal Khalifa to Manila to make contact with Abdurajak Janjalani, a Libyan-trained Filipino" terrorist. Thus, an Asian wing of bin Laden's sprawling Al-Qaeda network was born with Janjalani and Angeles the appointed beneficiaries of the Saudi construction billionaire's worldwide labyrinth of hidden wealth.

Two puritanical disciples of bin Laden entered the picture straightaway. Khalid Shaikh Mohammed, the architect of the future September 11, 2001, suicide airline hijackings, bankrolled Abu Sayyaf through Khalifa's purported charitable organizations based in Malaysia. Mohammed also served as a "conduit" to subsidize his nephew Ramzi Yousef's Manila cell. The man who would eventually climb Al-Qaeda's corporate ladder to CEO received his master's degree in the malevolent art of bomb building under the tutelage of the Central Intelligence Agency.

During the 1980s, Uncle Sam invested billions to arm the Mujahadeen rebel forces in Afghanistan's war to crush the invading Soviets. A young Ramzi Yousef joined the burgeoning ranks of Islamic enthusiasts pouring in from Saudi Arabia, Yemen, Pakistan, South Africa, Chechnya, Uzbekistan, and the Philippines. The CIA trained the twenty-five thousand strong army of "Afghan Arabs" in "guerilla tactics, bomb making, hijackings, and covert ops."

Like his handpicked point man Ramzi Yousef, Osama bin Laden's enigmatic influence as radical Islam's spiritual leader and financier traced back decades to the training grounds of the CIA-backed freedom fighters. During the hostilities, bin Laden set up stakes in the northern Pakistani border town of Peshawar where the International Islamic Academy recruited "young Muslim zealots" to enlist in the crusade. Terrorist alliances thicker than blood were forged in the battlefield trenches of Afghanistan giving rise to the devil's triangle—Ramzi Yousef, Osama bin Laden, and the blind Egyptian cleric, Sheikh Omar Abdel Rahman. The charismatic Sheikh served as the linchpin of Yousef's American-based terror cell and would later be convicted in a plot to blow up New York landmarks.

After driving out the Communist invaders, a radicalized faction of Mujahadeen soldiers became unemployed mercenaries poised to redirect their battle-honed skills in a terror war against countries, governments, and innocent civilians whom bin Laden deemed enemies of Islam. Henceforth, the network known as Al-Qaeda took form and shape. The United States sat squarely in its crosshairs with Ramzi Yousef assuming the role of fanatical general.

February 26, 1993, marked Yousef's first strike. A truck bomb erupted in the underground parking garage of the World Trade Center, fracturing America's towering pillar of prosperity. Miraculously, only seven people died, including a mother-to-be and her unborn baby. The low casualty count proved disappointing for the budding terrorist mastermind. He had hoped the death toll would soar as high as a quarter million in his ambitious plan to topple the North Tower into the South Tower. Survivors would live but a moment, as the failed plan went, condemned to asphyxiate amidst a poisonous cloud of cyanide gas.

The savvy, lethal mind of Yousef nurtured a bloodlust for murdering Americans and "infidels" that pulsated with every beat of his heart. But diabolical passion did not always translate into success. After foiled assassination attempts against President Bill Clinton and Pope John Paul II, Yousef added another colossal failure to his resume. In early 1995, authorities intervened as the Philippines-based bin Laden operative and his fellow Islamic "brothers," Abdul Hakim Murad and Wali Khan Amin Shah, prepared to implement the precursor to the 9-11 holocaust—a monstrous plan dubbed "Project Bojinka." The thwarted Bojinka conspiracy, which means "big noise" in Serbo-Croatian, involved the bombing of a dozen U.S.-bound commercial jetliners flying out of Asia in a forty-eight-hour murder spree over the Pacific Ocean.

The terrorist who engineered the delivery of a Ryder truck packed with a powerful fertilizer-fuel oil bomb to America's financial district likely orchestrated a similarly executed bombing in Oklahoma City. As head explosives trainer of Abu Sayyaf, Ramzi Yousef mentored onetime ringleader Edwin Angeles. When authorities nabbed Angeles in 1996, the Muslim terrorist opted to save his own skin and become a cooperating witness. It seemed there was no loyalty in the den of vipers.

During Angeles's interrogation, representatives dispatched from the Philippine National Police (PNP) and the Bureau of National Investigation (BNI) unearthed a "direct personal link between Yousef and Nichols." Dr. Coronel subsequently leaked the witness's sworn affidavit and debriefing summaries to the McVeigh defense team.

The incarcerated terrorist certified in writing that he had attended a meeting in the early 1990s (the specific dates differed in Angeles's various statements) at the Del Monte Labeling factory in Davao City on the island of Mindanao. Yousef and his field lieutenants Shah and Murad were all in attendance. The fourth invitee to the terrorist soirée was an American who "introduced himself as the farmer." The informant claimed the group gathered near a "place where Muslims were taught in bomb making." The topics of discussion included "bombing activities, providing firearms and ammunition, and training in bomb making and handling."

When Philippine officials asked Angeles why he attributed the Oklahoma bombing "to Muslim terrorists when, in fact, the arrested suspects were American, Angeles flatly stated that he knows Terry Nichols personally." He later drew a sketch of the "farmer's" face and provided a physical description that closely matched the Oklahoma City bomber.

The Abu Sayyaf guerilla also identified arms dealer Jack Sapihi. McVeigh's defense had developed information that Sapihi, a member of the Philippine terrorist organization known as the Moro Liberation Front, visited Nichols's Cebu City residence. More importantly, Angeles disclosed inside knowledge of bin Laden's connection to Pakistan's International Islamic Academy which was tasked with the indoctrination and training of Muslim terrorist cadres.

Edwin Angeles had unearthed Terry Nichols's footprints in the secret criminal underworld, but could the word of a reputed terrorist be trusted? The most obvious question had yet to be answered. Was the purported Philippine conference between Angeles, key Al-Qaeda operatives, and the American "cut out" logistically possible? Author Peter Lance obtained Philippine intelligence documents that confirmed both Ramzi Yousef and Abdul Hakim Murad had opportunity to visit the South Pacific islands during the general time frame reported by Angeles. McVeigh's investigators established Nichols's passport records indicated the meeting "dates are consistent with Nichols's being in the Philippines."

Proximity was just one of several intriguing coincidences in which the lives of the terrorist foursome (Yousef, Murad, Shah, and Nichols) vectored. According to Lance, both Yousef and Shah "applied for their final visas to the Philippines in Singapore on November 3, 1994." Within twenty-four hours, the Philippines consulate in Chicago issued Nichols his visa. Two weeks later, the "tourist" from America's heartland embarked on his last venture to Ramzi Yousef's corporate headquarters. Was it by fate or design that two terror brokers resided in the same out-of-the-way place during the same period?

And why would both flee the island nation almost simultaneously? A harrowing event ultimately sent Nichols streaking back to the sanctuary of U.S. borders. But what?

In time, critical facts would demystify the timing and peculiarity of Nichols's travels. I would obtain the dossier of sealed defense filings, confidential FBI reports, and the bombers' phone records which would eclipse the naïve persona Nichols's defense lawyers invented for his federal trial. Emerging from the body of evidence was a cold-blooded traitor acting in collusion with Middle Eastern intelligence based out of the Philippines.

## TELEPHONE TRAIL OF EVIDENCE

Terry Nichols's passport records documented at least five flights to the Philippines from August 1990 through January 1995. However, the convicted bomber took as many as twenty trips, ostensibly to search for a new bride and new life. In 1989, while embroiled in divorce proceedings, former spouse Lana Padilla discovered an expensive airline ticket to the South Pacific.

"How are you going to the Philippines? How are you going to afford this?" Padilla exploded. She was understandably annoyed at such a lavish expense in light of the couple's financial troubles.

"Tim bought it for me," Nichols sheepishly asserted. "He insisted I go."

During an undercover interview with KFOR-TV, Padilla theorized Nichols used his mail-order bride, Marife Torres, as a "cover story" to explain repeated excursions to the foreign venue. Josh Nichols said his father visited the Philippines several times a year without his young wife to vacation and lounge on the beach. Scraping together $2,000 cash for roundtrip airfare was no small feat for a traveling gun dealer, part-time ranch hand, and struggling farmer.

Ever the skeptic about McVeigh's ability to build the masterfully assembled Ryder truck bomb, lawyer Stephen Jones postulated bin Laden's prized talent, Ramzi Yousef, schooled Nichols in his pernicious craft.

"There is simply no evidence," Jones told writer Peter Lance, "that Terry Nichols or Tim McVeigh or anybody known to have been associated with them had the expertise, knowledge, skill, [and] patience to construct an improvised device that would bring down a modern nine-story office building."

Michael Fortier, the government's key witness in securing the bombers' federal convictions, testified McVeigh and Nichols set off relatively small pipe and bottle bombs. But the twosome failed miserably when experimenting with a milk jug containing an explosive mixture patterned after the one used to gut the Murrah Building.

McVeigh told Jones he learned the complex construction of a five thousand pound ammonium nitrate fuel oil (AMFO) bomb from a book he allegedly checked out of a Kingman, Arizona, library. Miffed by his client's insulting mockery and proven past deception on a polygraph examination, Jones decided to order his investigators to locate the so-called bombing manual. But no such publication existed. However, Jones did discover through FBI reports and his resourceful scouts on the ground in the Philippines that Nichols exercised no compunction in advertising his desire to make a bomb. The sworn statement of Nichols's former Filipino tour guide, Daisy Legaspi, said the American sightseer made his nefarious motives known.

"Terry asked if I knew someone who knows how to make bombs," Legaspi recounted. The Filipina sharply rebuked Nichols for posing such a "stupid" question.

McVeigh's lawyer, Stephen Jones, said he didn't have to look far to find proof that Nichols persisted in his destructive quest. "His own father-in-law, who is a Philippine policeman, said to us and to the Philippine police that he found books on explosives and bomb making in Terry Nichols's luggage at the house. Why would Terry Nichols carry books on explosives and bomb making to the Philippines?"

The bombing defendants' telephone records further connected the dots between the shores of the Pacific Far East and the plains of the American Midwest. In an attempt to cover their tracks, Nichols and McVeigh obtained a phone debit card issued under the alias "Daryl Bridges" to purchase bomb components. They also used the card to make a series of cryptic calls to untraceable numbers in the Philippines from public pay phones in Junction City, Kansas. Defense filings documented two hundred calls to the Philippines, seventy-eight of which were placed to a Cebu City boarding house that sheltered students from a local university well known for Islamic militancy. Nichols's Filipino bride, Marife, resided there for a brief period while taking some college courses in physical therapy. However, Nichols continued to phone that location after Marife returned to their Kansas home. In fact, on March 17, 1995, three days prior to Marife's departure from the Philippines, Nichols's lease on the guest house was inexplicably extended, even though the couple had no plans to continue living there.

From April 2 to April 10, an unidentified party placed thirteen calls to Nichols's Herington, Kansas, home from an untraceable number in the

Philippines. On April 21, two hours before Nichols surrendered to the FBI, he phoned this same Cebu boarding house which was owned by Saudi national Ernesto Malaluan. Phone logs exposed Nichols's frenzied attempts to reach an unnamed resident at Malaluan's lodge for Muslim students. Earlier that same year, on January 17, immediately following his hasty return from the Philippines, Nichols placed fifteen consecutive calls to the boarding house from his ex-wife's Las Vegas residence. No one answered, but he continued the manic barrage of calls over a relatively short time span.

On January 31, the curious sequence of calls to the Cebu dormitory repeated. One of the Oklahoma City bombers, most likely Nichols, dialed the international number nine times within nine minutes from a pay phone at a Texaco station in Junction City, Kansas. On the last ring, someone finally picked up. Two weeks later, on February 14, when news accounts broke internationally documenting the apprehension of Ramzi Yousef in Pakistan, Nichols dashed back to the phone at the local Texaco and frantically dialed the island boarding house using the Daryl Bridges debit card. He robotically placed twenty-two calls and patiently waited forty minutes before an unknown party answered.

February 28 ushered in another series of rapid-fire phone transactions. This time Nichols began the drill shortly after sunrise. At 6:28 A.M., he slipped into the phone booth at a Junction City convenience store, but no one answered. Nichols hung up and raced to the nearby Texaco. Only five minutes had passed since the last call. It was now 6:33 A.M., and Malaluan's Philippines business line jingled again and again and again. Nichols methodically punched in the lengthy overseas number thirteen more times. Thirty minutes ticked by. Still no answer.

Nichols drove to the UTS Waters Hardware store and made three additional attempts to contact Malaluan, but to no avail. He then phoned the residence of Pacific islander Naneth Jaraive. No one was home. Minutes later, at 7:16 A.M., the calls to the Philippines boarding house resumed. Over the next two hours, eighteen calls poured in, but no one picked up. Nichols scrambled to yet another payphone at a truck stop before the staccato battery of calls abated. Was this consecutive pattern of rings indicative of a code or covert form of communication? If so, such a clandestine method of sending messages would circumvent government monitoring of overseas phone conversations. More importantly, Nichols and McVeigh incorrectly assumed the use of public payphones and a debit card would render the evidence trail of calls invisible. Stephen Jones made discovery demands for classified information which included possible National Security Agency intercepts of

Nichols's international conversations to the South Pacific. The court refused his requests.

## FINAL FORAY, DEADLY SCARE

Nichols's final flight to Marife's native homeland of Cebu City lifted off on November 22, 1994. As mentioned earlier, Padilla says when she drove her ex-husband to the airport, he handed her a package and a stern admonishment. "If I'm not back in sixty days, open it and follow the instructions," he ordered somberly.

Padilla's curiosity gained the upper hand, compelling her to unseal the package. Inside she found a will, Nichols's life insurance policy with Marife named as the beneficiary, and instructions leading her to $20,000 cash sealed in a plastic bag taped to the bottom of her kitchen drawer. The signs were indicative of a man who did not expect to return alive. Nichols's farewell message to his son Joshua caused the boy to weep bitterly as he voiced dread over the likelihood he would not see his father again.

Why would Nichols express grave apprehension about a routine vacation? And more importantly, how did a man with a meager financial portfolio obtain large amounts of unexplained cash? The answers may be gleaned from an extraordinary timeline of events. Nichols happened to set foot on Philippine soil while the World Trade Center bomber deftly executed the test run for his upcoming Bojinka terror spree. On December 11, 1994, Ramzi Yousef boarded Philippines Airline flight 434 in Manila, planted an explosive device under his seat, and disembarked safely at a stopover in Cebu City. The timed bomb detonated as the jetliner continued its journey to Narita, Tokyo, killing a Japanese tourist who became the unfortunate passenger to take Yousef's seat.

A month later, on the evening of January 6, 1995, while tutoring his protégé Abdul Hakim Murad in assembling pipe bombs, the explosives expert goofed. Murad told authorities that Yousef "was burning some chemicals that were no longer needed" when the lethal compound spewed a dense cloud of caustic fumes, filling his kitchen at the Dona Josefa Apartments in Manila. By the time the fire department responded, the smoke had dissipated, and Murad and Yousef had bolted the scene. Mindful of a potential terrorist strike against the Pope during his upcoming visit, the Philippine National Police wisely decided to check out the incident. Detectives walked into a makeshift bomb factory and confiscated Yousef's laptop computer. The hard drive contained the encrypted blueprint for the Bojinka plot.

Minutes later, Murad returned to the scene of the crime, stunned to find the place swarming with cops. Investigators informed him he was wanted for questioning. Murad panicked and made a run for it. In his hasty escape, he clumsily tripped on the sidewalk and was subsequently captured and cuffed.

Once again, uncanny timing would snap another link in the chain of circumstantial clues. Authorities busted Murad, Yousef bolted to Pakistan where he would be nabbed a few weeks later, and Nichols abruptly ended his Philippines getaway and flew home to the U.S. refuge much earlier than originally planned. When Lana Padilla asked what precipitated his premature return, Nichols's eyes narrowed.

"Somebody could get killed down there," he growled. From that point forth, Nichols packed a concealed weapon. Was his unexplained trepidation related to Murad's detainment and Yousef's flight into hiding? If Nichols did, indeed, serve as an American conscript in the Islamic army of holy warriors, did he believe Murad would leak his name to Philippine police interrogators? There was no conclusive proof that the three reconnoitered during his final foray. However, the logbook for Ramzi Yousef's Manila apartment bore the signature of an occasional visitor named "Nick."

## INTELLIGENCE COUP

The takedown of the master bomb maker's sidekick, Abdul Hakim Murad, would net an intelligence coup. In his riveting analysis of the FBI's missteps that culminated in the September 11 massacre, reporter Peter Lance provided exclusive and frighteningly specific details from inside the interrogation room. The commander of the PNP's Special Investigations Group, Colonel Rodolfo Mendoza, was unwilling to cower in the face of evil. The daring investigator sparred with the immovable terrorist who had previously refused to crack under harsh questioning techniques that allegedly bordered on torture. But when the virtuoso of eliciting true confessions entered the game, Murad quickly melted under Colonel Mendoza's ego stroking and crafty ploys.

The student of Yousef's evil genius outlined plans to crash a small single engine aircraft packed with explosives into the CIA headquarters near Washington. The plot had been widely reported in the wake of 9-11. However, Peter Lance uncovered a more prescient confession in which

Murad confirmed Ramzi Yousef's maniacal desire to "hijack commercial air-lines" and dive bomb American targets that included the "CIA headquarters, the Pentagon, and an unidentified nuclear facility."

The FBI frantically scoured U.S. flight schools but failed to identify the Middle Eastern pilots handpicked to die as Allah's martyrs. Murad's cockiness made it impossible for him to resist taunting authorities. He challenged Colonel Mendoza to prevent the future kamikaze holy crusade—all the while relishing the knowledge of a truck bombing that was well underway in America's heartland. Yet apparently, his lips would not utter a hint, not until the morning of April 19.

Speculation that the strike on hometown U.S.A. was most likely imported from the Middle East saturated the airwaves. A correctional officer at the New York Metropolitan Detention Center listened to initial radio news reports that Islamic fundamentalist groups were lining up to tout credit. The intuitive prison guard decided to conduct some field research of his own. The thought suddenly occurred to him that an inmate on his watch, Abdul Hakim Murad, who awaited trial in the abortive Bojinka plot along with his nefarious partner Ramzi Yousef, might have tangential knowledge of the Oklahoma hit. He sauntered down to Murad's cell and solicited the caged terrorist's opinion.

"What do you think about the bombing in Oklahoma City?" the guard asked.

"I am responsible," Murad eagerly boasted. "As a member of the Liberation Army, I am responsible for the attack on the Oklahoma City federal building." Murad would not tolerate being discounted or ignored, so he scribbled his confession on paper and slipped the note through the bars to the stunned officer.

What exactly was the Philippine Liberation Army? The group's organizer, Ramzi Yousef, purposely cloaked the identity of the true sponsors during his February 1995 federal debriefing, alluding only to a vague tie to bin Laden's home base of Afghanistan. But shortly thereafter, bravado seized the day as he laid the bait to reel in the Al-Qaeda hook.

Yousef, the globe-trotting terrorist, traveled under an estimated ten aliases including a forged Pakistani passport issued in the name of "Abdul Basit." However, members of his New Jersey cell tasked with the first WTC bombing referred to the man of shifting nationalities as "Rashid the Iraqi" who entered the United States in 1992 on an Iraqi passport. Yet "Rashid" vehemently denied that he was an agent of Saddam during an April 1995 interview with the Arabic daily newspaper *Al-Hayat*. However, Yousef disclosed that his Liberation Army supported members of Egypt's Islamic Group (IG), Egypt's Islamic Jihad (EIJ), Hamas, Islamic Jihad, and Algeria's FIS (Islamic Salvation Front).

Investigator Peter Lance procured intelligence reports from the Philippine National Police that connected bin Laden to the IG and his chief Al-Qaeda henchman, Dr. Ayman Al-Zawahiri, to the EIJ. Philippine authorities purportedly remitted the documentary evidence to the FBI in the wake of Murad's extradition to New York to face trial. A year later, in September 1996, Murad and Yousef were convicted for the Bojinka conspiracy.

## UNEXPLOITED WEALTH OF SECRETS

The New York office of the FBI spared no time responding to the prisoner Abdul Hakim Murad's staggering admission. FBI Special Agent Francis Pellegrino and Secret Service Agent Brian Parr arrived at the correctional facility the afternoon of April 19. But according to the FBI's official record of the investigation, the federal officers chose not to speak to Murad himself or the prison guard to whom Ramzi Yousef's protégé confessed. Instead, they recorded a hearsay statement from a detention center supervisor, Lieutenant Philip Rajos, to memorialize what was arguably a watershed lead into a Philippines-Middle East connection.

The one-on-one interrogation of Murad would be mysteriously side-stepped, but more troubling was the federal officer's name recorded on the follow-up investigative report. One week prior to the Oklahoma City bombing, on April 12 and 13, inmate Murad voluntarily waived his rights to lay out his terrorist resume before the same FBI agent, Francis Pellegrino. But days later, following the deadliest terror attack to date, Agent Pellegrino did not see the need to question this man specifically about his claim of culpability in the Murrah Building bombing. During the previous debriefing, the Philippines-based operative opened the interview session by chronicling his lifelong friendship with Osama bin Laden's Asian theatre commander and Abu Sayyaf kingpin, Ramzi Yousef.

Murad elaborated about Yousef's role in the first World Trade Center bombing, the pair's explosives training in Lahore, Pakistan, to prepare for the destruction of U.S. commercial airliners originating out of Manila, and visionary details of a future scheme to hijack jumbo jets and convert them into flying missiles. One of the proposed targets, according to Murad, was CIA headquarters. He had previously disclosed to the Philippine National

Police that additional U.S. landmarks on the hit list included the Pentagon and an unspecified nuclear power plant.

Without doubt, the New York fed grasped the alarming implications of Murad's April 19 declaration. While rescuers filled fresh body bags from the cavernous bowels of the federal complex, Agent Pellegrino urgently began transcribing his week-old interview with the self-professed Middle Eastern engineer of the attack. He already had empirical confirmation that Murad had sounded an approaching death knell. Just a few weeks earlier, on February 13, 1995, Agent Pellegrino witnessed Ramzi Yousef define his role in the World Trade Center attack in a negotiated court proffer. The bomb maker's imperious nature prompted him to dazzle his audience with the chemical composition of "ammonium nitrate, nitromethane, and analite" that composed his "1500-pound" fertilizer-fuel explosive device. With cool composure he likened his terror campaign against New York's tallest skyscraper to "America's use of atomic bombs at Hiroshima and Nagasaki."

Just three months after Yousef imparted his combustible formula to the FBI, Timothy McVeigh transported and detonated a comparable deadly concoction in Oklahoma City's downtown district. Years later, the imprisoned McVeigh repeated the same demented philosophy as the WTC bomber, invoking Yousef's comparison to "Hiroshima and Nagasaki" in a published essay to justify his crime.

In summation, Abdul Hakim Murad proved he was intimately familiar with Yousef's 1993 bombing of New York's Twin Towers, the failed 1995 Bojinka plot, and a not yet formulated scheme to convert jumbo jets into bombs. But we are expected to discount this man's emphatic claim on April 19 that an Islamic terrorist group rooted in the Philippines orchestrated the Murrah building attack—the same individual, whom the former leader of Abu Sayyaf, Edwin Angeles, stated was present when Terry Nichols and Ramzi Yousef linked up in the southeast Asian nation to confer about the fine art of bomb making.

In light of the enormous national security implications of April 19, the reservoir of intelligence Agent Pellegrino extracted from Murad, coupled with his assertion of foreign sponsorship of the Oklahoma City operation, it was inconceivable the FBI would make only a token interview of the prison guard's boss. Apparently, the FBI had no intention of pursuing Middle Eastern complicity, no matter how well-placed and connected the source.

CHAPTER 17

# PRIOR WARNING

Though persuasive, the witnesses' testimonies did not satisfy my quest for evidence. I continued to search for additional proof which would show the harrowing attack was, in fact, plotted and sponsored by Middle Eastern terrorists. The final litmus test of truth was yet to be imposed. I desperately needed to eclipse the government's official version of *whodunit*. However, the only feasible means to achieve such a pivotal breakthrough would be to consult counterterrorism experts who circulated in the innermost corridors of international intelligence gathering operations. Establishing such a contact would be formidable, if not unattainable, to a journalist from a Midwestern state, far removed from the influential Byzantine network of Washington, D.C.

I had all but abandoned such a utopian mission when a friend recommended I read a recently published book that delved far beyond the headlines and court record regarding the upcoming trials of foreign terrorists charged in the 1993 World Trade Center bombing. I stared at the cover and paused in amazement. The word "terror" was scrolled across a blood red backdrop. The caption read: "Americans have awakened to find themselves targeted by fanatic Islamist terrorists. Holy war has come to American soil."

I thought, "Awakened to what?" On February 26, 1993, an explosives-laden Ryder van detonated in the financial epicenter of the United States and violently shattered America's innocence. For the first time, foreign terrorism hit home within our borders. But public outrage and concern soon waned. The criminal trials portrayed the perpetrators as a rogue group of radical Muslim extremists. However, the author of *Terror: The Inside Story of the Terrorist Conspiracy in America*, internationally renowned terrorism expert Yossef Bodansky, viewed the 1993 operation through the prism of state sponsorship. He issued a terrifying wake-up call, claiming the strike on New York was the handiwork of more than "fanatic malcontents."

Bodansky did not equivocate when assigning culpability. He imputed responsibility for the terror campaign to "Iran, Sudan, and their allies." The next statement, which was published less than a year before the Oklahoma City attack, would carry a measurable degree of prescience. "For those sponsoring governments, the terrorist operations in New York were instruments of state policy—and will not be the last ones they will attempt."

The author had sounded a clarion call about the future face of terrorism in the wake of the Persian Gulf War. While America rested comfortably under the perceived security of a sweeping military victory, our most virulent Islamic enemies throughout the Middle East set aside their religious differences and came together under the headship of the Armed Islamic Movement. Bodansky warned a foreboding merger between Iran and Iraq would usher in a new era of deadly holy war against the hated West. Bodansky solidified his belief in this unconventional alliance upon revealing that a few days before the 1993 World Trade Center bombing, two Iraqi experts came to New York to "coordinate the operation and ensure the technical details of the bombing." The majority of suspects seen with the Oklahoma City bombers were Iraqi soldiers. Had I stumbled upon the realization of Bodansky's vision?

My curiosity about the Washington insider intensified. Several Arab American and Muslim organizations debunked the Israeli native's credibility, labeling him a Zionist propagandist and extremist, even speculating he served as an agent of the Israeli Mossad. Regardless of his detractors, Mr. Bodansky's standing in the intelligence community could not be summarily dismissed. As a recognized authority on worldwide terrorism, as well as guerilla and unconventional warfare, Bodansky's track record in foreseeing the next terror campaign was notably impressive. He had previously served as director of research for the International Strategic Studies Association, senior editor for the Defense & Foreign Affairs group of publications, National Security Fellow of the American Security Council Foundation, and a visiting scholar in the Security Studies Program of Johns Hopkins University.

In 1999, the prolific analyst and former consultant to the Departments of Defense and State published the definitive study of the world's rising archterrorist entitled *Bin Laden: The Man Who Declared War on America*. Tragically, the American public paid little heed to the dire warnings laced in the text until Al-Qaeda's homicidal wrath of September 11 catapulted Bodansky's bin Laden book to the best-seller list, earning him international acclaim as a preeminent expert on the architect and financier of Al-Qaeda.

In 1996, when I was first introduced to the name Yossef Bodansky, I reasoned that as acting director of the Congressional Task Force on Terrorism and Unconventional Warfare, he was undoubtedly exposed to highly classified information that would indicate whether the Murrah Building had become the target of Mid-East sanctioned Islamic jihad against America, the "Great Satan."

## SCRATCHING IN THE RIGHT DIRECTION

Was I prepared to hear Bodansky's theory about who executed the bombing? Did he have reason to believe in a foreign connection or did he, like the nation's media, subscribe to the prosecution's case, which was open and shut with the arrest of discontented military dropouts? The answer would mark a defining moment in my pursuit of Middle Eastern suspects.

I dialed Washington, D.C., directory assistance to locate a business number for the Republican House Congressional Task Force. There was no listing. I decided to contact the organization's then ranking member, U.S. Representative Bill McCollum of Florida. A receptionist answered. I attempted to conceal a sudden wave of nervousness by lowering my voice.

"May I please speak to Mr. Bodansky?"

After an uncomfortable pause, the young woman declared to my surprise, "There is no one here by that name. May I ask who is calling?" I assumed she was screening the call. My hopes of getting through fell.

"My name is Jayna Davis. I am a reporter with KFOR-TV, the NBC affiliate in Oklahoma City," I answered. Instantly, I was placed on hold. Moments later, someone picked up the line.

An enigmatic voice with a distinguished Israeli accent opened our dialogue with a brief introduction, "This is Mr. Bodansky, how may I help you?" His cryptic tone fulfilled my mental image of an intriguing character created in the mind of a spy novelist. Consciously regaining my concentration, a surge of trepidation caused me to rapidly explain the purpose of my call.

"My name is Jayna Davis. I seem to be the only journalist who is seriously investigating a Middle Eastern connection to the Oklahoma City bombing. As a reporter for KFOR-TV, I have discovered several Iraqis residing in Oklahoma City whom various witnesses tied to the Murrah Building, Timothy McVeigh, and several getaway vehicles targeted by the FBI the morning of April 19. Channel 4 has provided confidential copies of this investigation to several Oklahoma congressmen. As director of the Congressional Task Force are you familiar with the material? And is it your professional opinion the Middle East may have played a role in this terrorist attack?"

"How shall I answer you?" Mr. Bodansky remarked. Silence followed as he contemplated his riposte. "Yes, no, yes, maybe, no, yes," he said lightheartedly. His uniquely timed humor immediately eased my obvious anxiety.

"Well, Mr. Bodansky, I'm overwhelmed by your candor and clarity. You've more than adequately answered all my questions," I feigned in accord with his jovial manner.

We broke into laughter as he quipped in a genteel manner, "My pleasure, my pleasure."

During the ensuing weeks, I learned that cultivating such an esteemed source would be tantamount to navigating a minefield. As director of the Task Force, Bodansky maintained a fierce commitment to federal laws which sealed matters of national security—rules he had sworn to uphold. It was unfathomable for him to open up his files and invite me to pull up a chair. However, Bodansky also exuded a passionate loyalty to the truth. When I inquired about the plausibility of eyewitness accounts that implicated Arab men in the Murrah Building bombing, he pondered his rejoinder with discernible caution.

"How shall I put it? You're scratching the tip of the iceberg. However, you're scratching the right place in the right direction," he said encouragingly.

I fired back in typical reporter-like fashion, "Do you believe we're on the right track concerning certain Middle Eastern suspects because you have viewed Channel 4's reports, or have you received similar information regarding specific names of suspects from independent sources?"

My hand clasped over the mouthpiece as I drew a deep breath and nervously awaited his response. He chose his words carefully. "I'm still doing my own investigation, and the stories that you're telling fit very closely with the stories that I have. I got the names in my own sweet way," he asserted with sagacious flair.

"And those names were tied to the bombing?" I pressed.

"I did not get them just because I'm trying to run a one man census of the Oklahoma City area," Mr. Bodansky remarked with a chuckle. Before long, I would grow accustomed to his witty, yet dry sense of humor.

Bodansky's point was unmistakable—the implications daunting. I sank into my chair overcome with relief. But the elation of the moment was overshadowed by perplexing thoughts. If my witnesses were corroborated by a man in the upper echelons of government intelligence, why would law enforcement ignore evidence of foreign participants? The notion of a cover-up had evolved from idle conjecture into a disheartening realization.

## OVERLAPPING SUSPECT LISTS

Yossef Bodansky confided in a personal meeting in May 1996 that he had independently targeted the same foreign conspirators in the initial stages of the investigation he conducted on behalf of the Congressional Task Force. Through rare circumstances, I was privileged to corroborate this assertion. Confirmation came through a memorandum documenting a phone conversation between the New York City division of the Federal Protective Services (FPS) and Bodansky. In the spring of 1997, I was privileged to hand copy the contents of the memo dated August 2, 1995, in which FPS Special Intel Agent Thomas E. Williams discussed KFOR-TV and Bodansky's belief that the television station had been pursuing the same suspects as the Task Force:

- As to Oklahoma—a lot of names overlap from NBC News affiliate reports and his [Bodansky's] lists.

- Immediately after the bombing, in the U.S. and abroad, the same network that was collecting money for Sheikh Rahman's legal defense sent out communications asking for donations for the legal defense fund for their "brothers" involved in the Oklahoma bombing.

I was astonished to learn that the Middle Eastern terrorist underground braced for the eventuality that its Muslim "brothers" would be criminally charged in the heartland attack. But even more stunning was the indisputable confirmation that Channel 4's investigative efforts had captivated the attention of an internationally recognized authority on terrorism and a key advisor to congressional House members. The sequence of events compounded the intrigue all the more. The FPS memo was dictated in August 1995; however, at that time, I had never heard of Yossef Bodansky. I did not contact the Congressional Task Force director until eight months later in April 1996. But evidently, the Task Force chief was already well aware of my probative journey into a local terror network.


## SOUNDING THE SILENT ALARM

In the years that followed, Mr. Bodansky disclosed sensitive intelligence documents that refuted the conventional wisdom that two disenfranchised army pals had the bomb making expertise to execute such a massive attack. On February 27, 1995, the Congressional Task Force on Terrorism issued a prior warning which stated there would be an "Iran-sponsored Islamic attack" on U.S. soil. Washington, D.C., topped the hit list. The primary targets were Congress and the White House, a foreshadowing of the infernal events of 9-11.

The warning was disseminated to the FBI and other federal intelligence agencies. Fortunately, increased security stymied the terrorists' original strategy to hit the nation's capitol, yet it did not diminish their resolve. A contingency plot immediately shifted the focus away from Washington, D.C., taking direct aim at the American Midwest. On March 3, 1995, the Task Force chief authored an updated warning that predicted the terrorists now planned to strike at "the heart of the U.S." Bodansky wrestled intensely with the decision to sound the silent alarm.

"It's a judgment call. It's the responsibility of the analyst to say this is where we are. This is for real," he explained.

"How often do you issue terrorism alerts like the ones the Congressional Task Force put out on February 27 and March 3 of 1995?" I asked.

"There has to be a tremendous amount of very precise evidence to warrant it," he stated with conviction and passion. "Information continued to flow and continues to flow that enabled us to understand that the other side [Middle Eastern terrorists] shifted attention to the heartland."

Government installations topped the list of objectives ahead of communication and transportation systems. Twelve cities were placed on the potential target list because of the radical Islamic groups and terrorist networks operating within those cities. In subsequent written correspondence dated September 1996, Bodansky expounded on the inflow of intelligence data that compelled him to narrow his list of possible terrorist targets to Oklahoma in the spring of 1995:

I did get, and later confirmed by numerous sources, certain criteria on how to better identify possible terrorist targets. By the time I mastered this "method," it was too late for Oklahoma City. However, going over and reconstructing relevant data (some of which arrived only after the bombing but had originated prior to the bombing) Oklahoma City was on the list of terrorist targets.

The Task Force chief's somber concession that "it was too late for Oklahoma City" roundly dispelled conspiracy theorists who propagated salacious rumors accusing federal lawmen of ignoring prior warnings. At no time did I, or for that matter, did Bodansky, come across a scintilla of information hinting a Ryder truck rigged with an AMFO bomb would be detonated at the Alfred P. Murrah Building during the height of the business morning on April 19, 1995. However, the intelligence director did know the delivery boys would be non-Arabs acting at the will of Islamic puppet-masters.

## RECRUITMENT OF "LILY WHITES"

After eighteen months of sifting, discarding, and corroborating reams of intelligence streaming into the Task Force from embedded informants and overt Arabic sources, such as news publications, the threshold of proof necessitated urgent notification of authorities to "prevent the Islamic threat from materializing." By February 1995, Bodansky comfortably prognosticated an imminent international terrorism offensive, sponsored by "Iran and Syria," to be launched inside the United States. The strike date would likely occur sometime after the "start of the Iranian New Year on March 21." Bodansky elucidated his reasons for taking the last resort step of disseminating the official alert:

> Other Iranian sources confirmed Tehran's desire and determination to strike inside the US against an object symbolizing the American government in the near future. They stressed that Tehran was adamant about launching the crucial strikes after the beginning of the Iranian New Year in order to ensure that the message is unambiguous—the wave of terrorism was a part of the Holy War between Tehran and Washington.

Throughout the intelligence gathering phase, information crossed the wire that, if true, would pose a new and daunting challenge in preempting the cadre of predators. The Task Force learned the Middle Eastern terrorists had recruited two "lily whites" to carry out the bombing of an American federal building. "Lily whites," in the lexicon of the intelligence community, refers to operatives who have no criminal history and no obvious ties to Middle Eastern terrorist organizations, thereby hamstringing law enforcement's ability to profile and track potential terrorists. Such was the case in Oklahoma City. Both Timothy McVeigh, a decorated Gulf War veteran, and Terry Nichols, a former soldier and Kansas farmer, fit the "lily white" criterion. Bodansky outlined in written correspondence to me the chilling intelligence he had collected before the Oklahoma atrocity. His prediction turned out to be deadly accurate:

> As for the warnings: (1) The Israeli warning [received by Bodansky] was actually that it will be an Islamist operation but will be carried out by non-Arabs. (2) One of the main reasons the Task Force narrowed down the warnings in the spring of 1995 to the heartland were indications—not absolute proof—that Lily Whites would be activated for the forthcoming operation. This meant that Oklahoma City should have been on the short list of objectives because of the known prominence of the local Islamist networks.

The visionary analyst had isolated a new modus operandi designed to mask the morphing face of terrorism. This inventive recruiting technique vastly broadened the candidate pool of global assassins. Outside-the-box thinking enabled Bodansky to recognize the deadly fusion between radicalized Muslims and lily whites—an epidemic trend to which the FBI declined publicly to lend credence until the post 9-11 era.

"We know this: The Al-Qaeda terrorist network remains the most serious threat to U.S. interests both at home and overseas," the Bureau's top counterterror official testified before the Senate Judiciary terrorism subcommittee on June 27, 2003. Assistant FBI Director Larry Mefford disclosed that agents were spanning forty U.S. states to root out Osama bin Laden's operatives. However, Mefford somberly warned that the method of identifying jihadists was greatly hindered by Al-Qaeda's recruitment of U.S. citizens and non-Arab operatives—lily whites who could easily "evade detection" when penetrating U.S. borders.

"They [Middle Eastern terrorists] understand the benefits of having this type of asset, somebody who can travel under the radar screen," Mefford announced to the Washington press following his terrorism briefing to the

Senate panel. Regardless of Mefford's acknowledgment of born and bred Americans fighting in the Islamic revolution, a spate of arrests and guilty pleas had effectively exposed an outbreak of the "lily white" phenomenon.

The most widely publicized case involved the capture of the man dubbed the "American Taliban." The U.S.-led coalition apprehended John Walker Lindh as he was fighting alongside Taliban and Al-Qaeda forces during the 2001 war in Afghanistan, the longtime base of operations for Osama bin Laden's terrorist empire. The native Californian was sentenced to twenty years incarceration for enlisting as a soldier in the Taliban militia and engaging in hostile actions against his fellow countrymen.

Two African American Muslim converts from Portland, Oregon, also pledged allegiance to the Taliban resistance. However, they were denied entry into the Afghan conflict in the wake of September 11 to fight on behalf of the enemy. Patrice Lumumba Ford and Jeffrey Leon Battle, a former Army reservist, confessed to waging holy war against the U.S. and allied forces. In October 2003, a federal judge condemned both defendants to eighteen years imprisonment.

A third Oregonian, James Ernest Thompson, who goes by the Islamic name "Ujaama," pleaded guilty to conspiring to provide "cash, computers, and fighters to the Taliban." Ujaama's plea agreement secured his testimony against Abu Hamza Al-Masri, the radical London cleric deemed a leading Al-Qaeda recruiter in Europe. Ujaama accused Al-Masri of enlisting his assistance in establishing a terrorist training camp in Bly, Oregon.

Jose Padilla, popularly referred to as the so-called "dirty bomber," also met the textbook definition of a lily white and classic prototype of an expendable asset. Padilla, a former Chicago gang member who was convicted of a juvenile murder, adopted the Muslim moniker Abdullah Al Mujahir. Authorities believe he may have been drafted into the terrorist movement while serving time in prison. Although an ex-felon, Padilla had no apparent ties to Arab terrorist organizations, and therefore, he was able to travel internationally without alerting authorities. In June 2002, when Padilla reentered the country following a Middle East excursion, the military detained the U.S. citizen and Muslim convert as an "enemy combatant." The suspected American/Al-Qaeda operative was allegedly tasked with detonating a conventional bomb laced with radioactive material in an undetermined city. Captured Al-Qaeda leader Abu Zubaydah divulged details of the "dirty bomb" plot during interrogation.

Heavy-hitters on both sides of the political aisle have stridently enlightened the public to the subversive proselytizing and recruitment taking place in

American prisons and the U.S. military. Senate Judiciary leaders have called for stricter screening of Islamic clerics who preach a fanatically violent doctrine known as Wahabbism, a virulent form of Islam based in Saudi Arabia. Most Al-Qaeda members subscribe to these militant, aberrant teachings.

Prisons are "becoming a ready-made forum for recruiting disaffected citizens," said Arizona Senator Jon Kyl, terrorism subcommittee chairman. "Our government needs to take this growing threat extremely seriously and take immediate steps to curtail it," he added.

"My fear is, if we don't wake up and take action now, those influenced by Wahabbism's extremist ideology will harm us in as of yet unimaginable ways," warned New York Senator Charles Schumer.

Army Captain James Yee quite possibly represented Senator Schumer's nightmarish prediction. In October 2003, the military charged the Muslim Army chaplain with improperly handling classified material in a wider espionage probe at the Guantanamo Bay Naval Station in Cuba where more than six hundred suspected foreign terrorists are imprisoned. Yee, also known as "Yousef," ministered to detainees with reputed ties to Al-Qaeda and the ousted Taliban regime in Afghanistan.

The Chinese American, who was reared in the Lutheran faith, graduated from the distinguished U.S. Military Academy at West Point, New York. Sometime after the 1991 Gulf War, while stationed in Saudi Arabia, he experienced a spiritual transformation and converted to Islam. Yee resigned his commission and studied his new found religion in Syria, then re-enlisted in the U.S. Army as a Muslim cleric.

Like Captain Yee, Timothy McVeigh underwent dramatic emotional changes during the same time frame. While McVeigh was never shown to be an adherent to Islamic doctrine, he and the terrorist brethren harbored a mutual disdain for the United States' military subjugation of Iraq. His patriotism soured, fostering a deep-seated resentment toward U.S. foreign policy, which he viewed as perverse and imperialistic.

In 1991, Bodansky received unconfirmed intelligence reports from "reliable sources" that the Arab terror networks were actively recruiting "soldiers of fortune" from the ranks of the U.S. military in the aftermath of Operation Desert Storm. The theory that McVeigh volunteered to conduct American-based terror operations while serving in the Middle East may be speculative; however, close proximity and McVeigh's profound regret over killing enemy troops during the Gulf crisis cannot be dismissed out of hand. Such a psychological disposition indeed made the embittered McVeigh plausibly an ideal candidate for recruitment by hostile foreign governments intent on bringing terrorism to U.S. soil. Moreover, McVeigh made no attempt to conceal his desire to make the leap from soldier to soldier or fortune. During the Persian Gulf War, he plainly stated to his army buddy, Greg Henry, that "he wanted to become a mercenary for the Middle East because they paid the most."

## THE BIN LADEN FACTOR

The 1995 Task Force warnings were generated from multiple sources in several Middle Eastern countries spanning an eighteen month period prior to the Oklahoma City bombing. Intelligence was also gleaned from international terrorist conferences which took place in the fall of 1994 and early 1995 in which Tehran's terror chieftains unveiled their agenda to levy an unconventional war inside U.S. borders. While Bodansky did not directly state that the Saudi billionaire orchestrated the Oklahoma City bombing under the umbrella of Iranian state sponsorship, strong indicators abounded in his chart topping book, *Bin Laden: The Man Who Declared War on America.*

Bodansky noted that a few days after the July 17, 1996, downing of TWA Flight 800, an editorial published by the London-based *al-Quds al-Arabi* Arabic newspaper reported that "the terrorism issue . . . has reached the United States, which has always been immune from terrorist operations." While such a statement only obliquely alluded to the destruction of the TWA jetliner, the Islamist terrorist leadership chose this timely opportunity to openly boast of responsibility for the 1993 attack on New York's Twin Towers and the "Oklahoma bombing," publishing this startling claim in the same article.

When assessing the meritocracy of the bold declaration, Bodansky wrote, "not only is *al-Quds al-Arabi* a highly respected Islamist newspaper, but the editor, Abdul-Bari Atwan, is also personally close to Osama bin Laden." Put simply, the world's pre-eminent organizer and financier of terrorism had unambiguously, albeit indirectly, claimed the April 19 massacre as a milestone achievement.

In developing his circumstantial body of evidence, Bodansky outlined intelligence that named Ayman Al-Zawahiri, bin Laden's closest confidant, as the field commander anointed with the execution of "spectacular" terrorist strikes on U.S. soil. In November 1993, Zawahiri established a major terrorist headquarters in Geneva, Switzerland, to avoid detection by the FBI, which at the time was investigating the New York City terrorist cell that perpetrated the first World Trade Center bombing. Bodansky explained the "Islamists feared the [FBI] investigation would lead to a crackdown on the other Islamist terrorist networks then dormant in the United States." Zawahiri's primary assignment included the insertion of "high-quality experts into the United States to oversee and conduct lethal terrorist operations under emergency circumstances."

A year later, beginning in October 1994, key Islamic terrorist organizations conducted an unusually large number of conferences throughout the Middle East. The clandestine meetings continued through April 1995, just prior to the bombing of the Murrah Building. Bodansky contended the Islamist network convened to strategize and study future terrorist operations to be carried out in the United States. "Following the fall 1994 conferences, the Sudanese sent high-level emissaries to the United Kingdom and the United States to notify the local Islamist leaders of the resolutions and to instruct them about future plans and their respective role in them."

The most frightening revelation outlined by Bodansky centered on an Iran-sponsored strategy to specifically target government buildings and related objectives on American turf. The diabolical plan was hatched in November 1994, at a summit in Larnaca, Cyprus, in which the participants studied firsthand the status of specific terrorist networks (in the U.S.) and the "ability of local Muslim communities to withstand the aftermath of major strikes."

## Osama's Oklahoma Outreach

Bin Laden's spiritual mentor and sword bearer, Abdullah Azzam, mesmerized audiences with his incendiary call to arms. The Palestinian jihadist served as the organizer of foreign volunteers harvested from the ranks of the Afghan Mujahadeen which later became the core of the Sunni Islamist terrorist movement. The fiery orator radiated a magnetic charisma that bewitched thousands of young men into abandoning their personal ambitions in order to train for holy war and the global expansion of Islam. In 1989, investigative journalist Steve Emerson videotaped Azzam delivering a rousing speech at an Oklahoma City Islamic conference.

In a private correspondence, the Task Force director disclosed the hidden agenda behind Azzam's presence in Oklahoma. "Azzam's invitation to Oklahoma City was organized by the local (clandestine) branch of an Islamic charity called Al-Kifah that served (and still serves!) as cover for the recruitment of, and other types of support for, Islamist terrorists in the U.S.," Bodansky wrote. Investigative journalist Richard Miniter, author of the 2003 book *Losing Bin Laden*, depicted the Al-Kifah Refugee Center in New York as a fund-raising front for the "most feared and hated terrorist of our time."

Osama's Oklahoma outreach crept in like a flood on the eve of the Murrah building bombing. Bodansky informed me of a popular Islamist conference that convened in Tulsa, Oklahoma, from April 14 through April 16, 1995. The convention, which attracted thousands of Muslim youth, offered legal and legitimate activities, but malevolence festered beneath the public façade. The congressional intelligence analyst pointed out that the conference organizers maintained a close relationship with the terrorist-sponsoring nation of Sudan and a grab bag of militant groups such as "Hamas, both FIS and GIA in Algeria, various Jihadist organizations in Egypt, and even Shi'ite Hizballah"—all spiders in bin Laden's venomous web of influence.

"I know that there were a few clandestine/covert Islamist operatives among the participants," Bodansky revealed. "People from Oklahoma City attended the (Tulsa) conference."

## CHICAGO TERRORIST TRAINING CAMP

In June 1998, the U.S. Department of Justice seized $1.4 million dollars in cash and assets owned by Mohammad Salah, a naturalized United States citizen born in Jerusalem. The FBI branded the suburban Chicago car salesman as a "high-level Hamas military operative" headquartered in the American Midwest. The government complaint alleged that Salah and the Quranic Literacy Institute in Oak Lawn, Illinois, a non-profit organization which translated and published sacred Islamic texts, served as conduits for Hamas funds. The terrorist monies allegedly financed the organization's recruiting, training, weapons acquisitions, and military operations in the occupied territories of the West Bank and Gaza Strip.

The FBI exposed Salah's work as a computer analyst for the Islamic religious foundation as a "cover story" to travel undetected as a Hamas courier. But Salah and representatives of the Quranic Literary Institute cried foul. They vehemently denied aiding and abetting Israel's archfoe. Salah charged the FBI egregiously mischaracterized his humanitarian mission to assist impoverished Palestinians.

"I'm not a member of Hamas, I'm not a supporter of them," the defendant told the *New York Times* in June 1998. "I am a person who likes to help poor people."

Federal investigators countered with evidence tracing the illicit funds to specific terrorist attacks, including the purchase of an M-16 rifle used in the 1992 murder of an Israeli soldier in Hebron. Moreover, bank records indicated Salah had received large infusions of cash from the political leader of Hamas, Abu Marzook. U.S. Attorney Scott Lassar said the case marked an unprecedented implementation of civil forfeiture laws, normally used against narcotics dealers and fraudulent stock traders, "to stop the flow of money through American financial institutes to support terrorist activity abroad."

The voluminous FBI affidavit which laid out the Chicago civil action stemmed, in part, from foreign intelligence and admissions the Illinois resident allegedly made during his previous incarceration. In January 1993, the Israeli secret police arrested Salah and another Arab American, Mohammed Jarad, during the pair's visit to Jerusalem. The *Jerusalem Post* reported that Israeli security forces nabbed the Middle Eastern tourists while they were in possession of huge "sums of cash, lists of activists, and plans for terrorist attacks."

While in custody, Salah reportedly held back nothing, confessing to Israeli officials that he was a Hamas recruiter of prospective candidates for a militant cell. The suspect also intimated the "outlawed" fundamentalist group, which opposed peacemaking negotiations with Israel, received tactical and financial support in the United States. On January 3, 1995, the *Chicago Sun-Times* reported the prisoner had identified several Virginia based Arab American organizations that acted as "fronts for Hamas."

More substantively, Salah's confession offered a rare glimpse into his training in "mixing poisons, developing chemical weapons, and preparing remote control explosive devices." Furthermore, the Israeli news agency disclosed that Salah admitted he had "organized training sessions in the United States for the preparation of explosive devices together with ten other Palestinians with U.S. citizenship. The group was to be sent to the (occupied) territories to carry out attacks, but the plan was foiled when Salah was arrested."

Salah later recanted. In an impassioned plea, he told the U.S. press he was "super innocent." The distraught Palestinian immigrant lamented that he manufactured his terrorist exploits under the duress of torture—an accusation the Israeli government strenuously denied. A prominent *New York Times* reporter and author, Judith Miller, witnessed a closed-circuit broadcast of Salah's interrogation inside Israel's high security prison in February 1993.

"The man I saw seemed to be quite relaxed and not under any obvious pressure," Miller told the *Chicago Sun-Times*. "This is not a man who seemed to be fearful of his life."

The criminal prosecution of the man dubbed the "world commander" of Hamas military campaigns did not hinge solely upon Salah's self-incrimination. During the Palestinian native's 1994 secret military trial, Israeli officials introduced the signed statement of Palestinian detainee Nasser Issa Jalal Hidmi. The former Kansas State University student said Salah invited him to attend a four-day retreat in the Chicago area in June 1990 where participants received explosive training and studied Hamas philosophy. Hidmi testified he met the accused on a second occasion in December of that same year at a Kansas City Muslim youth conference. Palestinian trainees underwent additional Hamas training in closed-door sessions with Salah allegedly assuming the role of instructor.

In 1995, an Israeli military court sentenced Salah to five years confinement for channeling funds collected primarily from Chicago's Arab community to the armed unit of Hamas. He was paroled after two years and settled back into his previous life as a family man in the Illinois community of Bridgeview. Before re-entering the United States, the federal government classified the middle-aged father of three as a "specially designated terrorist." His suspected accomplice, Mohammad Jarad, served six months in an Israeli prison on charges of aiding Islamic militants.

In the summer of 1998, Mohammed Salah's unsavory past came back to haunt him. The ex-convict found himself mired in yet another legal morass when the FBI froze his bank accounts and property holdings in an attempt to cripple his alleged support of terrorist activities. But the feds stopped short of pursuing a criminal indictment. Why? The mercurial political climate surrounding the culturally sensitive story might have ruled the day. Prominent Arab Americans decried Salah's "abusive" treatment at the hands of the Israelis, which, in turn, could have pressured the FBI to nail down an airtight case for prosecution. The evidence, quite possibly, was insufficient to file felony charges.

Was Salah's confession while in Israeli custody coerced fiction? Or, had the Chicagoan surrendered his intimate knowledge of Hamas operatives honing their deadly craft at clandestine terrorist training camps in his hometown? The answers would determine whether or not law enforcement slept while the enemy approached the gate. Deconstructing the Salah conundrum would lead me to an extraordinary FBI agent who battled relentlessly to bring this case before a jury—a lawman whose world would collide serendipitously with mine as I traveled the path of clues from the ashes of Oklahoma to the windy city of Chicago.

## THE CHICAGO-OKLAHOMA CROSSROADS

How did Hamas, Chicago, and the FBI's civil forfeiture against Mohammed Salah intersect with the calamity of April 19? Drawing upon his vast repository of intelligence, Congressional Task Force Director Yossef Bodansky scrutinized the probable links. If proven in a courtroom sense, then Bodansky had unearthed the dead bang connection between the Middle East, the strike on the heart of America, and a Hamas terrorist training camp that reportedly took place in Chicago in preparation for the Oklahoma blast.

"There are at least two young Arabs from Oklahoma City who were trained in 1993 in making car bombs of the type used in April 1995. They are not the only Islamists from Oklahoma City involved in international terrorism," Bodansky disclosed to me in September 1996.

His report traced the genesis of the Chicago terrorist curriculum as far back as 1988 when Iranian intelligence instructed Hamas to train Palestinian youths living in the United States. The goal was to develop a group of highly trained Arabs with U.S. passports or green cards who could then be inserted into Israel to replace local terrorist cadres arrested or killed by Israeli forces.

"The Iranians argued, and correctly, that Israel would treat Americans with kid gloves," Bodansky explained, "and it would be easier for them to enter Israel with U.S. documents."

The summer of 1990 ushered in the first round of military training. The freshman class of "Hamas activists" purportedly convened at an undisclosed staging ground in the Chicago area.

"All [participants] were given code names and forbidden to discuss where they were from, either in the U.S. or the Middle East," the congressional advisor wrote. "Training was conducted by Salah himself and five other instructors, one of them a Libyan American who was a veteran of the Marines."

Six months later, in December 1990, secret sessions devoted to leadership and command techniques were allegedly given under the "cover of a Hamas conference in Kansas City." Bodansky said several leading generals in the Hamas movement were in attendance, including a top official affiliated with the Holy Land Foundation for Relief and Development based in a Dallas, Texas, suburb. In the wake of the September 11, 2001, suicide hijackings, the Bush administration froze Holy Land's assets because the charitable organization was suspected of illegally channeling funds to Hamas.

In February 1991, the operational hierarchy met again in Kansas City at which time the briefings focused upon "supervising the construction of different types of explosives including car bombs of the type used in Oklahoma." Bodansky specified that the Hamas Political Committee included an Islamist from Oklahoma City.

In the fall of 1992, when the Immigration and Naturalization Service temporarily detained the 1993 World Trade Center mastermind, Ramzi Yousef, upon his entry into the U.S., the "Iranian and Islamist leadership" adopted a major policy change. In order to avoid the inevitable snarls with INS officials while attempting to insert experts from the Near East whose names appeared on international terrorism watch lists, the organizers decided to limit recruitment and training specifically to "lily whites." What came next, according to Bodansky's estimation, delivered a foreboding prelude to Oklahoma City:

• The most important course for about 30 lily whites was conducted in the summer of 1993 in the same summer camp site near Chicago. The material was even more specific than the 1990 course, including the latest on building massive car bombs from readily available materials . . . at least two of the participants were from Oklahoma City.

• Members of the network that includes Oklahoma and Texas, including a senior supervisor/commander from the Dallas area, took part in the [Islamist] conference in Tulsa, Oklahoma, the weekend before the Oklahoma City boom.

Bodansky's theory that "two Oklahoma City Islamists" graduated from the Chicago "academy" of assembling truck bombs from "off the shelf" materials unquestionably factored into his calculated decision to disseminate the 1995 prior warnings. Despite his precision in forecasting the impending doom of April 19, the terrorism scholar found himself a lone voice when categorizing Oklahoma City as a deadly instrument of state policy by foreign adversaries. But validation would come in short order.

World renowned bomb experts corroborated Bodansky's prognosis, delivering yet another blow to the government's fragile hypothesis that an army sharpshooter with minimal demolitions training cooked up the explosive home brew from recipes found in mail-order manuals. In April 1997, during the height of McVeigh's trial, the Justice Department's Office of Inspector General handed down a scathing repudiation of the FBI's Oklahoma City bomb analysis. The eighteen-month internal review of the Bureau's laboratory procedures sharply criticized the FBI's flawed judgment when assessing the bomb's weight, main ingredients, and trigger mechanism. The inspector general sharply derided explosives unit examiner David Williams for providing analyses that were "scientifically unsound, not explained in the body of the [Oklahoma City bomb] report, and biased in favor of the prosecution."

The government instantly scratched Williams from their expert witness list. However, while frantically dousing the flames of a credibility meltdown, federal prosecutors did not bank on shocking new evidence of the bomb's Middle Eastern design leaking out. It did, and I, like McVeigh's chief counselor, were among a handful of recipients.

## ISRAELI BOMB REPORT

In late April 1995, Bodansky issued a classified report outlining his steadfast belief that the heartland attack bore unmistakable parallels to Middle Eastern bombings in Argentina. In the portions of his written analysis that I was permitted to review, the congressional consultant postulated that the "initial forensic investigation in Oklahoma suggests strong similarities to bombing techniques used by Iran-sponsored Islamic terrorists."

He illustrated the uncanny analogy to the car bomb that destroyed the Amia Jewish Center in Buenos Aires, Argentina, on July 18, 1994. Not only was the bomb design remarkably similar, the Amia operation involved the Islamic terrorist recruitment of a "lily white" Caucasian who delivered the weapon of mass destruction, drawing a compelling comparison to another designated "mule" named Timothy James McVeigh.

"The Amia bombing in Argentina was specifically identified as a test run for the forthcoming terrorist campaign [Oklahoma bombing] in the U.S. by numerous sources in the Middle East," the Task Force director informed members of Congress in his official analysis. "Moreover, the 1992 bombing of the Israeli Embassy in Buenos Aires was also the test run for the 1993 Islamist terrorist bombing and plot in New York."

Two Israeli bomb experts personally inspected the federal complex and reached a professional conclusion echoing Bodansky's sentiments that the Oklahoma bombing bore indisputable earmarks of a Middle Eastern truck bomb. Doron Bergerbest-Eilon, then chief of security for the Israeli Embassy in Washington, D.C., accompanied by Yakov Yerushalmi, a civil engineer who worked as a consultant to the Israeli government, drafted a report outlining their observations of the blast damage. During a closed-door meeting in April 1996, a prominent Oklahoma City businessman, who served as the appointed escort for the Israeli envoys, detailed the "highly confidential" visit of Eilon and Yerushalmi with KFOR-TV's legal counsel and me.

The source was an Israeli American with dual citizenship. The Israeli government had bestowed upon him an honorary award for exposing the terrorist activities of an Iraqi arms dealer with putative ties to the 1988 bombing of Pan Am 103. During our private conversation, he expressed consternation over the notable absence of foreign arrests in the Oklahoma bomb case.

"The Israeli experts determined that the bomb which destroyed the Murrah building was constructed by Arab terrorists or people trained by Arab terrorists," he stated without compunction. "Yakov [Yerushalmi] told me pictures of the Amia Jewish Center in Argentina and the Israeli Embassy in London showed the same pattern of destruction. In both cases, the truck bombs were parked near the most vulnerable area of the target and detonated during peak occupancy."

The Israeli veteran of the 1967 Six Day War with familial contacts inside the Jewish nation's security and intelligence agencies exuded supreme confidence in the findings set forth by the two bomb experts. The duo reportedly illustrated how the strategic placement of the Ryder truck achieved maximum impact from the directional charge encased in the cargo hold. Determining the perfect spot and angle in which to park the bomb truck required the skill of an architectural engineer who must have studied the blueprints of the Murrah Building's design. Repositioning the truck just "two parking spaces away" would have greatly reduced the structural damage.

"Did you actually read the report or were you informed about its contents?" I asked.

The witness chuckled with amusement as he presented the business cards of his foreign guests. "The bomb analysis was typed on my laptop computer in my office. The final printed copy was three pages."

"Were federal authorities aware of their findings?"

"I would assume so," he answered. "It was my understanding the evaluation was performed in collaboration with the ATF. I was told that agency was given a copy of the report."

I pictured the distressed response from the ATF given the government's

penchant to establish the scenario in which a domestic, homegrown terrorist had engineered the explosive device. "Did the ATF agree with the Israelis'
conclusions?" I queried.

"Yakov [Yerushalmi] told me he asked an ATF supervisor why U.S
investigators thought McVeigh acted alone and had eliminated the possibility of Arab terrorist involvement."

"Really, what was the response?"

"Yakov said the head guy agreed with him that the bombing looked like
it was carried out by experts."

"To which experts did the ATF refer?" I asked myself. "McVeigh and
Nichols, two Army soldiers with no demolitions expertise, or Arab engineers
who had perfected the fine art of Middle Eastern bomb making?"

Two contacts with high-level access to Israeli security officials independently confirmed the Oklahoma City escort's story. Shortly after our
April 1996 rendezvous, McVeigh's attorney Stephen Jones interviewed my
confidential source before venturing off to Israel to personally ferret out the
facts.


## DODGE AND DENY

Not surprisingly, Jones had not received a copy of the dignitaries' written
evaluation—the leitmotiv to dodge and deny revisited. But he was resolved
to confirm the report existed and had been withheld. Israeli officials played
the courteous host to the American visitor, but were loath to admit to the
lead defense lawyer that Eilon and Yerushalmi had surveyed the bomb site.
Defense motions compelled the prosecution to cough up one page of the
Israeli experts' raw notes, which were absent the findings that the design of
the Ryder truck was Islamically inspired. Much to Jones's dismay, U.S.
District Judge Richard Matsch did not compel the ATF to produce the
entire three-page document which purportedly contained the key words
"Middle Eastern signature."

The courtroom tussle ended in a technical knockout, but in the final
round Father Time awarded Stephen Jones the title belt of ultimate truth.
Validation arrived in October 2001 when President Bush deployed U.S.
troops to eradicate the fanatical ruling Taliban in Afghanistan. Strewn across
the basement floor of a Kabul mansion which once housed a hideout and
makeshift headquarters for bin Laden loyalists was a do-it-yourself guide-
book to construct an "Oklahoma-style" bomb. A Bosnian soldier in the Al-

Qaeda army of terrorists had penned the step-by-step instructions and components needed to replicate the Murrah Building explosive device.

What a shocking discovery that Timothy McVeigh's legendary bomb-making skills were referenced halfway around the world, being emulated as an effective technique in the terrorists' toolbox! Imagine the incredulity on the faces of bin Laden's devotees upon hearing they would implement a bomb formula which McVeigh perfected through exhaustive research from a book checked out at a Kingman, Arizona, public library. In the sage words of Stephen Jones that McVeigh "couldn't blow up a rock," the Afghanistan find transformed the Justice Department's "lone bomber" theory into a work of science fiction.

# CHAPTER 18

# NEW YORK TIMES V. JAYNA DAVIS

Scorching winds of change whipped through the Channel 4 newsroom in the summer of 1996. The jet stream blowing in from the East Coast carried a stormy forecast for my professional future when the media giant, the New York Times Corporation, purchased KFOR-TV. The new ownership immediately spiked all stories on John Doe 2 and the Middle Eastern connection. My most loyal supporters, the news director and station manager, found employment in other television markets. I, too, moved on, tendering my resignation on the eve of Timothy McVeigh's federal trial in March 1997.

Upon learning I had left broadcasting, attorney Stephen Jones offered to hire me as a defense team consultant. I declined but accepted his proposal to work as a "consultant for a day." The proposition was obviously designed to entice me to come aboard.

At the Denver defense headquarters, I frantically sifted through a mountain of discovery documents. While scanning several memoranda from the New York branch of the Federal Protective Services (FPS), the name "Yossef Bodansky" jumped out at me. There it was—printed in black and white—the memo mentioned in the last chapter. Bodansky informed the FPS intelligence division that the list of suspects he had compiled in the bombing "overlapped" with the subjects profiled by the Oklahoma City "NBC affiliate." The phone conversation took place on August 2, 1995—eight months prior to my first call to Bodansky's Washington, D.C., office.

I nervously shuffled through the stack of related intelligence reports and discovered another FPS memo in which Bodansky described a terrorist threat aimed at Wall Street.

"Where's the prior warning of a pending attack in the heart of the U.S.?" I wondered. The realization hit me like a shock wave. The Task Force alerts had been unlawfully withheld during the discovery process. The defense team employee assigned to observe my review of the documents noted my bewildered expression.

"Is there something wrong?" he inquired.

Contemplating the legal ramifications of the missing evidence, I answered without thinking: "Several alerts about a pending Iran-sponsored Islamic attack targeting the American Midwest issued by the Congressional Task Force are missing from these records."

One unguarded moment came back to haunt me. A few weeks later, the defense team subpoenaed me to testify in the guilt/innocence phase of McVeigh's trial. Stephen Jones said he wanted me to enter into evidence a KFOR-TV story in which I had interviewed Kansas witnesses who tied McVeigh to a second Ryder truck. I perceived his reason to be a ruse that was rather transparent. I quickly ascertained from legal counsel that the law did not require me to take the stand in order to submit my broadcast report into the court record.

"I have a gut feeling Jones is conning me. He has no intention of asking me about a previous story I produced about the bombing. I believe his true motivation is for me to divulge what I know about the missing prior warnings from the Congressional Task Force," I speculated in a conversation with my lawyer Carl Hughes, a brilliant litigator with a riveting courtroom style that had swayed many a jury.

"We should immediately file a motion to quash your testimony or you will be obligated to reveal your confidential sources on the stand," Hughes cautioned.

"I assumed that Oklahoma newsman's privilege would preclude a journalist from having to divulge sources in open court," I responded.

"Oklahoma statutes will not carry much weight in a federal death penalty case," he shot back. "I cannot guarantee you will not be held in contempt."

Suddenly, the thought hit me—my predicament was a lot stickier than I had originally anticipated. In March 1996, Stephen Jones presented a list of

Oklahoma City witness reports which the FBI had remitted to the defense. KFOR-TV's attorney Robert Nelon and I carefully reviewed the names. We were stunned to learn that several of my confidential sources who had given statements to federal authorities had been excised from the record. Naturally, Jones desired I identify the missing witnesses, but I had pledged not to reveal their names to any third parties other than law enforcement.

Now I was holding a subpoena and McVeigh's lawyer held the power to compel me to talk, but Hughes, ever the wily tactician, suggested we lace the motion to suppress my testimony with overt references to my knowledge of Middle Eastern complicity. It was a high stakes gambit, but the only recourse. The scuttlebutt among the press corps indicated Judge Richard Matsch's tolerance for granting wide latitude to the defense in chasing down foreign conspiracies had run out.

In May 1997, I dialed Bodansky from a payphone on the ground floor of the Denver courthouse, poised to take the stand at any moment if my motion to quash was not granted.

"The prior warnings to the bombing that you issued through the Congressional Task Force were not turned over to McVeigh's lawyers," I anxiously explained in a soft tone so as not to be overheard. "If it was not an oversight, then withholding the alerts could constitute obstruction of justice, or in the worst case scenario, cause a mistrial."

Bodansky's normally witty, calm composure did not trump an overriding concern over the impending courtroom showdown. "You assure the judge that you are confident that person A, B, C, and D (Middle Eastern suspects) were involved in the bombing because the Congressional Task Force has confirmed your findings."

Bodansky, like attorney Carl Hughes, correctly assessed that Judge Matsch was not inclined to complicate the trial in the eleventh hour. Obviously, Stephen Jones held the same belief. I sat on a bench outside Matsch's chambers when Jones emerged reading the motion with a deflated look of defeat. He walked over to my lawyer and explained that he had temporarily withdrawn my subpoena. I had dodged the bullet.

## LEGAL FACE-OFF WITH THE NATION'S "NEWSPAPER OF RECORD"

"You owe the *New York Times* monetary damages if you walk out on your employment contract!" KFOR-TV's newly-appointed station manager barked across the desk at me. The face-off in the corporate head's office was obviously designed to intimidate me into withdrawing my March 1997 resignation. I stood my ground. I explained to the irate manager I could no longer work under the *New York Times* ownership. I had punched my ticket at one of the country's largest NBC affiliates, KCRA-TV in Sacramento, California, but after steep budget cuts and newsroom layoffs, I landed a position at KFOR-TV. Now, after more than a decade establishing my credentials as a solid investigative journalist, Channel 4 was sold to the *New York Times*, and the new management immediately relegated me to covering cub reporter assignments. I was convinced the undeclared but unmistakable demotion was tantamount to constructive termination.

The upcoming federal trials of McVeigh and Nichols also weighed heavily in my decision to leave the broadcast industry altogether. Blind obedience to management's cease and desist order concerning my investigation would have compelled me to report what I considered to be government half-truths in the prosecution of the Oklahoma City bombers. That scenario was simply unconscionable; therefore, I resigned.

The *New York Times* had purchased KFOR-TV prior to my departure. However, the previous owner, Palmer Communications, retained financial and legal interest in the ongoing Al-Hussaini libel lawsuit. The Palmer family had demonstrated unshakable support of my reporting despite the flurry of negative publicity surrounding the charges of defamation. Offering an out-of-court settlement to Al-Hussaini was out of the question. Therefore, I felt obligated to my former employer to remit to the safekeeping of my attorneys the confidential source interviews, the linchpin in the defense of the case. Regardless, *Times* management insisted I return the tapes to Channel 4.

Abundantly aware that chaotic newsroom operations, compounded by pressing deadlines, created a fertile environment for lax security, I expressed my concerns to Channel 4's general manager that the witnesses' unpublished statements could be inadvertently broadcast. I had a personal and professional duty to maintain their collective anonymity and to prevent disclosure of their testimonies without their written consent or legitimate intervention by law enforcement. The witnesses understandably feared retribution by the active terrorist network if publicly identified.

To ensure the sanctity of my First Amendment pledge as a journalist, I proposed the *Times* management sign a waiver absolving me of legal liability if my sources' names or statements were released. My request for indemnification and a compromise agreement, which was plainly stated in several letters written by me as well as my lawyer, was categorically ignored.

However, the *Times* legal representative informed Carl Hughes and me on two separate occasions that the company had no interest in the confidential source recordings that were germane to the Al-Hussaini litigation. But the implicit approval for me to maintain custody of the raw, unedited tapes would be reversed in May 1997 when the doorbell rang, and I was handed a subpoena to testify at McVeigh's trial.

The *Times* rejected my plea when I reached out for legal representation to quash my testimony. Instead, their corporate attorneys filed a lawsuit, accusing me of misdemeanor theft of station property. However, I was powerless to resolve the legal morass. Before the *New York Times* initiated legal action, Bodansky requested I send the confidential source recordings to the Task Force, suggesting in a polite but firm tone that a federal subpoena would be forthcoming if I did not comply. Unemployed and expecting my first child, I cooperated, realizing that challenging Congress could drain an already tight personal budget. After obtaining the consent of the witnesses, I shipped the sensitive box of evidence to Capitol Hill.

Despite legal pleadings before the court confirming I no longer possessed the tapes, the *Times* persisted in its courtroom bully tactics. The owners were unfazed by revelations Congress maintained control of the investigative evidence. A sympathetic local attorney, Dan Woska, who would later represent me in Al-Hussaini's libel case, generously donated pro bono work on the *Times* lawsuit, but the burden of proof was on me. Ironically, a non-profit organization established by the *New York Times* to extend free legal advice to journalists provided the bedrock of my defense.

## CREDIBLE COURTROOM ALLY

The year of 1997 was emotionally trying, fighting legal battles on two fronts—one lawsuit filed by a man I firmly believed to be a terrorist, and the second initiated by my former employer, which threatened to violate the anonymity of the witnesses. Throughout the ordeal, Yossef Bodansky remained supportive but was advised not to become entangled in the litigation. I steadfastly maintained his confidentiality in the court record, omitting references to the highly sensitive intelligence he had shared with me. However, when it appeared my defense against the *New York Times* might be teetering on shaky ground, Bodansky thrust himself into a precarious position by offering to assist.

On October 5, 1998, he drafted a letter to Oklahoma State District

Judge Bryan Dixon outlining the significance of the congressional examination of Channel 4's investigation and the "possibility of foreign involvement" in the April 19 bombing. As the Task Force director, Bodansky straightforwardly expressed his high regard for the trustworthiness of the evidence:

> The Congressional Task Force on Terrorism and Unconventional Warfare is conducting its investigation of the April 1995 Murrah Building bombing. Most sensitive issues, such as the possibility of foreign involvement, are still being studied. For this investigation, I sought, and still seek, every bit of information from both U.S. and foreign sources. It was in this context that former KFOR-TV reporter, Ms. Jayna Davis, contacted me in April 1996. Ms. Davis subsequently advised me that she had compiled tape-recorded interviews of several substantive witnesses identifying Middle Eastern suspects as being involved in various stages of the bombing plot.
>
> This evidence is of great importance to the Task Force's investigation. Therefore, in the spring of 1997, at my request, she forwarded those tapes to my congressional office for review and safekeeping. At the time, Ms. Davis was informed that this material could have been subjected to a congressional subpoena if necessary.
>
> The Task Force maintains custody of the raw tape-recorded interviews as evidence in an on going congressional investigation. . . .
>
> Having studied the material provided by Ms. Davis very closely, I consider it most sensitive, reliable, and important evidence for the Task Force investigation . . .
>
> Having carefully studied these tapes, as well as other work of Ms. Davis, I'm convinced that the witnesses she had interviewed provide credible testimony. It is my professional conclusion, based on lengthy experience with, and expertise in, international terrorism, that these witnesses are, in fact, justified in fearing for their lives in the event their recorded statements are compromised. As already mentioned above, the Task Force keeps these tapes and all related material secure. We don't even advertise the conduct of this investigation because of its great sensitivity.

The Congressional Task Force letter was to be presented to Judge Dixon during an en camera (meaning closed-door) hearing and not to be distributed to any third parties. In the final hour, I instructed my attorneys to hold back Bodansky's correspondence, which I deemed unnecessary for the court to issue an objective determination as to whether or not I had acted lawfully when upholding my journalistic commitment to shield confidential sources.

Moreover, revealing my professional relationship with Bodansky at that point in time, no matter how discreet, also presented potentially detrimental consequences for the intelligence source I had promised to keep anonymous. As it turned out, my gut instinct was on the mark.

After two years of waging legal war in a David versus Goliath battle against the media giant, I prevailed. On March 23, 1999, Judge Dixon ruled that the *Times* owned the witnesses' testimonies but with strict conditions attached. While the publishing company rightfully retained ownership of the physical property, consisting of the plastic casings and metallic tape, it could not disseminate the information memorialized on those tapes without the expressed written consent of the witnesses. Judge Dixon upheld my newsman's privilege to protect my sources until such time that law enforcement authorities solicited their cooperation in bringing the guilty parties to justice. The hollow victory for the nation's "newspaper of record" turned out to be a landmark case in which the court permitted a journalist to withhold confidential source information even from his or her employer.

CHAPTER 19

# CASE CLOSED

Raging legal brush fires set the year of 1997 ablaze. In March, Hussain Al-Hussaini dropped his state defamation lawsuit against KFOR-TV while reserving the right to re-file within a year, which he did. While riding the crest of a short-lived victory, KFOR-TV's new owners lowered the axe on my exploration of foreign involvement. The story was summarily shelved without explanation. I walked out in protest, and weeks later, I was slapped with a subpoena to testify in McVeigh's trial.

Entering the Denver courtroom would have forced me to disclose my witnesses and testify to the existence of the 1995 congressional alerts that were withheld from the defense teams, perhaps illegally. When the *New York Times* learned of my predicament, it offered no assistance in suppressing my testimony in order to shield confidential sources. The company promptly sued me for the return of witness interview tapes that were out of my possession and control. By that time, the Congressional Task Force maintained custody of the recorded statements. Thankfully, my attorneys, Carl Hughes and Kyle Goodwin, filed an ingeniously crafted motion that rescued me moments before I was scheduled to be sworn in.

Needless to say, the whirlwind events eroded my fundamental faith in the execution of justice for the lost souls of April 19. But who could have fathomed that the firewall obstructing my path in exposing the truth had just begun to burn. In September 1997, a subpoena arrived, ordering me to testify before the Oklahoma County Grand Jury which had been impaneled to examine the possibility of additional culprits. I was less than enthused at the prospect. My previous attempts to surrender the witness testimonies to the Oklahoma County prosecutor in charge of the grand jury probe in early January 1997 had elicited a tepid, almost hostile reception.

During the ensuing eight months, the office of District Attorney Bob Macy flatly ignored the witnesses' statements, making no attempt to prove or disprove the veracity of their stories. Although officials assured me the D.A. investigator intended to speak to the witnesses, none was contacted until my attorney unleashed a letter-writing campaign documenting the agency's inaction. Henceforth, only a handful of the twenty-two were interviewed, and in each case, the witnesses remarked that the token line of questioning communicated perceptible hostility. Now, months later, I was staring at a grand jury subpoena, which given the D.A.'s abysmal enthusiasm for the evidence I had already surrendered, looked to be a butt-covering maneuver.

The scope of the grand jury's probe also dimmed my hopes of accomplishing any good. The panel had been sifting through the testimonies of more than one hundred witnesses who espoused a slew of outlandish conspiracy theories, the most egregious of which included allegations John Doe 2 was an undercover government informant and that the CIA or some other covert operative sanctioned by the feds planted multiple charges inside the Murrah Building. Lastly, the grand jury was probing the unsubstantiated belief that law enforcement deliberately stood down in the face of prior warnings to carry out an undercover sting operation that went awry. These claims represented utter insanity in my judgment, but nevertheless, I cooperated with the subpoena.

As it turned out, I testified on three separate occasions, reading into the record the most critical aspects of the witnesses' testimonies and outlining how the strangers' stories uncannily overlapped. Obviously, I had made an impression. The grand jury wrote several letters to my attorney requesting to speak to my sources. All agreed to comply if summoned, despite the inherent danger of parading before a battery of news cameras to testify in the hidden chambers of the Oklahoma County jail.

On October 5, 1998, the District Attorney's office claimed it would honor my written request to hand-deliver the witness affidavits, twenty-two in all, to the jurors. The eighty pages of sworn statements laid out in excruciating detail Timothy McVeigh's collusion with men of Middle Eastern extraction. A peculiar silence followed. No subpoenas were issued to call forth the frightened, yet duty-bound Oklahomans who had articulated their willingness to testify in personal letters to the panelists. Weeks later, a surprise witness dispatched from the halls of the Justice Department would "officially" eradicate the presence of foreign suspects.

## SURPRISE WITNESS

On the heels of media-saturated coverage regarding my grand jury appearances, the FBI began lobbying U.S. District Judge Richard Matsch and the Tenth Circuit Court of Appeals to allow the lead bombing investigators to testify before the panel in order to lay to rest "reckless claims that the federal government had prior knowledge of or involvement in the Murrah Building bombing." After months of legal wrangling, permission was finally granted in November 1998.

A reliable source close to the proceedings briefed me on the Bureau's generalized, glossed over dismissal of my investigation before the panel. The constantly invoked mantra, "We found no credible evidence of a Middle Eastern connection" became a recurring theme as an FBI agent glibly mischaracterized the evidence I had compiled with condescending authoritativeness. How else could he have convinced his audience that the feds had thoroughly checked out KFOR-TV's findings when he either mistakenly or purposely failed to mention the testimonies of seventeen of my witnesses? Instead, he addressed only five, and in so doing, he delivered inaccurate or outright false portrayals of their statements to the FBI. I had personally reviewed the FBI 302s of several witnesses he did mention. In each case, the written record grossly misrepresented the facts that the individual subjects said they had relayed to federal investigators.

It was no wonder the panel adjourned in December without hearing from my witnesses; yet when issuing its final verdict, the group of citizen investigators confessed its profound frustration in declaring last rites over the participation of unknown perpetrators.

"However, in spite of all the evidence before us," the jurors wrote, "we cannot put full closure to the existence of John Doe II."

Obviously, some of the panelists remained dubious about the FBI's broad brush impeachment of nearly two dozen people, many of whose very existence the Bureau failed to acknowledge. According to my source, an assistant district attorney specifically asked the FBI agent during his testimony,

"Regarding Jayna Davis and a Mideast connection, did she provide you with a list of witnesses?"

"I'm not aware of such a list. I did not have a conversation with Jayna Davis," the agent asserted in an artfully parsed response. "I'm not aware such a list was turned over, but I can't say if it wasn't turned over." That statement was accurate. In November 1998, when the agent testified before the grand jury, my witness affidavits were not in the Bureau's custody for one simple reason—the FBI point-blank refused to take the evidence when I freely offered it.


## SHOCKING REFUSAL

The quest to initiate a legitimate inquiry by federal authorities proved equally as exasperating and futile. My encounters with the FBI began in the spring and summer of 1995. KFOR-TV's management and I initially discussed our findings with federal agents, but their zest for our information evaporated when the third terrorist, John Doe 2, inexplicably vanished from the Bureau's radar screen.

In the fall of 1997, upon the advice of my lawyer, I set an appointment with an FBI agent to surrender all twenty-two witness statements and hundreds of pages of corroborative documentation. Upon arriving at the Oklahoma City field office accompanied by notary public, Pam Nance, I was rebuffed. The FBI brazenly refused to take receipt of the investigative file.

When I demanded an explanation for such an absurdity, one of the lead prosecutors for Terry Nichols's approaching federal trial informed my attorney, Tim McCoy, that the Justice Department did not want any more "documents for discovery" to turn over to the defense teams. Shocked by the response, McCoy requested written documentation confirming their phone conversation. However, the prosecutor audaciously refused to disclose his private business fax number unless my lawyer agreed to redact any written references to the "Oklahoma City bombing" and my attempts to turn over "witness testimonies." The resulting statement sounded simply ludicrous: "The United States (DOJ) has not made any investigative demands for any knowledge Jayna Davis may or may not have."

I was dumbfounded. The federal government's capital investment in resources and manpower to track down the killers in the Oklahoma bombing was historically unparalleled. But the FBI slammed the door on a reporter from the mainstream media who desired to share credible information that needed to be investigated.

In 1999, I returned to the FBI headquarters in Oklahoma City. Dan Vogel, a courageous FBI agent, agreed to take custody of the twenty-two witness affidavits. Despite Agent Vogel's obvious concern that the Bureau speak to the witnesses, there was no investigative follow-up to vet the legitimacy of their testimonies. Moreover, the FBI stubbornly refused to question Hussain Al-Hussaini, the man whom multiple witnesses identified as John Doe 2. Eventually, the elaborate runaround and suppression of evidence would play out in an Oklahoma courtroom and on the national airwaves.

CHAPTER 20

# AMERICAN HERO

My quest to exhaust all legal channels to bring about a thorough investigation into the Middle East's role left me disillusioned. I had all but abandoned hope of ever breaking through until a newscast in September of 2000 turned the tide. Chicago attorney David P. Schippers was making the rounds on the cable news networks discussing his explosive best-seller, *Sellout: The Inside Story of President Clinton's Impeachment.* As chief investigative counsel of the House Judiciary Committee for the 1998 impeachment trial, the lifelong Democrat and veteran federal prosecutor held the nation's rapt attention with his eloquent and intrepid summary of the evidence that indicted a sitting president. His spellbinding presentation prompted the December 19, 2000, vote on the floor of the U.S. House of Representatives that would resound in history.

But the man who once spearheaded Attorney General Robert Kennedy's Organized Crime and Racketeering Unit, convicting notorious mobsters such as Sam Giancana and Sam Battaglia, was not going to retreat from Capitol Hill quietly. During his brief stint as chief impeachment prosecutor, he had confronted "lies, hypocrisy, cynicism, butt-covering, and amorality" from members of Congress on both sides of the political aisle, and he was determined to raise the bar of accountability—an American hero who uncompromisingly upheld the rule of law.

I reasoned if a lawyer with such grit and acumen could be convinced of the truth of my investigative efforts, then I would gain a formidable ally in bringing this case to the American people. After all, David Schippers had proven his mettle by his willingness to take on the thankless job of impeaching a popular but scandal-ridden president with anemic support from Congress. I figured the Chicagoan and I shared a common adversary. Schippers's profound disgust with the stonewalling from the Department of Justice and party loyalists mirrored my run-ins with several Oklahoma congressmen who cowered from my research, compounded by the stiff-arm offered by the FBI and the Oklahoma County District Attorney's office. At that point in time, David Schippers represented the only light in my dark world.

So I commenced assembling a comprehensive investigative dossier. I then prepared an introductory letter with a thumbnail sketch of my findings supported by key evidentiary exhibits. The no-nonsense attorney was understandably skeptical at first. However, after months of studious review and consultation with several law enforcement sources, he graciously agreed to meet with my husband Drew and me the afternoon of March 15, 2001.

His impeccably groomed silver beard, classic distinguished features, and resonant voice composed a penetrating countenance. Concealing my initial intimidation, I embarked on an exposition of the evidence, laying on his desk three large black binders which contained twenty-four hundred documents establishing my thesis of foreign complicity. The marathon meeting ended with an appointment for the next day so that the Chicago lawyer could glance through the additional materials I had hand-delivered to his office.

"I'm going straight to the top," Schippers exclaimed. "I'm going to request to meet with the Attorney General John Ashcroft himself!"

"He thinks this is credible," I excitedly told myself, internally unwinding from the intense pressure to gain his confidence. The indefatigable impeachment lawyer moved directly to the next order of business, strategizing ways to invigorate the intractable FBI to take a serious look at this case. I suggested focusing upon the prior warning issued by the Congressional Task Force—ammunition that promised to deliver quite a jolt.

A light tap on the office door interrupted our conversation as a tall, imposing man with a handsome allure entered the room. Schippers introduced the youthful looking stranger as "Bob" and asked if I would mind if he listened to my recitation of the investigation. I perceived the obvious hint not to explore the reason for Bob's interest and resumed discussing intelligence shared by the Task Force director, Yossef Bodansky.

"Bodansky discovered two Islamic militants from Oklahoma City traveled to Chicago in the summer of 1993 to attend a Hamas terrorist training camp," I assured my attentive audience. "Imagine this: The terrorists learned to construct the Murrah Building truck bomb right here in your city!"

I then presented a stack of confidential e-mails Bodansky sent to me in the summer of 1998 which predicted the FBI was preparing to file a civil complaint against the alleged operator of the training camp, Mohammed Salah. I recounted a brief history of the case beginning with Salah's 1993 arrest after authorities discovered him carrying large amounts of unexplained cash during a trip to Israel. The Arab American was tried and convicted of funding Hamas activities. The most incriminating evidence presented at trial was the defendant's confession in which he purportedly admitted to recruiting and training Islamic militants in "mixing poisons, developing chemical weapons, and preparing remote control explosive devices."

The Israelis offered the testimony of a Palestinian student who attended the University of Kansas as independent confirmation of terror training camps in the American Midwest. The student testified Salah invited him to attend covert training facilities in Chicago and Kansas City in 1990. He was reportedly schooled in Hamas philosophy and the assembly of explosives during those sessions. However, when Salah was released from prison, he claimed the Israelis tortured him and forced him to give a false confession. After returning to his suburban life in Chicago as a used car salesman, the FBI seized $1.4 million dollars of Salah's cash and property under civil forfeiture and seizure laws commonly used to go after drug dealers.

"Take note of the dates on Mr. Bodansky's e-mails," I instructed. "The record proves the Congressional Task Force director knew a Chicago FBI agent was preparing to freeze Salah's assets weeks before the charges were filed in federal court. He also claims the agent was frustrated because the Bureau shut down his efforts to open a criminal probe into allegations Salah was running a terror training facility right here in Chicago."

David Schippers's steel blue eyes flickered with stunned amazement as he scanned the Bodansky correspondence. "Do you know the name of the Chicago agent who spearheaded the Mohammed Salah investigation?" He asked with a sly smile.

"I'm afraid the news articles never specifically identified the agent," I answered, wondering what struck him as so humorous.

"His name is Robert Wright. He's the man seated next to you!" he howled with laughter.

Stealing a quick glance at the grinning agent, my face flushed with embarrassment. I broke into a nervous giggle. But the levity of the moment belied the career-threatening battle the veteran terrorism investigator had been waging within his own agency.

In the wake of September 11, 2001, the hidden persona of the agent who knew too much entered the public spotlight. During an emotionally charged press conference, the thirty-eight-year-old Wright entreated the American people to forgive the "fatal failures of the FBI intelligence mission," lamenting the Bureau's abject inability to prevent the next wave of terror. The man who held the professional distinction as the only FBI agent nationwide to crack down on the flow of suspected terrorist funding through charitable front operations prior to 9-11 elicited ire, not accolades, from the agency's power structure. He cautiously parsed his words, divulging the FBI's suppression of his criminal probe into a purported terrorist training camp in suburban Chicago. Moreover, he accused his supervisors at the FBI's Intelligence Division of ordering him not to arrest suspected terrorists.

But it didn't take long for Bob's righteous indignation to trump his fear of legal retaliation from his employer. Under the camera's glare of ABC's news magazine show, *Primetime Live*, the incensed agent lambasted the FBI's efforts to quash his pre-2001 pursuit of one of Osama bin Laden's chief Saudi financiers, Yassin Kadi, and vented his outrage over an Arab FBI agent who audaciously refused to surreptitiously record several suspected Muslim terrorists.

"September 11 is a direct result of the incompetence of the FBI's International Terrorism Unit," Wright passionately charged during an interview with ABC's Chief Investigative Correspondent Brian Ross. "No doubt about that. No doubt about that."

## TELEVISED TELL-ALL

I received a subpoena from Terry Nichols's defense lawyers hours before boarding my flight to Chicago. Evidently, the convicted bomber's attorneys became aware of the FBI's alleged improprieties concerning its refusal to receive and investigate the witnesses' testimonies from my 1997 sealed testimony before the Oklahoma County Grand Jury. Now I was being summoned to appear at a March 20, 2001, preliminary hearing in Nichols's state murder case to outline the Bureau's apparent malfeasance. If convicted at the trial that is scheduled to begin in March 2004, McVeigh's only criminally charged accomplice will confront the prospect of execution.

During the Chicago rendezvous with David Schippers, I handed him my subpoena. Without hesitation he phoned the nation's hottest cable news host, the Fox News Channel's Bill O'Reilly of *The O'Reilly Factor*. His call was returned less than an hour later by O'Reilly himself, impressing me as one who had an enormous respect for David Schippers.

"Bill, are you interested in an exclusive story about the FBI's possible suppression of evidence which implicates the Middle East in the Oklahoma bombing?" Schippers proposed with a tantalizing flair. "Sitting in front of me is the only reporter in the country who has compiled one of the finest investigative dossiers I've ever seen." Seconds later, Schippers thrust the receiver in my direction. "Tell Bill O'Reilly what you know, Jayna."

Panic and trepidation caused my palms to sweat. The brilliant but brusque talk show host on the other end of the line had mastered the art of skillful interrogation. With a hard swallow, I tackled Bill O'Reilly's rapid-fire questions, offering to send materials for his review.

"If David Schippers deems you to be credible, so do I," he interjected. "Why don't you come on my show and outline the facts in your own words?"

Within twenty-four hours, I sat before the cameras at the Fox News Channel studios in Chicago, summarizing six years of research in a seven-minute news window. Bill O'Reilly hammered away at the reasons for the apparent cover-up, but I held my ground, unwilling to indulge in unproven speculation.

"Their reasons, their motivations, that's a question for the Department of Justice and the former attorney general," I calmly reiterated, deflecting his tenacious and repeated attempts to elicit a politically controversial answer. My interview was pre-taped and slated to air in the next few days.

Upon returning to Oklahoma City, I endured three hours of prosecutorial grilling in a closed-door hearing in Nichols's state murder proceedings as I unveiled the prior warning and intelligence which placed the 1995 bombing under the umbrella of foreign sponsorship. Three of my attorneys, notary public Pam Nance, and my husband Drew took the stand to corroborate my testimony that the FBI brazenly turned me away in 1997 when I tried to surrender the evidence I had collected. Two years later, in 1999, FBI Agent Dan Vogel took custody of the witness affidavits. But after he passed the information along to his superiors, the documents were never seen again.

Hours after departing the courthouse, my previously recorded interview with Bill O'Reilly debuted with a combustible introduction before a nationwide audience of fifteen million viewers. "Investigative Reporter Jayna Davis, who worked for the NBC affiliate in Oklahoma City, uncovered evidence that Nichols had ties to the terrorist Osama bin Laden."

"The evidence we gathered definitely incriminates McVeigh and Nichols," I clarified. "However, it really is a foreign conspiracy masterminded and funded by Osama bin Laden according to my intelligence sources."

"You took your information to the FBI, you told me. What happened?" O'Reilly inquired, anticipating the answer would infuriate his viewers.

"Well, what happened was they turned me away and refused to take it," I declared.

"Really?" O'Reilly urged.

"I was flabbergasted. I couldn't even speculate why they wouldn't take this information. They had hundreds of agents on this case. They had millions of dollars of property damage. They had 171 victims. Why wouldn't they want the information from a reporter who had sworn witness statements implicating others unknown in the Oklahoma City bombing?"

Bill O'Reilly wrapped up the interview with his trademark confrontational style, "Of course, the former attorney general is Janet Reno. We called the FBI and they refused to comment, as usual."

## Fox News Fallout

David Schippers phoned the next morning. "The phone lines are lighting up like a Christmas tree at Fox News. It seems *The O'Reilly Factor* has been barraged with inquiries from Congress," he beamed with delight. "We've got their attention, Jayna, but we are not talking to staffers. Believe me, I've learned the hard way that if you want something done in Washington, you deal directly with the congressmen and senators."

The Fox News broadcast replayed three more times over the next thirty days, inflicting untold pressure on the FBI for its inexcusable behavior. At last, the Department of Justice was compelled to admit to Bill O'Reilly that the Bureau rejected my investigative dossier because it did not want any more documents to remit to the defense lawyers before the federal trials. A former U.S. Army prosecutor and assistant U.S. attorney candidly admitted to me that withholding evidence of additional suspects in a death penalty case could constitute "obstruction of justice."

Not surprisingly, the criminal implications of my allegations did not prompt elected officials to reach out from inside the beltway; but little did I know the historic ricochet that would follow. In May 2001, just two months after my testimony in Nichols's pre-trial hearing and my charges of governmental misconduct on the national airwaves, the FBI made a staggering admission. The criminal case touted as the Bureau's "crown jewel" had been tarnished by the "inadvertent" withholding of four thousand discovery documents from the lawyers who represented the convicted bombers. The belated disclosure was egregious enough to halt McVeigh's imminent execution and prompted the Department of Justice Office of Inspector General to launch an internal investigation. Yet even after the discovery documents were dispensed, the affidavits which I gave to Agent Vogel in 1999 were still officially classified as missing.

"What would fuel such bureaucratic madness?" I asked a trusted federal law enforcement source. "Why would the FBI deep-six twenty-two witness affidavits which I gave the Bureau in the presence of my attorney?"

The career investigator smiled wryly, then offered me an abridged education in the art of evidence suppression, "Jayna, if the FBI does not possess your investigative file, agents can swear under oath the documentation never existed. Therefore, the Bureau is under no legal obligation to open a national security investigation into the Middle Eastern connection."

## Missing Evidence

In October 2001, the legal drama reached a crescendo when retired FBI Agent Dan Vogel was subpoenaed to testify in Nichols's Oklahoma pre-trial proceeding which stemmed from the missing evidence debacle. In a court proffer, the defendant's lawyers told Oklahoma State District Judge Ray Dean Linder that Agent Vogel readily admitted "he received twenty-two affidavits from reporter Jayna Davis in January 1999," but after he turned the materials over to the FBI legal department in the Oklahoma City field office, the sworn declarations disappeared. Government prosecutors argued the federal officer's oath of office prohibited him from testifying. The judge agreed and barred him from delivering his statement in open court.

In the wake of the September 11 terrorist onslaught, the troubled FBI agent unburdened himself in a rare interview with *Indianapolis Star* columnist James Patterson.

"We may have been in a position to start a massive investigation deep down in the Oklahoma City office based on the information that Jayna Davis had come up with on this Middle Eastern connection. Whether or not there was a connection didn't really matter. What really mattered was the fact that there was something very sinister going on with these individuals just because of the information that Jayna had gathered," Agent Vogel ruminated with perceptible grief. "Jayna Davis was giving us a warning back as early as 1997 and we didn't do anything with it. We just refused to take the documents. And I don't know to this day what happened to the documents."

## "THEY'RE GOING TO BLOW UP LOWER MANHATTAN"

Calling upon courageous souls with whom he once served side-by-side in the trenches of the impeachment battle, David Schippers confronted an unspoken code of silence. Not even the fiercest and the finest wanted to broach the subject of Oklahoma City and Middle Eastern complicity. His tireless efforts to generate interest in a congressional inquiry fell on deaf ears.

"But why?" I pondered. "The suppression of the Middle Eastern link took place under a Democratic administration."

Then it hit me. The answer had been right in front of me all these years. The director of the Congressional Task Force, Yossef Bodansky, reported to House Republicans when he distributed terrorist alerts in February and March of 1995. His forethought was summarily dismissed as "Zionist propaganda," and in the end, the arrest of foreign nationals would have solidified and validated his prediction. One unintended consequence involved Congress and law enforcement bearing the onus of liability for failure to evacuate the Oklahoma City federal building. It didn't matter that there was simply not enough information to isolate the target and stop the bomb. I theorized that those involved could not risk the fallout of negative public perception and incendiary political spin.

More significantly, Yossef Bodansky had retained the confidential recordings of my witness interviews since 1997 and Congress had not called hearings. Then, in 1998, the Task Force chief authored correspondence to the presiding judge in the *New York Times* lawsuit against me in which he confirmed the "highly sensitive congressional examination" of KFOR-TV's investigation and the "possibility of foreign involvement" in the April 19 bombing. Bodansky's letter proved that Congress had possession of the witnesses' statements long before September 2001 but failed and/or refused to act on the evidence. As a result, the very mention of the Yossef Bodansky's name induced instant memory loss from Washington insiders, in spite of his frequent appearances on cable news networks as an eminent authority on Osama bin Laden.

"It's like nothing I've ever experienced," Schippers mused. "The guy is the director of the Congressional Task Force on Terrorism, but none of the

Republicans with whom I have spoken has ever heard of him. Bodansky is either a phantom or a spook hiding in plain sight."

Undaunted by the institutional apathy, the dogged advocate resolved not to give up until he spoke to the man in charge at the Department of Justice.

"I want a meeting with General Ashcroft," David Schippers demanded in a June 2001 phone conversation with a high ranking deputy attorney general in Washington, D.C. "I have in my office volumes of credible evidence indicating Middle Eastern involvement in the Oklahoma City bombing, and quite frankly, it scares the hell out of me. If nothing is done, I'm afraid these terrorists are going to blow up Lower Manhattan."

"Well, sir, we don't normally start our meetings at the top," the DOJ official cautioned as he delivered the bureaucratic brush-off. "But I'll see what I can do and get back to you."

That call never came. Three months later, Schippers's warning proved prophetic. Hijacked airliners, transformed into guided missiles, dive-bombed the New York Trade Center and Pentagon. September 11 would eclipse Pearl Harbor in the annals of infamy, with Iraq's sponsorship being seriously considered. Despite exhaustive efforts, the Bush administration's CIA and FBI found no conclusive connection to the president's principal nemesis, Saddam Hussein. However, before long the common thread weaving Oklahoma to the kill zones of New York and Washington materialized with all roads pointing to the "Butcher of Baghdad."

## History Repeated

The kamikaze invasion from our skies unleashed a riptide of anger and wrenching pain, the kind of hurt that seeps into one's bone marrow. The unstoppable human spirit that embodied David Schippers withered and wept on September 11. The drumbeat of the coming holy war had been pounding for months, but he was among the rare few to detect the approaching rumble.

"It is a tragic day in American history when three thousand people have to die for Congress to wake up to the mortal threat of radical Islam," he bemoaned.

"What do we do now?" I asked. Until then, I had been muzzled by the pending civil lawsuit with Hussain Al-Hussaini. Schippers volunteered to speak in my stead.

"There's no holding back. We owe it to the American people to tell all we know."

In no time, his 2002 calendar was booked. Schippers sacrificially put his demanding law practice on hold to fulfill back-to-back speaking engagements and to appear on popular coast-to-coast radio talk shows. He patiently addressed the myriad of objections raised by disbelieving print journalists, all the while, the engaging orator argued the tragic miscarriage of justice in the heartland with the fiery conviction of a defense attorney fighting to spare his client the death penalty. But uniquely in the case of Oklahoma City and the ensuing encroachment of Muslim terrorism, Schippers considered himself an advocate of the people, protecting the rights of uninformed citizens.

"I tried the House. I tried the Senate. I tried the Department of Justice," Schippers told a Pittsburgh radio audience. In the next breath, he accused the FBI of squelching information from the April 1995 bombing that provided the springboard for bin Laden's 2001 terror spree. That allegation prompted a call from a representative from the office of House Speaker Dennis Hastert.

"I have at least two and maybe three witnesses that should be subpoenaed to come out there and testify in executive session and tell you what I'm talking about," Shippers told the man who had the ear of the most influential elected official in the House of Representatives.

"OK, we'll get back to you," Hastert's staffer vowed—a pledge that would inevitably be unfulfilled. But the Chicago native's message resonated with the influential *Wall Street Journal* and other respected mainstream journalists, most notably, *LA Weekly* reporter Jim Crogan and *Indianapolis Star* editorial writer James Patterson.

"The man who fell just a few votes shy of removing a president from office is now on another crusade," Patterson wrote in his October 13, 2001, column. "Schippers wants to know what happened to a boatload of affidavits and other information turned over to Oklahoma FBI Special Agent Dan Vogel by Jayna Davis, a former KFOR-TV reporter in Oklahoma."

The intrepid and discerning journalist latched onto my story, tackling the alleged cover-up by introducing new and riveting evidence in his weekly columns. Behind the scenes, Patterson gently nudged Indianapolis's hometown U.S. representative, Dan Burton, then chairman of the Government Reform Committee, to investigate my claims. To Burton's credit, he asked Schippers to spearhead the probe, but career lawyers with the committee denied Schippers's request for Congress to fund independent investigator Jeff Pavletic, an Illinois attorney who served as Schippers's co-counsel during

President Clinton's impeachment trial. In March 2002, Schippers and Pavletic flew to Washington, D.C., to spar face-to-face with committee attorneys who unabashedly let their impatience with the whole affair be known.

"The handwriting is on the wall," Schippers somberly warned. His solemnity and resignation foreshadowed the disappointment that lay ahead. "No one in Washington wants to unearth such a colossal cover-up."

Radio host Glenn Beck echoed those same sentiments in August 2002 while interviewing Schippers and me for his nationally syndicated show.

"Too many bodies to exhume," Beck astutely observed when a listener asked why President George Bush's administration would not seize the opportunity to indict Iraqis accused of collaborating with McVeigh and Nichols.

## ARROGANCE AND APATHY—AMERICA AT RISK

From February through November 2002, Representative Dan Burton's staffers feigned interest under the watchful eye of James Patterson's relentless coverage in Indiana's most influential newspaper. After all, it was an election year. During the interim, investigators flew to Oklahoma City to meet the witnesses personally—meetings that would have never taken place had these Oklahomans not rearranged their schedules with just twenty-four hours notice. As it turned out, their sacrifice and effort seemed pointless. All the witnesses complained that the congressional representatives came across as apathetic, posing only superficial questions, avoiding the topic of possible FBI malfeasance altogether.

"It was comical," said witness Jesse Pearce, who, on April 19, glanced inside the Ryder truck at John Doe 2 when Timothy McVeigh pulled into a downtown tire store to ask for directions. "The investigators asked me one or two questions about my testimony over a barbecue sandwich. They were more interested in lunch than in what I had to say. That's hardly the attitude I expected from Congress."

"The whole ordeal was a complete farce!" fumed Georgia Hammerstein, the former Cactus Motel clerk who rented McVeigh a room the night before the bombing. "I firmly believe Burton's people had not read one word of my affidavit before they came to question me. I told the lead attorney, 'I live with the guilt of April 19 because I failed to see the warnings when these Arabs visited the Cactus Motel; but if you don't do anything to get these guys now, the next time they blow up a building, the blood will be on your hands!'" That encounter would mark Georgia's only opportunity to inform authorities of her testimony. She passed away from surgery complications in October 2002.

The congressional inquiry soon fizzled out just as Schippers had foreseen. On August 15, 2002, the committee's chief investigator, in a patronizing tone, asserted that "innocent explanations" could easily dispel the theory of Middle Eastern complicity. In his informed opinion, all twenty-two witnesses were simply wrong. But after five months of trudging through the avalanche of evidence I had unloaded on the Government Reform Committee, staffers could not convincingly dismiss the people and events which inculpated Iraqi soldier Hussain Al-Hussaini as John Doe 2 and cast the FBI's actions in a dubious light. I make such an assertion unreservedly after having posed a litany of interrogatories to Representative Burton in a letter dated September 4, 2002.

I have yet to receive an "innocent explanation" to the following questions: Why has the Justice Department/FBI not issued an official on-the-record statement exonerating Hussain Al-Hussaini in the Oklahoma City bombing? Has the DOJ provided Congress with Hussain Al-Hussaini's whereabouts for the critical hours of the morning of April 19, 1995? Why did the FBI never question Hussain Al-Hussaini about the bombing? Why did the FBI previously suspect Al-Hussaini's employer of ties to the Palestinian Liberation Organization? Why were the original Cactus Motel registration logs where witnesses testified McVeigh checked in with Al-Hussaini's Iraqi cohort the evening of April 18, 1995, never returned to the establishment's owner? Whatever happened to the brown Chevrolet pickup that was seen carrying Middle Eastern suspects from the bomb site? The Oklahoma City police found fingerprints inside the recovered truck; to whom did they belong? Why did the Bureau rebuff my efforts to surrender the witness statements and supporting evidence in September 1997? Why did the FBI withhold from the defense teams the twenty-two witness affidavits that I delivered to FBI Special Agent Dan Vogel in January 1999? Why were the prior warnings issued by the Congressional Task Force on Terrorism and Unconventional Warfare that predicted an Islamic attack in the heart of the U.S. disregarded as an indicator of foreign participation?

Tragically, the absence of vigilant public pressure on Congress to push for real answers permitted the committee to jettison the unwelcome burden of "exhuming the bodies" of Oklahoma City. This was not just a dismissal of penetrating facts surrounding the Murrah Building blast itself, but also the deeper question of how the horror of 4-19 could be linked to the final outrage in the war against America, 9-11.

# CHAPTER 21

# NEXUS: 4-19 AND 9-11

As the passenger-filled jumbo jets sliced through the towering twin sky-scrapers, haunting questions that did not yield simple answers reverberated in my head. Did the failure to examine a Middle Eastern signature in Oklahoma City embolden Islamic extremists in their unhindered mission to commit wholesale murder on a scale the world had never seen? Saddam Hussein's lust to avenge his mortifying Gulf War defeat quite possibly spawned the first attack on the World Trade Center in 1993; however, the grandiose scheme to topple the parallel structures failed miserably, killing only six people, when thousands could have perished. Did the Iraqi dictator, backed by Osama bin Laden and a host of terrorist sponsoring nations, dis-patch their operatives a second time in 1995 and again in 2001 to satisfy an insatiable appetite to settle the score?

Within days of the aerial raids manned by Muslim suicide squads, the finger of blame pointed to bin Laden as the diabolical architect. But accord-ing to Yossef Bodansky, the director of the Congressional Task Force on Terrorism and Unconventional Warfare, the Saudi tycoon was not a transna-tional, borderless agent of terror as characterized by many in intelligence cir-cles. Instead, the freelancer operated under the guidance and support of Iran, Syria, Sudan, and Iraq. In 1996, I received several confidential intelligence reports from Bodansky that implicated bin Laden as the financier of the

NEXUS: 4-19 AND 9-11    297

Oklahoma attack. At the time, the devout Muslim was riding the crest of his meteoric rise to spiritual leader of radical Islam.

Although bin Laden had openly declared war against America, the strikes on New York and Washington, D.C. had not been linked to Oklahoma City in any fashion. The widely reported story that two of the four ill-fated flights had originated from Boston Logan International Airport kept coming to my thoughts in the days following the 9-11 atrocity. Scouring through a sea of documentary evidence, I searched for a reference to Boston Logan. The location somehow sounded familiar to me. Hussain Al-Hussaini's psychiatric records, which I compelled to be released to me during the lengthy litigation, affirmed my suspicions.

## "IF SOMETHING WERE TO HAPPEN THERE, I WOULD BE A SUSPECT."

In November 1997, Al-Hussaini confided to his psychiatrist he was con-templating whether to quit his job at Boston Logan International Airport stating, "If something were to happen there, I would be a suspect." The doctor's notations described the Iraqi patient's strong desire to "look for another job because he feels unsafe in the environment he works in, i.e. the airport, given the recent events involving his being previously suspected of involvement in the Oklahoma bombing." Al-Hussaini reiterated the pecu-liar disclosure to his doctors during his 1998 deposition stating that if "something else were to happen, they [airport authorities] would point the finger at me."

Al-Hussaini's seemingly innocuous complaint to his psychiatrist four years before suicidal disciples of Allah commandeered the cockpits of American jumbo jets suddenly leapt from the page. One can only imagine why Al-Hussaini's apprehension about a terrorist strike at that particular air-port coincided with the 1997 genesis of the September 11 plot.

Officials with the Massachusetts Port Authority, which managed per-sonnel at Logan International, declined to verify Al-Hussaini's specific air-port duties, access to secured areas, and current employment status. But the Iraqi soldier's connection to the exact airport used to execute an unprece-dented major terrorist assault on U.S. soil stretched the boundaries of mere coincidence. That disturbing fact, coupled with the slew of evidence accu-mulated against Al-Hussaini in the Oklahoma bombing, made him either the most unlucky individual on the planet or a diabolical player who had a hand in two harrowing terrorist hits against American targets.

I gleaned more incriminating clues while scanning through the Al-Hussaini litigation files—personal information that would have remained buried had he not sued me and been compelled to comply with discovery. I found it particularly intriguing that upon the Iraqi immigrant's August 1994 arrival to Boston from the Middle East, Al-Hussaini resided with two brothers, Abu and Marwan Mahmud. The pair served in Saddam's military and had engaged in combat against American troops during the 1991 Gulf War.

As the November 1994 Thanksgiving holiday approached, Abu Mahmud personally escorted Al-Hussaini to start a new life in Oklahoma City. Curiously, Abu prearranged his employment and place of residence in a city where Al-Hussaini professed to know no one. The Iraqi chaperone remained in Oklahoma for several months, taking a temporary job at Dr. Abdul's property management company while Al-Hussaini settled in. During his 1998 deposition in the KFOR-TV lawsuit, Al-Hussaini testified that Abu eventually returned to his previous employment in food catering services for the commercial airlines at Boston Logan International Airport. Federal investigators theorized food suppliers secretly planted the box cutters that the 9-11 hijackers used to subdue the flight crews and passengers.

## FBI Asks Al-Hussaini for Assistance

Hussain Al-Hussaini's association with Boston area Iraqis flashed across the FBI radar screen long before the Oklahoma City bombing. While being deposed, Al-Hussaini disclosed, with a degree of reluctance, that federal agents interviewed him in August 1995. However, the inquiry did not focus on his possible involvement in the Murrah Building attack, but rather, investigators questioned him about a Boston acquaintance, a man reportedly named "Mohammad Altaflawi." Al-Hussaini claimed to have met the Iraqi expatriate through the International Rescue Committee when he immigrated to the United States, contending he had no idea why the FBI was interested in Altaflawi. But most intriguing was the timing of the federal probe into the Boston Iraqi, which coincided with the FBI's 1995 survey of aviation schools nationwide in an effort to corroborate the confession of jailed terrorist Abdul Hakim Murad.

The FBI arrested Murad in early 1995 for conspiring with reputed Iraqi intelligence operative Ramzi Yousef in "Project Bojinka," a thwarted plot to detonate bombs aboard twelve U.S. airliners originating in the Philippines in a murderous rampage over the Pacific Ocean. While being interrogated, the Middle Eastern terrorist hinted at a future scheme (paradigm for the 9-11 strikes) in which Muslim fundamentalists would train at U.S. flight schools to learn to hijack commercial jetliners. One plan involved the recruitment of suicide pilots to dive bomb the Virginia-based CIA headquarters aboard general aviation aircraft rigged with explosives.

After conducting a perfunctory investigation, Murad's far-fetched tale of unspeakable carnage to come dissolved into the file of "false" leads. The stratospheric intelligence failure would not fully sink in until the FBI retraced the domestic flight instruction of the nineteen Al-Qaeda executioners. Their aviation skills were not only made in the U.S.A., but several were previously flagged as visa violators and suspected terrorists who melted through the so-called safety net of intelligence gathering.

Yet even in death, their soulless eyes proved inescapable as their photographs dominated the international airwaves. Three men in particular instantly jogged the memory of the motel owner where Timothy McVeigh and Terry Nichols once met with their Middle Eastern handlers.

"Jayna, I've toiled with coming forward with this, but I can't shake the image of their faces," Cactus owner Randy Christian said with timid sincerity. "I'm positive three of the 9-11 hijackers visited my motel a month before the attacks."

## TWIN TOWERS/TERRORIST MOTEL INTERSECTION

Just four days after the World Trade Center disintegrated on live television, Randy recounted his fantastic story. The self-styled ringleader Mohammed Atta, his dutiful sidekick Marwan Al-Shehhi, and the surviving would-be hijacker Zacarias Moussaoui entered the Cactus Motel lobby in early August of 2001. The trio inquired about renting a room with a kitchenette, but the owner cordially explained there were no vacancies.

Acting as the group's decision maker, Atta sauntered across the room, standing an arm's length from the owner. "We're going to be attending flight school in Norman and would really like to stay at your motel because we have heard such good things about it," the slight framed man insisted as he broke into a broad smile.

Randy considered Atta's persistence quite peculiar given the ample avail-ability of discount motels that provided convenient proximity to the Norman aviation schools.

"Our motel is at least a thirty mile drive, one-way. I'm sure you will have no problem renting a room at a reasonable rate much closer," Randy gra-ciously suggested. But Atta, conspicuously clad in a heavy leather flight jacket on a blistering hot summer day, was not dissuaded. He gushed with compliments about the "outstanding" reputation of Randy's motel. In hind-sight, the men appointed to die in a few short weeks, intended to deliver yet another humiliating slap in the face to American law enforcement by sign-ing their names to the register at the very motel that served as the staging grounds for their Middle Eastern predecessors, as if to say, "Ignore us at your own peril."

Shortly after the World Trade Center disaster, Randy reluctantly prom-ised me, "I'm going to report this to the FBI. But given my past history with the Murrah Building attack, I don't expect they will want to hear from me, much less take my statement. Regardless, I know it's the right thing to do."

"Did anyone else witness the meeting?" I inquired.

"Yes. The desk clerk on duty that day remembers the arrival of three men who pressed for a discounted rate to rent a kitchenette, but he does not recall what they looked like," he explained.

As expected, Randy's recorded voice message at FBI headquarters in Oklahoma City was ignored for several months. However, federal investiga-tors exhibited a fortuitous change of heart after one of my law enforcement sources pressured Oklahoma City Police Sergeant Jerry Flowers, a ranking member of the newly formed Oklahoma Joint Terrorism Task Force, to check into Randy Christian's testimony. On December 19, 2001, Sgt. Flowers and an FBI agent debriefed Randy about his unforgettable encounter with Atta, Al-Shehhi, and Moussaoui.

When Randy contacted me in September 2001, the international trav-els and movements of the 9-11 terrorists inside the U.S. had not yet been reported. But the official indictment against suspected Al-Qaeda operative, Zacarias Moussaoui, would yield a windfall of eagerly awaited corroboration. The government's prosecutorial evidence trail established that Moussaoui remained in Oklahoma through August of 2001, the same time frame in which Atta and his terrorist comrades purportedly visited the Cactus Motel. Moussaoui arrived in the Sooner State in February to attend Airman Flight School in Norman. The training lasted until May, but the French citizen of Moroccan descent resided in Oklahoma through the summer months to receive a $14,000 transfer from train stations in Dusseldorf and Hamburg, Germany. Bin Laden chieftain, Ramzi Bin Al-Shibh, wired the funds to Moussaoui on August 1 and 3, 2001.

## FBI—FUMBLING BUMBLING INVESTIGATIONS

The July 2003 omnibus congressional report into pre-September 11 intelligence failures admonished the Oklahoma City FBI field office as a repeat offender in the maddening chain of missed clues. The thread to America's heartland unravels to August 16, 2001, and a pivotal opportunity squandered in the string of government blunders. Federal authorities detained and charged Zacarias Moussaoui for an expired visa, but immigration violations merely opened a legal gateway to make the arrest. Moussaoui, a flight student with no pilot's license, less than fifty hours in the cockpit of civil aircraft, and no instruction on sophisticated commercial jets, paid $6800 cash to train on a Boeing 747 simulator. The Islamic fundamentalist expressed an "ego boosting" desire to learn to fly from Heathrow Airport in England to John F. Kennedy Airport in New York.

Minnesota FBI agents were frantically seeking evidence to warrant logging on to the potential hijacker's computer hard drive. Urgency in this case could not be overstated. The Oklahoma City field office was commissioned to assist. On August 23, two agents assigned to the international terrorism squad were dispatched to Airman Flight School in Norman where Moussaoui previously attended, but it wasn't their first visit. In 1999, the Oklahoma field office made inquiries about Osama bin Laden's chief pilot who had received training at the same aviation facility. Unfortunately, that pertinent fact slipped the lead FBI agent's mind when conducting the Moussaoui probe, depriving the Minnesota field office of critical information in its quest to obtain a search warrant.

Congress isolated yet another intelligence gaffe during its inquiry. In August 2001, when INS officials nabbed Moussaoui and his roommate, Hussein Al-Attas, a notorious individual attempted to post bond for Al-Attas. That individual had been "the subject of a full-field FBI international terrorism investigation in the Oklahoma City Field Office." Apparently, this unnamed former or current Oklahoma resident had impressive terrorist credentials that included "Vice President of Overseas Operations and Recruiting for Al-Fatah" as well as membership in the Muslim Brotherhood. The FBI "person of interest" was depicted as a close associate of the Muslim cleric who reportedly administered spiritual guidance to two of the 9-11 hijackers. The Justice Department invoked the "national security" shield when refusing to confirm or deny if the Oklahoma City FBI probe into the Al-Fatah recruiter was still active.

## CACTUS CONNECTION TO AL-QAEDA COMRADE

The trail of Oklahoma missteps may trace as far back as April 19, 1995. On October 11, 2001, the FBI arrested Mujahid Abdulqaadir Menepta of Norman, Oklahoma, as a material witness in connection with the terror campaign of September 11, charges that were never proven. Federal authorities detained the fifty-one-year-old Menepta because of his close friendship with alleged conspirator, Zacarias Moussaoui. The twosome socialized during Moussaoui's training at Airman Flight School. In an October 2, 2001, interview with the *Daily Oklahoman*, Menepta vehemently defended Moussaoui, calling him a "scapegoat."

"I saw him daily at the mosque. We'd eat together sometimes. I don't think he is a terrorist," Menepta said. "I understand terrorism quite well. I am a victim of terror, America's terror. I am a descendent of slaves." The Missouri native changed his name from Melvin Lattimore to Mujahid Menepta after converting to the Muslim faith in 1989. One year later, he traveled to Pakistan to study Islam.

The FBI confiscated three weapons and six hundred rounds of ammunition during the October 2001 search of Menepta's Norman home. Weeks later, the former felon pleaded guilty to illegal possession of firearms. But the ensuing courtroom drama made it abundantly clear that the weapons charges provided a means to keep Menepta in custody after federal investigators failed to tie the ex-convict to the 9-11 attacks.

According to the November 7, 2001, federal court testimony of ATF Agent Jeffrey Whitney, a government informant who characterized Menepta as "violent," surfaced within twenty-four hours of the 1995 Murrah Building bombing. The source told the FBI Menepta was a member of a radical Islamic group in Norman and St. Louis that spewed vitriol against the United States and advocated destroying government targets, killing police officers, and committing terrorist acts. The informant also claimed he witnessed Menepta threatening to shoot any police officer who entered the prayer area of a St. Louis mosque where he worshipped.

Agent Whitney also testified that several telephone numbers traced from cell phones seized during a search of Menepta's car and home were associated with "ongoing criminal investigations in St. Louis, Kansas City, Detroit, El Paso, Texas, and Oklahoma City." The investigations involved organized crime, drugs, and money laundering. Additionally, Agent Whitney informed the court that Menepta claimed the Secret Service told him a conspirator in the 1993 World Trade Center bombing had used his passport number, although his account could not be confirmed.

"Why does this guy look so darn familiar?" former Cactus Motel manager Gary Hammerstein mused aloud while examining a photo line-up of several African American males. He singled out the picture of Mujahid Menepta. "Let me think a minute. I know it will come to me."

Several moments of pensive reflection brought about a revelation. Gary snapped his fingers. "I got it. This man was definitely a guest at the motel."

"How long ago did this sighting occur?" I asked.

"It must have been years, but I know it was right before my hip surgery because I was still walking with a cane. I cannot give you an exact date, but I'm pretty certain this man stayed several weeks at the motel in the spring of 1993."

I had come to know Gary as a no-nonsense, straight shooter, but the alleged encounter took place quite a few years earlier. "You've slept a few nights since 1993. What makes you so certain this is the same man?" I queried.

"Because the man spent no less than three hours a day drinking coffee and talking to me in the motel lobby. He stayed at the Cactus for two to three weeks," he answered. "But what really stands out in my mind was his peculiar behavior and the bundles of cash stuffed in his pockets."

"Why do you consider it so unusual to carry around a lot of cash?" I inquired.

"This guy passed himself off as a construction worker, but I sensed that somebody was giving him a lot of money. When he bought a thirty-five cent cup of coffee, he always pulled out a stack of fifty and hundred dollar bills. The money was so bulky, it would not fit in his wallet," Gary recalled.

After purchasing coffee, Menepta would settle into a chair in front of the registration counter, watch television, and make small talk with Gary. For hours on end, the two discussed superficial topics such as the economy, sports, and the weather, but Menepta never mentioned where he was from, his family, or his profession. The light complexioned black male came across as intelligent and well spoken.

Gary noticed that the ubiquitous customer closely observed his daily routine and listened intently to his conversations on the motel switchboard.

Whenever a motel guest entered the office, Menepta quickly slipped out the door, sending the implicit message he did not want to be noticed by strangers. His skittish behavior initially alarmed Gary, who suspected the talkative patron of casing the Cactus to stage a heist when business traffic had slowed down. While working at another hotel chain, Gary was robbed at gunpoint. From that point forward, Gary was especially observant of the clientele.

While Gary was somewhat apprehensive about Menepta's motives, he soon realized that his actions did not forebode the planning of a crime. Even though Menepta immediately departed when guests arrived, he did not mind the presence of maintenance staff. He began to speculate that Menepta might have been a lonely construction worker, but that theory did not hold up to scrutiny either. Every morning, Menepta arrived in a freshly laundered white shirt, but his pants and boots displayed the same pattern of dried red clay. When he returned in the afternoon, his T-shirt appeared unsoiled, indicating he had not been traipsing around a construction site. In hindsight, Gary hypothesized that Menepta wore mud-spattered jeans to give the impression he had a construction job.

"Now as I look back on things, I think that man's purpose was to watch everything that went on at the motel and report back to somebody. To whom, I have no idea," Gary opined. "But it's my belief, in light of all that happened at the motel with Timothy McVeigh and his Middle Eastern friends, that this motel guest might have been scouting the place out for a future operation."

## DARK CONFESSION

The nexus between 4-19 and 9-11 extended beyond the borders of the Oklahoma City terrorist motel. Another witness handed me the key to a Pandora's Box, unlocking the innermost secrets of a member of the Iraqi terrorist cell which I had been investigating since 1995. Stacy McBride, the niece of Rita Edwards—the witness whom I had dubbed the "insider"— broke her silence. The emotional burden of "Black Tuesday" convinced the young woman she could no longer ignore a still, calm voice within, urging her to flee her seven year live-in relationship with Hussain Al-Hussaini's Iraqi cohort, Majid Ajaj. While watching the ghastly television images of the 9-11 annihilation, Majid disgorged bone-jarring, insensitive remarks.

"Do you know who did this?" Stacy daringly inquired with unmistakable accusation.

Unruffled by the inference of guilt, Majid shrugged, then answered with detached inflection, "This kind of thing happens in my country all the time."

"What he really means is terrorist acts are committed by fundamentalist Iraqis," Stacy surmised under her breath as she continued peppering the ex-Iraqi soldier with penetrating questions.

Majid grew impatient, flashing an agitated glower her direction. "If the FBI comes looking for me, tell them you don't know where I am," he ordered.

For years, Stacy had endured Majid's unprovoked beatings, verbal tirades, and perennial unfaithfulness, but his paranoia about federal authorities suspecting him of terrorist ties was something new, a side of his personality he had never exposed before. She began contemplating the unspeakable. "Is the man whom I once loved, the father figure to my children, in reality, a terrorist, a ruthless killer?"

An intoxicated Majid delivered the gut-wrenching answer just days later. Before the sun dipped below the horizon on the evening of September 17, 2001, Majid combusted into uncontrolled fury.

"I am going to burn down your mother's house with your mother and your sister in it. You know I'll do it 'cause you know what I did. I had something to do with the bombing," Majid growled at Stacy over the cell phone. She could hear a chorus of shrill male voices in the background barking orders in Arabic for Majid to "shut up."

"I have to let you go," he whimpered. The line went dead. Stacy stared at the receiver, trying to mentally process his spontaneous confession.

Her mother, sister, and brother-in-law sat motionless, bracing to hear what triggered her stunned expression. "Majid just confessed to being involved in the Oklahoma City bombing and quite possibly the attacks on New York and Washington," the quivering blonde announced to the anxious audience. The phone rang again, causing everyone's heart to race.

"It's Majid calling back," Stacy said as she glanced at the caller identification. "What should I do?"

"Answer it, but act like the confession didn't even register with you," her sister Jennifer advised. "He's obviously drunk and didn't mean for that to slip out."

Stacy punched the speakerphone button, broadcasting Majid's deadly intentions to the roomful of witnesses. "I'm going to get your family. I'm going to burn their house down. I don't care if the police come. I don't care if I die. I'm already dead."

Battle-weary from Majid's invective outbursts, the family sought sanctuary at a local motel. Slumped behind the wheel of her car, Stacy kept watch throughout the dead of night, convinced Majid would follow through on his threat and torch her home. Shrouded in darkness and silence, she came to terms with their tumultuous relationship.

As if awakening from a daydream, naïveté gave way to suspicion. Stacy reflected upon seven years of strange occurrences which included out-of-state visitors from Phoenix where several of the 9-11 hijackers had received flight training, mysterious trips to undisclosed destinations, shady business ventures with automotive garages that appeared to function as shell companies, unexplained sources of income without steady employment, and his frequently sneaking off to payphones to make untraceable calls overseas with a phone debit card. She shuddered as she relived how she had assisted Majid's criminal exploits such as staging automobile thefts and accidents to collect illicit insurance settlements—money which Majid routinely sent home to Iraq.

Images of a simmering hot day in June 1995 traveled to the fore of her thoughts. She could still hear the knock at the door. An FBI agent had come to the couple's home to inquire about Ali's whereabouts for the morning of April 19. During the interrogation, the agent disclosed that the FBI had recorded phone intercepts of a man they believed to be Majid discussing the construction of a bomb with contacts in Boston. That call, according to the stern-faced agent, took place shortly before the heartland massacre. Majid nervously denied the allegation, but astonishingly, he did not reject the agent's claim that such a phone conversation had originated from his residence. Instead, he named his former roommate, Abu Mahmud, as the guilty party.

At the time, the implicit accusation that her boyfriend was a terrorist struck Stacy as inconceivable, but as morning rays warmed the dashboard of her car, she saw everything clearly. She was resolved to set aside her fear and convince someone, anyone, in law enforcement to take action.

Stacy bore witness to the indubitable fact that April 19 had sounded the alarm that went unheeded. The nightmare that lay ahead communicated the unambiguous message that the buried skeletons surrounding this travesty of justice would never be exhumed. Stacy's sworn statement detailing Majid's dark confession and her complicity in his felonious scams was hand delivered to the Oklahoma City FBI headquarters in October 2001. But no one would listen—no one but me.

I, too, had witnessed a confession of sorts, seated just feet away from the man whom I had come to know as the third terrorist. Unlike Majid Ajaj's inebriated outburst, Hussain Al-Hussaini exuded calm composure as he unknowingly turned his civil deposition into a damning, criminal admission. In the fall of 1998, he freely volunteered during questioning that he had visited the Oklahoma City bar where two witnesses had identified him as Timothy McVeigh's drinking companion. He asserted that a Middle Eastern associate had recognized the establishment from KFOR-TV's June 1995 broadcasts, so the pair decided to check it out. That declaration presented a major dilemma for the Iraqi litigant. Channel 4 did not name the bar in its reports and went to great lengths to conceal its location. So how could Al-Hussaini have known where the sighting of John Doe 2 with the Oklahoma City bomber had taken place?

Even more incriminating was Al-Hussaini's recounting of the unconventional manner in which he surveyed the tavern. He claimed he was riding in the passenger seat of his friend's car when the vehicle pulled up to the rear exit of the nightclub. He leaned forward and peered inside through an open door, but he and the driver never entered the building. The startled bartender, Elizabeth Brown, had relayed an identical description of the encounter three years prior to the deposition—unbeknownst to the Iraqi soldier. Her testimony was memorialized in an affidavit, which was safeguarded by my attorneys, but the story was never reported. The unusual unfolding of events upon Al-Hussaini's purported return to the Oklahoma City tavern were known only to the witness Elizabeth Brown and Hussain Al-Hussaini—the man whom she observed socializing with McVeigh four days prior to the deadly attack.

## DERELICTION OF DUTY AND JUSTICE DENIED

The axiom that persistence pays has one exception—the Oklahoma City bombing. I had come to believe that the evidence of Middle Eastern sponsorship wielded the destructive power of "Kryptonite"—the imaginary substance that could debilitate the fictional champion of truth and justice, Superman. No one in law enforcement wanted to lay eyes upon my investigative dossier. Possession constituted responsibility to investigate. That was clearly not an option.

In 1997, the FBI sent me packing when I attempted to surrender the witness statements, claiming that the U.S. Department of Justice "did not want any more documents for discovery" that could complicate the prosecution of Terry Nichols. In 1998, the Oklahoma County Grand Jury probing the specter of "others unknown" submitted several requests to speak to my confidential witnesses but abandoned the mission after an FBI agent "discredited" the notion of foreign complicity in confidential testimony before the panel. In 2002, Senator Arlen Specter and Congressman Dan Burton took possession of the documentary file when popular *Indianapolis Star* columnist James Patterson and Philadelphia radio personality Michael Smerconish made the public offer too politically risky to ignore. The superficial congressional investigation that followed failed to address the FBI's shameless refusal to interview nearly two dozen witnesses and the man they collectively identified as John Doe 2.

KFOR-TV's high profile stories, which plainly exposed an Arab terrorist cell operating in the city where the unprecedented attack occurred, shockingly yielded no sustained interest from law enforcement. Although the news coverage stirred up a whirlwind of public controversy and included the dismantling of the Iraqi soldier's alibi on regional newscasts, the FBI refused to officially clear Hussain Al-Hussaini as a bombing suspect. Larry Johnson, a former CIA analyst and deputy director of counterterrorism for the U.S. Department of State, succinctly summarized the enormity of the evidence before a nationwide audience in March 2002—one year before the commencement of Operation Iraqi Freedom.

"Do you and your CIA friends think that this is legit material?" asked *Fox News* anchor John Gibson.

"Absolutely," Johnson began. "Listen, I compared it [KFOR-TV's investigation] to all the human intelligence I have looked at, and in comparing that to classified material, this is not just from one witness. This is not just from two witnesses. You're talking about twenty-three people. You're talking about at least ten people that put Tim McVeigh with Hussain Al-Hussaini before the Oklahoma City bombing. Two people who identify Hussain Al-Hussaini in a bar on April 15. Three people who identify Hussain Al-Hussaini running from the federal building early in the morning at 5:30 A.M. as he is practicing timing himself. You have two witnesses that put Tim McVeigh with Hussain Al-Hussaini in the Ryder truck. You have one witness inside the Murrah Building who sees Hussain Al-Hussaini getting out of the truck. You have other individuals, and there is more than just Mr. Hussain Al-Hussaini. There are other individuals identified."

But the trail of incriminations did not stop there. Downtown witness, Rachel Sealy, recounted how she stared directly into the rage-filled eyes of Al-Hussaini as he nearly ran her over in a brown Chevy pickup during a mad dash from the blazing federal complex. A host of evidentiary facts led the FBI to initially deduce that a recovered truck, which had been discovered abandoned in the wake of the blast, was likely the same getaway vehicle that carried several Middle Eastern suspects. But for some arcane reason, the notorious pickup, which had been stolen from a Norman, Oklahoma, business in December 1994, was hastily handed back to the original owners. Before dumping this pivotal exhibit of forensic evidence, the FBI recovered three sets of fingerprints from the driver's side of the cab. Agency officials contended the prints were worthless because they did not match any criminal databases. But what about those contained in the immigration files of Hussain Al-Hussaini and two Arab associates whom several witnesses directly linked to the infamous brown Chevy pickup before, during, and after the Murrah Building attack?

"The FBI has not thoroughly, fully investigated this. It is an outrage. I went along for many years thinking they covered this. They have not," Larry Johnson frankly stated on *Fox News* the afternoon of March 20, 2002.

The idealistic scenario that the FBI would arrest Al-Hussaini, interrogate him regarding his whereabouts for the morning of April 19 and the multiple sightings placing him in the presence of Timothy McVeigh, round up his confederates, and unearth a Middle Eastern plot (which possibly could have led to war against the sponsoring countries) was not to be. Instead, federal officials within the Clinton administration stood by, acting as spectators, while Al-Hussaini, flanked by his legal hired guns, announced at a statewide news conference the filing of a lawsuit against me and my employer KFOR-TV—the most flagrant abuse of our civil courts one could ever imagine. Although the Tenth Circuit Court of Appeals vindicated my journalistic integrity and the veracity of my findings on March 26, 2003, the tragic failure of our government authorities at all levels betrays every American, even more so, the victims and families of 4-19.

The Bureau was derelict in its duty to "pursue every lead" as Attorney General Janet Reno had solemnly promised. FBI agents were never dispatched to test the veracity of the witnesses. *Fox News* talk show host John Gibson explored the motivations behind the Bureau's inexplicable behavior when presenting insightful commentaries that aired on March 20 and March 22, 2002:

Even if the federal prosecutors bet their careers there was no such person as John Doe 2, and even if that idea prevailed at the trial and among the jurors who condemned Tim McVeigh, that was then and this is now.

We need to know if that person seen with McVeigh was an Iraqi agent who manipulated the Oklahoma City bombing and could have been involved in 9-11.

Why wouldn't McVeigh say anything about his Iraqi pal, if it were true? I think McVeigh was happy to go to his death as a martyr in the anti-big-government movement, but he was not willing to die as a collaborator with the enemy he fought in the Gulf War. That is treason and would have deeply embarrassed Tim McVeigh. Now, maybe somebody should find Mr. Al-Hussaini. We need to go over a few things with him once and for all.

John Gibson's practical view of how things ought to be contrasted my reality. Yes, the FBI did finally accept the sworn witness statements in January 1999 because FBI Special Agent Dan Vogel, to his credit, dared to take receipt of the evidence. But despite the veteran agent's keen determination to follow through and talk to the witnesses, that too, was not to be. The documents were passed up the chain of command and simply vanished. To this day, the materials are classified as "missing." Years later, in the aftermath of 9-11, Agent Vogel courageously summed up the potential dreadful consequences of the Bureau's bovine complacency toward my research during a candid interview with *LA Weekly* reporter Jim Crogan.

"What they [FBI] did was unconscionable," Agent Vogel said as he reflected upon the FBI's outrageous refusal to investigate the testimony memorialized in the twenty-two affidavits. "The American people deserved the truth and the Bureau needed to look into this Middle East network here in Oklahoma City. If they had, maybe they would have come upon the network behind the September 11 attacks. But I guess that now, we'll never know."

## ACKNOWLEDGMENTS

More times than I would like to admit, I desired this tumultuous ordeal to simply vanish. But my family heritage beckoned me back into the fight. I am a daughter of the American Revolution. My forefathers shed their blood at Valley Forge to give birth to this great nation. My grandfather, William Christensen, received four Purple Hearts for wounds suffered on the battlefields of World War II. From childhood, I learned the enduring value of military discipline under the example set forth by my father, Captain Paul Edwards (U.S. Navy, retired), a former naval aviator who flew anti-submarine warfare missions over the Northern Arctic Ocean during the Cold War. My husband, Drew Davis, a Gulf War veteran of the U.S. Army, always told me "courage is the ability to act in spite of your fear." Fear, I had plenty of. But Drew was right, and during the rare moments when I seriously considered abandoning my investigation, he instilled in me the faith to press on.

My mother, Georgia, has been a soldier in this crusade in the truest sense, offering a well-timed pep talk when my grueling undertaking seemed almost unbearable.

This project was not intended for the faint of heart. Joseph Farah, David Dunham, Joel Miller, and the rest of the team at WND Books merit the highest regard for their valor in bringing this story to print.

First and foremost, I recognize my cherished friends, David and Jackie Schippers, whose heartfelt concern for the gravity of my case and its impact on all Americans propelled them to stake their personal reputations on my behalf.

Jim Woolsey, former director of the Central Intelligence Agency, thank you for vetting my research, and in so doing, bestowing upon me the credibility that a distinguished public servant of your stature brings.

Larry Johnson, the no-nonsense CIA analyst and former deputy director of counterterrorism for the U.S. Department of State, your guidance and brilliant insight have been priceless. It took a heap of guts to back my investigative work on national television. Your homerun sound bites were spectacular!

Colonel Patrick Lang, the intrepid former chief of human intelligence for the Defense Intelligence Agency, who admirably served in the jungles of Vietnam to the halls of the Pentagon advising the commander-in-chief, I offer my deepest gratitude for deconstructing the murky past of *The Third Terrorist*.

I am especially indebted to Frank Gaffney Jr., a former deputy assistant secretary of defense who indisputably ranks at the top of his class among defense and foreign policy experts.

Dr. Constantine Menges, a senior fellow at the Hudson Institute, who once served as special assistant to the president for national security affairs, I am so very grateful for your gracious reception and support.

Dan Vogel, FBI special agent, retired, thank you for your uncompromising service to the rule of law.

I salute an extraordinary breed of journalists who exercise loyalty to the truth in a day of rampant distrust of the media. Though "courageous" has become an overused term when describing maverick reporting, it is the only word that embodies the journalistic integrity of the late Robert Bartley, the legendary editor of the *Wall Street Journal*, and his senior editorial writer, Micah Morrison. These two fine men gave my investigative dossier a judicious review, followed by an arduous, five-month validation process. On September 5, 2002, they presented my case to the American people at a moment in history when we as a nation were seeking a legitimate motive for toppling Saddam Hussein in our war against terror.

Included in this rare class of reporters are Jim Crogan of the *LA Weekly*, James Patterson of the *Indianapolis Star*, Jon Doughtery of *WorldNetDaily*, nationally syndicated radio host Glenn Beck, and Philadelphia radio personality Michael Smerconish. All you gentlemen have made immeasurable contributions in advancing my story.

Bill O'Reilly, you granted me a voice to millions before anyone else would listen. Thank you.

And to the small cadre of people whom I call friends: I appreciate how you have donated your time and talents to this cause. I am beholden to David Schippers's wonderfully gifted assistant, Nancy Ruggero, Bill Chatfield for his warm Washington, D.C., introductions, my former news director Melissa Klinzing for her guts and grit, my station manager Bill Katsafanas for believing in me early on, the Palmer family for moral fortitude in standing against an unjustified legal onslaught, Pam Nance for her research and notary services, Paul Baumann for his creative Web site design, Kelly McCord for her faith and conviction, bombing survivor Arlene Blanchard for her heart of gold, Phyllis Schlafly, Bunny Chambers, the Feist family, and Todd and Jill Utz.

I also extend a bow to my stellar team of legal eagles—Dan Woska, Dan Nelson, Steve Martin, Carl Hughes, Kyle Goodwin, Robert Nelon, Jon Epstein, and Tim McCoy.

I cannot quantify how much I relied upon the love and encouragement extended by my uncle Wayne, cousin Brian, mother-in-law Gaye, niece Georgia, and nephews Cole and Pryce. My sister Laura never failed to answer the call for "S.O.S." babysitting services, and my brother Craig proudly held his restaurant employees and customers hostage in front of the TV set during my nationally televised appearances.

And last, but by far the most dear to me, my beloved son Jacob Michael, you have been a trooper throughout mom's demanding work schedule. You never failed to make me laugh, including the moment when you uttered your first three-syllable word: "terrorist."

# NOTES

*The number of sources for this project was immense, and so, rather than cluttering the manuscript with multitudinous reference numbers, I have simply divided the endnotes here by chapter, arranging them, for the most part, in the order in which they are referenced.*

## CHAPTER 1: A VIEW OF HELL

1. Daina Bradley, interview with author, audiotape and notes, August 1995 and July1999.
2. Clark Peterson, interview with author, notes, September 1999.
3. Clark Peterson, personal essay entitled, "Blasted Unto A Pile of Rubble."
4. Steve Bowers, interview with author, audiotape and notes, May 2000.
5. Dorothy Henry, interview with author, audiotape and notes, January 2000.
6. Transcript and videotape, KFOR-TV Channel 4 Oklahoma City, April 19-21, 1995.
7. Transcript, KOCO-TV Channel 5 Oklahoma City, April 19-21, 1995.
8. Transcript, KWTV Channel 9 Oklahoma City, April 19-21, 1995.
9. Henry Hurt, "Horror in the Heartland," *Reader's Digest*, May 1996.
10. Oklahoma County Medical Examiner's reports that documented the cause of death for bombing victims.
11. Project Recovery OKC, Inc., *Oklahoma City: The official commemorative volume, In Their Name* (New York: Random House, 1995) pp. 52-54, 56-57, 59, 65, 76-79, 84-85, 162.
12. Nancy Gibbs, "The Blood Of Innocents: In The Bomb's Aftermath, Tales Of Horror And Heroism," *Time*, May 1, 1995.
13. Transcript, testimony of Dr. Andy Sullivan, *United States of America v. Timothy James McVeigh*, United States District Court for the District of Colorado, Criminal No. 96-CR-68-M, June 5, 1997.
14. Transcript, testimony of Daina Bradley, *U.S. v. McVeigh*, May 23, 1997.

## CHAPTER 2: MANHUNT

1. Dr. Claudia Rossavik, interview with author, audiotape and notes, August 1999. Dr. Rossavik served as the translator for bombing witness Manuel Acosta during his interview with the FBI the morning of April 19, 1995. Acosta resided at Rossavik's medical clinic for a year while waiting to be subpoenaed to testify in the bombing case. The summons never

arrived despite promises by federal authorities the witness would be required to appear before the federal grand jury. Acosta returned to Mexico in 1996.

2. Manuel Acosta interview, FBI 302 Serial No.174A-OC-56120-4556 viewed and hand-copied by author, FBI Special Agent James E. Strickland, April 20, 1995.

3. Material Witness Warrant, Affidavit of FBI Special Agent Henry C. Gibbons, *United States v. Abraham Abdallah Ahmed*, United States District Court Western District of Texas, Magistrate No. 95-94-H, April 20, 1995.

4. Videotape and transcripts, KFOR-TV, KWTV, and NBC News, April 19, 1995.

5. Transcript, 10:00 P.M. newscast, KFOR-TV, May 22, 1995. The news report broadcast police radio dispatches of the FBI all-points bulletin that targeted Middle Eastern suspects making their getaway in a brown Chevrolet pickup.

6. FBI confidential letter addressed to Senator Arlen Specter, FBI Section Chief of Government Relations Eleni P. Kalisch, November 5, 2002. In the correspondence, the FBI officially confirmed the Bureau's Teletype that was issued at 11:56 A.M. on April 19, 1995 for a brown Chevy truck that carried foreign suspects. However, the Bureau claimed "no further information was found regarding the cancellation of the all-points bulletin."

7. Affidavit of author, Defendants' Motion for Summary Judgment, *Al-Hussaini Hussain v. Palmer Communications, Inc. d/b/a KFOR-TV, Jayna Davis, Brad Edwards, and Melissa Klinzing*, United States District Court for the Western District of Oklahoma, Case No. Civ-97-1535-L, December 16, 1998.

8. Lee Hancock, "Manhunt Targets 2 Suspects; Bombing Death Toll Stands at 52 as Hope for Survivors Fades; Possible Link with Dallas Downplayed," *Dallas Morning News*, April 21, 1995.

9. Alexei Barrionuevo, "Raid Targets Possible Suspect's N. Dallas Apartment," *Dallas Morning News*, April 21, 1995.

10. Jim Polk, CNN news bulletin disseminated to broadcast affiliates nationwide, April 20, 1995.

11. Sharon Cohen, "Two Sought in Bombing; Death Toll Hits 52 – Deadliest in U.S. History," Associated Press, April 21, 1995.

12. Photocopy, Oklahoma Highway Patrol all-points bulletin that targeted a blue Chevrolet Cavalier and Blazer with Middle Eastern occupants, April 19, 1995. The Texas license tag, PTF-54F, which law enforcement verified had been attached to the suspicious Blazer, was registered to a blue Chevrolet Cavalier leased by National Car Rental System, Inc. at the Dallas/Ft. Worth International Airport.

13. Rodney Uphofe, Barbara Bergman, and Barry Schwartz, state defense and federal appellate lawyers for Terry Nichols, interview with author in which author's attorney, Dan Woska, was present, June 22, 2000. Nichols' legal counsel confirmed that the FBI drafted several interview reports, which documented the interrogation of several men of Arab descent, who were apprehended in Dallas and Oklahoma City in the wake of the bombing.

14. Joseph A. Gambardello and Pete Bowles, "The Blast/Day of the Suspects; 2 Queens Brothers Released," *Newsday.com*, April 22, 1995.

15. Jack Douglas, "Dallas FBI Files Believed to Detail Two Arrests," *Ft. Worth Star Telegram*, May 16, 2001.

16. Transcripts, FBI press conferences, April 19-20, 1995.

17. Transcript, Attorney General Janet Reno's press conference, April 20, 1995.

18. "Britain Returns American in Oklahoma Bombing; Bags Found in Rome," London Associated Press, April 20, 1995.

## Chapter 3: 48 Hours

1. Indictment, *United States v. Timothy James McVeigh and Terry Lynn Nichols*, United States District Court for the Western District of Oklahoma, Criminal No. 95-11, August 10, 1995.

2. Transcripts, CBS Evening News and CNN, April 19, 1995.

3. Petition for Writ of Mandamus of Petitioner-Defendant, Timothy James McVeigh and Brief in Support, *U.S. v. McVeigh*, United States Court of Appeals for the Tenth Circuit, Criminal Case No. 96-CR-68, March 25, 1997, pp. 14-15, 82-85.

4. Motion for Disclosure of Discoverable and Exculpatory Intelligence, Rule 16 Material and Brief in Support, *U.S. v. McVeigh*, November 1996, pp. 22, 26.

5. Photocopy, U.S. Department of Army memorandum documenting an FBI request for ten U.S. Army Arabic linguists to assist in translating documents and tapes for the Oklahoma City bombing investigation, Department of Army Headquarters Forces Command, Fort McPherson, Georgia, April 19, 1995.

6. Photocopy, U.S. Department of Army memorandum documenting a request by FBI Director Louis Freeh to Defense Secretary William Perry to change the Arabic linguists' mission to monitoring live wire taps to protect the life of President Clinton during his Oklahoma visit, Department of Army Headquarters Forces Command, Fort McPherson, Georgia, Captain Mark E. Austin, April 22, 1995.

7. Brian Duffy, "Terror in the Heartland," *U.S. News and World Report*, May 1, 1995.

8. Ed Godfrey and John Parker, "Nichols Charged in Bombing; Evidence Has Been Mounting, Prosecutor Says – Suspect Taken From Wichita to El Reno," *Daily Oklahoman*, May 11, 1995.

9. Affidavit of FBI Special Agent Henry C. Gibbons, *U.S. v. Ahmed*, April 20, 1995.

10. Defendant McVeigh's Fourth Supplemental of Specification of Materiality of Requested Classified Information Ex Parte and Under Seal, *U.S. v. McVeigh*, September 30, 1996, pp. 3-4, 10-16.

11. Norman Kempster, "Terror in Oklahoma City; Man Returned to United States Is Not a Suspect; Controversy: The Jordanian-born U.S. Citizen Was in the Wrong Place at the Wrong Time," *Los Angeles Times*, April 22, 1995.

12. Transcript, interview with former U.S. Representative Dave McCurdy, CNN, April 19, 1995.

13. Ed Godfrey and John Parker, "Heartland Easy Target, McCurdy Says," *DailyOklahoman.com*, April 20, 1995.

14. William M. Savage, Jr., "For Bomb Coverage, Local TV Reporters Outdo Ex-politicians," *Oklahoma Gazette*, May 11, 1995.

15. Dave McCurdy, "U.S. Wise Not to Falsely Judge Islam Or Ignore Terrorist Tactics," *Oklahoma Gazette*, May 25, 1995.

16. Judith Colp Rubin, "Islamic Terror Stalks America," *Jerusalem Post International Edition*, August 26, 1995.

17. Steve Emerson, *Jihad in America*, PBS, 1994.

18. Sam Vincent Meddis, Bruce Frankel, and Carol Castaneda, "Oklahoma Learns 'No Safe Place;' Bomb Consistent With Mideast Terror Tactics," *USA Today*, April 20, 1995.

19. A.M. Rosenthal, "Israel's Prime Minister Has Duty To Battle Terrorism," *Daily Oklahoman*, October 15, 1997.

20. Helen Kennedy, "Scores Feared Killed In Oklahoma City Blast," *Boston Herald*, April 20, 1995.

21. Transcript, interview with Steve Emerson, *Today Show*, NBC News, April 20, 1995.

22. Mark Mathews and Tom Bowman, "Attack Bears Mark Of Mideast Terrorism; Experts Refuse To Rule Out Anyone," *Baltimore Sun*, April 20, 1995.

23. Arnold Hamilton, "Oklahoma City Car Bomb Kills At Least 31; Scores Missing In Rubble Of Office Building," *Dallas Morning News*, April 20, 1995.

24. "World Watches Terror Attack," Associated Press, April 20, 1995.

25. Transcript, *World News Tonight*, ABC News, April 19, 1995.

26. Vincent Cannistraro interview, FBI 302 Serial No. 174A-OC-56120-Sub E-6998, FBI Special Agent Kevin Foust, April 19, 1995.

27. Petition for Writ of Mandamus of Defendant Timothy McVeigh, *U.S. v. McVeigh*, March 25, 1997, pp. 82-85.

28. Stephen Jones and Peter Israel, *Others Unknown: Timothy McVeigh and the Oklahoma City Bombing*, (New York, Public Affairs, 2001) pp. 229-230, 232-233, 235-237.

29. Defendant McVeigh's Fourth Supplemental of Specification of Materiality (Volume II), *U.S. v. McVeigh*, October 30, 1996, pp. 1- 4.

30. Letter addressed to Timothy McVeigh's defense counsel, Stephen Jones, from Assistant U.S. Attorney Beth Wilkinson, September 27, 1996.

31. FBI interview with redacted source, FBI 302 Serial No. 174A-OC-56120-Sub D-15284, April 19, 1995.

32. Oklahoma County Reserve Deputy Sheriff Don Hammons, interview with author, audio-tape and field notes, August 2000.

33. Don Hammons, personal written statement documenting his experience while guarding the bombsite on April 19, 1995.

34. Oklahoma County Reserve Deputy Sheriff David Kochendorfer, personal written statement documenting his experience while guarding the bombsite on April 19, 1995.

35. Affidavits of Don Hammons and David Kochendorfer.

36. Howard Pankratz, "Wild Claims in OKC," *Denver Post*, January 16, 1998.

37. Diana Baldwin and Ed Godfrey, "Grand Jury To Meet Monday – Key Wants To Hear Uncalled Witnesses," *DailyOklahoman.com*, June 29, 1997.

38. Bill McAllister, "Oklahoma Grand Jury to Hear Cover up Charge; State Lawmaker Sees Bombing Conspiracy," *Washington Post*, June 13, 1997.

39. Transcript and audiotape, *The Mike McCarville Show*, KTOK 1000 AM Oklahoma City, January 15, 1998.

40. Yossef Bodansky, Director of Congressional Task Force on Terrorism and Unconventional Warfare, interview with author, audiotape, May 18, 1996.

41. Prior warning issued by the Congressional Task Force on Terrorism and Unconventional Warfare, which was published on February 27, 1995.

42. Yossef Bodansky, written correspondence addressed to author, May 18, 1996.

43. Abraham Ahmad, interview with author, KFOR-TV videotape, April 22, 1995.

44. Transcripts, 5:00 P.M. and 10:00 P.M. newscasts, KFOR-TV, April 22, 1995.

45. Abraham Abdallah Ahmad interview, FBI 302 Serial No. 174A-OC-56120-Sub D-3939, FBI Special Agents Richard K. Ruminski and J. Charles Miller, April 19, 1995.

46. Abraham Abdallah Ahmad interview, FBI 302 Serial No. 174A-OC-56120-3354, FBI Special Agents Paul Geiger, Basil C. Doyle, Michael Nund, Brent Beaver, April 20-21, 1995.

47. Evidence log of items the FBI discovered in Abraham Abdallah Ahmad's luggage, FBI 302 Serial No. 174A-OC-56120-Sub D-230, Legal Attache Walter Mangiacotti, ALAT George R. Kiszynski, April 21, 1995.

48. Quitclaim Deed, Oklahoma County Tax Assessor's records documenting Abraham Ahmad's

purchase of his home from Dr. Anwar Abdul (pseudonym), 1820 N.W. 40<sup>th</sup> Street, Oklahoma City, Oklahoma, December 30, 1994.

49. Affidavit of Darby Williams (pseudonym).

50. Micah Morrison, "The Iraq Connection," *Wall Street Journal*, September 5, 2002.

## CHAPTER 4: "HOMEGROWN" TERRORISM

1. Darby Williams (pseudonym), interview with author, KFOR-TV videotape and field notes, April 30 and May 8, 1995.

2. Affidavits of Darby Williams (pseudonym), Bernie Stanton (pseudonym), and author, Defendants' Motion for Summary Judgment, *Al-Hussaini v. Palmer Communications*, December 16, 1998.

3. Material Witness Warrant, *U.S. v. Ahmed*, April 20, 1995. The FBI requested to hold Abraham Ahmed as a material witness without bail to secure his testimony before the Federal Grand Jury.

4. Manuel Acosta interview, FBI 302, April 20, 1995.

5. Criminal Complaint, *U.S. v. McVeigh*, April 21, 1995.

6. Eldon Elliott interview, FBI 302 Serial No. 174A-OC-56120, FBI Special Agent R. Scott Crabtree, April 19, 1995.

7. Vicki Beemer interview, FBI 302 Serial No. 174A-OC-56120, FBI Special Agent R. Scott Crabtree, April 19, 1995.

8. Tom Kessinger interview, FBI 302 Serial No. 174A-OC-56120-Sub D-119, FBI Special Agent R. Scott Crabtree, April 19, 1995.

9. Lea McGown, interview with author, KFOR-TV videotape, September 1995 and April 1996.

10. Transcript, 10:00 P.M. newscast, KFOR-TV, September 27, 1995.

11. Transcript, 5:00 P.M. newscast, KFOR-TV, April 15, 1996.

12. "Final Report on Oklahoma City Bombing," Oklahoma County Grand Jury, December 30, 1998.

13. Photocopy of Timothy McVeigh's signed registration card from the Dreamland Motel in Junction City, Kansas, April 14, 1995.

14. "McVeigh's First 48 Hours After Arrest Documented," *Dallas Morning News*, September 11, 1995.

15. Transcript, testimony of Oklahoma Highway Patrolman Charlie Hanger, *U.S. v. McVeigh*, April 28, 1997.

16. Dana Williamson, "No Tag Led Trooper To Stop Oklahoma City Bomber," *Baptist Messenger*, April 20, 2000.

17. Transcript, 12:00 P.M. newscast, KFOR-TV, May 1, 1995.

18. Diana Baldwin and Robert E. Boczkiewicz, "Nichols' Lawyer Expects Charges In Bombing," *DailyOklahoman.com*, May 10, 1995.

19. Transcripts, *The Dennis McQuistion Show*, PBS, June 10 and June 12, 2003.

20. Terry Nichols interview, FBI 302, FBI Special Agents Stephen E. Smith, John F. Foley, Scott Crabtree, and Daniel Jablonski, *United States v. Terry Lynn Nichols*, United States District Court for the District of Colorado, Criminal Case No. 96-CR-68, April 21, 1995.

21. Evidentiary exhibit, *U.S. v. McVeigh*, photographic image taken from Regency Apartment Complex lobby surveillance camera located at 333 NW 5<sup>th</sup> Street, Oklahoma City, Oklahoma, videotape recorded on April 16, 1995.

22. Tim Talley, "FBI Agent Testifies In Nichols Hearing," *WashingtonPost.com*, May 10, 2003.

23. "Nichols, Bomb Materials Linked," *DailyOklahoman.com*, May 12, 1995.

24. Nolan Clay, "Jurors View Alleged Bombing Map," *Daily Oklahoman*, November 8, 1997.

25. Nolan Clay and Robby Trammell, "Getaway Map Found At Nichols' Home," *DailyOklahoman.com*, September 8, 1996.

26. Tim Talley, "Man Testifies On Theft In Nichols Case," *WashingtonPost.com*, May 7, 2003.

27. Nolan Clay and Penny Owen, "Nichols Used Fertilizer Customer's Name, Jury Told," *Daily Oklahoman*, November 7, 1997.

28. Transcript, testimony of FBI Special Agent Larry Tongate, *U.S. v. Nichols*, November 10, 1997.

29. Transcript, testimony of FBI Special Agent James Cadigan, *U.S. v. Nichols*, November 7 and 10, 1997.

30. Transcript, testimony Martin Marietta Rock Quarry employee, Allen Radtke, *U.S. v. Nichols*, November 7, 1997.

31. Transcript, opening arguments presented by Assistant U.S. Attorney Larry Mackey, *U.S. v. Nichols*, November 3, 1997.

32. Diana Baldwin, Nolan Clay, Robby Trammell, and Randy Ellis, "Fortier Different After Army, Friends Say," *Daily Oklahoman*, August 13, 1995.

33. Transcript, interview with Michael Fortier, CNN, May 1995.

34. Paul Queary, "Attention Focuses on Fortiers," Associated Press, August 8, 1995.

35. Robby Trammell, Nolan Clay, Diana Baldwin, Randy Ellis and John Parker, "Fortier Agrees to Take Stand at Bomb Trial," *Daily Oklahoman*, August 9, 1995.

36. Transcripts, testimony of Michael Fortier, *U.S. v. Nichols*, November 1997.

37. "U.S. Court Refuses to Lower Oklahoma Bomb Sentence," Reuters, June 12, 2001.

38. Rae Tyson, Robert Davis, and Dennis Cauchon, "McVeigh's Life One Of Anger, Turbulence," *USA Today*, April 24, 1995.

39. "Factual Statement in Support of Plea Petition," handwritten confession of Michael Fortier, *United States v. Michael J. Fortier*, United States District Court for the Western District of Oklahoma, Criminal No. 95-111-R, August 1995.

40. Indictment, *U.S. v. Fortier*, August 10, 1995.

41. Transcript, testimony of Michael Fortier, *U.S. v. McVeigh*, May 1997.

42. Transcript, opening arguments presented by Assistant U.S. Attorney Joseph Hartzler, *U.S. v. McVeigh*, April 24, 1997.

43. Transcript, testimony of Arkansas gun collector, Roger Moore, *U.S. v. Nichols*, November 18, 1997.

44. Transcript, opening statements of defense attorney Michael Tigar, *U.S. v. Nichols*, November 3, 1997.

45. Nolan Clay, "Arkansas Gun Collector Tells Jurors Of Robbery," *Daily Oklahoman*, November 19, 1997.

46. Nolan Clay, "Ready for 'Any Just Sentence,' Fortier Hopes For Short Term," *Daily Oklahoman*, May 18, 1997.

47. Nolan Clay and Penny Owen, "Nichols Reluctant To Mix Bomb, Fortier Tells Jury," *Daily Oklahoman*, November 14, 1997.

48. Transcript, *Primetime Live*, ABC News, April 25, 1995.

49. Lou Michel and Dan Herbeck, *American Terrorist: Timothy McVeigh and the Oklahoma City Bombing*, (New York: Regan Books, 2001) pp. 7, 14, 19, 21, 23-24, 74-76, 80, 82, 86, 91, 132, 200, 321.

50. Timothy McVeigh, "An Essay On Hypocrisy," *Media Bypass*, May 30, 1998.

51. Nolan Clay, "Jury's Mercy Sought, Waco Fueled Ire, McVeigh Panel Told," *Daily Oklahoman*, June 7, 1997.

52. Timothy McVeigh, Letter to the Editor, *Union Sun & Journal*, February 11, 1992.

53. Nolan Clay and Penny Owens, "Nichols Trial Focuses On Friend's Oddities," *Daily Oklahoman*, November 23, 1997.

54. Ed Godfrey and John Parker, "Nichols Charged In Bombing; Evidence Has Been Mounting, Prosecutor Says – Suspect Taken From Wichita To El Reno," *Daily Oklahoman*, May 11, 1995.

55. Nolan Clay, "Four Testify As Nichols Hearing Opens," *DailyOklahoman.com*, May 6, 2003.

56. Kenneth R. Timmerman, "Iraq Connection To The Oklahoma Bombing," *Insight*, April 15, 2002.

57. Petition for Writ of Mandamus, *U.S. v. McVeigh*, March 25, 1997.

58. Lana Padilla, interview with author, KFOR-TV videotape, July 1995. KFOR-TV's lawyers deemed it legal to surreptitiously record the interview with Lana Padilla in a Las Vegas casino where signs were posted warning patrons they could be recorded on videotape or audiotape. Moreover, station management obtained the permission of the Sands Casino management before the hidden camera interview with the witness was recorded.

59. Transcript, 10:00 P.M. newscast, KFOR-TV, July 13, 1995.

60. Passport of Terry Lynn Nichols documenting five trips to the Philippines from August 1990 through January 1995.

61. Defendant McVeigh's Fourth Supplemental of Specification of Materiality, *U.S. v. McVeigh*, September 30, 1996, p. 35.

62. Defendant McVeigh's Fifth Supplemental Specification of Materiality, *U.S. v. McVeigh*, November 8, 1996, p. 8.

63. Transcript, testimony of Lana Padilla, *U.S. v. Nichols*, November 19, 1997.

64. Robby Trammell, Nolan Clay, "Nichols Got Cold Feet Before Bombing, Witnesses Say," *Daily Oklahoman*, March 9, 1996.

65. Confidential handwritten investigative report by Dr. Oscar P. Coronel, Chief of Intelligence Division, Bureau of Immigration, Department of Justice, Republic of the Philippines, March 1, 1996.

66. Timothy McVeigh, "McVeigh's Letter To Fox News," *FoxNews.com*, April 27, 2001.

67. Carl Limbacher, "McVeigh Cites Osama Bin Laden In Letter To Fox News," *NewsMax.com*, April 27, 2001.

68. Ed Bradley, "McVeigh Vents," *60 Minutes*, CBS News.com, March 12, 2000.

69. Transcript, 6:30 P.M. newscast, KFOR-TV, October 23, 1995.

70. Vincent Cannistraro interview, FBI 302, April 19, 1995.

71. Transcript, 10:00 P.M. newscast, KFOR-TV, July 11, 1995.

72. Transcript, 10:00 P.M. newscast, KFOR-TV, July 12, 1995.

73. Timothy McVeigh, bombing convict's published letter addressed to *Houston Chronicle*, May 2, 2001.

74. Paul Bedard, "Washington Whisper: McVeigh's Ghost," *U.S. News & World Report*, October 29, 2001.

75. Sam Tanenhaus, "Bush's Brain Trust," *Vanity Fair*, July 2003.

76. Indictment, *U.S. v. McVeigh and Nichols*, August 10, 1995.

77. Nolan Clay, "Some Jurors Convinced Others Involved; Nichols Trial Renews Speculation Concerning John Doe 2," *Daily Oklahoman*, January 11, 1998.

78. Dale Hurd, "Oklahoma City Cover-up: The Iraq Connection," *CBNNews.com*, October 22, 2002.

79. Diana Baldwin and Judy Kuhlman, "Bombing Case Remains Open, FBI Agent Says," *Daily Oklahoman*, March 27, 1998.

80. Kevin Johnson, "John Doe Enigma May Help McVeigh, Nichols," *USA Today*, April 18, 1996.

## CHAPTER 5: REFUGEES OR AGENTS OF SADDAM?

1. Abraham Ahmad, interview with author, KFOR-TV videotape, April 22, 1995.

2. Transcripts, 5:00 P.M. and 10:00 P.M. newscasts, KFOR-TV, April 22, 1995.

3. Norman Kempster, "Terror In Oklahoma City; Man Returned To United States Is Not A Suspect," *Los Angeles Times*, April 22, 1995.

4. William Booth, "Nightmare of a Stopover in London; Arab American Describing Ordeal of Detention, Says People Were Quick to Judge," *Washington Post*, April 24, 1995.

5. Defendant McVeigh's Fourth Supplemental Specification of Materiality, *U.S. v. McVeigh*, September 30, 1996, pp. 10-16.

6. Abraham Ahmad interview, FBI 302s, April 19, 1995.

7. Transcript, 5:00 P.M. newscast, KFOR-TV, April 20, 1995.

8. Ute Draper, interview with author, videotape and field notes, April 20, 1995.

9. Bernie Stanton (pseudonym), interview with author, videotape and field notes, April 23 and May 2, 1995.

10. Larry Monroe (pseudonym), interview with author, field notes, April 23, 1995.

11. Affidavits of Bernie Stanton (pseudonym) and author, Defendants' Motion for Summary Judgment, *Al-Hussaini v. Palmer Communications*, December 16, 1998.

12. Response to Presentence Report, *United States of America v. Dr. Anwar Abdul* (pseudonym), United States District Court for the Western District of Oklahoma, Criminal Action **-***, January **, 19**.

13. Guilty Plea, *U.S. v. Abdul* (pseudonym), February **, 19**.

14. Partial Summary Judgment, Findings of Undisputed Fact, *Al-Hussaini Hussain v. Palmer Communications, Inc.*, Civil Case No. 97-1535-L, November 17, 1999.

15. Affidavit of Darby Williams (pseudonym).

16. Darby Williams (pseudonym), interview with author, KFOR-TV videotape and notes, May 8-9, 1995.

17. Author interview, FBI 302 Serial No. 174A-OC-56120-Sub D-5029, FBI Special Agents James E. Strickland and James E. Judd, May 4, 1995.

18. Defendants' Answers to Plaintiff's First Set of Interrogatories, *Al-Hussaini v. Palmer Communications*, December 16, 1998.

19. Transcripts, FBI press conferences, April 20-21, 1995.

20. Transcript, Attorney General Janet Reno's press conference, April 20, 1995.

21. Transcripts, 10:00 P.M. newscasts, KFOR-TV, May 22 and June 7, 1995.

22. FBI Special Agent Dan Vogel, interview with author, field notes, May 22, 1995.

23. FBI confidential letter addressed to Senator Arlen Specter, November 5, 2002.

24. Oklahoma County Medical Examiner's official list of dead and missing in April 19, 1995 bombing of Alfred P. Murrah Building, Associated Press, April 28 and May 6, 1995.

25. Darby Williams (pseudonym) interview, FBI 302 Serial No. 174A-OC-56120-Sub D-3783, FBI Special Agents Scott A. Billings and David S. Swanson, May 5, 1995.

26. Oklahoma County Medical Examiner's report confirming cause of death of Karen Abdul (pseudonym), Office of the Chief Medical Examiner, June 18, 1995.

27. Decree of Divorce, *Karen Abdul v. Anwar Abdul* (pseudonyms), Oklahoma State District Court, Case No. **-**-****, February **, 19**.

28. Dr. Anwar Abdul (pseudonym), hidden camera interview with Bernie Stanton (pseudonym), KFOR-TV videotape, June 6, 1995.

29. Subpoena for testimony of Darby Williams (pseudonym), Oklahoma Employment Security Commission (OESC), March 1, 1996.

30. State of Oklahoma Unemployment Compensation Tax Warrant issued to Dr. Anwar Abdul (pseudonym) for non-payment of unemployment compensation taxes, interest and penalties totaled $26, 508.13, March **, 19**.

31. Josh Nichols, interview with author, audiotape, July 7, 1995.

32. Lana Padilla, interview with author, KFOR-TV videotape, July 1995.

33. Lana Padilla and Josh Nichols, interview with author in El Reno, Oklahoma, field notes, July 6, 1995.

34. Photocopy, phone records for Terry Nichols's Herington, Kansas residence (913-258-3400), *U.S. v. Nichols*, November 1997.

35. Helen Abdul (pseudonym), interview with author, field notes, May 1995.

36. Ira O'Brien (pseudonym), interview with author, field notes, May 1995.

37. Micah Morrison, "The Iraq Connection," *Wall Street Journal*, September 5, 2002.

## CHAPTER 6: DEAD RINGER

1. Surveillance videotapes of Hussain Al-Hussaini and his Iraqi co-workers, KFOR-TV videotape, April 24, May 5, and May 9, 1995.

2. Robby Trammell, Diana Baldwin, Randy Ellis, and Nolan Clay, "FBI Combs Vinita, Issues New Sketch of 2nd Suspect," *Daily Oklahoman*, May 2, 1995.

3. Arnold Hamilton and Lee Hancock, "Trial Ordered for Bombing Suspect; Judge Orders McVeigh Held Without Bail," *Dallas Morning News*, April 28, 1995.

4. Affidavit of Debbie Nakanashi, witness who assisted FBI sketch artist Jean Boylan in drafting profile drawing of the bombing suspect, John Doe 2.

5. Warrant for Arrest, *United States v. John Doe 2*, United States District Court for the Western District of Oklahoma, Criminal Case No. 95-93-H, April 20, 1995.

6. FBI profile sketch of bombing suspect John Doe 2 released on May 1, 1995.

7. Affidavit of author, Defendants' Motion for Summary Judgment, *Al-Hussaini v. Palmer Communications*, December 16, 1998.

8. Partial Summary Judgment, Findings of Undisputed Fact, *Al-Hussaini Hussain v. Palmer Communications*, November 17, 1999.

9. Bernie Stanton (pseudonym), interview with author, KFOR-TV videotape and field notes, May 2, 1995.

10. Affidavits of Bernie Stanton (pseudonym) and Darby Williams (pseudonym).

11. Videotape of Hussain Al-Hussaini's tattoo, 10:00 P.M. newscast, KFOR-TV, June 9, 1995.

12. Transcript, 10:00 P.M. newscast, KFOR-TV, June 22, 1995.

13. Jose Gonzales (pseudonym), interview with author, field notes, May 1995.

14. Jose Gonzales (pseudonym), surreptitiously recorded interview with Bernie Stanton (pseudo-nym), audiotape, May 1995.
15. Defendant McVeigh's Fourth Supplemental Specification of Materiality *U.S. v. McVeigh*, September 30, 1996, pp. 14-16.
16. Author interview, FBI 302, May 4, 1005.
17. Transcript, en camera testimony of author, *State of Oklahoma v. Terry Lynn Nichols*, Criminal Case No. CF-99-1845, Oklahoma State District Court, March 20, 2001.
18. Darby Williams (pseudonym) interview, FBI 302, May 5, 1995.
19. Bernie Stanton (pseudonym) interview, FBI 302 Serial No. 174A-OC-56120-Sub D-785 viewed and hand copied by author, May 10, 1995.
20. Darby Williams (pseudonym), interview with author, KFOR-TV videotape and notes, May 8-10, 1995.
21. Employee records of Dr. Anwar Abdul (pseudonym), viewed and hand-copied by author. The employee list was included in the discovery documents that were remitted to Timothy McVeigh's defense team in November 1996.
22. Confidential source, interview with author in which the source presented a March 1996 letter signed by Assistant U.S. Attorney Joseph Hartzler. In the correspondence, Mr. Hartzler denied that witness Darby Williams (pseudonym) had provided the FBI a company list of Dr. Anwar Abdul's (pseudonym) Middle Eastern employees. However, the list was eventually turned over to Timothy McVeigh's defense team in November 1996.
23. Transcript, FBI press conference, May 8, 1995.
24. Transcript, testimony of FBI Special Agent Jon Hersley, *U.S. v. McVeigh*, April 27, 1995.
25. Arnold Hamilton and Selwyn Crawford, "McVeigh Remains Stoic During Hearing," *Dallas Morning News*, April 28, 1995.
26. FBI Teletype, Serial No. 174A-OC-56120, FBI Special Agent Thomas P. Ravenelle, May 1995. The specific date on which the FBI Teletype was issued was not noted in the bulletin. However, FBI Special Agent Dan Vogel confirmed the interoffice memorandum was valid.

## CHAPTER 7: BREAKTHROUGH

1. Affidavit of Bernie Stanton (pseudonym), Darby Williams (pseudonym), and author, Defendants' Motion for Summary Judgment, *Al-Hussaini v. Palmer Communications*, December 16, 1998.
2. Helen Abdul (pseudonym), interview with author, field notes, May and June 1995.
3. Transcript, KFOR-TV broadcast story scripted by author, May 8, 1995.
4. FBI Special Agent James Strickland, interview with author, field notes, May 1995.
5. Partial Summary Judgment, Findings of Undisputed Fact, *Al-Hussaini Hussain v. Palmer Communications*, November 17, 1999.
6. FBI confidential letter addressed to Senator Arlen Specter, November 5, 2002.
7. Crime Report, Oklahoma City Police Department, Arrest of Hussain Hashem Al-Hussaini, Case No. 95-05224, Case No. 95-5775954, Case No. 95-5775963, June 3, 1995.
8. Dr. Anwar Abdul (pseudonym), hidden camera interview with Bernie Stanton (pseudonym), KFOR-TV videotape, June 6, 1995.
9. Oklahoma County Medical Examiner's report confirming cause of death of Karen Abdul (pseudonym), June 18, 1995.
10. Author interview, FBI 302, May 4, 1995.

11. Darby Williams (pseudonym) interview, FBI 302, May 5, 1995.

12. Ira O'Brien (pseudonym), interview with author, field notes, May 1995.

13. Transcript, 10:00 P.M. newscast, KFOR-TV, June 7, 1995.

14. Elizabeth Brown (pseudonym), interview with author, KFOR-TV videotape and notes, June 7, 1995.

15. Johnny Wilborn (pseudonym), interview with Channel 4 reporter Brad Edwards, KFOR-TV videotape, June 7, 1995.

16. Affidavits of Elizabeth Brown (pseudonym) and Johnny Wilborn (pseudonym).

17. Transcript, en camera testimony of author, *Oklahoma v. Nichols*, March 20, 2001.

18. FBI Special Agent James Strickland and FBI Special Agent Dan Vogel, telephone conference call with author in presence of KFOR-TV attorney Robert Nelon, Channel 4 reporter Brad Edwards, and KFOR-TV news director Melissa Klinzing, field notes, June 7, 1995.

19. Transcript, 10:00 P.M. newscast, KFOR-TV, June 9, 1995.

20. Eldon Elliott interview, FBI 302, April 19, 1995.

21. Vicki Beemer interview, FBI 302, April 19, 1995.

22. Jeff Davis, interview with author, KFOR-TV videotape and field notes, April 1996.

23. Transcript, 10:00 P.M. newscast, KFOR-TV, April 18, 1996.

24. Transcript, *World News Tonight*, ABC News, April 18, 1996.

25. Sally Streff Buzbee, "Artist Uses Pencil Sketches To Draw In Crime Suspects," *DailyOklahoman.com*, May 2, 1995.

26. Nolan Clay and Penny Owen, "Defense Hints Extra Left Leg Was Bomber's – Witness Sure Of 169th Victim," *DailyOklahoman.com*, May 23, 1997.

27. "Nichols Prosecutors Rest, Defense Begins In Denver," *DailyOklahoman.com*, December 7, 1997.

28. Jeff Davis interview, FBI 302 Serial No. 174A-OC-56120, Lead Control No. 14723-D-15335, FBI Special Agent Larry G. Tongate, April 26, 1996.

29. Confidential source, interview with author in which the source disclosed a comprehensive list of Oklahoma City witness statements turned over to the defense counsel in the discovery process prior to the trial of Timothy McVeigh. KFOR-TV's legal counsel, Robert Nelon, was present at the time the author viewed the witness list.

30. Rachel Sealy (pseudonym), interview with author, KFOR-TV videotape, June 9, 1995.

31. Transcript, testimony of Rachel Sealy (pseudonym), *Oklahoma v. Nichols*, March 21, 2001.

## CHAPTER 8: POSITIVE I.D.

1. Rachel Sealy (pseudonym), interview with author, KFOR-TV videotape and notes, June 9, 1995.

2. Transcripts, 10:00 P.M. newscasts, KFOR-TV, June 7, June 9, and September 27,1995.

3. Affidavit of author, Defendants' Motion for Summary Judgment, *Al-Hussaini v. Palmer Communications*, December 16, 1998.

4. Partial Summary Judgment, Findings of Undisputed Fact, *Al-Hussaini v. Palmer Communications*, November 17, 1999.

5. Transcript, testimony of Rachel Sealy (pseudonym), *Oklahoma v.Nichols*, March 21, 2001.

6. Transcript, en camera testimony of author, *Oklahoma v. Nichols*, March 20, 2001.

7. Elizabeth Brown (pseudonym), interview with author, field notes, June 12, 1995.

8. Affidavits of Elizabeth Brown (pseudonym), Johnny Wilborn (pseudonym), Darby Williams (pseudonym), and Rachel Sealy (pseudonym).

9. Crime Report, Oklahoma City Police, Burglary 2 at Darby Williams's (pseudonym) residence, Case No. 95-******, July **, 1995.

10. Crime Report, Oklahoma City Police, unlawful discharge of weapon in drive-by shooting at Darby Williams's (pseudonym) home, Case. No. 95-******, July **, 1995.

11. Darby Williams (pseudonym), interview with author, videotape and field notes, July 3, 1995.

12. Confidential witness, Darby Williams's neighbor who requested anonymity, interview with author, videotape and field notes, July 1995.

13. Summons and Forcible Entry Retainer to evict witness Darby Williams (pseudonym) from rental property owned by Dr. Anwar Abdul (pseudonym), Case No. SC- ****** June **, 1995 and July **, 1995.

14. Permanent Protective Order, *Darby Shaw v. Dr. Anwar Abdul* (pseudonyms), Case No. PO-95-****, State of Oklahoma District Court, August 1, 1995.

## CHAPTER 9: NO ALIBI

1. "FBI Identifies, Clears John Doe 2," *DailyOklahoman.com*, June 15, 1995.

2. Videotape and transcript, 6:00 P.M. newscast, KWTV, June 15, 1995.

3. Transcripts, 10:00 P.M. newscasts, KWTV, June 15-16, 1995.

4. Transcripts, 10:00 P.M. newscasts, KFOR-TV, June 12, June 14, and June 22, 1995.

5. United States Department of Justice press release, Washington DC headquarters, June 14, 1995.

6. Transcript, 5:00 P.M. newscast, KOCO-TV, June 15, 1995.

7. FBI Facial Identification Fact Sheet, FBI sketch artist notes regarding witness Tom Kessinger's description of John Doe 2, *U.S. v. McVeigh*, April 20, 1995.

8. Warrant for Arrest, *U.S. v. John Doe 2*, April 20, 1995.

9. Transcript, testimony of FBI Special Agent Jon Hersley, *U.S. v. McVeigh*, April 27, 1995.

10. Exhibit, letter written by Assistant U.S. Attorney Joseph Hartzler to Timothy McVeigh's attorney, Stephen Jones, *U.S. v. McVeigh*, March 25, 1996.

11. Nolan Clay and John Parker, "John Doe 2 Still Sought, Letter Says; Prosecutors Doubt Witnesses Mistaken," *Daily Oklahoman*, May 2, 1996.

12. Nolan Clay, "Debate Continues Over Another Bombing Suspect," *Daily Oklahoman*, February 23, 1997.

13. Howard Pankratz and George Lane, "McVeigh Linked to Bomb Truck," *DenverPost.com*, May 10, 1997.

14. Nolan Clay, "Bombing Witness Admits Mistake," *DailyOklahoman.com*, January 30, 1997.

15. Eldon Elliott interview, FBI 302, April 19, 1995.

16. Vicki Beemer interview, FBI 302, April 19, 1995.

17. Maurice Possley, "2 Tie McVeigh to Truck in Oklahoma Bombing; Witnesses recall a 2nd Man While Renting Vehicle," *ChicagoTribune.com*, February 19, 1997.

18. Nolan Clay, "Witness Recalls Renting Truck To Murrah Bomber," *DailyOklahoman.com*, May 8, 2003.

19. Sally Streff Buzbee, "Artist Uses Pencil Sketches To Draw In Crime Suspects," *DailyOklahoman.com*, May 2, 1995.

20. Robby Trammell, Diana Baldwin, Randy Ellis, and Nolan Clay, "FBI Combs Vinita, Issues New Sketch Of 2nd Suspect," *Daily Oklahoman*, May 2, 1995.

21. Arnold Hamilton and Lee Hancock, "Trial Ordered For Bombing Suspect; Judge Orders McVeigh Held Without Bail," *Dallas Morning News*, April 28, 1995.

22. Transcript, Erin Hayes, "Some Suspect More People Involved In Oklahoma City Bombing," *World News Tonight*, ABCNews.com, May 30, 2001.

23. Transcript, *The Dennis McQuistion Show*, PBS, June 12, 2003.

24. Affidavit of author, Defendants' Motion for Summary Judgment, *Al-Hussaini v. Palmer Communications*, December 16, 1998.

25. George Lang, "Out On A Limb, KFOR Story 'Identifying' John Doe 2 Sparks Firestorm Of Controversy," *Oklahoma Gazette*, June 22, 1995.

26. Partial Summary Judgment, Findings of Undisputed Fact, *Al-Hussaini v. Palmer Communications*, November 17, 1999.

27. Immigration records of Hussain Hashem Al-Hussaini, U.S. Department of Justice, Immigration and Naturalization Service, August 1994.

28. International Rescue Committee records of Hussain Hashem Al-Hussaini, Massachusetts Refugee Resettlement Program, Case No. SA-031-105, August 31, 1994.

29. Mas'ood Cajee, "Muslim Community Calls For Healing After KFOR-TV 4's Hasty Accusations," *Oklahoma Gazette*, June 22, 1995.

30. Material Witness Warrant, *U.S. v. Ahmed*, April 20, 1995.

31. Crime Report, Oklahoma City Police Department, arrest of Hussain Hashem Al-Hussaini, Case No. 95-05224, Case No. 95-5775954, Case No. 95-5775963, June 3, 1995.

32. FBI Special Agent Dan Vogel, interview with author, audiotape and field notes, June 7 and June 20, 1995.

33. Assistant U.S. Attorney Steve Mullins, interview with author, audiotape and notes, June 20 and August 30, 1995.

34. Defendants' Answers to Plaintiff's First Set of Interrogatories, *Al-Hussaini v. Palmer Communications*, December 16, 1998.

35. U.S. Department of Justice Spokesman Carl Stern, interview with author, field notes, August 30, 1995.

36. U.S. Department of Justice press release, Washington DC headquarters, June 14, 1995.

37. Robby Trammell, Randy Ellis, Diana Baldwin, Chris Casteel, and John Parker, "Pair In Missouri Free; FBI Keeps Looking," *Daily Oklahoman*, May 3, 1995.

38. Robert L. Jackson and Ronald J. Ostraw, "Nichols Talks Of Bomb Tests, FBI Agent Says," *Los Angeles Times*, May 3, 1995.

39. Susan Steinberg, "Man Resembling 'John Doe' To Be Tried On Other Charges," *Los Angeles Times*, May 3, 1995.

40. Tim Talley, "Dutch Reports To Be Investigated By McVeigh's Attorneys," Associated Press, January 4, 1996.

41. Transcripts, 5:00 P.M. and 6:00 P.M. newscasts, KFOR-TV, December 29, 1995.

42. Letter addressed to author's attorney, Dan Woska, from Senator Jim Inhofe's chief of staff, Herb Johnson, September 22, 1998.

43. Herb Johnson, interview with author, field notes, May 1995.

44. Senator Jim Inhofe's public information officer Tom Alexander, interview with author, audiotape and field notes, May 1995.

45. "McVeigh's Attorney Wants Trial Moved," *DailyOklahoman.com*, June 10, 1995.

46. FBI Special Agent Jeffrey Jenkins, interview with KFOR-TV private investigator, audiotape, June 1995.

47. FBI Special Agent Jenkins, interview with author, field notes, June 2001.

48. Defendants' Responses to Plaintiff's First Set of Interrogatories, *Jayna Davis v. Gazette Media, Inc.*, Oklahoma State District Court, Case No. CJ-2000-191-66, May 2, 2000.

49. Phil Bacharach, "Liar, Liar," *Oklahoma Gazette*, July 29, 1998.

50. Transcript, deposition of *Oklahoma Gazette* reporter Phil Bacharach, *Davis v. Gazette*, February 2, 2001.

51. Letters addressed to *Oklahoma Gazette* editor, Bill Bleakley, from author's attorney, Dan Nelson, requesting a retraction for the article entitled, "Liar, Liar," August 27 and September 15, 1998.

52. Letter addressed to *Oklahoma Gazette* attorney, Michael Minnis, from author's attorney, Dan Nelson, September 28, 1998.

53. Objection to Inspection or Copying of Materials Designated in Subpoena of Phil Bacharach, *Al-Hussaini v. Palmer Communications*, September 14, 1998.

54. Petition, *Davis v. Gazette*, January 12, 2000.

55. Dismissal Without Prejudice, *Davis v. Gazette*, March 12, 2001.

56. Larry Monroe (pseudonym), interview with Bernie Stanton (pseudonym), audiotape, June 18, 1995.

57. Larry Monroe (pseudonym), interview with author, field notes, April 23, 1995.

58. Affidavits of Bernie Stanton (pseudonym), Debbie Nakanashi, Elvin Devers, and Darby Williams (pseudonym).

59. Jose Gonzales (pseudonym), surreptitiously recorded interview with Bernie Stanton (pseudonym), audiotape, May 1995.

60. Jose Gonzales (pseudonym), interview with author, field notes, May 1995.

61. Helen Abdul (pseudonym), hidden camera interview with Bernie Stanton (pseudonym), KFOR-TV videotape, June 1995.

62. Employment records of Hussain Hashem Al-Hussaini, Western Sizzlin Steak House of Oklahoma City and Metro Area, November 1994 through June 1995.

63. Affidavit of Western Sizzlin Assistant Manager Henry Johnson (pseudonym), Defendants' Motion for Summary Judgment, *Al-Hussaini v. Palmer Communications*, December 16, 1998.

64. Plaintiff's Answers to Defendant Jayna Davis' First Set of Request for Admissions, *Al-Hussaini v. Palmer Communications*, October 15, 1998.

65. Transcript, deposition of Hussain Al-Hussaini, *Al-Hussaini v. Palmer Communications*, October 27-30 and November 17-19, 1998.

66. George Lang, "Iraqi Refugee Sues KFOR Over John Doe 2 Report," *Oklahoma Gazette*, August 30, 1995.

67. Rob Frazier, U.S. Department of State official who was assigned to the embassy in Riyadh, Saudi Arabia, interview with author, audiotape, notes, and e-mail correspondence, October 23, November 18, 2002 and April 3, 2003.

68. Jim Crogan, "Borderline Logic: Immigration Lessons From The First U.S. War With Iraq," *LA Weekly*, December 27, 2002.

69. James Patterson, "No Need To Look Overseas If Enemy Lives Among Us," *Indianapolis Star*, January 11, 2003.

70. Bill Gertz, "Saddam Seen Using Proxy Groups To Attack The U.S.," *Washington Times*, February 25, 2003.

71. Dan Eggen, "FBI Has War Plans To Mobilize Agents Against Terrorists," *Washington Post*, March 17, 2003.

72. Dan Eggen, "Missing Iraqis Sought, FBI Hunts For Thousands Here Illegally," *Washington Post*, January 27, 2003.

73. Kelly Arena, "DOJ Plans To Detain Dozens Of Iraqis," *CNN.com*, March 19, 2003.

74. Transcript and videotape, 10:00 P.M. newscast, KFOR-TV, June 9, 1995.

75. Colonel Patrick Lang (U.S. Army retired), former Chief of Human Intelligence for the Defense Intelligence Agency, interview with author, audiotape and field notes, July 2002.

76. Memorandum, endorsed by Colonel Patrick Lang, military intelligence analysis of Hussain Al-Hussaini's tattoo, March 2002.

77. Micah Morrison, "The Iraq Connection," *Wall Street Journal*, September 5, 2002.

78. Transcript, interview with the former Deputy Director of Counter Terrorism for the U.S. Department of State Larry Johnson, *The O'Reilly Factor*, Fox News, May 7, 2002.

79. Major Lin Todd (U.S. Army retired), former U.S. Department of Defense analyst and war planner, interview with author, field notes, October 10, 2002.

80. Abraham Ahmad, interview with author, audiotape, June 20, 1995.

81. Crime Report, Oklahoma City Police Department, arrest of Hussain Al-Hussaini, Case No. 95-059971, June 24, 1995.

## CHAPTER 10: COUNTDOWN TO 9:02 A.M.

1. Transcript, 10:00 P.M. newscast, KFOR-TV, June 14, 1995.

2. Mike Benton (pseudonym), interview with author, field notes, June 26, 1998.

3. Cindy Preston (pseudonym), interview with author, field notes, June 26, 1998.

4. Letter addressed to Oklahoma County Grand Jury from Cindy Preston (pseudonym) in which the witness verified her April 19, 1995 encounter with a mysterious jogger near the Alfred P. Murrah Building, July 6, 1998.

5. Joan Whitley (pseudonym), interview with author, June 28, 1998.

6. Jesse Pearce (pseudonym), interview with author, KFOR-TV videotape, audiotape, and field notes, August 1995.

7. Transcripts, 10:00 P.M. newscasts, KFOR-TV, August 7 and August 17, 1995.

8. Affidavits of Jesse Pearce (pseudonym), Mike Benton (pseudonym), Lance Carmichael (pseudonym), Dan Nelson, and Rachel Sealy (pseudonym).

9. Jesse Pearce (pseudonym) interview, FBI 302 Serial No. 174A-OC-56120-Sub D-68 viewed and hand copied by author, FBI Special Agent John Elvig, April 21, 1995.

10. Transcript, testimony of FBI Special Agent Jon Hersley, *U.S. v. McVeigh*, April 27, 1995.

11. Lance Carmichael (pseudonym) interview with author, KFOR-TV videotape and field notes, August 1995.

12. Lance Carmichael (pseudonym) interview, FBI 302 Serial No. 174A-OC-56120-Sub D, FBI Special Agent John M. Elvig, May 11, 1995.

13. Transcripts, 10:00 P.M. newscasts, KFOR-TV, June 9, June 22, August 9, August 14, September 5, and September 27, 1995.

14. Daina Bradley, interview with author, KFOR-TV videotape, audiotape, and field notes, August 1995, and September 1995.

15. Jerry Nance (pseudonym), interview with author, KFOR-TV videotape, audiotape, and field notes, August 1995.

16. Jerry Nance (pseudonym) interview, FBI 302 Serial No. 174A-OC-56120-D-245 viewed and hand-copied by author, FBI Special Agent John T. Risenhoover, transcribed on April 24, 1995.

17. Videotape and transcript, KFOR-TV, April 19, 1995.

18. Rachel Sealy (pseudonym), personal essay documenting witness' encounter with the driver of a speeding brown Chevrolet pickup in the wake of the Murrah Building bombing. Timothy McVeigh's attorney Stephen Jones and Terry Nichols' state defense counsel confirmed for the author that Rachel Sealy's (pseudonym) FBI 302 had been withheld from the defense teams.

19. Rachel Sealy (pseudonym), interview with author, KFOR-TV videotape and field notes, June 9, 1995, June 22, 1995, September 1998, October 2000, and September 2001.

20. Tiffany Green (pseudonym), interview with author, field notes, August 1995.

21. Transcript, testimony of Dr. Andy Sullivan, *U.S. v. McVeigh*, June 5, 1997.

22. Transcript, *Good Morning America*, ABC News, April 20, 1995.

23. Transcript, FBI press conference, April 20, 1995.

24. Transcript, *Today Show*, NBC News, April 20, 1995.

25. Daina Bradley interview, FBI 302 Serial No. 174A-OC-56120-Sub D, FBI Special Agent Angela Byers, May 3, 1995.

26. Daina Bradley interview, FBI 302 Serial No. 174A-OC-56120-Sub D-3525, FBI Special Agents Nancy Houston and John E. Osa, May 21, 1995.

27. Brent Martin (pseudonym), interview with author, field notes, August 7, 1995.

28. Brent Martin (pseudonym) interview, portions of witness's FBI 302 viewed and hand-copied by author, April 21, 1995.

29. Defendant McVeigh's Fifth Supplemental Specification of Materiality, *U.S. v. McVeigh*, November 8, 1996, pp. 27-28.

30. Robby Trammell and Nolan Clay, "FBI Downplays Man's Account of Truck Driver," *DailyOklahoman.com*, August 16, 1995.

31. "Brush With Bomb Suspects Described," *DailyOklahoman.com*, April 29, 1998.

32. Transcript, deposition of Hussain Al-Hussaini, *Al-Hussaini v. Palmer Communications*, October 27, 1998.

33. Transcript, CNN reporter Robert Vito's interview with Jesse Pearce (pseudonym), CNN, August 14, 1995.

34. Mark Eddy, "Others with McVeigh, Bomb Witnesses Say More Than 2 Involved," *Denver Post*, June 16, 1996.

35. Jo Thomas, "Sightings of John Doe No. 2: In Blast Case, Mystery No. 1," *New York Times*, December 3, 1995.

36. "Three Witnesses Say Others Were With McVeigh Before Bombing," Denver Associated Press, June 17, 1996.

37. Peter Gelzinis, "Memory of Terror Truck Haunts Oklahoma Witness," *Boston Herald*, April 16, 1996.

38. Grand juror Hoppy Heidelberg, interview with author, audiotape and notes, October 1995.

39. Letter addressed to U.S. District Judge David R. Russell from grand juror Hoppy Heidelberg, October 5, 1995.

40. Indictment, *U.S. v. McVeigh and Nichols*, August 10, 1995.

41. Transcript, 6:00 P.M. newscast, KFOR-TV, August 10, 1995.

42. Transcript, 10:00 P.M. newscast, KFOR-TV, October 26, 1995.

43. "Grand Juror Dismissed from Bombing Panel," Associated Press, October 26, 1995.

44. Letter addressed to grand juror Hoppy Heidelberg from U.S. District Judge David R. Russell, October 24, 1995.

45. Nolan Clay, "Fate Picks Bombing Witness; Man Saw Driver of Truck," *Daily Oklahoman*, January 16, 1997.

46. Kevin Flynn, "Prosecutors Drop Eyewitness; The Only Person To Place Defendant McVeigh At Bomb Scene Won't Be Called To Testify," *RockyMountainNews.com*, February 15, 1997.

47. John Parker, "FBI Revealed New Evidence at Preliminary Hearing," *DailyOklahoman.com*, April 30, 1995.

48. Betsy Travis (pseudonym), interview with author, field notes, October 1995.

49. Author interview, FBI 302 Serial No. 174A-OC-56120-Sub D-11351, FBI Special Agent Dan Vogel, October 27, 1995.

50. Transcript, 12:00 P.M. newscast, KFOR-TV, May 1, 1995.

51. Daina Baldwin and Robert E. Boczkiewicz, "Nichols' Lawyer Expects Charges in Bombing," *DailyOklahoman.com*, May 10, 1995.

52. KFOR-TV videotape of Arkansas license plate that witness Betsy Travis (pseudonym) recovered on April 21, 1995.

53. Phillip Douglas (pseudonym), interview with author, field notes, October 1995.

54. Nolan Clay, "Trial Held Up FBI to Scrutiny," *DailyOklahoman.com*, December 24, 1997.

55. "Accomplice Mystery Grows," *DailyOklahoman.com*, June 18, 1995.

56. Jones and Israel, *Others Unknown*, pp. 270-271.

57. Kevin Johnson, "McVeigh's Fingerprints Not Found On Some Evidence," *USAToday.com*, May 19, 1997.

58. Transcript, testimony of Daina Bradley, *U.S. v. McVeigh*, May 23, 1995.

59. Nolan Clay, "Eyewitness Now Says 2 Men Fled Bomb Truck," *Daily Oklahoman*, May 24, 1997.

## CHAPTER 11: THE ABANDONED PICKUP: FBI EVIDENCE DUMPING

1. Virginia King (pseudonym) and Joe King (pseudonym), interviews with author, KFOR-TV videotape and field notes, June and November 1995.

2. Affidavits of Virginia King (pseudonym) and Joe King (pseudonym), Bernie Stanton (pseudonym), Darby Williams (pseudonym), and Rachel Sealy (pseudonym).

3. Affidavit of author, Defendants' Motion for Summary Judgment, *Al-Hussaini v. Palmer Communications*, December 16, 1998.

4. Incident report documenting the discovery of a stolen vehicle, Bureau of ***** *****, Inc., security guard Nick Migliorato, April 27, 1995.

5. Impound Report, Oklahoma City Police Department, police report which confirmed the Oklahoma City Police took custody of a stolen pickup that the FBI Command Post suspected of possible involvement in the April 19, 1995 bombing, Case No. 95-******, April 27, 1995.

6. Surveillance videotapes of Hussain Al-Hussaini and his Iraqi co-workers, KFOR-TV videotape, April 24, May 5, and May 9, 1995.

7. Luke Conner (pseudonym) and Lori Conner (pseudonym), interviews with author, audiotape and field notes, July 2003.

8. Stolen Vehicle Incident Report, Norman, Oklahoma Police Department, Case No. 94-******, December 5, 1994.

9. Letter addressed to Luke and Lori Conner (pseudonyms) from the FBI, which documented

the reimbursement for damages incurred during the Bureau's inspection of the couple's 1983 GMC pickup, August 28, 1995.

10. Letter addressed to Luke Conner (pseudonym) from the FBI Oklahoma City field office. The letter documented the return of Conner's 1983 GMC pickup which had been stripped of its vehicle identification numbers and High Sierra emblems, July 11, 1995.

11. Photographs and videotape of Luke and Lori Conner's (pseudonyms) 1983 GMC pickup after the FBI returned the vehicle in May 1995.

12. Letter addressed to Luke Conner (pseudonym) from Norman, Oklahoma Police Department, Records division employee John Spillmeier, April 18, 1996.

13. Affidavit of FBI confidential letters addressed to Senator Arlen Specter, November 5 and November 21, 2002.

14. Transcript, 10:00 P.M. newscast, KFOR-TV, May 22, 1995.

15. Transcript, FBI press conference, April 20, 1995.

16. FBI Special Agent Dan Vogel, interview with author, field notes, May 1995.

17. Photocopy of handwritten verification authored by FBI Special Agent James Elliott which confirmed Luke and Lori Conner (pseudonyms) owned the stolen pickup that the FBI had inspected in connection with the Murrah Building bombing, May 28, 1995.

18. Transcripts, *The Michael Smerconish Show*, WPHT 1210 AM Radio, Philadelphia, Pennsylvania, October 2, 2002, October 10, 2002, and March 19, 2003.

19. Rose DeWolf, "Specter Asks Probe Of Iraq Links To WTC-Oklahoma Attacks," *Philadelphia Daily News*, October 5, 2002.

20. "Specter to FBI: Probe Iraq Involvement in OKC, WTC '93 bombings," *NewsMax.com*, October 5, 2002.

21. Michael Smerconish, "Specter and the John Doe 2 Connection," *Philadelphia Daily News*, October 10, 2002.

22. Micah Morrison, "The Iraq Connection," *Wall Street Journal*, September 5, 2002.

23. Editorial, "Making the Iraq Case," *Wall Street Journal*, September 5, 2002.

24. James Langton, "Iraqis Linked to Oklahoma Atrocity," *London Evening Standard*, October 21, 2002.

25. Frank J. Gaffney, Jr., "Lurking in the Jayna Davis Files," *Washington Times*, November 19, 2002.

26. Frank J. Gaffney, Jr., "Bush's Hour to Shine," *Washington Times*, January 28, 2003.

27. Transcript, interview with author, *The O'Reilly Factor*, Fox News, March 20 and May 14, 2001.

28. Transcript, interview with author, *The Big Story with John Gibson*, Fox News, June 20, 2001.

29. Transcript, interview with former Deputy Director of Counter Terrorism for the U.S. Department of State Larry Johnson, *The O'Reilly Factor*, Fox News, May 7, 2002.

30. Transcript, interview with former Deputy Director of Counter Terrorism for the U.S. Department of State Larry Johnson, *The Big Story with John Gibson*, Fox News, March 20, 2002.

31. Transcripts, interview with author, *On the Record with Greta Van Susteren*, Fox News, June 21 and September 9, 2002.

32. Transcript, interview with author, *Lou Dobbs Moneyline*, CNN, September 9, 2002.

33. John Gibson, "Let's Find Tim McVeigh's Pal John Doe No. 2," *The Big Story with John Gibson*, FoxNews.com, March 22, 2002.

34. John Gibson, "Tim McVeigh and a Possible Iraqi Connection," *The Big Story with John Gibson, FoxNews.com*, June 20, 2002.

35. Partial Summary Judgment, Findings of Undisputed Fact, *Al-Hussaini v. Palmer Communications*, November 17, 1999.

36. "Final Report on Oklahoma City Bombing," Oklahoma County Grand Jury, December 30, 1998.

37. Manuel Acosta interview, FBI 302, April 20, 1995.

38. *LA Weekly* reporter Jim Crogan, interview with author regarding Crogan's discovery of the return of the stolen brown pickup to the vehicle's owners, Luke and Lori Conner (pseudonyms), field notes, July 2003.

39. Supplemental Report, Norman, Oklahoma Police Department, Case No. 94-******, May **, 1996.

40. Transcript, 10:00 P.M. newscast, KFOR-TV, June 9, 1995.

## CHAPTER 12: THE TERRORIST HOTEL

1. Affidavits of Randy Christian (pseudonym), Georgia Hammerstein (pseudonym), Gary Hammerstein (pseudonym), David Elmore (pseudonym), Cole O'Brien (pseudonym), Ken Banks (pseudonym), Rosanna Elmore (pseudonym), Richard Parnell (pseudonym), and Virginia King (pseudonym).

2. Randy Christian (pseudonym), interview with author, audiotape and field notes, October 1995, November 1995, December 1995, January 1996, May 1996, September 2001, and March 2003.

3. Georgia Hammerstein (pseudonym), interview with author, audiotape and field notes, November 1995 and June 2000.

4. Gary Hammerstein (pseudonym), interview with author, audiotape and field notes, November 1995.

5. Ken Banks (pseudonym), interview with author, audiotape and field notes, March 1997.

6. Cole O'Brien (pseudonym), interview with author, KFOR-TV videotape and notes, June 1996.

7. Evidence log documenting items recovered from Timothy McVeigh's Mercury Marquis, *U.S. v. McVeigh*.

8. David Elmore (pseudonym), interview with author, audiotape and field notes, November 1995 and January 1997.

9. Richard Parnell (pseudonym), interview with author, audiotape and field notes, November 1995.

10. Photocopy, Oklahoma Highway Patrol all-points bulletin for Middle Eastern suspects, April 19, 1995.

11. Sharon Cohen, "Two Sought in Bombing; Death Toll Hits 52 – Deadliest in U.S. History," Associated Press, April 21, 1995.

12. Jim Polk, CNN bulletin disseminated to network affiliate KFOR-TV, April 20, 1995.

13. "Terror in the Heartland," *DailyOklahoman.com*, April 22, 1995.

14. "U.S. Offers $2 Million for Capture; Islamic Militants May Not Have Been Involved," *Sacramento Bee*, April 21, 1995.

15. Transcript, 10:00 P.M. newscast, KFOR-TV, May 22, 1995.

16. FBI confidential letter addressed to Senator Arlen Specter, November 5, 2002.

17. Jack Douglas, Jr., "Dallas FBI Files Believed To Detail 2 Arrests Of Arabs In OKC Bombing," *Ft. Worth Star Telegram*, May 16, 2001.
18. Nolan Clay, "Cashier Nixed As Witness in Bomb Trial," *DailyOklahoman.com*, May 12, 1997.
19. Exhibit, Medical examination records of Fred Skrdla, Worker's Compensation Claim No. 811866-92-1-2, *U.S. v. McVeigh*, January 1997.
20. Transcripts, *U.S. v. McVeigh*, March-June 1997.
21. Photocopies of Cactus Motel (pseudonym) registration logs dated March through April 1995. The FBI withheld the original guest registration logs for April 18, 1995 and the sign-in sheets dated December 1994 through April 1995.
22. FBI Insert Serial No. 174A-OC-56120-Sub D-10105, ATF Serial No. 53200-95-0005W, the document confirmed that federal agents confiscated the Cactus Motel (pseudonym) registration logs dated December 1994 through April 1995, ATF Special Agent Doug C. Moore, transcribed on May 26, 1995.
23. FBI letter addressed to witness Randy Christian (pseudonym), Co-Director Richard L. Huff, U.S. Department of Justice, Office of Information and Privacy, Washington DC, July 15, 1996.
24. Letter addressed to the FBI from Randy Christian (pseudonym) in which the witness submitted a written Freedom of Information Act (FOIA) request for the release of the original Cactus Motel (pseudonym) registration logs dated December 1994 through April 1995, May 1, 1996.
25. FBI letter addressed to Randy Christian, FBI Special Agent Thomas Kuker, June 10, 1996.
26. Randy Christian interview (pseudonym), FBI 302 Serial No. 174A-OC-56120-D-11935, FBI Special Agent Jon R. Hersley, December 5, 1995.
27. Randy Christian interview (pseudonym), FBI 302s Serial Nos. 174A-OC-56120-D-12827, D-12828, and D-12845, FBI Special Agents Jon R. Hersley and Floyd M. Zimms, January 22, 1996.
28. Confidential source, interview with author, field notes, March 1996 and June 2000. Author's attorneys, Robert Nelon and Dan Woska, were present during several meetings in which the confidential source provided documentation and verbal confirmation that several FBI 302s documenting interviews with the author's witnesses had been excised from the bombing investigative archive.
29. Darby Williams (pseudonym), FBI 302, May 5, 1995.
30. Daina Bradley interview, FBI 302s, May 3 and May 21, 1995.
31. Lance Carmichael (pseudonym) interview, FBI 302, May 11, 1995.
32. Jerry Nance interview (pseudonym) FBI 302, April 24, 1995.
33. Nolan Clay, "McVeigh Carried Political Writings," *DailyOklahoman.com*, November 4, 1995.

## CHAPTER 13: THE INSIDER

1. Transcript and videotape, 10:00 P.M. newscast, KFOR-TV, June 7, 1995.
2. Rita Edwards (pseudonym) interview with author, audiotape and field notes, June 1997.
3. Affidavits of Rita Edwards (pseudonym) and Stacy McBride (pseudonym).
4. Attorney Daniel Woska's letter addressed to the Wichita attorney Kenneth Clark requesting Clark's law firm conduct research into Kansas DWI arrest of Majid Al-Saad (pseudonym).
5. Stacy McBride (pseudonym), interview with author, audiotape and field notes, September 2001.
6. Transcript, deposition of Hussain Al-Hussaini, *Al-Hussaini v. Palmer Communications*, October 1998, pp. 158-159, 162-163, 375.

## CHAPTER 14: DEATH THREAT

1. Oklahoma Tax Commission, interview with author in which tax commission officials revealed that International Auto Mechanics (pseudonym) was suspended for non-payment of taxes in June 1995, notes, July 1996.
2. Priscilla Gutierrez, Ali Kamel's (pseudonym) former business partner and donut shop employee, interview with author, field notes, July 1996.
3. Freeman Armstrong, interview with author, field notes, July 1995. Mr. Armstrong owned the building in which Ali Kamel's (pseudonym) garage, International Auto Mechanics (pseudonym), was housed.
4. Rizwan Sidiqqi (pseudonym), interview with author, audiotape and field notes, July 14, 1996.
5. Oklahoma Secretary of State corporation registration records that reveal Rizwan Sidiqqi (pseudonym) incorporated International Auto Mechanics (pseudonym) under his name in 1994. The new owners, two Pakistani nationals, then changed the name of the garage. The company service agent was listed as Adnon Khan (pseudonym). The Oklahoma corporate registration for the garage was suspended in June 1996 for failure to meet franchise tax requirements.
6. Ali Kamel (pseudonym), interview with author, audiotape and field notes, July 7, 1996.
7. Leon Rhodes (pseudonym), interview with author, field notes, July 1996.
8. Oklahoma Department of Motor Vehicles records, the license tag VBG-220 that the author witnessed on Ali Kamel's (pseudonym) automobile was registered to a 1983 Pontiac Grand Prix. However, the vehicle's owner was listed as Myrna Morrissey who resided at 4500 N.W. 43rd Street, Oklahoma City, Oklahoma. The street address was invalid.
9. Thelma Rains (pseudonym), interview with author, field notes, July 1996.
10. Photocopy of check bearing the name of a donut shop owned by Ali Kamel (pseudonym) that Kamel endorsed to Tim Rains (pseudonym) as a partial investment in a restaurant business. The twenty-five hundred dollar check was stamped "insufficient funds."
11. Lease application for tenant Rizwan Sidiqqi (pseudonym) to rent an Oklahoma City apartment managed by Tim Rains (pseudonym), February 15, 1995.
12. Adnon Khan (pseudonym), phone interview with Drew Davis witnessed by the author, field notes, July 14, 1996.
13. Transcript and audiotape, telephone answering machine recording of an anonymous threatening call placed to author's home phone in the early morning of July 16, 1996.
14. Oklahoma County property records that documented the sale of Ali Kamel's (pseudonym) Oklahoma City residence, *Journal Record*, July 1997.
15. Oklahoma State Bar Complaint filed against Ali Kamel's (pseudonym) Oklahoma City attorney on charges of moving out of state without notifying his clients and failing to provide a forwarding address, January 16, 1997.
16. Affidavit of Ali Kamel's (pseudonym) lawyer that was filed with the application for an order to approve the attorney's resignation from Oklahoma State Bar Association, July 3, 1996.

## CHAPTER 15: CIVIL WEAPON

1. Indictment, *U.S. v. McVeigh and Nichols*, August 10, 1995.
2. Transcript and videotape, press conference in which Hussaini Al-Hussaini announced his libel lawsuit against KFOR-TV, August 24, 1995.

3. Oklahoma Bar Association disciplinary ruling against attorney William C. Donovan III in which the accused voluntarily surrendered his law license for five years, January 21, 1997.

4. Affidavit of author, Defendants' Motion for Summary Judgment, *Al-Hussaini v. Palmer Communications*, December 16, 1998.

5. Partial Summary Judgment, Findings of Undisputed Fact, *Al-Hussaini v. Palmer Communications*, Case No. Civ-97-1535-L, November 17, 1999.

6. Affidavits of Elizabeth Brown (pseudonym), Johnny Wilborn (pseudonym), Daina Bradley, Rachel Sealy (pseudonym), Randy Christian (pseudonym), Georgia Hammerstein (pseudonym), Gary Hammerstein (pseudonym), David Elmore (pseudonym,) Cole O'Brien (pseudonym), and Rosanna Elmore (pseudonym) and Rita Edwards (pseudonym), Bernie Stanton (pseudonym), and Elvin Devers.

7. FBI confidential letter addressed to Senator Arlen Specter, November 5, 2002.

8. Plaintiff's Dismissal Without Prejudice, *Al-Hussaini v. Palmer Communications*, Case No. CJ-95-5761-63, April 17, 1995.

9. Oklahoma County Grand Jury Subpoena for author, Oklahoma State District Court, Case No. CJ-95-7278, September 18, 1997.

10. Amended Complaint, *Al-Hussaini v. Palmer Communications*, Case No. Civ-97-1535-L, October 3, 1995.

11. Summary Judgment, *Al-Hussaini v. Palmer Communications*, Case No. Civ-97-1535-L, September 29, 2000.   U.S. District Judge Timothy Leonard dismissed Al-Hussaini's libel claim against KFOR-TV on November 17, 1999 and subsequently dismissed the plaintiff's claims of false light invasion of privacy and intentional infliction of emotional distress on September 29, 2000.

12. Docketing Statement, *Al-Hussaini v. Palmer Communications*, United States Court of Appeals for the TheTenth Circuit, Case No. 00-6366, November 14, 2000.

13. Plaintiff's/Appellant's Opening Brief, *Al-Hussaini v. Palmer Communications*, Case No. 00-6366, March 6, 2001.

14. Order and Judgment, *Al-Hussaini v. Palmer Communications*, Case No. 00-6366, March 26, 2003.

15. Notice of Deposition, *Al-Hussaini v. Palmer Communications*, Case No. Civ-97-1535-L, June 16, July 21, and October 8, 1998.

16. Letter addressed to Al-Hussaini's lawyer Vic Grider from author's attorney Dan Woska, documenting plaintiff's stonewalling on scheduling deposition, June 12, 1998.

17. Letter addressed to author's attorney Dan Woska from Al-Hussaini's attorney, Vic Grider, confirming Al-Hussaini's deposition would take place on July 29, 1998, July 16, 1998.

18. Plaintiff's Motion to Quash Notice to Take Deposition, *Al-Hussaini v. Palmer Communications*, July 28, 1998.

19. Letter addressed to Al-Hussaini's lawyer, Vic Grider, from author's attorney, Dan Woska, confirming that Al-Hussaini cancelled the August 4, 1998 deposition date because his psychiatrist advised that the plaintiff suffered from a mental problem which prohibited his traveling to Oklahoma City, July 23, 1998.

20. Letter addressed to KFOR-TV attorney Robert Nelon from Al-Hussaini's legal counsel, Gary Richardson, advising that his deposition had been postponed until August 19, 1998, August 4, 1998.

21. Letter addressed to Al-Hussaini's lawyer, Gregory Cole, from author's attorney, Dan Woska,

advising that the author refused to authorize any further postponements of the plaintiff's deposition, September 1, 1998.

22. Letter addressed to Al-Hussaini's lawyer, Vic Grider, from author's attorney, Dan Woska, requesting the plaintiff's immigration records, July 27, 1998.

23. Letter addressed to Al-Hussaini's lawyer, Gregory Cole, from author's attorney, Dan Woska, requesting the plaintiff's medical records, September 1, 1998.

24. Letter addressed to Al-Hussaini's lawyer, Gary Richardson, from author's attorney, Dan Woska, requesting the plaintiff's immigration records, birth certificate, court records verifying Al-Hussaini's claims of arrest and imprisonment in Iraq, and photo identifications of plaintiff that had been issued by U.S. authorities, August 11, 1998.

25. Letter addressed to Al-Hussaini's lawyer, Gary Richardson, from author's attorney, Dan Woska, reminding the plaintiff's counsel that the defendants still had not received Al-Hussaini's immigration file, August 21, 1998.

26. Letter addressed to Al-Hussaini's lawyer, Greg Cole, from author's attorney, Dan Woska, requesting Al-Hussaini's immigration, medical, and Iraqi imprisonment records, September 14, 1998.

27. Letter addressed to Al-Hussaini's lawyer, Greg Cole, from KFOR-TV attorney, Robert Nelon, setting October 19, 1998 deadline to produce the plaintiff's psychiatric records, October 8, 1998.

28. Exhibit, Medical records of Hussain Al-Hussaini regarding his psychiatric therapy at The Arbour Hospital and The Quincy Center, *Al-Hussaini v. Palmer Communications*, October 1997 through February 1998, pp. 1-641.

29. Immigration records of Hussain Hashem Al-Hussaini.

30. International Rescue Committee records of Hussain Al-Hussaini.

31. Exhibit, letter addressed to Oklahoma County Assistant District Attorney Suzanne Lister-Gump from the plaintiff's psychiatrist, Dr. Frank Kahr, *Al-Hussaini v. Palmer Communications*, January 15, 1998.

32. Transcript, deposition of Hussain Al-Hussaini, *Al-Hussaini v. Palmer Communications*, October 27-30 and November 16-19, 1998.

33. Handwritten notes documenting attorney Dan Woska's interview with defendant's expert witness, Dr. Michael J. Mufson, concerning his professional assessment of Hussain Al-Hussaini's mental condition following his October 26, 1998 psychiatric evaluation and personal interview with the plaintiff.

34. Exhibit, handwritten notes of Hussain Al-Hussaini listing his prescribed medications for mental health, *Al-Hussaini v. Palmer Communications*, November 17, 1998.

35. Transcripts, 10:00 P.M. newscasts, KFOR-TV, June 7, June 9, June 14, June 22, and December 29, 1995.

36. Press release issued by Al-Hussaini's attorney, Gary Richardson, to the Oklahoma City media announcing the filing of the libel lawsuit against KFOR-TV, August 23, 1995.

37. Transcripts, 10:00 P.M. newscasts, KWTV, June 15-16, 1995.

38. Transcript, 10:00 P.M. newscast, KOCO-TV, June 16, 1995.

39. George Lang, "Out On A Limb, KFOR Story 'Identifying' John Doe 2 Sparks Firestorm Of Controversy," *Oklahoma Gazette*, June 22, 1995.

40. Larry Monroe (pseudonym), interview with Bernie Stanton (pseudonym), audiotape, June 18, 1995.

41. Jose Gonzales (pseudonym), surreptitiously recorded interview with Bernie Stanton (pseudonym), audiotape, May 1995.

42. Defendants' Answers to Plaintiff's First Set of Interrogatories, *Al-Hussaini v. Palmer Communications*, Case No. CJ-95-5761-63, March 18, 1997.

43. Status Report, *Al-Hussaini v. Palmer Communications*, Case No. Civ-97-1535-L, July 6, 1998.

44. Helen Abdul (pseudonym), hidden camera interview with Bernie Stanton (pseudonym), KFOR-TV videotape, June 1995.

45. Darby Williams (pseudonym), interview with author, audiotape and field notes, June 15, 1995.

46. FBI Special Agent Dan Vogel, interview with author, audiotape, June 20, 1995.

47. Assistant U.S. Attorney Steve Mullins, interview with author, audiotape and notes, June 20 and August 30, 1995.

48. U.S. Department of Justice Spokesman Carl Stern, interview with author, notes, August 30, 1995.

49. U.S. Department of Justice press release, Washington DC headquarters, June 14, 1995.

50. "FBI Identifies, Clears John Doe 2," *DailyOklahoman.com*, June 15, 1995.

51. Robert L. Jackson and Ronald J. Ostraw, "Nichols Talks of Bomb Tests, FBI Agent Says," *Los Angeles Times*, May 3, 1995.

52. Susan Steinberg, "Man Resembling 'John Doe' to be Tried on Other Charges," *Los Angeles Times*, May 3, 1995.

53. Tim Talley, "Dutch Reports to be Investigated by McVeigh's Attorneys," Associated Press, January 4, 1996.

54. Crime Report, Oklahoma City Police Department, arrest of Hussain Hashem Al-Hussaini, Case No. 95-05224, Case No. 95-5775954, Case No. 95-5775954, Case No. 95-5775963, June 3, 1995.

55. Crime Report, Oklahoma City Police Department, arrest of Hussain Al-Hussaini, Case No. 95-059971, June 24, 1995.

56. Traffic Citations issued to Hussain Al-Hussaini, Oklahoma City Police Department, Case No. 95-6026846, Case. No. 95-6026855, June 2, 1995.

57. Bench Warrant for arrest of Hussain Al-Hussaini for failure to appear, Oklahoma City Municipal Court, Case No. 95-5775963, Case. No. 95-5775954, June 28, 1995.

58. Bench Warrant for arrest of Hussain Al-Hussaini for failure to appear, Oklahoma City Municipal Court, Case No. 95-6236533, Case No. 95-6026855, Case No. 95-6026846, August 5, 1995.

59. Crime Report, Irving, Texas Police Department, arrest of Hussain Hashem Al-Hussaini, Case No. 96-004384, February 14, 1996.

60. Warrant for Arrest for Hussain Al-Hussaini, Dallas County Municipal Court, Case No. M-96-30972-0, June 20, 1996.

61. Traffic Citation issued to Hussain Al-Hussaini, Failure to Show Insurance, Oklahoma City Municipal Court, Case No. 94-5293678, December 29, 1994.

62. Traffic Citation issued to Hussain Al-Hussaini, Violation of License Restriction, Oklahoma City Municipal Court, Case. No. 94-4953630, January 10, 1995.

63. Traffic Citation issued to Hussain Al-Hussaini, FTY/Private Drive, Oklahoma City Municipal Court, Case No. 94-495366-X, January 10, 1995.

64. Traffic Citations issued to Hussain Al-Hussaini, Driving Without a Driver's License, Disregarding a Traffic Light, City of Edmond, Oklahoma Municipal Court, Case No. T167029, January 19, 1995.

65. Notice of Suspension of Driver's License for Hussain Al-Hussaini, Oklahoma State Department of Public Safety, Case No. 235100000, February 13, 1995.

66. Traffic Citation issued to Hussain Al-Hussaini, Oklahoma City Municipal Court, Case No. 95-582858-X, May 26, 1995.

67. Notice of Suspension of Driver's License for Hussain Al-Hussaini, Oklahoma City Municipal Court, Case No. 95-6025846, Case No. 95-60256855, August 17, 1995.

68. Director of Congressional Task Force on Terrorism and Unconventional Warfare Yossef Bodansky, interview with author, audiotape and field notes, April 1996 and November 1998.

69. Colonel Patrick Lang (U.S. Army retired), former Chief of Human Intelligence for the Defense Intelligence Agency, interview with author, audiotape and field notes, July 2002.

70. Memorandum, endorsed by Colonel Patrick Lang, military intelligence analysis of Hussain Al-Hussaini's tattoo, March 2002.

71. Micah Morrison, "The Iraq Connection," *Wall Street Journal*, September 5, 2002.

72. Application to Shorten Time for Plaintiff to Produce Documents Pursuant to F.R. Civ. P. 34 Prior to Deposition, *Al-Hussaini v. Palmer Communications*, September 15, 1998.

73. Motion to Require Plaintiff to Submit to Mental Examination, *Al-Hussaini v. Palmer Communications*, September 15, 1998.

74. Joint Application of Parties for Vacation of Protective Order, *Al-Hussaini v. Palmer Communications*, April 4, 2001.

75. Order granting vacation of a protective order, *Al-Hussaini v. Palmer Communications*, April 4, 2001.

## CHAPTER 16: THE FARMER MEETS THE TERRORIST

1. Nolan Clay, "Some Jurors Convinced Others Involved; Nichols Trial Renews Speculation Concerning John Doe 2," *Daily Oklahoman*, January 11, 1998.

2. Nolan Clay and Penny Owen, "Terry Nichols Guilty; Conspiracy Convicts Allows Death Penalty," *Daily Oklahoman*, December 24, 1997.

3. Nolan Clay, "Matsch to Decide Nichols' Fate; Jury Fails to Determine Sentence in Bomb Case," *Daily Oklahoman*, January 8, 1998.

4. Nolan Clay, "Nichols' Words Could Avert Life Sentence," *Daily Oklahoman*, March 26, 1998.

5. Robby Trammell, "Pair Recount Nichols' Trips to Philippines," *DailyOklahoman.com*, March 9, 1996.

6. "Nichols, Terrorist Met, McVeigh's Ex-Lawyer Says," *DailyOklahoman.com*, October 13, 1998.

7. Jones and Israel, *Others Unknown*, pp. 51-54, 146-173.

8. Defendant McVeigh's Fourth Supplemental of Specification of Materiality, *U.S. v. McVeigh*, October 30, 1996, pp. 4, 6.

9. Defendant McVeigh's Fifth Supplemental Specification of Materiality, *U.S. v. McVeigh*, November 8, 1996, pp. 1-8.

10. Memoranda authored by Thomas Black (pseudonym) which detailed his investigative findings as a contract consultant for KFOR-TV, March 13, March 25, and April 10, 1996.

11. Confidential, original handwritten investigative report by Dr. Oscar P. Coronel, Chief of Intelligence Division, Bureau of Immigration, Department of Justice, Republic of the Philippines, March 1, 1996.

12. Thomas Black (pseudonym), interview with author in presence of KFOR-TV attorney Robert Nelon, field notes, March 1996.

13. Thomas Black (pseudonym), interview with author, audiotape and field notes, November 1996.

14. Transcript, interview with Timothy McVeigh defense attorney Stephen Jones, *The O'Reilly Factor*, Fox News, May 7, 2001.

15. Exhibit L, investigative report documenting Edwin Angeles' interview with Philippine authorities on November 3, 1996, Defendant McVeigh's Fifth Supplemental Specification of Materiality, *U.S. v. McVeigh*, November 8, 1996.

16. Handwritten affidavit of Abu Sayyaf co-founder Edwin Angeles, November 1996.

17. Peter Lance, *1000 Years for Revenge, International Terrorism and the FBI – The Untold Story*, (New York: Reagan Books, 2003), pp. 4-5, 9, 13, 24-26, 81-82, 93, 108, 200, 265-267, 274, 278-279, 312-322,

18. Defendant McVeigh's Fourth Supplemental of Specification of Materiality, *U.S. v. McVeigh*, September 30, 1996, pp. 1, 32-33, 35, 44-47.

19. Yossef Bodansky, *Bin Laden: The Man Who Declared War on America* (California: Prima Publishing, 1999) p. 33.

20. Richard Miniter, *Losing Bin Laden:How Bill Clinton's Failures Unleashed Global Terror*, (Washington DC: Regnery Publishing, Inc., 2003), pp. 19-22.

21. Laurie Mylroie, *Study of Revenge: The First World Trade Center Attack and Saddam Hussein's War Against America*, (Washington DC: The AEI Press, 2001) pp. 78-82, 173-175.

22. Abdul Hakim Murad interview, FBI 302, FBI Special Agents Francis J. Pellegrino and Thomas G. Donlon, April 12-13, 1995, Appendix I: *1000 Years for Revenge*, pp. 499-517.

23. Petition for Writ of Mandamus, *U.S. v. McVeigh*, March 25, 1997, p. 91.

24. Passport of Terry Lynn Nichols issued by the Philippine Consulate in Chicago on November 3, 1994.

25. Passport of Terry Lynn Nichols which documented five trips to the Philippines from August 1990 through January 1995. His final trip to the Philippines bore an arrival date of November 24, 1995. He returned to the United States on January 16, 1995.

26. Lana Padilla, interview with author, KFOR-TV videotape and field notes, July 1995.

27. Transcript, 10:00 P.M. newscast, KFOR-TV, July 13, 1995.

28. Josh Nichols, interview with author, audiotape, July 7, 1995.

29. Kenneth R. Timmerman, "Iraq Connection to the Oklahoma Bombing," *Insight*, April 15, 2002.

30. Transcript, *The Dennis McQuistion Show*, PBS, June 10, 2003.

31. Transcript, testimony of Michael Fortier, *U.S. v. McVeigh*, May 12, 1997.

32. Serapin Uy interview, Manager of Philippine Starglad International Lumber Company, FBI 302 Serial No. 174A-OC-56120, Alat Ronald E. Ward, April 28, 1995. Serapin Uy told investigators that Nichols's father-in-law, Eduardo Torres, found a book on making explosives in Nichols's luggage.

33. Sworn statement of Daisy Yvonne B. Legaspi, former tour guide for Paradise Sheton Tours in Cebu City, October 3, 1996.

34. Dale Hurd, "Oklahoma City Cover-up: The Iraq Connection," *CBNNews.com*, September 14, 2003.

35. Transcript, opening arguments presented by Assistant U.S. Attorney Larry Mackey, *U.S. v. Nichols*, November 3, 1997.

36. U.S. Department of Justice phone records which documented calls placed on the "Daryl Bridges" Spotlight prepaid phone debit card and calls placed from the homes of Terry Nichols and his ex-wife Lana Padilla, *U.S. v. Nichols*, exhibits 01074-010923.

37. U.S. Department of Justice phone logs tracking calls placed to Terry Nichols's Herington, Kansas residence from untraceable numbers in the Philippines on April 2-10, 1995, exhibits 010836-010839.

38. U.S. Department of Justice phone records documenting calls placed from Terry Nichols's Herington, Kansas residence, exhibit 010844.

39. U.S. Department of Justice phone records documenting calls charged to "Daryl Bridges" phone card on January 17, 1995 from Lana Padilla's Las Vegas home, exhibits 010773-010774.

40. U.S. Department of Justice phone records documenting calls charged to "Daryl Bridges" phone card on January 31, February 14, and February 28, 1995, exhibits 010778-010779, 010783-010784, 010788-010790.

41. Transcript, testimony of Lana Padilla, *U.S. v. Nichols*, November 19, 1997.

42. Exhibit, *United States v. Ramzi Ahmed Yousef et al.*, the log book of Philippine Dona Josefa Apartments, December 1994-January 9, 1995. Evidentiary exhibit was obtained by author Peter Lance, *1000 Years for Revenge*, p. 314.

43. Jim Gomez and John Solomon, "Authorities Warned of Hijack Risks," Associated Press, March 5, 2002.

44. Lt. Philip Rojas interview about April 19, 1995 statement of Abdul Hakim Murad, FBI 302 Serial No. 174A-OC-56120-Sub D-15285, FBI Special Agent Francis J. Pellegrino and U.S. Secret Service Agent Brian G. Parr, April 19, 1995.

45. Raghida Dirgham, "Ramzi Yousef Discusses WTC Bombing, Other Activities," *Al Hayat*, translated in FBIS-NES-95-097, April 12, 1995.

46. Timothy McVeigh, "An Essay on Hypocrisy," *Media Bypass*, May 30, 1998.

## CHAPTER 17: PRIOR WARNING

1. Yossef Bodansky, *Terror: The Inside Story of the Terrorist Conspiracy in America*, (New York: S.P.I Books/Shapolsky Publishers, Inc., 1994), pp. 13, 18, 44, 66, 79-81, 188.

2. Yossef Bodansky, *Bin Laden: The Man Who Declared War on America*, pp. 100-104, 181, 183.

3. Yossef Bodansky, interview with author, audiotape notes and field notes, April 24 and May 18, 1996.

4. Memorandum dated August 2, 1995 which memorialized a phone conversation between Yossef Bodansky and Thomas E. Williams, Special Agent Intel, New York Branch of Federal Protective Services. The memo was viewed and hand-copied by the author.

5. Prior warning issued by the Congressional Task Force on Terrorism and Unconventional Warfare, published on February 27, 1995. Intelligence sources were redacted from the documents provided to author.

6. Transcript, interview with U.S. Representative Jim Saxton (R-New Jersey) in which he discussed the dissemination of the Congressional Task Force alert to federal law enforcement agencies, *Rivera Live*, CNBC, April 20, 1995.

7. Written correspondence addressed to author from Yossef Bodansky, May 18 and September 1996.

8. Transcript, *This Week With David Brinkley,* ABC News, June 9, 1995.

9. Written correspondence by Yossef Bodansky, September 1996.

10. Yossef Bodansky's intelligence analysis of April 19, 1995 terrorist operation entitled: "Between Oklahoma and Amia" issued after the Murrah Building attack in the spring of 1995.

11. Letter addressed to Oklahoma State District Judge Bryan Dixon from Yossef Bodansky, October 5, 1998.

12. Curt Anderson, "FBI Hunts Al-Qaeda Agents in 40 States," Associated Press, June 27, 2003.

13. Written Congressional Statement of Assistant FBI Director of Counterterrorism Larry Mefford, June 27, 2003.

14. Tarek Al-Issawi, "Americans, Britons Held in Attacks on Forces in Iraq," Associated Press, September 17, 2003.

15. Larry Margasak, "John Walker Lindh to Plead Guilty," Associated Press, July 15, 2002.

16. Neil Lewis, "American Who Joined Taliban Pleads Guilty," *New York Times,* July 15, 2002.

17. "Text of John Walker Lindh's Deal," Associated Press, July 15, 2002.

18. "U.S. Charges Six With Terrorism," *NewsMax.com,* October 5, 2003.

19. Teresa Carson, "Two More Oregon Pro-Taliban Suspects Plead Guilty," Reuters, October 16, 2003.

20. Andrew Kramer, "Two Oregon Men Plead Guilty in Terror Case," Associated Press, October 16, 2003.

21. "U.S. Charges Six With Terrorism," *NewsMax.com,* October 5, 2003.

22. Mike Carter and Steve Miletich, "Ujaama Pleads Guilty to Conspiring to Support Taliban," *Seattle Times,* April 14, 2003.

23. Patrick J. McDonnell and Josh Meyer, "Links to Terrorism Probed in Northwest," *Los Angeles Times,* July 13, 2003.

24. Gina Holland, "Supreme Court Bides Time in Terror Cases," Associated Press, October 14, 2003.

25. Kevin Johnson, "2nd Wave of Terror Attacks Probed," *USA Today,* March 30, 2003.

26. Richard Willing, "Pursuit of Al-Qaeda Keeps Coming Back to Florida," *USA Today,* June 15, 2003.

27. Phil Hirschkorn, "Attorney Visits No Closer for Enemy Combatant," *CNN.com,* March 27, 2003.

28. Frank Davies, "Screening of Muslim Chaplains Urged," *Knight Ridder Newspapers,* October 14, 2003.

29. Paisley Dodds, "Guantanamo Troops Must Surrender Laptops," Associated Press – Latin America, October 21, 2003.

30. "Chaplain Who Counseled Gitmo Prisoners Detained," Associated Press, September 20, 2003.

31. Will Dunham, "U.S. Army Chaplain Yee Charged in Guantanamo Case," Reuters, October 10, 2003.

32. Timothy McVeigh, "An Essay on Hypocrisy," *Media Bypass,* May 30, 1998.

33. Michel and Herbeck, *American Terrorist,* pp. 74-76, 80, 82, 91.

34. Dale Hurd, "Oklahoma City Cover-up: The Iraq Connection," *CBNNews.com,* October 22, 2002.

35. Richard Miniter, *Losing Bin Laden*, pp. 8, 37.
36. Steve Emerson, *Jihad in America*, PBS, 1994.
37. Cam Simpson, "Feds Seize Home, $1 Million; Owner Linked To Terrorists," *ChicagoSunTimes.com*, June 10, 1998.
38. Cam Simpson and Alex Rodriguez, "Area's Ties To Terrorists," *ChicagoSunTimes.com*, June 11, 1998.
39. Margot Dudkevitch and Mohammed Najib, "FBI Seizes $1.4 Million From Hamas Official," *Jerusalem Post*, June 11, 1998, http://www.jpost.com/.
40. David Johnston, "U.S. Prosecutors Suspect an American Citizen of Financing Hamas Terror," *New York Times*, June 14, 1998.
41. Tom Hundley, "Chicagoan is Charged by Israel with Heading Hamas Militants," *Chicago Tribune*, October 23, 1993.
42. Matt O'Connor and Sarah Downey, "FBI Seizes $1 Million Linked to Terrorism; Bridgeview Resident, Literacy Group Alleged to Have Helped," *ChicagoTribune.com*, June 10, 1998.
43. Dan Perry, "Israeli Prison Awaits Convicted Suburb Man; Arab-American fromBridgeview Guilty of Funding Islamic Militants," *Chicago Tribune*, January 3, 1995.
44. Cam Simpson, "How Car Salesman Got Tag As Terrorist," *ChicagoSunTimes.com*, June 14, 1998.
45. Stephen Franklin, "U.S. Probing Chicago Connection to Hamas, Israeli and the State Department Contend Chicago is Training Center of Cash and Training for Militant Palestinians, But Hard Evidence is Difficult to Come By," *Chicago Tribune*, November 16, 1994.
46. Stephen Franklin, "The Prisoner No One Wants; Jailed Hamas Leader's Deft Legal Move Has World in Check," *Chicago Tribune*, March 16, 1997.
47. Molly Sullivan, "Salah States His Case As Man Of Peace," *Daily Southtown*, June 17, 1998.
48. Lisa Myers, "FBI probes Hamas presence in U.S.; Agent Charges Investigation Of Group Has Been Mishandled," *MSNBC.com*, June 2, 2003.
49. Sharman Stein, "Grocer Ties to Terrorists Comes Home," *Chicago Tribune*, July 28, 1993.
50. Mary Houlihan-Skilton, "Arab Americans Seek A Fairer Role In Society," *ChicagoSunTimes*, June 18, 1998.
51. Molly Sullivan, "Area Arabs Battle Back Against Bias; Muslims Say They're Forced To Protect Own Civil Rights," *Daily Southtown*, August 6, 1998.
52. Tom Hundley, "Chicagoan Denies Israeli Charges Terror Group Suspect: Confession Obtained Under Duress," *Chicago Tribune*, June 23, 1993.
53. Scott Lindlaw, "Bush Freezes Suspected Terror Assets," Associated Press, December 4, 2001.
54. Judith Miller, "Group Sues Over Frozen Assets, Saying U.S. Violated Rights," *New York Times*, March 9, 2002.
55. Defendant McVeigh's Fourth Supplemental Specification of Materiality, *U.S. v. McVeigh*, September 30, 1996, pp. 16-17.
56. Confidential source, interview with author with KFOR-TV attorney Robert Nelon present, field notes, April 1996. The confidential source shared the same testimony with defense attorney Stephen Jones, who recorded the phone interview and submitted the transcript in a sworn affidavit filed with the court, *U.S. v. McVeigh*, September 30, 1996.
57. Jo Thomas, "Prosecution Setbacks Abound in Bomb Case," *New York Times*, April 17, 1997.
58. Richard A. Serrano, "FBI Issued Flawed Bomb Analysis, U.S. Probe Finds," *Los Angeles Times*, March 21, 1997.

59. Written report submitted by confidential intelligence source employed as KFOR-TV consultant. Report corroborated the conclusions contained in the Israeli bomb report, July 9, 1996.
60. Jones and Israel, *Others Unknown*, pp. 155-158, 160-161.
61. Nick Fielding, "Secrets Of Al-Qaeda: Network Studies Oklahoma-Style Bomb," *London Sunday Times*, November 18, 2001.
62. Lance, *1000 Years for Revenge*, p. 315.

## CHAPTER 18: NEW YORK TIMES VS. JAYNA DAVIS

1. Second Amended Answer and Counterclaim, *The New York Times v. Jayna Davis*, Oklahoma State District Court, Case No. CJ-97-4657-63, March 20, 1998.
2. Author's resignation letter dated March 3, 1997 addressed to KFOR-TV General Manager Tim Morrissey, Defendant's Objection to the Plaintiff's Cross Motion for Summary Judgment, *Times vs. Davis*, October 20, 1998.
3. Stephen Jones, interview with author, field notes, March 1997. Author traveled to Denver, Colorado at Jones's invitation in March 1997 and was permitted to review defense materials at Timothy McVeigh's defense headquarters.
4. Memorandum dated August 2, 1995, which memorialized a phone conversation between Yossef Bodansky and Thomas E. Williams, special agent intel, New York branch of the Federal Protective Services, viewed and hand-copied by author.
5. Yossef Bodansky, interview with author, audiotape and field notes, April 24 and May 1996.
6. Memorandum dated February 17, 1995, which memorialized a phone conversation between Yossef Bodansky and John G. Crowe, special agent in charge, New York branch of the Federal Protective Services, viewed and hand-copied by author.
7. U.S. Marshals Service warning issued by Eduardo Gonzales entitled, "Potential Threat to U.S. Marshal Service Personnel and Property," viewed and hand copied by author, March 15, 1995.
8. Subpoena for Jayna Davis to Appear and Testify, *U.S. v. McVeigh*, May 18, 1997.
9. Motion to Quash Subpoena for Jayna Davis to Appear and Testify, *U.S. v. McVeigh*, May 23, 1997.
10. Letter addressed to U.S. District Judge Richard P. Matsch by author's attorney, Kyle Goodwin, May 23, 1997.
11. Affidavit of author, *The Times v. Davis*, August 31, 1998.
12. Letter addressed to *New York Times* legal counsel, Michelle Johnson, from the author's attorney, Carl Hughes, which memorialized April meeting between KFOR-TV General Manager Tim Morrissey and the author, May 30, 1997.
13. Defendant's Objection to the Plaintiff's Cross Motion for Summary Judgment, *The Times v. Davis*, October 20, 1998.
14. Defendant's Motion for Partial Summary Judgment, *The Times v. Davis*, August 31, 1998.
15. Letter addressed to the author from KFOR-TV General Manager Tim Morrissey, March 11, 1997.
16. Letter dated March 27, 1997 addressed to KFOR-TV General Manager Tim Morrissey from the author, *The Times v. Davis*, August 31, 1998.
17. Sworn affidavits signed by twenty-two witnesses who objected to the court releasing their recorded interviews to *The New York Times* Company, *The Times v. Davis*, August 31, 1998.
18. Letter addressed to *The New York Times* lawyer, Michelle Johnson, from the author's attorney, Dan Woska, December 12, 1997.

19. Letter addressed to attorney Michelle Johnson from author's lawyer, Carl Hughes, on May 30, 1997, *The Times v. Davis*, August 31, 1998.

20. Letter addressed to author from attorney Carl Hughes documenting a conversation with *New York Times* legal representative, Robert Nelon, in which *The Times* granted permission for Hughes to maintain custody of the recorded interviews of the author's confidential sources, *The Times v. Davis*, August 31, 1998.

21. Affidavit of attorney Robert Nelon, *The Times v. Davis*, October 20, 1998.

22. Petition, *The Times v. Davis*, July 2, 1997.

23. Defendant's Objection to Request for Order of Delivery of Property, *The Times v. Davis*, July 9, 1997.

24. Letter addressed to Oklahoma State District Judge Bryan Dixon from the Director of Congressional Task Force on Terrorism and Unconventional Warfare Yossef Bodansky, October 5, 1998.

25. Journal Entry of Judgment, *The Times v. Davis*, March 23, 1999.

## CHAPTER 19: CASE CLOSED

1. Plaintiff's Dismissal Without Prejudice, *Al-Hussaini v. Palmer Communications*, Case No. CJ-95-5761-63, April 17, 1995.

2. Affidavit of author, *The Times v. Davis*, August 31, 1998.

3. Defendant's Objection to Request for Order of Delivery of Property, *The Times v. Davis*, July 9, 1997.

4. Letter addressed to Oklahoma State District Judge Bryan Dixon from Yossef Bodansky, October 5, 1998.

5. Motion to Quash Subpoena for Jayna Davis to Appear and Testify, *U.S. v. McVeigh*, May 23, 1997.

6. Letter addressed to U.S. District Judge Richard P. Matsch from author's attorney, Kyle Goodwin, May 23, 1997.

7. Oklahoma County Grand Jury subpoena for author, September 18, 1997.

8. Written statement submitted to Oklahoma County Grand Jury during author's testimony, September 18, 1997.

9. Letter addressed to author's attorney, Dan Woska, from Assistant Oklahoma County District Attorney Patrick Morgan, June 25, 1997.

10. Letter addressed to Oklahoma County District Attorney Bob Macy from author's lawyer, Dan Woska, August 13, 1997.

11. Transcript, testimony of author before Oklahoma County Grand Jury, sealed testimony of September 18-19, 1997 and January 26, 1998.

12. Letters addressed to Oklahoma County Assistant District Attorney Suzanne Gump from author's lawyer, Dan Woska, January 15, 1998 and May 20, 1998.

13. Memorandum, which memorialized a phone conversation between Oklahoma County Assistant District Attorney Patrick Morgan and author's lawyer, Dan Woska, June 4, 1998.

14. Letter addressed to Assistant District Attorney Patrick Morgan from author's attorney, Dan Woska, June 10, 1998.

15. Letter addressed to author's attorney Dan Woska from Assistant District Attorney Patrick Morgan, June 11, 1998.

16. Diana Baldwin, "Lead Private Investigator Meets Bomb Grand Jury," *DailyOklahoman.com*, March 11, 1998.

17. Diana Baldwin, "Bombing Grand Jury Hears Ex-Informant," *DailyOklahoman.com*, October 9, 1997.

18. Diana Baldwin and Ed Godfrey, "Grand Jury to Meet Monday – Key Wants to Hear Uncalled Witnesses," *DailyOklahoman.com*, June 29, 1997.

19. Bill McAllister, "Oklahoma Grand Jury to Hear Cover-up Charge; State Lawmaker Sees Bombing Conspiracy," *Washington Post*, June 13, 1997.

20. Ed Godfrey, "Judge Refuses to Bar Subpoena of Ex-Reporter," *Daily Oklahoman*, September 12, 1997.

21. Letters addressed to author's attorney, Dan Woska, from Oklahoma County Assistant District Attorney Suzanne Gump, December 10, 1997, June 18, 1998, June 29, 1998, and December 4, 1998.

22. Letter addressed to Oklahoma County Grand Jury c/o Assistant District Attorney Suzanne Gump from author, October 1, 1998.

23. Copies of letters that the confidential witnesses wrote to the Oklahoma County Grand Jury in June and July 1995 which were hand delivered to the panel through courier employed by author's attorney, Dan Woska, July 7, 1998.

24. Letter addressed to Oklahoma County District Attorney Bob Macy from author, October 1, 1998. The preceding two letters and accompanying packet of witness affidavits were hand delivered by the author's attorney, Dan Nelson, on October 2, 1998.

25. Letters addressed to Oklahoma County Grand Jury c/o Assistant District Attorney Suzanne Gump from author, June 15, 1998 and July 7, 1998.

26. Nolan Clay and Diana Baldwin, "Ban Lifted on Federal Help in State's Bombing Case," *Daily Oklahoman*, July 1, 1998.

27. Diana Baldwin, "Baby Interrupts Agent's Long-Awaited Testimony," *Daily Oklahoman*, November 18, 1998.

28. Nolan Clay, "Blast Prosecutors Seek OK to Aid Grand Jury," *Daily Oklahoman*, May 16, 1998.

29. Diana Baldwin, "FBI Agent Ends Grand Jury Testimony," *DailyOklahoman.com*, November 25, 1998.

30. "Final Report on Oklahoma City Bombing," Oklahoma County Grand Jury, December 30, 1998.

31. Confidential source, interview with author, field notes, March 1996. The source disclosed information taken directly from the grand jury sealed transcript of an FBI agent's testimony regarding author's investigation and witnesses.

32. Transcript, en camera testimony of author, *Oklahoma v. Nichols*, March 20, 2001.

33. Transcripts, testimonies of author's attorney, Tim McCoy, author's notary public, Pam Nance, author's attorney, Dan Nelson, and Drew Davis, *Oklahoma v. Nichols*, March 20-21, 2001.

34. Memorandum addressed to Assistant U.S. Attorney Sean Connelly from author's attorney, Tim McCoy, September 12, 1997.

35. Memorandum addressed to FBI Special Agent James Strickland from attorney Tim McCoy, September 12, 1997

36. "Nichols Attorneys Argue Double Jeopardy," Oklahoma City KOCO-TV, March 20, 1997, http://www.channeloklahoma.com/.

37. Nolan Clay, "Nichols Team Wants More Access to Reports," *DailyOklahoman.com*, March 21, 2001.
38. Jon Dougherty, "FBI Refused 22 Eyewitness Testimonies, Evidence Implicating Mideast Connection Created Discovery Problems," *WorldNetDaily.com*, May 16, 2001.
39. Affidavit of Dan Nelson.
40. Court proffer entered on behalf of FBI Special Agent Dan Vogel confirming he took receipt of twenty-two witness affidavits from the author, *Oklahoma v. Nichols*, October 29, 2001.
41. James Patterson, "Justice Department Won't Let Agent Testify," *Indianapolis Star*, November 3, 2001.
42. James Patterson, "Missing Evidence From Oklahoma City," *Indianapolis Star*, November 17, 2001.
43. FBI confidential letter addressed to Senator Arlen Specter, November 5, 2002.

## Chapter 20: American Hero

1. David P. Schippers and Alan P. Henry, *Sellout: The Inside Story of President Clinton's Impeachment*, (Washington DC: Regnery Publishing Inc., 2000) pp. 201-248, 257.
2. Letter and evidence dossier addressed to David Schippers from the author, September 29, 2000.
3. David Schippers, interview with author, field notes, March 2001, April 2001, May 2001, June 2001, September 2001, January 2002, March 2002.
4. Prior warning issued by the Congressional Task Force on Terrorism and Unconventional Warfare, published on February 27, 1995.
5. Written correspondence addressed to author from Yossef Bodansky, May 18, 1996.
6. E-mails addressed to the author from Yossef Bodansky, September 1996 and July 3, 1998.
7. Transcript, press conference of FBI Special Agent Bob Wright, Federal News Service, May 30, 2002.
8. Brian Ross, "Called Off The Trail; FBI Agents Probing Terror Links Say They Were Told Let Sleeping Dogs Lie," *Primetime Live*, December 19, 2002, http://www.ABCNews.com/.
9. Jim Crogan, "Another FBI Agent Blows the Whistle; New Evidence That The Bureau Quashed Another Terror Probe Before 9/11," *LA Weekly*, August 2, 2002.
10. "Terror Insubordination? FBI Agent Probed After Criticism," ABCNews.com, June 12, 2003.
11. Glen R. Simpson, "Muslim FBI Agent Is Accused Of Not Taping Terror Suspects," *Wall Street Journal*, November 26, 2002.
12. Transcripts, interview with author, *The O'Reilly Factor*, Fox News, March 20 and May 14, 2001.
13. Photocopy of letter addressed to Timothy McVeigh's defense counsel, Robert Nigh, Nathan Chambers, and John Richilano, from Special Attorney to the Attorney General Sean Connelly, May 9, 2001.
14. Transcript, public statement of Attorney General John Ashcroft regarding the FBI's withholding of discovery documents from the defense teams representing Timothy McVeigh and Terry Nichols, May 24, 2001.
15. Richard Serrano and Eric Lichtblau, "More McVeigh Files Found; FBI Orders Massive Search," *Los Angeles Times*, May 15, 2001.
16. "Judge Won't Delay McVeigh Execution," Associated Press, June 6, 2001.

17. Karen Gullo, "Ashcroft: McVeigh Documents Turned Over," Associated Press, May 24, 2001.

18. Summary of U.S. inspector general's report, U.S. Department of Justice, March 19, 2001. The U.S. inspector general's report referenced the author's public allegations that the FBI refused her evidence of Mideastern complicity, pp. 121-122.

19. Jerry Seper, "FBI Supervisor In Oklahoma City Probe To Step Down," *Washington Times*, April 18, 2002.

20. John Solomon, "Report Details McVeigh Case Errors," Associated Press, March 19, 2002.

21. James Patterson, "A Few Questions Before FBI Agent Exits," *Indianapolis Star*, April 20, 2002.

22. Transcript, FBI Special Agent Dan Vogel, phone interview with *Indianapolis Star* reporter, James Patterson, audiotape, November 9, 2001.

23. Transcript, en camera testimony of author, *Oklahoma v. Nichols*, March 20, 2001.

24. Transcripts, testimonies of author's attorney, Tim McCoy, author's notary public, Pam Nance, author's attorney, Dan Nelson, and Drew Davis, *Oklahoma v. Nichols*, March 20-21, 2001.

25. Court proffer entered on behalf of FBI Special Agent Dan Vogel confirming he took receipt of twenty-two witness affidavits from the author, *Oklahoma v. Nichols*, October 29, 2001.

26. James Patterson, "Justice Department Won't Let Agent Testify," *Indianapolis Star*, November 3, 2001.

27. James Patterson, "Missing Evidence from Oklahoma City," *Indianapolis Star*, November 17, 2001.

28. FBI confidential letter addressed to Senator Arlen Specter, November 5, 2002.

29. James Patterson, "The Impeachment Lawyer Smells A Rat," *Indianapolis Star*, October 13, 2001.

30. Letter addressed to Oklahoma State District Judge Bryan Dixon from the Director of Congressional Task Force on Terrorism and Unconventional Warfare Yossef Bodansky, October 5, 1998.

31. James Patterson, "Ex-CIA Agent Believes In John Doe 2," *Indianapolis Star*, March 23, 2002.

32. James Patterson, "Congress Steps In To Probe 1995 Bombing," *Indianapolis Star*, April 6, 2002.

33. James Patterson, "The FBI Knew '95, Why Didn't We?" *Indianapolis Star*, May 25, 2002.

34. James Patterson, "Burton's Panel Finds Links To Foreigners In Oklahoma Blast," *Indianapolis Star*, August 24, 2002.

35. James Patterson, "Exploring Iraq Link To Pre-September 11 Acts," *Indianapolis Star*, September 7, 2002.

36. James Patterson, "Let FBI And CIA Agents Talk About Links To Terrorism," *Indianapolis Star*, March 22, 2003.

37. Jim Crogan, "Mcveigh Et Al.; Congressional Hearing To Examine Possible Middle East Link To Oklahoma City Bombing," *LA Weekly*, April 5, 2002.

38. Jeff Pavletic, interview with author, field notes, March 2002.

39. Transcript, *The Glenn Beck Show* broadcast on KTOK 1000 AM Radio, Oklahoma City, Oklahoma, August 15, 2002.

40. Letters addressed to U.S. Representative Dan Burton (R- Indiana) from the author, September 4 and September 13, 2002.

## Chapter 21: Nexus 4-19 and 9-11

1. Dan Eggen and Vernon Loeb, "U.S. Intelligence Points to Bin Laden," *Washington Post*, September 12, 2001.

2. Dan Eggen and Bob Woodward, "U.S. Develops Picture Of Overseas Plot; Hijackers Spent $500,000; At Least 4 Trained In Afghan Camps," *Washington Post*, September 29, 2001.

3. Prior warning issued by the Congressional Task Force on Terrorism, February 27, 1995.

4. Written correspondence addressed to the author from Yossef Bodansky, May 18, 1996.

5. FBI press statement, FBI National Press Office, Washington DC, September 14, 2001.

6. Exhibit, Medical records of Hussain Al-Hussaini regarding his psychiatric therapy at The Arbour Hospital and The Quincy Center, *Al-Hussaini v. Palmer Communications*, October 1997 through February 1998, pp. 313, 725.

7. Transcript, deposition of Hussain Al-Hussaini, *Al-Hussaini v. Palmer Communications*, October 27-30 and November 16-19, 1998.

8. Johanna McGeary and David Van Biema, "Inside The Conspiracy: The New Breed Of Terrorist," *Time*, September 24, 2001.

9. Randy Christian (pseudonym), interview with author, videotape and field notes, September 13 and December 2001.

10. Jim Crogan, "The Terrorist Motel; The 1-40 Connection Between Zacarias Moussaoui And Mohammed Atta," *LA Weekly*, July 26, 2002.

11. Indictment, *United States v. Zacarias Moussaoui*, United States District Court of Eastern Virginia, Alexandria Division, December 2001.

12. Congressional Report on pre-September 11, 2001 intelligence failures, July 24, 2003. pp. 315-322.

13. Transcript, 4:00 P.M. newscast, KKNG 93.1 FM Radio, Oklahoma City, Oklahoma, July 2003.

14. Nolan Clay, "Norman Man Accused Of Islamic Extremist Ties," *DailyOklahoman.com*, November 8, 2001.

15. Nolan Clay, "Moussaoui Friend Pleads Guilty To Weapons Charge," *DailyOklahoman.com*, December 19, 2001.

16. Gary Hammerstein (pseudonym), interview with author, audiotape and field notes, December 2001.

17. Stacy McBride (pseudonym), interview with author, audiotape and field notes, September 15, 2001.

18. Affidavits of author, Stacy McBride (pseudonym), Elizabeth Brown (pseudonym), and Rachel Sealy (pseudonym).

19. Stacy McBride's mother, sister, and brother-in-law, interviews with author, audiotape and field notes, September 2001.

20. Rita Edwards (pseudonym), interview with author, field notes, September 2001. Rita Edwards verified that she hand delivered Stacy McBride's affidavit and supporting documentation to the FBI Oklahoma City field office in October 2001.

21. Transcript, Deposition of Hussain Al-Hussaini, *Al-Hussaini v. Palmer Communications*, pp. 618-623.

22. Transcript, interview with former Deputy Director of Counter Terrorism for the U.S. Department of State Larry Johnson, *The Big Story with John Gibson*, Fox News, March 20, 2002.

23. Transcripts, *The Big Story with John Gibson*, Fox News, March 19-22, 2002.

24. Transcript, Attorney General Janet Reno's press conference, April 19, 1995.

25. Transcript, FBI Special Agent Dan Vogel interview with *LA Weekly* reporter, Jim Crogan, September 2001.

# INDEX

U.S. Department of State,
121, 157, 237, 308

Van Susteren, Greta, 158
*Vanity Fair*, 60
Vogel, Dan, 69, 94, 104, 110,
115, 143, 155, 209, 283,
288, 290, 293, 295, 310

*Wall Street Journal*, 157, 293
*Washington Times*, 122, 157
Webster, William, 37
Whitley, Joan, 7, 125, 135

Whitney, Jeffrey, 302
Wilborn, Johnny, 7, 92-93,
95, 97, 102
Williams, Darby, 7, 45-46,
68-74, 81, 82-83, 90-91,
102-3, 117, 119, 199, 221,
223
Williams, Thomas E., 255
Wolfowitz, Paul, 60
Woolsey, James, 122, 157
World Trade Center bombing
(1993), 39, 249, 251-52,
262, 303

*WorldNetDaily*, 157
Woska, Dan, 212, 223, 276
WPHT Radio
(Philadelphia), 158
Wright, Robert, 286-87
Yee, James, 260
Yousef, Ramzi, 2, 58, 239-43,
245-50, 260, 267, 299

Zubaydah, Abu, 259